SURVIVING REVOLUTION

SURVIVING REVOLUTION

BOURGEOIS LIVES AND LETTERS

DENISE Z. DAVIDSON

CORNELL UNIVERSITY PRESS
Ithaca and London

This book is freely available in open access editions thanks to the generous support of Emory University and the Andrew W. Mellon Foundation. The open access editions are available through the Cornell Open initiative.

First published 2025 by Cornell University Press

Librarians: A CIP catalog record for this book is available from the Library of Congress.

ISBN 9781501783401 (hardcover)
ISBN 9781501784880 (paperback)
ISBN 9781501783425 (pdf)
ISBN 9781501783418 (epub)

GPSR EU contact: Sam Thornton, Mare Nostrum Group B.V., Mauritskade 21D, 1091 GC, Amsterdam, NL, gpsr@mare-nostrum.co.uk.

In loving memory of Marguerite Davidson
née Melanson (1919–2017)

Contents

Acknowledgments

Like the people discussed in this book, scholars depend on networks of family, friends, and colleagues to accomplish their goals. During the many years I was researching and writing this book, large numbers of people and institutions offered advice and support in various ways. It is a pleasure to express my gratitude here.

Georgia State University provided me with financial support on multiple occasions and funded an early foray into the archives with a Research Initiation Grant. Since then, I have received summer research support from the History Department several times, including the Ellen L. Evans History Faculty Enrichment Endowment, which paid for a trip to the archives as I was finishing the book. I completed the bulk of my research during a year spent working in the archives in Lyon funded by a Fulbright Research Grant that was "topped off" by the Georgia State College of Arts and Sciences. Two years later, a National Endowment for the Humanities Summer Stipend allowed me to make significant progress on my writing. That was followed by a year at the National Humanities Center (NHC) funded by an American Council of Learned Societies Burkhardt Grant. I drafted a first version of this book that year in the beautiful surroundings of the NHC while benefiting from the intellectual stimulation of my cohort of fellows, and where the NHC staff, especially the librarians, were extremely helpful.

I have also benefited from the opportunity to present my work in a wide range of contexts. I appreciate the invitations I received to discuss early chapter drafts at the Charlotte Area French Studies Workshop, the Triangle Area French Studies Workshop, the Modern France Workshop at the University of Chicago, the Ecole Normale Supérieure in Lyon, and the Laboratoire en Recherches Historiques Rhône-Alpes. It is such a pleasure to be a part of the collegial French history community; I have felt so welcome and have made so many wonderful friends whose ideas and encouragement have shaped my thinking in countless ways. I have presented my research on a wide variety of panels at the annual conferences of both our US-based professional societies: the Society for French Historical Studies and the Western Society for French

Historical Studies. My involvement in a third professional society, the Consortium on the Revolutionary Era, 1750–1850, has brought opportunities to benefit from the expertise of scholars working both within and beyond the field of French history.

Most of my research was done at the Municipal Archives of Lyon, whose former director, Jeanne-Marie Dureau, told me about the Fonds Vitet soon after they acquired it. Knowing I was interested in female sociability (a subject addressed in my first book), she even permitted me to consult Catherine Arnaud-Tizon's letters before the collection had been processed. By the time I returned to complete my research, the archives had moved from the seventeenth-century former bishops' lodgings they had long overgrown to a new spacious, modern, and well-lit building. The staff at the archives have always been amazingly friendly and helpful, particularly André Maire (now retired) and, more recently, Gilles Bernasconi. I would also like to express my gratitude to the staff at the Departmental Archives in Lyon and Rouen and at the National Archives in Saint Denis. This book could never have been completed without the rich holdings of these archives and the generous assistance and knowledge of the people who work there.

Now I'd like to turn to the many friends and colleagues whose support has been indispensable, starting with those in Lyon. My brilliant coauthor, Anne Verjus, played an essential role as I developed my ideas on the history of the family and of marriage. During my year of research in Lyon, Serge Chassagne welcomed me into his research center and even shared his archival notes with me. He also connected me with a descendant of the Arnaud-Tizon family, Monique Augustin-Normand, who generously invited me to her home in Le Havre and allowed me to photograph letters in her private collection. The Lyonnais historian Paul Feuga also shared his extensive notes on both the Arnaud-Tizon and Vitet families and invited me to his home, where some of the portraits that appear in this book were hanging on his walls. Finally, Magali Vital made multiple visits to the Municipal Archives in Lyon to help with ordering images during the last stages of preparing this book for publication.

Here in the United States, many mentors, friends, and colleagues have offered advice, more than I can possibly name here. Paul Hanson, Jennifer Heuer, and Jennifer Popiel generously read and provided feedback on chapter drafts, while Suzanne Desan, Mette Harder, Carol Harrison, and Jeff Horn engaged with drafts of other materials that eventually made it into the book. Others who have offered advice and support at various stages of my research and writing include Bryan Banks, Rafe Blaufarb, Lauren Clay, Rachel Fuchs, Dena Goodman, Beatrice de Graaf, Christine Haynes, Lynn

Hunt, Lloyd Kramer, Lynn Lees, Jann Matlock, Tip Ragan, William Reddy, Ronen Steinberg, Victoria Thompson, Leslie Tuttle, Charles Walton, and Whitney Walton. Closer to home, conversations with my Georgia State History Department colleagues as well as opportunities to share works in progress have influenced my thinking. The current department chair, Jared Poley, has a been a dear friend and source of limitless advice and assistance for more than twenty years. I am also grateful to the previous chairs, Michelle Brattain and Hugh Hudson, and appreciate the advice of many colleagues, including Duane Corpis, Ian Fletcher, Cliff Kuhn, Joe Perry, Tiffany Player, David Sehat, Jake Selwood, Wendy Venet, Nick Wilding, and Jeffrey Young. Georgia State friends and colleagues outside my department have also contributed to my thinking, particularly Maria Gindhart (now at Marshall University) and the many faculty I have gotten to know through my work as director of the Humanities Research Center (HRC), including all the HRC fellows, whose work has inspired me to read and think more broadly, as well as the regular attendees of the HRC's Writing Power Hours. I have appreciated being part of such a supportive community of writers and scholars. I've also been fortunate to have had several wonderful doctoral students and graduate research assistants who contributed in various ways to this book, including Whitney Abernathy Barnes, Xavier Barrow, Gloria Calhoun, Eduardo Meija, Medha Prasad-Mediratta, Sally Stanhope, Michael Stevens, Allyson Tadjer, and Dennise Turner. Lastly, my cherished friend and former student and colleague, Michelle Howell, generously provided feedback on parts of the manuscript as it was entering production.

Even closer to home, I must thank my loving and supportive family, starting with our three brilliant and beautiful children, now entering adulthood: George, Caroline, and Leila. My incredibly good-natured husband and partner in everything, Georges, has always been there to help with translations and rereading my French-language publications, joining me on research trips, caring for our home and our children, and, through it all, making me laugh. When my mother was around, she also enjoyed reading and helping me with French-language materials. Having francophone family members certainly helps when one is a French historian! My beloved cousin, Diane D'Esterre Hall, who has always felt like a second mother to me, and who even came to visit Lyon while I was doing my research there, has been a constant source of emotional support.

Finally, I would like to thank the publishers who granted me permission to reuse previously published versions of some of the material in this book. Parts of chapter 4 appeared as "'Happy' Marriages in Early Nineteenth-Century France," *Journal of Family History* 37, no. 1 (2012): 23–35; parts of chapter 8 appeared as "The New (Emotional) Regime: Bourgeois Reactions to the Turmoil of 1814–1814," *French Historical Studies* 42, no. 4 (2019): 595–621; parts of the conclusion appeared as "Bourgeois Families and Their Survival Strategies," *H-France Salon* 16, no. 5 (2024); and sections of an article that I coauthored with Anne Verjus, "Generational Conflict in Revolutionary France: Widows, Inheritance Practices, and the 'Victory' of Sons," *William and Mary Quarterly* 70 (Spring 2013): 399–424, appear in chapters 5 and 6.

I will end by thanking my editor at Cornell University Press, Bethany Wasik, who has been wonderfully supportive and efficient throughout the various stages of seeing this book into press, and the anonymous readers whose reports contained many valuable suggestions that I did my best to implement. Of course, whatever errors remain are my own.

Abbreviations

AAT	Amélie Arnaud-Tizon née Thiébault
ADR	Archives Départementales du Rhône
ADSM	Archives Départementales de la Seine-Maritime
AHR	American Historical Review
AML	Archives Municipales de la Ville de Lyon
AN	Archives Nationales
AV	Amélie Vitet née Arnaud-Tizon
CAT	Catherine Arnaud-Tizon
CLAT	Claude Arnaud-Tizon
CM	Contrat de mariage
FHS	*French Historical Studies*
JJB	Jacques-Juste Barbet (de Jouy)
LAT	Ludovic Arnaud-Tizon
LV	Ludovic Vitet
MV	Marguerite Vitet
PMAT	Pierre-Marie Arnaud-Tizon
PV	Pierre Vitet
PVCJ	Pierre Vitet's Correspondence Journal

Cast of Characters

Pierre Jean Vitet (1772–1854)
Louis Vitet: Pierre's father (1736–1809)
Jeanne Marguerite Vitet née Faulin: Pierre's mother (1745–1820)
Amélie Marie Josèphe Vitet née Arnaud-Tizon: Pierre's wife (1785–1860)
Louis (Ludovic) Vitet: Pierre and Amélie's son (1802–1873)
Amélie Jeanne Claudine (Mimi) Vitet: Pierre and Amélie's daughter (1822–1897)
Claude Arnaud-Tizon: Amélie's father (1753–1834)
Catherine Françoise Arnaud-Tizon née Descheaux: Amélie's mother (1764–1832)
Pierre Louis (Ludovic) Arnaud-Tizon: Amélie's brother (1787–1862)
Amélie Arnaud-Tizon née Thiébault: Ludovic's wife (1794–1839)
Claudine Victoire Barbet née Arnaud-Tizon: Amélie's sister (1790–1874)
Jacques-Juste Barbet (de Jouy): Victoire's husband (1785–1864)
Adèle Riocreux née Arnaud-Tizon: Amélie's sister (1798–1833)
Jean Christophe Riocreux: Adèle's husband (1786–d?)
Pierre-Marie Arnaud-Tizon: Amélie's uncle (1752–1840)
Anne-Françoise Arnaud-Tizon née Vincent: Pierre-Marie's wife (1760–1817)
Françoise Adélaïde (Adèle) Suchet née Arnaud-Tizon: Amélie's cousin (1783–1866)
Gabriel Catherine Suchet: Françoise Adélaïde's husband (1773–1835)
Vital Roux: Lyonnais banker in Paris, partner of Jacques Fournel (1766–1846)
Françoise Roux-Montagnat: wife of Vital Roux, celebrated artificial flower maker
Jacques Fournel: Lyonnais banker in Paris, partner of Vital Roux
Louis Gabriel Suchet: Napoleonic marshal and childhood friend of Pierre Vitet (1770–1826)

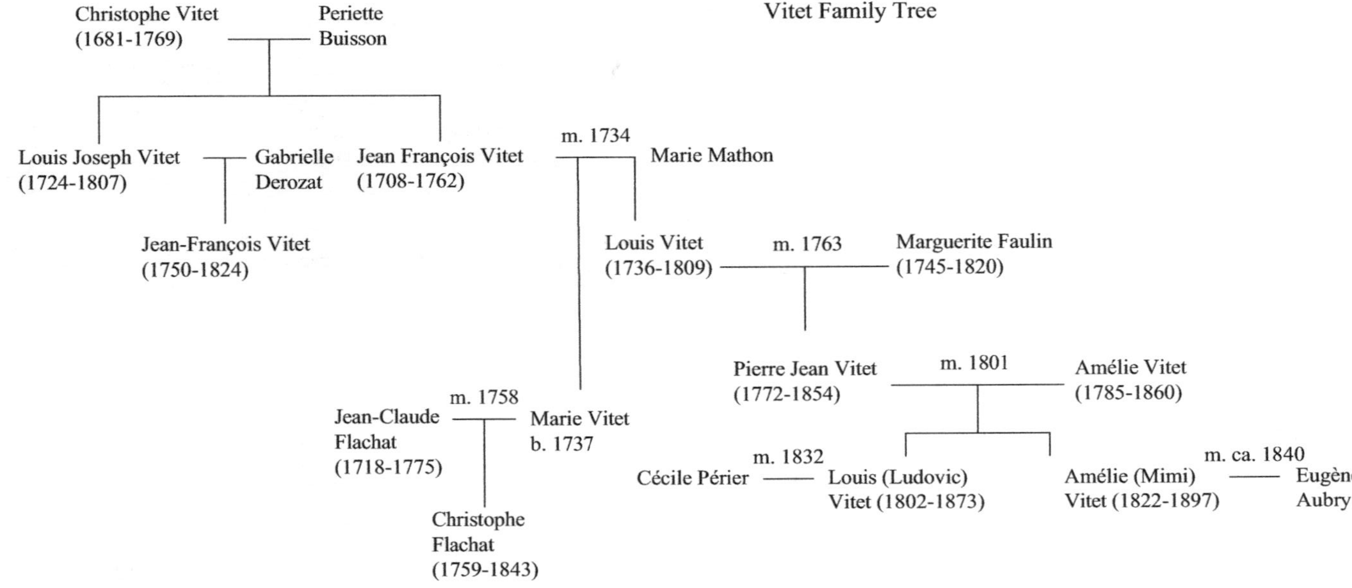

FIGURE 1. Vitet Family Tree.

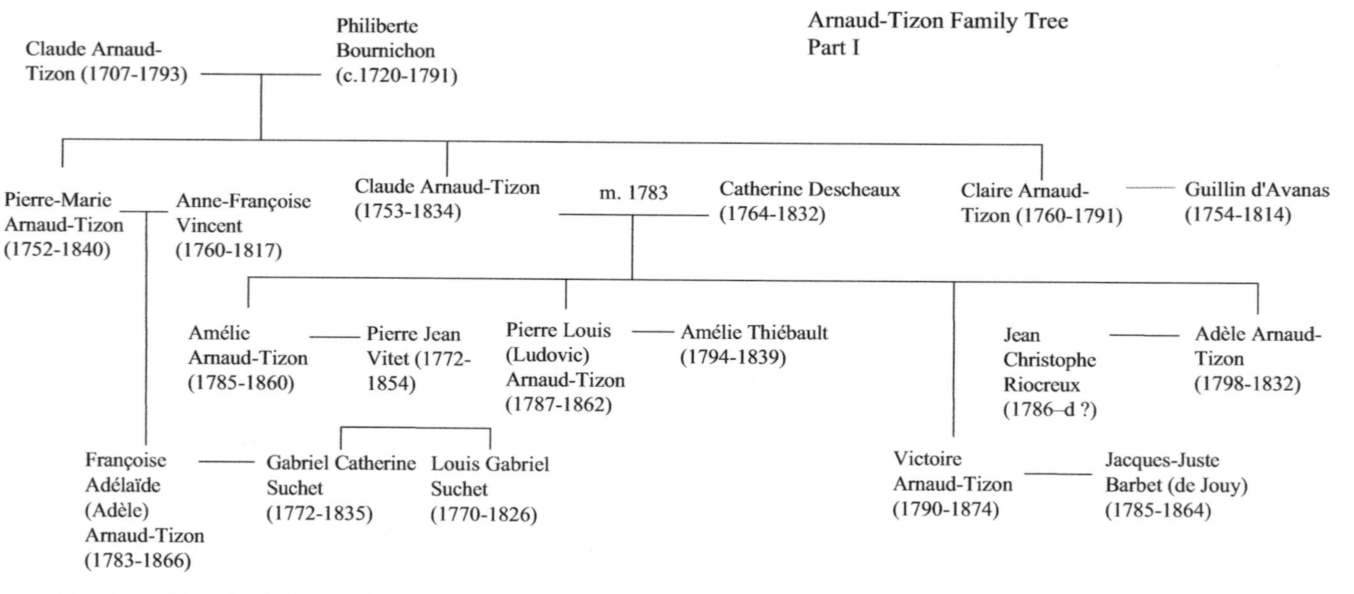

FIGURE 2. Arnaud-Tizon Family Tree, part I.

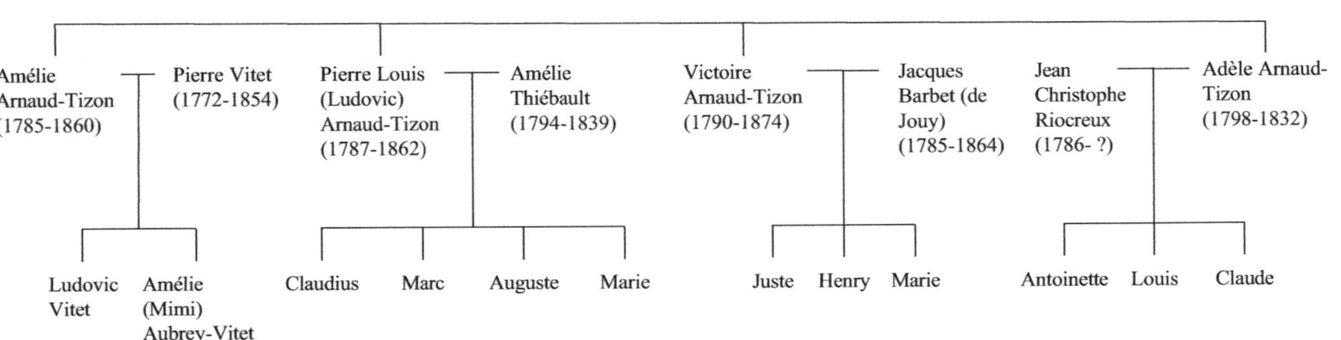

FIGURE 3. Arnaud-Tizon Family Tree, part II.

SURVIVING REVOLUTION

Introduction
A Life in the Shadows

Pierre Vitet was seventeen years old when the French Revolution began. His future mother-in-law, Catherine Arnaud-Tizon née Descheaux, was twenty-five and the mother of two young children. Both lived in the same central Lyonnais parish, Saint Nizier. The son of a prominent Lyonnais doctor and professor of medicine, Pierre was the fourth of ten babies his mother brought into the world and was the only one to survive to adulthood. The orphaned daughter of a textile manufacturer, Catherine married a man from the same milieu when she was eighteen and would eventually have four children. It is unclear if Pierre and Catherine met before 1789, but their families must have known of each other. Starting in fall 1790, Pierre's father, Louis, and Catherine's husband, Claude, worked together in the municipal government—Louis as mayor and Claude as a municipal official. As colleagues and collaborators, they, and possibly their family members, must have gotten to know each other well.

Unlike his father (and later his son), both of whom held public office and published widely, Pierre Vitet chose a more discreet existence, becoming what the French call a *rentier*, someone whose properties provide enough income that they can afford not to work (see fig. 4). He had attended one of Lyon's most prestigious schools along with several men who would go on to prominent careers during and after the Revolution, but he did not follow such a path. Instead, Pierre stayed by his father's side, going into exile

FIGURE 4. Pastel portrait of Pierre Vitet as a young man. Ville de Lyon, Archives Municipales, 5 PH 31976, photo by Jacques Gastineau.

with him in Switzerland in 1794 and then serving as his secretary when they moved to Paris in 1795. They eventually bought a former convent behind the Saint Roch church near the Tuileries that became their longtime home. It was there that Pierre would spend most of his adult life, along with his wife, Amélie, whose family had moved to Rouen. Pierre and Amélie married in 1801. He was twenty-nine; she was sixteen. Their son, Louis (who went by Ludovic), was born ten months after the wedding, in October 1802, and a daughter, also named Amélie (whom they called Mimi), came twenty years later. Pierre and Amélie had a close, seemingly happy relationship, spending much of their time together. The few letters they exchanged during their rare moments of separation suggest that they felt deep affection for each other.

More surprising perhaps is the close relationship that took shape between Pierre and his mother-in-law, Catherine. Soon after his wedding, he began communicating with her regularly. Aside from the summaries he recorded in his correspondence journal, most of Pierre's letters to Catherine have been lost, but he carefully preserved her letters to him, as did succeeding generations of the family. It was Catherine's nearly six hundred letters that first attracted me to the collection of letters now known as the Fonds Vitet. They are an incredibly rich source of information about bourgeois families—their activities, strategies, and attitudes—all from the perspective of a woman who had lived through the Revolutionary decade while trying to raise her young children and watching her husband take an active role in politics. Her voice and her sense of who she was and her role in the family as they attempted to roll with the punches that life brought them during these chaotic years dominate the story told here (see figs. 5 and 6).

It is interesting to contemplate the meaning of this intense epistolary relationship between a man and his mother-in-law. Catherine's daughters did not enjoy writing. She often complained about their laziness while expressing gratitude to Pierre for his reliability: "It is always you, my dear Vitet, who picks up your quill; our *petites dames* will end up forgetting how to write. It is wonderful of you to serve as your dear wife's secretary, but to do the same thing for your sister[-in-law] is too much."[1] Her daughter Victoire was visiting with Pierre and Amélie in Paris when Catherine wrote these words, so her flattering language may have been a way to reprimand Victoire for her silence. A month later, she made similar comments: "I received your letter my dear son. You thank me for the trinkets it pleases me to send you, when it is I who should thank you for your untiring fidelity [*complaisance*] in sending me your news, and in making up for the laziness of our *petites dames* whom I cannot convince to get in the habit of writing. You are spoiling them my dear Vitet. You authorize their laziness through your exactitude. It is you I am scolding, and I charge you with inflicting their punishment by kissing them tenderly for me."[2] Although there are no indications that any kind of romantic feelings between them, Catherine clearly appreciated the epistolary relationship she had developed with her dear Vitet, who was only eight years younger than her, a situation that was quite common, as the men in these families tended to marry younger women. Despite their closeness in age, she apparently felt no qualms about referring to Pierre as her son, though she always addressed him with *vous*, the formal version of *you* in French.

Pierre participated in many of the major decisions made by his extensive kinship network, and letter writing permitted him to contribute to those processes and served as the primary tool for building and maintaining that network. At the center of this network was his own family—his mother, aunt, and cousins in Lyon. Other nodes included his wife's much larger family, the spouses of her siblings, and the mostly Lyonnais friends and allies with whom he socialized in Paris. Handling that correspondence must have taken up many hours of his time and merited great effort and attention to

FIGURE 5. Miniature portrait of Madame Arnaud-Tizon. Ville de Lyon, Archives Municipales, 5 PH 31986, photo by Jacques Gastineau.

FIGURE 6. Miniature portrait of Monsieur Arnaud-Tizon. Ville de Lyon, Archives Municipales, 5 PH 31986, photo by Jacques Gastineau.

detail. Pierre's methodical approach to communicating with friends and family, demonstrated by the detailed correspondence journal he maintained, resembles practices found in the worlds of business and diplomacy more than the supposed affective realm of the family. That said, the letters are filled with emotion—expressions of love, concern, fear, trust, pity, anger, and many other feelings run through their missives. And sentiment was not something that mattered purely in family life; business, politics, and other supposedly rational components of life were imbued with emotion.[3]

The French Revolution contributed to the rise of the modern world, particularly in the realm of politics, and caused incredible turmoil (emotional and otherwise) that impacted people's lives in both concrete and more intangible ways. Europeans across the continent experienced a sense of bewilderment, as they could no longer rely on tradition to provide a reliable roadmap with which to plan their lives.[4] This book focuses on the consequences of that chaos on everyday life and explores how a handful of well-off and well-connected men and women responded to these remarkable, unprecedented changes. How did people cope with the turmoil taking place around them? How did they strategize when the very foundation of their world seemed to be collapsing? Where did they find solid ground? One answer is that they sought refuge in their families, in the comforts and calm of domestic life.

Pierre's life choices reflect attempts to find peace and tranquility in a sea of storms by remaining in the shadows. Aside from his voluminous correspondence and the legal documents he signed when passing through significant moments of transition—marriage, births, deaths, and buying and selling property—his life left few traces. Yet, what a correspondent he was! In addition to reading, responding to, and carefully filing away the letters he received, he meticulously recorded an entry in a correspondence journal for every letter he wrote.[5] The more than three thousand entries in his journal, which cover the years 1795 to 1835, range from "responded to my mother" to several paragraphs summarizing the contents of long, complicated letters about business arrangements, political developments, and networking strategies. That journal and the letters and other documents he saved are held in the Fonds Vitet at the Lyon Municipal Archives, with some from the later years of his life housed at the National Archives.[6]

This is a book about survival strategies and network building as well as the emotional bonds forged through the correspondence practices that lay at the heart of both. When family, friends, and allies wrote to each other, they reinforced their sense of connection. Even if the contents of these letters might seem rather trivial, the very act of writing could carry huge significance. At other times, the contents are anything but banal, as when crises emerged to engulf the family in tensions and fears. Momentous events such as a marriage or an impending bankruptcy brought an intense exchange of letters. Letters could also help allies gain access to political or professional positions by plugging into networks that had similarly been forged through writing and socializing. In addition to this functional component, letter writing played a role in the expression and construction of a sense of self.[7] And as women often served as the principal correspondents in these families, letters allow us to consider how they understood and expressed their subjectivity while rendering visible their contributions to this work of kinship.[8]

Although letters can be a rich source of information about everyday life and emotions, it is important to recognize their limitations, including their often-formulaic nature and the fact that some issues were deemed too sensitive or risky to preserve in writing.[9] Many topics were simply never broached. Letter writers knew their letters would be shared with the family and maybe even read aloud. If they wanted to send more confidential information, they would include a separate sheet that could be removed from their standard letter prior to sharing it. And recipients would have burned any letters that contained overly private or politically sensitive information. Pierre was saving his letters for posterity; he knew that his children and perhaps later generations would be seeing them. If he had any letters from a mistress or some other person in his life that he preferred his family not know about, he would not have saved them, and he would not have recorded entries for such correspondence in his journal. If Pierre ever sent Amélie a letter describing his burning desire for her, that probably would have been destroyed as well.

Matters related to sex and sexuality were almost never discussed explicitly or even implicitly, except in oblique ways, as when announcing news of a pregnancy. Was Pierre a faithful husband? We cannot know, just as we cannot know what kinds of sexual experiences he may have had prior to his marriage. What kind of sex life did Pierre and Amélie have? Were they passionately in love or simply compatible enough to find life with each other comfortable? We do know that they slept in the same bed, which suggests that they experienced a degree of intimacy that many upper-class couples seem to have lacked.[10] They also used the informal *tu* with each other, another sign of intimacy. They expressed love and affection in their letters but never sexual desire. Only one letter from Pierre comes close to hinting at their sex life. While away on a trip in 1810, he wrote while still in bed one morning: "My dear Amélie. It is seven o'clock. I am just waking up, and my first thoughts are naturally of you. Since I do not have you at my side to chat with and kiss, I am going to try to make myself feel better by writing to you about all that I have seen and done that merits your interest."[11]

In today's hyperconnected world, the nature of communication in eighteenth- and nineteenth-century France may seem limited and slow. Letters were sent through a variety of means. There was a reliable postal system with regular times and locations to drop off and pick up mail, and with mail delivery to people's homes available in larger cities.[12] A letter between Paris and Lyon, today a two-hour ride on France's high-speed train, typically took four days, and weather conditions or other problems could slow things down considerably. Families who maintained regular contact with people in other cities depended on men who spent their lives on the road carrying mail and packages for their clients. Pierre and his mother relied on a courier named Peuch, who traveled between Paris and Lyon every week. When they were discussing something urgent, the rhythm of their letter writing followed his; they wrote *courier-par-courier*, meaning that they would reply to each other's letters in time to send their response back with Peuch. Pierre and Catherine sent their letters via stagecoach, and since Rouen was only a day's ride from Paris, they could communicate more frequently. They wrote their letters on one sheet of paper folded in half to create four sides, with one side left blank for the address of the recipient, which was added once the sheet was folded and before sealing it with wax (see fig. 7). This method of folding meant they did not need to use envelopes, which did not come into regular use until later in the century.

Although their letters frequently treat quite ordinary—even banal—topics, matters of everyday life reflect broader and deeper concerns and allow us to consider how these families understood the world around them and their place in it. For regular correspondents like Pierre and Catherine, letter writing served as a vital link to share news and make plans to ensure the well-being of the larger family.[13] Because an illness or accident could quickly become catastrophic, any delay in responding to a letter could inspire great anxiety and thus necessitated an apologetic opening. Letters were designed to soothe rather than raise concerns, which meant that only good news was generally shared, unless the situation appeared so grave that it became necessary to prepare a person for the worst. During moments of duress, such as the chaotic period between Napoleon's first abdication in 1814 and the second Bourbon Restoration in 1815, their letters reveal a surprising degree of emotional restraint, encouraging perseverance rather than panic. Letters dating from such moments allow us to see how ordinary people responded to the extraordinary events of this period and to imagine their private conversations.

Not all of Pierre's correspondents have been forgotten to history. Pierre's father, Louis Vitet, was a prominent Lyonnais doctor and professor of medicine before the Revolution. After 1789, he held public office, serving as mayor

1er / 24 Sept.

Rouen le 23 septembre

je voulois remettre hier une lettre a l'oncle
mon cher ami, mes a mon grand regret
je ne pu trouver un moment pour vous
ecrire et je viens ce matin m'en dedomager
et vous donner des details sur la toute
gracieuse visite du Marechal; je recu a
Bapaume Dimanche votre billet qui m'anoncoit
son arrivée et dont je vous remercie
beaucoup; je serois allée desuitte a Rouen
pour y attendre son passage, mais nous
avions plusieurs marchands a dinner et
il fallut remettre le depart a sept heures
nous nous croisames sur la route et
arrivée chez moi avec le papa Ludovic
et adele on nous dit que trois Mrs
dont l'un avoit plusieurs decorations etoient
venu nous demander et sur la reponse
que toute la famille etoit a Bapaume
ils en avoient pris la route, (ma cuisiniere
croyoit mon frere et Mr vincent avec nous
ils avoient du y venir mes mon frere
ayant pris une medecine le samedy il avoit
craint la fraicheur de la vallée)
arrivés a Bapaume ces Mrs decendirent donnerent
un coup d'oeuil a la fabrique et le
Domestique leur dit qu'il nous trouveroit
chez Madame vincent ou il devoit

FIGURE 7. First page of one of Catherine Arnaud-Tizon's letters, September 23, [1814]. Ville de Lyon, Archives Municipales, 84II/12, photo by author.

of Lyon for two years. He then served as a deputy in the National Convention, where he sided with the Girondins and voted against the execution of the king, and later sat on the Council of 500. Another well-known figure of the Napoleonic period had been childhood friends with Pierre: Louis Gabriel Suchet, later Marshal Suchet. In a classic maneuver of bourgeois networking, Pierre helped to orchestrate the marriage of Suchet's younger brother to his wife's cousin, a step that reinforced his own connection to this high-ranking officer and brought his in-laws greater prestige. Suchet's origins, however, resembled those of Pierre's in-laws—all were wealthy textile manufacturers from Lyon. As such, they fit the classic Marxist definition of the bourgeoisie.

The loaded term *bourgeois*, which can be translated somewhat inaccurately as "middle class," requires some explanation. Ever since Marx defined the French Revolution as a bourgeois revolution, historians have been debating the extent to which the bourgeoisie participated in and benefitted from the events of 1789 to 1815. The current consensus is that class antagonism was not the driving force of the Revolution and that bourgeois class consciousness was more a consequence of the Revolution than one of its causes.[14] Going further, the historian Sarah Maza has argued that the French bourgeoisie never existed as a self-conscious class, except perhaps briefly during the 1820s, when political developments encouraged the formation of such an identity due to shared opposition to the Bourbon Restoration.[15] The term *bourgeois* nonetheless appeared with regularity throughout the eighteenth century, and the families whose words and lives are at the heart of this book fit the prevailing sense of bourgeois values and ways of life, including its "cult of domestic life and family happiness."[16] At its origin, *bourgeois* signified a citizen of a city, like *burgher* in German. By the mid-eighteenth century, the term suggested several key characteristics—simplicity of manners, frugality and economic conservatism, hard work, virtue, and morality—all in contrast to clichés about aristocratic lives of leisure, conspicuous consumption, and dissoluteness. One important consequence of the Revolution was a growing awareness of society as a concept and how people fit into it—in other words the "social imaginary," including the idea of the bourgeoisie as a group apart, separate from the aristocracy and the working classes.[17]

Whereas in the eighteenth century, bourgeois men and women did all they could to grow rich and purchase titles of nobility, in the postrevolutionary period, we see a reverse phenomenon, as even kings tried to live like bourgeois. Louis Philippe, who reigned between 1830 and 1848, became known as the "bourgeois monarch" because of the simplicity of his dress and his more modest, domestic lifestyle. The historian Adeline Daumard explored the significance of the term *bourgeois* in those years: "For a Guizot or a Rémusat, among others, belonging to the bourgeoisie required at least a superficial understanding of humanist culture; mastery of necessary social skills, which were typically passed on through familial traditions; and finally leisure time, without which it was difficult to participate in social life or to take on civil responsibilities."[18] Daumard's examples are well chosen for our purposes here: François Guizot and Charles de Rémusat were close friends and allies of Pierre's son, Ludovic Vitet. In addition, Daumard's definition of the bourgeoisie, like that of the anthropologist Béatrix Le Wita, emphasizes family life as essential for providing the skills and knowledge needed to master the rituals and gestures that characterized bourgeois life.[19]

The families discussed here originated in Lyon and thus give a Lyonnais perspective on bourgeois values, attitudes, and lifestyles. In contrast to the Parisian upper classes, whose socializing often brought them into contact with large numbers of acquaintances, the Lyonnais tended to keep to themselves and limit their networking to close friends. The historian Catherine Pellissier quotes a nineteenth-century university professor who wrote that the Lyonnais bourgeoisie preferred to socialize with "a circle of friends whose trustworthiness had been tested over many years."[20] A lawyer named Emmanuel Vingtrinier, a descendant of a man who makes a brief appearance in this story, described the traditional Lyonnais approach to sociability as "large families [and] social relations limited to a circle of close friends and allies."[21] A Lyonnais tendency to distrust outsiders put family even more at the center of social and business relations than might have been the case for bourgeois from other cities.

Among the essential characteristics of bourgeois families was a desire to plan everything, particularly all that related to family wealth, or what the French call *le patrimoine.* How is it that the bourgeoisie always seemed to be rising? They carefully strategized to ensure that each generation would improve the family's economic and social standing.[22] Until the Revolution, they built those plans in a world whose legal, economic, and social system they knew and understood. The Revolution created new opportunities while introducing obstacles and risks to their financial, social, and emotional well-being. One of the most important features of the postrevolutionary period was the emergence of previously unimaginable uncertainty. For example, how were these families supposed to strategize as they had in the past when they could no longer count on marriage and inheritance laws to remain the same from one generation to the next? How could they make well-informed investment decisions when tariff policies, taxes, and even property ownership were in constant flux, and all in the context of nearly constant warfare? It is this thoroughgoing uncertainty that differentiates the postrevolutionary period from the Old Regime. In response, they developed strategies and practices to help them succeed in this new world. Yet, most of those strategies built on those they and previous generations had mastered before the Revolution, particularly their reliance on networks of family and friends ready to help in any unanticipated circumstance.[23] These networks functioned largely through letter writing and socializing, spaces where emotional and practical ties could be built and reinforced, with men and women alike contributing to them.[24]

The concept of separate spheres—the idea that men were more suited to the activities of the public worlds of business and politics and that women's natures made them more suitable for the nurturing activities situated within the domestic realm—has played a prominent role in historical studies of the Revolutionary era, which corresponds as well to the first phases of industrialization. More recent work has challenged that model, however, and the findings presented here reinforce those challenges.[25] Although some traces of a gendered division of labor and responsibilities is visible in these letters, for the most part, the separation between public and private remained blurry in France until later in the nineteenth century. And to the extent that the domestic sphere came to be seen as a separate space, it was not yet associated with a purely female world of activities.[26] Men also relished the safety and tranquility of family life during these years of chaos. Pierre Vitet seems to have chosen to lead a largely domestic existence, devoting most of his energies to raising and educating his son and to developing his skills as an amateur artist, with a particular interest in landscape painting (see fig. 8).[27] His life choices reflect new understandings and images of the "good father" that historians have traced to the late eighteenth century.[28] Private, familial spaces shaped both men's and women's worldviews; it was in the home that they read and discussed books, the arts, and politics.

FIGURE 8. Painting of Ile Barbe by Pierre Vitet, Ville de Lyon, Archives Municipales, 5 PH 31981, photo by Jacques Gastineau.

This focus on the family, the heart of the bourgeoisie in every sense of the term, enables the overlapping nature of politics and friendship, business and intimate relationships, and male and female spheres of activity to come into view. The late eighteenth and early nineteenth centuries were marked by intense sentimentalism, a trend visible in romanticism in the arts as well as in less obvious genres and activities.[29] Although most of the letters examined here kept emotions subdued, there were some exceptions to that rule, particularly when a family's honor was at stake. As part of a highly gendered "invisible code," honor was an essential component of bourgeois identity.[30] Bourgeois men and women made decisions informed simultaneously by the economic logics of the market and the cultural logics of codes of sentiment and honor.

In giving voice to a set of largely forgotten men and women who lived through a tumultuous period in French and world history, this book traces the views, practices, and coping mechanisms implemented by these families as they faced the uncertainties of the new world taking shape around them. Part I contains three chapters that provide context and a brief overview of these families' lives. These chapters cover the major events of the period and trace the trajectories of the men and women who are the focus of this story. Incorporating sometimes lengthy passages from their letters, the five chapters in part II explore the perspectives and life choices of these family members as they worked to navigate through this new world while doing their best to position their loved ones for happiness and success. These chapters take a thematic approach, treating the strategies these families applied to handling marriage, child-rearing, property and business, socializing and networking, and finally politics, thus moving from the most private to the most public aspects of their lives. In all these arenas, the most essential strategies were communication, collaboration across the genders and the generations, and reliance on trusted, long-standing friends and allies. But collaboration does not mean they always agreed, and in some cases, their letters reveal generational distinctions and tensions.

Before I launch into these families' lives, it seems worthwhile to consider the meaning of the word *surviving*. I am using the term literally and figuratively to mean both managing to stay alive at moments when their lives were at risk *and* maintaining their social positions and wealth—despite the upheavals of the period. So, *survival strategies* included doing whatever was necessary to avoid imprisonment and death *and* rethinking how to approach major decisions such as where to live, what investments to make, choosing spouses for children, and selecting business partners, all in the name of positioning oneself and one's family members for success. The largest subset of Pierre Vitet's collected correspondence, Catherine Arnaud-Tizon's letters permit us to enter her world and to examine the perspective of a bourgeois wife, mother, and grandmother who had survived the chaos and confusion of Revolutionary Lyon only to find herself and her family living through war, economic crises, and multiple changes of regime. The strategies that she and other family members implemented to navigate the new world created by the Revolution included many that resembled eighteenth-century practices, such as a reliance on patronage networks, but also newer ones, such as emotional restraint and a focus on family and domestic life. To begin, we will enter their world by examining the place where virtually all these men and women had their roots: eighteenth-century Lyon.

Part One

Two Families Across Three Generations

Chapter 1

Eighteenth-Century Lyon

Two Families Experience Revolution

Often called France's "second city," Lyon has served as an important site for trade since the days of the Roman Empire, thanks in part to its location on the route to Switzerland and Italy. Long known as a center for printing, by the eighteenth-century, Lyon had developed a thriving silk industry. The men who most profited from that industry were the *négociants*: businessmen who sold the goods produced in weavers' workshops. They oversaw production and defined quality and pay regulations through an institution that functioned like a guild, the Fabrique, which brought together all those involved in the silk industry.[1] Unlike cities that housed *parlements* (high courts) with ennobled judges enlarging the size and wealth of the local aristocracy, Lyon was dominated by these wealthy merchants and other professionals. A small number of old aristocratic families lived in and near the city, but merchants and other "bourgeois" rarely mingled with them. One historian concluded that "relations between nobles and rich bourgeois—even members of consular families—were uneasy and often rancorous, and they became, it seems, more and more distant."[2] One matter that divided the city's diverse elites was how to deal with public disorders. During the 1770s and 1780s, an economic crisis resulted in numerous uprisings, the largest of which took place in 1786. The memory of that bloody event would play a role in the way the events of 1789 would be interpreted on a local level.[3]

In terms of its physical characteristics, the city was known for its narrow, dark streets, a consequence of the buildings in which the silk weavers lived and worked, as they needed high ceilings to accommodate their looms. One aspect of the city's layout that visitors admired were the open areas near the two rivers, the Rhône and the Saône, which meet in the city, creating a V-shaped area of land called the Presqu'île. In the 1780s, the population of the city numbered about 150,000.[4] Until the mid-nineteenth century, when the city began to expand beyond its longtime borders, Lyon's inhabitants resided within the Presqu'île and along the right bank of the Saône, a narrow strip of land suitable for building between the river and a very steep hill.[5] By the 1780s, a project to build a new neighborhood on the left bank of the Rhône had begun, preceded by the construction of a bridge over the rapidly flowing river, but the Revolution brought those efforts to a halt.[6] At the top of a hill to the north of the Presqu'île was the Croix-Rousse, a neighborhood where many silk workers began living starting in the late eighteenth century. These were the famous *canuts*, whose protests roiled the city in the early 1830s. This was the world that the Vitets and Arnaud-Tizons inhabited.

Virtually all the men and women whose stories appear here originated in Lyon, many in Saint-Nizier, the city's third wealthiest parish as measured by property values.[7] Born in Lyon in 1736, Pierre Vitet's father, Louis, was the son of Jean François Vitet (1708–1769), a surgeon from Condrieu, a town about a day's carriage ride south of Lyon. Categorized as artisans because they worked with their hands, surgeons mostly pulled teeth and set broken bones. Over the course of the eighteenth century, however, the status of surgeons in larger towns was rising, a trend epitomized by Jean François Vitet, who purchased a title of nobility; he was *secrétaire du roi*, a position that had few responsibilities and little significance other than prestige.[8] In contrast to surgeons, whose training resembled that of artisans, doctors' university education brought them higher status. Louis Vitet attended France's prestigious medical school in Montpellier. After defending his thesis in Paris in 1759, he returned to Lyon, where he became a professor of medicine.[9] His first cousin, also named Jean-François Vitet (1750–1824), built a similarly successful career as a lawyer and magistrate. Both men benefitted from their ancestors' wealth and connections to launch their careers and climb the social hierarchy.

Louis quickly became a prominent member of Lyon's medical community. He taught chemistry and pharmacology in the charity hospital and had a large following of patients. Doctors visited patients in their homes; they had no set fees and were paid whatever their patients chose to give them. One anecdote suggests that Louis cared a great deal about his patients. Not long after beginning his practice, Louis felt such guilt when one of them died that he stopped seeing patients for several years, focusing instead on research and teaching.[10] His two passions became midwifery and veterinary medicine. In the 1770s, he founded a veterinary school and published a book on the subject, *Médecine vetérinaire*. Then came another influential study, *Pharmacopée de Lyon*, published in 1778. In the 1780s, Louis directed Lyon's school of midwifery. Under his leadership, the school provided a three-year course on "the art of giving birth" to six women who received training at a clinic that offered free treatment to women deemed "poor, healthy, and of good morals."[11] Along with his close friend and collaborator Jean-Emmanuel Gilibert (1741–1814), Louis contributed to the period's cutting-edge scientific research, including work on electricity and magnetism.[12] In recognition of his scientific work, Lyon's Académie des Sciences, Belles-Lettres et Arts invited Vitet to join that august body in 1786. There, he mingled with Lyon's intellectual and social elites, something he would have done through his involvement in Freemasonry as well (see fig. 9).[13] When the Revolution

FIGURE 9. Pastel portrait of Louis Vitet, Ville de Lyon, Archives Municipales, 5 PH 31985, photo by Jacques Gastineau.

began, Louis had been working on a book about illnesses that afflicted the poorer inhabitants of his city, a reflection of his philanthropic approach to medicine.[14] Though he would have to put aside that study because of his political activities, he picked up the project again later in life.

A few years after completing medical school and returning to Lyon, Louis married Jeanne Marguerite Faulin, daughter of a *négociant*. Their ages when they married in 1765—twenty-nine and twenty, respectively—were typical for their social milieu. According to their marriage contract, the bride brought a sizable dowry of 40,000 livres; Louis's family contributed twenty thousand.[15] Little is known about their early family life, except for the fact that Marguerite gave birth to ten children, of whom only the fourth, Pierre Jean, survived.[16] Infant mortality rates were high in eighteenth-century France; one out of four children died during their first year of life. But the Vitet couple lost many more children than the average family, something that seems even more striking given the fact that Louis was a doctor. Their children mostly died young while in the care of wet nurses in the countryside. The parish records in Lyon list their births but not their deaths, suggesting they died outside the city.[17] It was common practice for mothers to send their children to wet nurses, and babies fed by wet nurses were more likely to die than those nursed by their mothers.[18] Still, the Vitet couple seemed particularly unlucky. It is impossible to know why so many died. Perhaps the couple carried a recessive gene that made their children sickly; perhaps they hired inexpensive wet nurses who did not properly care for the babies. What is certain is that the one surviving child must have been deeply cherished by both of his parents.

Pierre Vitet's baptism record, which is dated April 29, 1772, when he was one day old, shows that his godfather was Pierre Souchay, *écuyer* (squire), and his godmother was Jeanne Faulin, his mother's sister, who would later marry into the Morel family. Aside from that document, we have few sources of information on Pierre's childhood and nothing that comes directly from him or his parents. One nineteenth-century source indicates that Pierre "studied classical literature at the Oratoire with the Périer and Jordan [sons]," two prominent families that gained national prestige during the early nineteenth century.[19] The College de l'Oratoire, also known as *le grand collège*, was run by a religious order that had taken over the institution after its founders, the Jesuits, were expelled from France in 1763.[20] Although it was close to his family's home, Pierre boarded at the school, as it was assumed that boys benefited from the discipline they would learn while living in such institutions. When he finished, he took steps toward a degree in medicine but never completed his studies. Then, in 1789, when Pierre was seventeen, the Revolution abruptly changed the course of both his and his father's lives. It is from that point forward that the documentary evidence allows us to retrace the details of their experiences, but first I must introduce the second family whose lives this book traces.

Like Pierre's maternal grandfather, the men in the Arnaud-Tizon family were *négociants*. Their unusual hyphenated name, which is sometimes spelled as one word and sometimes as *Tison* instead of *Tizon*, may reflect an ancestor's Italian origins, with *Tizoni* evolving into *Tizon*. The historian Serge Chassagne has traced the family's roots back to the mid-seventeenth century in the Champsaur Valley in the Southern Alps; the ancestors of the family discussed here settled in and near Lyon by the late seventeenth century.[21] A textile merchant (*marchand-toilier*) in Lyon, Claude Arnaud-Tizon (1707–1793) was the man whose business savvy brought the family to prominence. He and his wife, Marie Philiberte Bournichon (c. 1720–1791), had two sons and a daughter. The daughter, Claire (1756–1791), married a local aristocrat, Hugues Guillin d'Avenas (1754–1814).[22] The Arnaud-Tizons's eldest son, Pierre-Marie, married Anne-Françoise Adélaide Vincent, the eldest daughter of a *négociant* from Rouen, in 1779, when he was twenty-seven and she was eighteen.[23] The couple spent the first two or three years of their marriage with her family and then settled in Lyon. It was common for the families of young brides to stipulate in marriage contracts that their daughters would remain with their parents for a certain amount of time following the wedding.[24] When Pierre-Marie's sister, Claire, married in 1781, he and his wife did not sign her marriage contract, which suggests they were still in Rouen at that point. Traces of Pierre-Marie's presence in Lyon begin to appear in Lyonnais notarial documents starting in 1782, with further confirmation of the couple's location dating from June 1783, when Anne-Françoise gave birth to their only daughter, Adèle, in the city.[25]

That same year, Pierre-Marie's younger brother, Claude, married Catherine Françoise Descheaux. Her mother, Marie Anne Franzoni, had died when Catherine was young, and by the time she married, Catherine's father, Dominique Descheaux, a *négociant*, had died as well. At the time of her marriage, Catherine was living with her stepmother, her father's widow. Claude was twenty-nine when he married Catherine; she was eighteen. As a minor, she married with the permission of her legal guardian, her cousin, Joseph Dominique Bergasse, a *négociant*.[26] The couple signed their marriage contract in Lyon on January 23, 1783, and married the same day at the Saint-Pierre / Saint-Saturnin parish church in the northern part of the Presqu'île, the neighborhood where Catherine spent her childhood.[27] Twenty signatures appear on the documents, including those of Claude's father, uncle, brother, sister, and brother-in-law. On Catherine's side, her paternal grandmother, stepmother, guardian, and several cousins appeared. The large number of witnesses attests to the prestige of both families and the desire among all involved to voice their support for this alliance.

What was it like for a couple to marry in the 1780s? The signing of the marriage contract was the most significant step, as it was there that the parties involved certified the exchange of property that took place with the marriage. Making their vows at church with the priest recording the ceremony in the parish registry came next. That could only happen after the publication of banns, announcements of the upcoming wedding meant to give community members the opportunity to express possible obstacles to the wedding (a practice that continues to this day). Spouses typically had little direct contact before the wedding, with girls kept in the dark until the financial and other arrangements had been finalized by both families. Only then did parents introduce them to their potential husband. A young woman could, in theory, refuse a proposed suitor, but that happened extremely rarely, in part because girls were raised to accept their parents' authority over them. We cannot know what Catherine Descheaux thought of the man who became her husband and with whom she would share a long, eventful life. All we have is her signature on a page. Did she look forward to her new life with anticipation or fear? She probably felt a combination of both as she took this important step in the transition toward adulthood. The daughter and granddaughter of *négociants*, she likely assumed her life would follow a similar path to that of earlier generations. She would give birth to and raise her children while praying that she and they would survive, care for her household, oversee domestic servants, and assist in running the family business.

Although this couple was not atypical for their milieu, economically they were far above the average Lyonnais. Like his siblings, Claude *fils* (the son) received 110,000 livres from his father, while an uncle, Jean-Baptiste Arnaud-Tizon, promised him an inheritance of 30,000 livres. Catherine's dowry was just over 100,000 livres—half from her deceased mother's dowry and half from her inheritance from her father. Aside from 9,000 livres she received to use at her discretion, the money went directly to her husband, who then became responsible for ensuring that her dowry would be passed on to their children. Dowries of 100,000 livres were extremely rare, even among Lyon's wealthy *négociants*. The average size of dowries among that social group in 1780–1789 was less than 40,000 livres.[28] Claude Arnaud-Tizon *père*'s (the father's) August 1791 will gives an indication of the family's wealth.[29] The total value of his business investments, properties, furniture, and cash was 910,000 livres, from which nearly 100,000 needed to be deducted to pay creditors. This was an extremely wealthy family.

We know little about the family's activities during the 1780s. Claude and his brother formed a partnership, Frères Arnaud-Tizon et Compagnie, and lived and worked alongside their families near the Place Saint Nizier. It would have been a busy life for the young wives, now sisters-in-law—Anne, far from her family in Rouen, and Catherine, in her native city but now living in her husband's household. The two women became close friends, as we know from their later lives, and would always refer to each other as sisters. They raised their children together and helped to care for their husbands' parents. Claude *père* died at home on May 27, 1793; his wife had died two years earlier. The signers of Claude's death registry were two of his employees, Antoine Bournichon (his wife's nephew) and Antoine Mouton.

Like most couples, Claude and Catherine quickly became parents. Their first child, Claudine Françoise Félicité, born in January 1784, only survived for a month. Amélie Marie Josèphe came next, in April 1785. The significance the family attached to her and later births is demonstrated by the number of signatures that appear on the baptism records. Amélie's godfather was Catherine's cousin, Joseph Dominique Bergasse, the man who had served as her guardian. (He would die on the guillotine in Lyon in 1793.) The godmother was Marie Philberte Bournichon, the child's paternal grandmother. Following the signatures of the godparents are those of about a dozen family members.[30] We can imagine the grandparents, parents, aunts, and uncles of this baby gathered in the church on this spring day as they attended the baptism and signed their names in the registry. A child's baptism and the selection of godparents served as a moment to reinforce family ties and strengthen alliances. As a rule, parents chose one godparent among the father's close relatives and the other from the mother's side.[31] Claude and Catherine's next child, Pierre Louis (whom they called Ludovic), arrived two and a half years later, in 1787, suggesting that Catherine breastfed her children, as that would explain the relatively long period between births. Ludovic was baptized six days after his birth, while Amélie's baptism took place when she was only one day old. The godfather was Pierre-Marie, the baby's uncle, and the godmother was Catherine's stepmother. Fewer people appeared as witnesses this time, and Catherine's name is not among the signers. This may have been a difficult birth, with the mother needing to rest longer and the baby kept at home for health reasons. Their second daughter to survive infancy, Victoire, came in November 1790. Her godfather was her paternal grandfather, Claude, and her godmother was her mother's sister, Catherine Victoire Descheaux. In contrast to the Vitet couple's unfortunate progeny, most of Catherine's children survived infancy, another indication that she likely nursed them herself.

Like Louis Vitet, the Arnaud-Tizon brothers became prominent local officials. In 1786, Pierre-Marie acceded to a position that carried significant prestige: Recteur de la Charité.[32] Lyon housed two hospitals, the Hôtel-Dieu and the Charité, each run by a board whose members were known as rectors. Eighteen rectors oversaw the administration of la Charité. They held two-year terms, at the beginning of which they were required to deposit between 10,000 and 16,000 livres, which were returned to them when they stepped down. On top of this expense, the rectors had numerous responsibilities, including raising funds, visiting poor houses, and overseeing the wet-nursing system established for abandoned babies. Maurice Garden notes the significance of serving as rector: "There was a respectability associated with the title of rector that came not only with the prerogatives of the position, but even the status of the town as a whole. It would not be false to write that Lyon's hospital boards served, for the *négociants* and bourgeois of Lyon, as their sovereign space, their *Parlement*."[33] As one might expect, the importance of this institution meant that rectors paid great attention to ceremony and ritual. When a new rector was elected, he received a book with detailed instructions on those ceremonies. As Garden explains, "respect for social position was central. . . . 'The rectors [were] required to appear in their offices at fixed times. They [had] to listen to all the opinions in silence and offer their opinion only when it [was] their turn to speak, according to their rank on the board.'"[34] Pierre-Marie's participation in this elite institution both reflected and enhanced the family's status.

Claude Arnaud-Tizon *père*'s flourishing business and accumulated wealth meant that his sons were able to enter the highest realms of Lyonnais society. On the eve of the Revolution, they were among Lyon's richest families and had gained access to the city's most prestigious institutions. Their sister had even married into a noble family. The Arnaud-Tizon brothers clearly knew how to maneuver successfully through the hierarchical world of eighteenth-century France, and Lyon in particular. The next step, had the Revolution not intervened, would have been to purchase an office that brought a hereditary title of nobility.[35] They were probably not far from accomplishing that feat, as they had enough money and local prestige to do so. Like the Vitets, the Arnaud-Tizon family had mastered the strategies needed to succeed in their world.

The Shock of Revolution

Then came 1789. A cataclysmic event for the entire country, the French Revolution was particularly traumatic for the inhabitants of Lyon. From early on,

Lyon gained a reputation as a center of counterrevolution, a place where aristocrats could hide by melding into the large populace.[36] The majority of the city's wealthy property owners kept their distance from politics. Following their usual conservative approach to life and taking only calculated risks, most preferred to sit back and observe the transformations taking place and consider how best to profit from them. Both Louis Vitet and Claude Arnaud-Tizon *fils* were exceptions to these tendencies. Both typified the men of the Third Estate; they were rich, well-educated property owners. As a doctor, Louis Vitet was a member of the liberal professions that were well represented among the deputies to the Estates General.[37] As textile manufacturers, the two Arnaud-Tizon brothers may have seen the Revolution as a chance to improve their status and expand their wealth.

The promise of change electrified these men; they attended political meetings several times a week and emerged as key players in municipal politics.[38] Louis was among the founding members of the Société des Amis de la Constitution, which was created in December 1789 and went by the name Société du Concert. Louis's wealthy cousin, the lawyer François Vitet, was also a member of the Société du Concert.[39] This club was the Lyonnais branch of what would become known as the Jacobin Club in Paris, until it broke from the Jacobins in July 1793. Its membership fees excluded workers and artisans, prompting one historian to describe the meetings as "genteel" gatherings of "well known citizens" and as "essentially a rich man's debating club."[40] In late 1790, neighborhood clubs known as the *sections*, thirty-two of them in all, emerged as a new, more popular voice in Lyonnais politics. Louis and Claude probably attended both their neighborhood sectional meetings and those of the Club Central, where representatives from the sections met. The Club Central composed lists of candidates for elected office, most of whom would then succeed in their bids for election. These clubs were precursors to modern political parties, as they helped to organize the slates of candidates. However, the line between organizing electoral lists and fixing elections easily blurred.[41]

The Revolution changed these men's lives forever, forcing them to respond to the new world taking shape around them. Louis Vitet's first official position was as a "notable," which meant he served on a committee that advised the mayor. As leading citizens, the two Arnaud-Tizon brothers and their father appeared on the lists of eligible voters that were created in February 1790. That same month brought popular disturbances inspired by demands to expand the suffrage beyond the wealthiest citizens. Louis Vitet, who often served as a mediator between the elites who controlled the municipality and the popular classes, was sent by the Consulate, a local governing body created to protect the silk trade, to preach law and order among the poor.[42] In March 1790, the Revolutionary government created the modern administrative divisions of France, departments, with each department divided into districts. Vitet became president of the district of Lyon, a position that put him in direct conflict with the mayor, Palerne de Savy, who was known for his opposition to the Revolution. He then won the first mayoral elections held in December 1790. Claude *fils*, too, became active in Revolutionary politics, serving on the municipal council from around the same time. Although the Revolution offered new opportunities to these men and transformed their circumstances, it had little effect on their values, preferences, or attitudes. They remained committed to holding on to their wealth and the elite status their families had been slowly accruing for generations.

Unflinching supporters of the Revolution, Louis Vitet and Claude Arnaud-Tizon were members of a group known as the *patriotes*. Over time, however, the significance of that label evolved. Vitet, along with his close ally Jean-Marie Roland, supported the early stages of the Revolution and later the transition from monarchy to republic.[43] Like Roland, Vitet believed in a limited form of democracy under which wealthy and educated citizens would serve as leaders working in the best interests of their poorer compatriots. He went on to serve as mayor of Lyon for two years, until September 1792. National and local political developments moved at a rapid pace during those years, and Vitet and his *patriote* allies managed to maintain control and avoid violent disorder thanks to a combination of good luck and political skill. Liked and respected by the *menu peuple*, he steered a middle course between the forces of democracy and popular politics on the one hand and the efforts of wealthy property owners who sought to limit the political influence of the popular classes on the other.[44] Vitet's attempts at pursuing a policy of moderation between these forces proved less successful as the divisions between these opposing groups grew increasingly irreconcilable.

Political turmoil led to personal tragedy for Claire Arnaud-Tizon, the sister who married into an aristocratic family. Claire died in Lyon on February 25, 1791, leaving behind two young children, Antoine and Agathe.[45] A contemporary source says she committed suicide while her husband was defending his family's chateau from attack. Although the account cannot be verified, and its bias is quite evident, it is worth quoting at length for its passionate depiction of her breakdown.

> While he rushed off to help his father, Guillin d'Avenas left his tender and interesting wife in Lyon. Already overwhelmed by anxiety about the disaster that menaced the family that had adopted her, she allowed

> her concern for her husband's well-being to overwhelm her. She could no longer stand the anxiety. Her reason was not strong enough to overcome the violence of her fears. Her heart broken by the pain, her spirit crushed by hopelessness, this young heroine of conjugal love threw herself from the window of her apartment. Her tragic and premature death resulted from an excess of *sensibilité*.[46]

This highly sentimental account by a prominent counterrevolutionary must be taken with a large grain of salt, but its emphasis on the private suffering caused by political violence typifies contemporary attitudes.

The Guillin family never comes up in the Arnaud-Tizon family's later correspondence, even though they seem to have been on good terms up until Claire's death. However, those family ties must have been difficult to manage, as Claire's brothers actively supported the Revolution, while her husband and his family came under attack as nobles. The emotional strain may have become too much for her. It is not surprising that her brothers and sister-in-law would not have brought up the scar left by Claire's suicide in letters written many years later to Pierre, who likely knew the whole story. The one exception to this silence is a passing reference in Pierre's correspondence journal, in which he recorded the March 1814 death of Guillin d'Avenas while in Paris, where he had come to enroll his son in the elite military school Saint Cyr.[47] That one line suggests that the two families had remained in touch.

Throughout 1791 and 1792, Claude *fils* continued to serve as a municipal officer, attending daily meetings of the municipal council, a six-member board that typically met every morning and afternoon. He was in charge of finances; among his other duties, he oversaw the melting down of an equestrian statue of Louis XIV in November 1792.[48] He also briefly served as interim mayor, during which time he blocked Joseph Chalier's proposal to put Lyon's newly arrived guillotine on permanent display.[49] Claude was voted off the council in November 1792, and we find little trace of his activities for several months. While Claude held public office, his wife, Catherine, was no doubt busy with their three young children. As mentioned earlier, the spacing between births suggests that she breastfed her children. How involved in raising her children was she? Like most bourgeois families, they no doubt had servants who did much of the real work of running the household. The wife's role was largely to supervise the servants and ensure that the household ran smoothly. Catherine may also have taken her husband's place in the family business while he was so involved in politics.

Unfortunately, there are no documents from this period to give a sense of Catherine's main occupations or the degree to which she followed political developments. She may have accompanied Claude to meetings of political clubs, such as the Société Populaire des Amis de la Constitution, which women attended in large numbers.[50] Lyonnais women, like those in several other provincial cities, also founded a woman's club where they discussed political texts.[51] A satirical play performed at the Théâtre des Célestins in the winter of 1791–1792 titled *Le club des bonnes gens* ridiculed the clubs and their members but drew particular attention to women who were depicted as "talking endlessly [and] lecturing their husbands on revolutionary principles."[52] Catherine was an avid observer of political developments later in life, a passion that probably dated to this period, but there are no traces of her views and activities during this time, other than her marriage contract and her name on the birth records for her children. What we can know with certainty is that she was a young wife and mother whose husband was deeply involved in local politics. She also no doubt worried about the consequences of his political activities, particularly as the Revolution entered its more radical phase.

National events often overshadowed local politics. In June 1791, Louis XVI tried to flee the country and was caught in the village of Varennes in northeastern France. He left behind incriminating documents proving that he had lied repeatedly when he had said he was willing to serve as a constitutional monarch. When Louis returned to Paris in disgrace, the crowds welcomed him with stunned silence. The idea of making France into a republic, which had been barely mentioned up until that point, began to seem like a desirable option to a growing portion of the population.[53] The members of the National Assembly nonetheless moved forward with the constitution they had been working on for nearly two years; it went into effect that fall, even though everyone now knew that the king was an unwilling participant.

Developments in Paris had an immediate impact in Lyon, where the radical *patriote* Joseph Chalier began to emerge as an influential voice in the sections. A populist who detractors suggest may have been mentally unstable, Chalier used his formidable skills as an orator to encourage the popular classes of Lyon to exercise their political power.[54] In January 1792, the departmental administration ordered that Chalier be suspended from his position as a municipal officer and organized a search of his home. Louis Vitet voiced his support for Chalier but probably felt relieved to have this extremist out of the way.[55]

Debates about religion inspired much of the violence that broke out in Lyon as elsewhere. In July 1791, the National Assembly passed the Civil Constitution of the Clergy, which required priests to sign an oath of allegiance to the Revolutionary government. Those who refused to sign were labeled "refractory priests," and as enemies of the Revolution, they were eventually denied the right to serve as parish priests. Many went into hiding, while others left the country. In Lyon, the members of the departmental administration supported the refractory priests, while Vitet was working to close churches that did not have "constitutional priests" to serve them. In the context of this conflict, Chalier returned to his spot on the municipal council and voiced criticism of the mayor's policies. He stirred up the popular classes to attack anyone who seemed insufficiently enthusiastic for the Revolution.

In August 1792, Vitet sent a letter to Roland, expressing his concerns about Chalier's calls for violent insurrection: "The day before yesterday Monsieur Chalier stood at the podium of the Club Central and said . . . that it was necessary to give the people all its sovereignty by cutting off the heads of all the refractory priests and aristocrats. It is only in seeing their impure blood streaming everywhere that you will acquire tranquility, security, and happiness. He stirred up the popular classes so much that we can no longer contain them, and horrific scenes will soon be taking place."[56] Vitet's prediction was on the mark: on September 9, 1792, a massacre of military officers and refractory priests being held in the prison of Pierre-Scize took place. Chalier had encouraged the crowds to enter the prison, but Vitet appeared partially responsible as well, having ordered the arrests of these people in the first place.[57] Though Vitet accused Chalier of encouraging this violence, these kinds of events occurred in many towns across France. It is thus inappropriate to assign blame solely on him or any other individual. Regardless of the immediate causes of this crisis, Louis Vitet's policy of moderation seemed to have failed. He stepped down as mayor on September 15 but did not give up on politics. Instead, he took a seat as deputy to the National Convention and then traveled back to Lyon in October as a representative on mission with the goal of bringing law and order to the city. While in Lyon that fall, Louis complained about the *négociants* and their unwillingness to support the Revolution. In a letter to Roland, he wrote that they "preferred to be slaves than to earn less money."[58]

After spending a few months in Lyon, in January 1793, Louis Vitet returned to Paris, where he participated in the Convention's deliberations and trial accusing Louis XVI of high treason. He voted for the king's guilt but not his immediate execution, supporting instead a national referendum on the king's fate. During the king's trial, Vitet responded to four questions posed to the deputies:

1. Is Louis guilty? Vitet: Yes
2. Should there be a referendum? Vitet: Save the republic and escape from the emerging factions. I say yes, and I say it because the people think and act better than we do.

3. Should there be a delay in making judgment on Louis Capet? Vitet: Yes
4. What punishment should Louis receive? Vitet: Imprisonment and banishment of *la race des Bourbons*.[59]

Vitet's language suggests that while he was a committed republican, he hoped to avoid the domestic and diplomatic consequences of executing the king.

In the end, more radical voices in the Convention carried the vote. The repercussions of the king's beheading on January 21, 1793, reverberated widely and led to growing factional division in the Convention. Claiming illness, Vitet left Paris in late February and settled in his country home in Longes, a village in the Pilat mountains about twenty-five miles south of Lyon.[60] By the spring, the Montagnards, the most radical members of the Convention, took control and eventually purged the leading Rolandins (later labeled the Girondins) from the Convention. Many fled to Caen in Normandy, where Charlotte Corday, inspired by their plight, began to lay her plans to assassinate the radical Parisian journalist Jean-Paul Marat.[61] Large numbers of Vitet's political allies, including the Rolands, would not survive the Terror. A combination of luck and timing, as well as a reliance on friends and family who helped him hide and eventually escape France, permitted Louis to avoid a similar fate.

Political Divisions Intensify

The Lyonnais upper classes, particularly the wealthy *négociants*, who had largely remained out of politics until this point, now felt compelled to act. Chalier's incendiary language and calls for open insurrection, which seemed to have as their goal the complete overthrow of the social order, stirred the Lyonnais elite to action. As the historian Bill Edmonds explained, "Nothing could have been better calculated to provoke a counter-attack from those men of property who had previously avoided local political affairs. Unfortunately for Lyon, this enhanced consciousness of the threat from below reinforced its élites' antagonism to popular involvement in politics just when national policy was being reshaped by radical democrats in Paris who regarded popular political involvement as essential to the defense of the Revolution."[62] In early May, the president of Lyon's now anti-Jacobin Committee of Public Safety, Louis Vitet's longtime collaborator Jean-Emmanuel Gilibert, published a notice in which he "warned of the 'anarchists' in Paris who were 'arming the poor against the rich' and 'crime against virtue.' He hastened to assure citizens that tranquility would be restored and civil war averted."[63]

The anti-Jacobins decided that it was in their best interests to take control of the municipality, which they managed to do on May 29, 1793. They then arrested Chalier, who was executed in July. With Chalier's opponents in control, the Jacobins in Paris sent troops to suppress the city's declared revolt against the National Convention.

Claude Arnaud-Tizon *fils* remained on the sidelines during these months of political turmoil. He had dropped off the municipal council in fall 1792, around the time that Louis Vitet stepped down as mayor, and there is no record of Claude's involvement in either the Chalier-led municipality or the regime set up by his opponents. His ailing father died two days before Chalier's overthrow. Thus, Claude may have chosen to reduce his public duties because of business and family responsibilities. Whatever the reason, he does not seem to have participated in municipal politics during either of these episodes, a fact that may have made him an appealing option once a new municipality took shape a few months later.

Beginning in late July 1793, Jacobin troops laid siege to the city and bombed it repeatedly, destroying homes and killing hundreds. Facing famine due to the siege, the Lyonnais accepted defeat in early October. Once the Jacobins took control, they executed nearly two thousand Lyonnais for taking part in the revolt.[64] On October 12, the Convention issued its famous decree, "Lyon made war against liberty; Lyon is no more." National forces then began to demolish the homes of wealthy residents near the Place Bellecour, though in the end, they did not destroy many of them.[65] As the Jacobin representatives on mission regained control over the city, they installed new leaders, including Claude, who once again became a municipal officer, this time under Antoine-Marie Bertrand, an ally of Chalier who had been serving as mayor before the anti-Jacobin takeover. Claude attended municipal council meetings virtually every day of that difficult year when Lyon's name was officially changed to Commune-Affranchie (Freed City) and the Terror was in full operation. In most cases, his name appears first on the list of signers to the minutes, right after that of the mayor.[66]

Claude served on the *comité de subsistances*, which meant that he was one of three men responsible for ensuring that Lyon's inhabitants would have access to sufficient food. Grain shortages had been a problem since the beginning of the Revolution, and various solutions were attempted, including subsidizing the cost of bread. In the months before the siege, the municipality introduced a system in which bakers could make two kinds of bread—"white bread and an inferior 'pain national'"—with poor families receiving subsidies to help them pay for the cheaper bread.[67] Local officials hoped that if the bakers could profit from the white bread, they would lower the price for the cheaper variety. Another option, which Paris Jacobins instituted in spring 1793, was the Maximum, a system of price controls on grain and bread. The Maximum was implemented temporarily in Lyon but lasted only a few weeks. The anti-Jacobin municipality believed that setting prices too low could result in reduced grain supply. After the siege, the Jacobin-controlled municipality reinstituted the Maximum, and Claude was among those responsible for enforcing the price controls and ensuring adequate supplies of bread.

Choosing Flight

While Claude stayed in Lyon and held public office under the Jacobins, many tried to flee the city. His brother, Pierre-Marie, received permission to travel to Rouen with his wife, daughter, and a servant in January 1794.[68] Louis and Pierre Vitet chose a different route: exile. They spent the first half of 1793 in Longes. Louis had inherited a house and agricultural lands in the village from his father and then bought more land and another house when they came up for auction as *biens nationaux* (church-owned property confiscated and sold by the Revolutionary government).[69] While there, the Vitets hosted two of Pierre's close friends, the Suchet brothers, one of whom would go on to an illustrious career in the military. The brothers left Lyon after the overthrow of the Chalier municipal council in May and stayed in Longes for a few days before heading to their father's native region, the Ardèche, where they joined the Revolutionary army.[70]

Louis chose to remain in Longes while his native city rose in insurrection against the Jacobin-dominated government in Paris. Pierre explained his father's thinking in a memoir he composed later in life:

> In these stormy circumstances, we were still in the country, and we were happy that our retirement had saved us from playing any role in the current crisis for which we could see the dangerous consequences. Our security seemed so assured that we were not even troubled by the new decree that placed my father *en état d'arrestation*. We were convinced that the Assembly had acted in error in his regard, since he had been on medical leave and had been living in the country for five months, and that separated at this distance from the city no one could suspect him of being in contact [with the insurgents in Lyon].[71]

According to Pierre, Louis took no precautions for his safety "and waited for the Convention to withdraw its decree once properly instructed" on his whereabouts during the insurrection in Lyon.[72] When news came that Jacobin troops were heading for Lyon, with some nearing Longes, Pierre and his father fled just in time to avoid arrest, leaving behind Marguerite, who had to face the "disrespectful behavior of the detachment" that arrived to search their property.[73]

While circling around Lyon, Pierre and Louis were arrested by municipal forces and brought into the city. Though quickly freed, they became trapped once the siege began. When the city fell to the Jacobins, Louis and Pierre knew they were in real danger. After spending a few days in hiding, they managed to leave the city under cover of darkness, but not before observing many atrocities, as the Jacobins began arresting so-called traitors and counterrevolutionaries. Pierre recalled their suffering in his memoirs:

> I had by this point left my first refuge and after living for a few days with some respectable people . . . I finally settled with our brave tenant, Colfavrot Tourneur, with whom I lived tranquilly and without bringing any suspicion upon him. They had even put seals on our apartment, which I had taken care to empty ahead of time. . . . It was during this period of house searches that my venerable grandfather (M. Faulin) was arrested. Imprisoned . . . without consideration for his age and virtue, he succumbed two months later from sorrow and misery.[74]

Sadness and fear dominate Pierre's account of this time spent hiding in a village on the outskirts of the city.

Shortly afterward, Pierre and Louis arranged for a guide to accompany them to the Swiss border. Pierre's account of their exile in Switzerland serves as both an adventure tale and a reflection on human nature, as he discussed how they were treated and mistreated. They left on January 6 and, after traveling on foot much of the way, arrived in Geneva five days later. From there, they headed to Coppet, a village bordering Geneva, where Louis XVI's former finance minister, Jacques Necker, lived in his chateau. However, Pierre and Louis received a poor welcome from local officials and did not stay. "I was told that the clerk at the office was ill-disposed to my father and me and had hesitated about whether to give us a *laissez-passer*. Trying to understand what was happening, we spoke with the office chief and explained our situation, our misfortune, and our intensions; we tried to make it clear that we had been misrepresented by an émigré who was an enemy of my father. Worrying that this slander would spread and that these unfavorable opinions of us would reach Lausanne, we decided to leave right away."[75] They boarded a stagecoach for Lausanne, where they found friends willing to help them. After passing through several other towns, they settled down in early February, with Pierre in Zurich working for an apothecary and his father in hiding in a small village with two friends, Conventionnels in exile like Louis.[76] The fact that Pierre later wrote a lengthy account of his and his father's actions and motivations during this difficult year suggests how much the experience of facing political persecution and being forced into exile affected him.

Then came 9 Thermidor (July 27, 1794), when Maximilien Robespierre and his closest collaborators on the Committee of Public Safety were overthrown and executed, ending the period now known as the Terror. Mass confusion accompanied this transition, labeled the Thermidorian Reaction, which included purging the "Robespierrists" from their offices. The French population as a whole struggled to make sense of the previous year and to comprehend its consequences on their collective psyche.[77] Discussing the Thermidorian period in Lyon, Paul Hanson explained that "the Jacobins who came to local office during the Terror stood as easy marks for the murderous vengeance of the White Terror, and they were killed not only for their own alleged crimes, but for having served as pawns of Paris during the Year II."[78] Claude was one such local official. For Louis and Pierre, Thermidor brought an end to their forced exile. They returned to Lyon and began working to have their sequestered property returned to them. Louis did not stay very long, as he was elected to serve as deputy for the department of the Rhône in the Council of 500, the lower house of the legislature as defined by the constitution of 1795.

Claude may have survived both the Red and the White Terror, but he did not come out unscathed. He was among those who were purged from Lyon's municipal council when the Jacobin-led government fell. From one day to the next, in late August 1794, the mayor and all the municipal officers who had served during the Terror were replaced by others who had remained out of politics since the end of the siege. Claude was arrested along with several of his colleagues from the municipality in October.[79] They were to be imprisoned first in Lyon and then sent to Paris, where Claude was apparently set free.[80] Soon after his arrest, municipal authorities searched and sealed his apartment, paying special attention to the papers they found in Claude's office. Two "business associates," Francoal and Bournichon, observed the search and signed the document listing the contents of Claude's home.[81] The document makes no mention of Claude's wife and children.

It is unclear where Catherine and her three children were when their family home was being searched. In the chaos of late summer and fall of 1794, with Robespierre dead and the Terror giving way to the White Terror, Catherine must have faced some of the most harrowing experiences of her life.[82] Her three children were nine, seven, and four years old when her husband was arrested and sent to Paris to await judgment. Claude could have easily been executed as part of the general purge of Jacobins that took place in the summer and fall of 1794, but he somehow escaped that fate. Instead, he and his family built lives for themselves in a new city. Although the documentary evidence is thin for these years, based on later comments in one of her letters, Catherine must have joined her "dear brother and sister" in Rouen in 1795 or 1796. Like Louis Vitet, Claude Arnaud-Tizon managed to survive this tumultuous period through a combination of luck and timing, and perhaps with the assistance of close friends and allies who may have orchestrated his release from prison.

Chapter 2

Recovery

Rebuilding Lives after the Terror

In the aftermath of the Terror, the French in general and these two families in particular worked to rebuild their lives after the chaos and trauma they experienced during the Year II. Politically, this meant writing a new constitution, a process that led to the creation of a government known as the Directory, named after its five-person executive committee of "Directors." Creating a stable political and economic system proved difficult. Both monarchists on the right and Jacobins on the left staged attempted coups against the government as it struggled to steer a middle course. The new paper currency the Revolutionary government had created, the *assignats*, quickly lost value, and runaway inflation made ordinary life difficult. Problems with food shortages and brigandage also remained unresolved. In the end, it was a military strongman, Napoleon Bonaparte, who would emerge as a savior for France. He began making a name for himself as a general in the mid-1790s. After invading Egypt in 1798, he returned to France and launched a coup d'état, bringing an end to the Directory regime and creating a more authoritarian government. The Napoleonic years brought greater stability to France, but at the cost of individual liberties, as strict censorship and a heavy police presence were the main tools to maintain order.

Confusion and turmoil marked the period immediately following the Terror; most people went into survival mode. For former Jacobins, or those presumed to have been Jacobins, such as Claude Arnaud-Tizon, the best strategy was to avoid the limelight. Moving to a city where he was largely unknown certainly made sense for Claude, and Rouen was an obvious choice, as the family already had a network in place there thanks to Pierre-Marie's in-laws. Claude nonetheless returned frequently to Lyon to oversee his business there.

By 1796, the Arnaud-Tizon brothers and their wives and children had settled in Rouen, a city in Normandy that is today about an hour's train ride from Paris. Like Lyon, Rouen is a city on a river (the Seine) surrounded by hills and whose dominant industry was textiles, but cotton rather than silk. It was also smaller than Lyon, with about eighty thousand inhabitants.[1] Pierre-Marie and Anne-Françoise left Lyon in February 1794, moving onto the same street as her parents, the Vincents, and her married sister, who had married into the Ballicorne family.[2] Catherine Arnaud-Tizon and her children joined them later. They all lived close together on a narrow street in central Rouen, the rue aux Ours, probably in buildings owned by the Vincent family, as there are no records of the Arnaud-Tizon men purchasing or renting property there.[3] Their homes were likely two-story, timber-framed dwellings, with commercial space on the ground floor, a courtyard, and living spaces above.[4]

In September 1798, two years after settling there, Catherine gave birth to her fourth child, Adèle. Claude did not sign the birth registry, which listed his address as rue de Sirène, Lyon.[5] For well over a decade, Claude and later his son Ludovic traveled back and forth between the two cities on a regular basis. Catherine, however, stayed in Rouen for the most part, along with her daughters, living side by side with her sister- and brother-in-law. After 1811, when they sold the last of their Lyonnais properties, Claude and Ludovic Arnaud-Tizon settled in Rouen as well. It is impossible to say whether the Arnaud-Tizons would have remained in Lyon had the Revolution not taken place, but their activities in Lyon during the Revolution, particularly during the period of Jacobin domination, no doubt contributed to their decision to transplant their families. This family's trajectory thus illustrates one of the less recognized consequences of the French Revolution: increased internal migration.[6]

Similarly, for both personal and political reasons, Pierre and Louis Vitet also settled into a new city: Paris. Leaving France had allowed them to keep their heads, but they returned to find their lives and property in disarray. How did Pierre's mother survive during their time in exile? Their house in Longes, la Jurary, was sealed soon after Pierre and Louis fled, as was their apartment on the rue Port Charlet near Lyon's Hôtel Dieu. Marguerite seems to have spent those months in or near Lyon, perhaps with her sister, Jeanne Morel. Soon after Robespierre's fall, she began the work of gaining access to their homes; it is her name that appears on those first official requests. The Lyonnais authorities officially removed the seals on Louis's properties in January 1795.[7] A month later, Pierre received permission to travel to Paris to study medicine, though he seems to have been more interested in studying art.[8] In March, Marguerite and her sister signed the document lifting the seals on their apartment on the rue des Bouchers, from which, they declared, some of their silverware had been stolen when the rooms were searched.[9] Though such losses no doubt caused some frustration, at least their lives were getting back to normal.

From 1795 to 1799, Louis served as a deputy to the Directory regime's lower house, the Council of 500, with Pierre serving as his assistant. We know that Pierre handled his father's correspondence, because the journals he left from these years are filled with summaries of letters received and copies of letters he wrote on behalf of his father. He also kept careful records of their income and expenses. Having their sequestered properties returned to them was relatively easy, but getting their finances in order took several years, in part because of the more general problem of currency during these years. In December 1789, the Revolutionary government began circulating assignats, a kind of paper money backed by the sale of national properties. Within a few years, the assignats' value crashed, which meant that inflation, along with efforts to hoard hard currency, added to the chaos of those years.[10] Pierre wrote frequently to his mother about how to maximize the value of their properties and investments, strategizing about how to handle their apartments and tenants, while she did the legwork in Lyon. He was also in regular contact with the farmers working their land in Longes and kept track of the family's country estate, even sending seeds to the gardener and lists of what to plant, including asparagus and artichokes.[11]

Other challenges peppered Pierre's time in Paris. In autumn 1797, he endured two operations to remove hemorrhoids, and it took him several months to recover.[12] Around the same time, he and his father took an important step: they purchased property in Paris. In January 1798, Louis signed the paperwork to buy a building on the rue neuve Saint Roch (today the rue Saint Roch), where Pierre and eventually his wife and son would live for many years.[13] The previous owner, Jean Marie Joseph Blondel, had purchased the building two years earlier as a *bien national* and sold it to Vitet for 25,500 livres. It had five floors plus an attic, a garden behind it, and an additional smaller structure alongside the garden. Parts of the building were rented out as apartments. It was a former convent located behind the Saint Roch Church, not far from the Tuileries. Following the 1801 Concordat, the man who became the priest at Saint Roch was a longtime family friend from Lyon,

Claude Marie Marduel, a former refractory priest and émigré. While maintaining their emotional and financial ties with Lyon and their fellow Lyonnais, both the Vitet and Arnaud-Tizon families were establishing roots and creating new routines and networks in the cities to which they had relocated.

A City Destroyed

In May 1798, Pierre traveled to Lyon for the first time in three years. During his trip, he corresponded frequently with his father, sending him news about the people he visited, the condition of their native city, and the actions he took regarding their properties. Upon his arrival, Pierre sent a long letter to his father describing his voyage and his first impressions upon seeing Lyon. His account brings to life this difficult and confusing moment when the Directory government was struggling to bring political and economic stability to an exhausted population.

> I am hurrying to inform you of our safe arrival in Lyon. . . . The roads, which were passable at this time of year, must be awful during the winter, and make one desire the prompt installation and useful consequences of new tolls. Tollbooths have already been constructed at the entry of several towns, but they are still unmanned. The posts are well manned, especially near Paris. The evening of our departure . . . we arrived at Fontainebleau where we spent the night. The next night we slept at Vermenton and the following one at Dijon where Mr. Audiffret had some business to handle. We admired the beauty and fertility of Burgundy, and at Baume my companion paid tribute to our admiration by buying twelve bottles of excellent wine. We finally arrived in Lyon on the morning of the 26th having made only a brief stop at Macon. We stayed on the road most of the last night to be able to travel with some other carriages heading in the same direction.[14]

Banditry remained a problem throughout the Directory. Having several carriages travel together offered some protection from attack.[15] Pierre's passing reference to other carriages reminds us of the dangers of travel in these years, though most of the letter emphasized the positive.

When Pierre turned to his reactions to Lyon, he sounded less sanguine: "As I was entering Lyon, I was struck by the solitude and inactivity that reigns in the streets. It is certain that this sensation was not simply the effect of the contrast with the immense city of Paris which I had just left, but that in reality the population and activity of Lyon have greatly diminished and that to sojourn here has become less pleasant."[16] He then provided an account of various sites that had been destroyed and took note of some slight improvements that had been made to the quays. Overall, Lyon compared poorly to the capital. "That's all that I have been able to see for the moment, having spent most of my time at the house and the rest of the day with my mother and our friends Davallon and Jautet. I did not find the trip tiring, having taken the precaution to eat only healthy food and washing every evening. I will be sure to continue this routine."[17] Pierre wanted to reassure his father that he was taking good care of himself.

After describing the city, Pierre spoke of his mother and their house and then shared his plans. "I found my mother in good health and happy to see her son and to receive news about her husband. The preparations for my arrival produced more orderliness in our apartment than I would have thought possible. I noticed that our third floor was in good condition. The kitchen has been repaired correctly; all together there has been little damage [from the fire]. . . . I will include details on all of this in my next letters."[18] Much of the letter discussed the people he had seen. The purpose of the trip seemed to include interacting with the right people to accomplish some unstated goal. "I will be able to play a role here as I have already been visited by the dignitaries of the town . . . as well as our friend Marduel. I do not know if my arrival was trumpeted, but to avoid so many visits, I have informed the servant [not to admit guests], and soon I will leave for the countryside."[19] It is unclear what his "role" was, but Pierre's reference to "dignitaries" suggests there was something he hoped to accomplish besides checking on their properties. The letter's closing offers a glimpse into the relationship that existed between this father-and-son team, two men who had lived side by side for many years: "Adieu my dear father. Take care of your health and send me your news, and if there is any interesting political news, please tell me about it. Your devoted son, Vitet."[20] There was a strong sense of cohesion and familiarity between them.

Pierre's journal indicates that he wrote to his father every few days during this stay in Lyon. Unfortunately, we cannot be certain how often Louis responded, because most of his letters have been lost. However, one of the few letters Louis addressed to Pierre that has been conserved in the archives dates from this period. It includes details about some of the changes he was making to the new house in Paris. He had workers adding windows and expanding the attic over the chapel. Before closing the letter, Louis mentioned that he had dined with the younger Suchet brother and "your good [female] friends" (*tes bonnes amies*) and that they had drunk to Pierre's health.[21] Louis and Pierre seem to have socialized together as well as collaborating on Louis's political and other projects. We cannot know who those friends were, but the passing reference to Suchet suggests that he was someone they saw regularly. It seems they mostly socialized with fellow Lyonnais, a practice Pierre would continue even after many years in Paris.

After spending about four months in Lyon, from mid-May until early September 1798, Pierre returned to Paris and then submitted an official request to remain in the capital. He had to get a statement from the police of his arrondissement attesting to his good behavior, and his father, who was still a member of the Council of 500, endorsed the request, which was granted in November 1798. On the back of that document is Pierre's physical description at the time: "26 years old, 5 feet 6 inches tall [*5 pieds, 6 pouces*]; brown hair and eyebrows, ordinary forehead, brown eyes, aquiline nose, average size mouth, round chin, long face."[22] Although the document used feet and inches to describe his height, those measurements are not equivalent to those used today in the United States. The translation of eighteenth-century French measurements into meters gives him the height of 1.79 meters, or about 5 feet 10 inches, which would have been quite tall for this period. The average height of conscripts in the eighteenth century was 169 centimeters, but most of those men came from poor families who struggled to provide their children with enough food.[23] Wealthy families tended to have taller children because they were better fed. So, while Pierre was much taller than the average man in this period, he may not have stood out (so to speak) that much among men of his social standing.

In 1799, not long after receiving permission to stay in Paris, Pierre lived through another common experience of men in these years: he was drafted and ordered to report to the headquarters of the Army of Italy, then under the command of General Barthelémy Joubert (1769–1799).[24] The document describes Pierre as an *officier de santé* (a health officer), a term that referred to medical practitioners who had completed "an abbreviated program of study and who could practice limited forms of medicine in specific places."[25] He was a young man; France was at war. It was almost inevitable that he would be called to serve in the military. Pierre's childhood friend, Louis Gabriel Suchet, rose through the ranks in the Army of Italy and was promoted to *général de division* and chief of staff to General Joubert in July 1799.[26] Had Pierre joined the army, he might have served under his friend. But he avoided military service by taking advantage of a common practice among wealthy men: hiring a replacement. In an April 1800 letter to his mother, Pierre described the difficulties he had faced in finding a replacement before announcing this news that no doubt made her happy.[27] The Vitet family's wealth and connections permitted Pierre to remain in Paris pursuing his passion for art and managing the family's properties. Pierre was beginning his chosen lifestyle—that of a comfortable *rentier* with enough resources to opt out of a "real" career.[28]

Political and Personal Transitions

A few months later, political events once again transformed the Vitet men's lives. When Napoleon Bonaparte launched a successful coup d'état against the Directory in November 1799, Louis Vitet voiced staunch opposition to the coup and then chose to drop out of politics altogether.[29] Sixty-three years old at that point, he retired from public life and returned to writing, publishing two books in 1803, *La Médecine expectante* and *Matière médicale* (with Pierre listed as coauthor), and another, *Le Médecin du peuple*, in 1804.[30] His last book, *Traité de la sangue médicinale*, appeared posthumously in 1809.

A momentous event in Pierre's life took place in December 1801, when he got married at the age of twenty-nine. Pierre traveled to Lyon in the summer of that year, perhaps to explore matrimonial possibilities, even speaking with his future father-in-law, Claude Arnaud-Tizon. Unfortunately, there are no letters or journal entries to indicate who initiated the discussions or how. What is certain is that as soon as he returned to Paris, Pierre left for Rouen to meet Amélie and her family.[31] He was at the age to marry at this point. When men reached the age of thirty without marrying, people began to wonder about them, just as twenty (or even eighteen!) was the line drawn in the sand for young women.

Although we cannot know exactly how Pierre came to marry Amélie, some clues allow us to construct a plausible scenario, namely that mutual friends initiated the discussions of marriage, most likely the Roux couple. Vital Roux and his wife, Françoise Montagnat, came from the same Lyonnais milieu as the Arnaud-Tizon family. Claude Arnaud-Tizon and Vital Roux were in much the same situation in Lyonnais politics during and after the Terror. Both collaborated with the Jacobins and were subsequently forced to leave their native city.[32] The Roux family settled in Paris in 1798. Shortly thereafter, Vital Roux opened a bank with another Lyonnais, Jacques Fournel.[33] Madame Roux, who was known as Roux-Montagnat, ran a flourishing business making artificial flowers, eventually becoming the official flower maker of the emperor.[34] Pierre and Louis knew the Roux and Fournel families from their days in Lyon and numbered among their closest friends in Paris.

Families typically worked through intermediaries when negotiating a potential marriage, avoiding direct contact with the families of potential spouses on the chance that the plans fell through. No one wanted rumors to spread about why the marriage did not take place. The Roux couple would have served as the ideal interlocutors, as they were old friends of both families, and since they were in Paris, they could talk to Pierre and his father in person. They would have been able to lay out the financial side of the agreement and to describe Amélie as they remembered her. Once the initial details had been ironed out and it seemed as though all was in order, Pierre traveled to Rouen to meet Amélie and the rest of her family. That initial visit must have gone well, as they were married a month later.

Pierre and Amélie probably met for the first time during his trip to Rouen in November 1801. If they had seen each other earlier, it would have been in Lyon prior to 1793, when Amélie was a young child. It is possible that their fathers had remained in touch and even that Louis contributed to getting Claude released from prison. He (and perhaps Pierre) may, in that context, have had reason to be in touch with his wife. However, there is no trace in Pierre's papers that he ever wrote to any member of the Arnaud-Tizon family prior to his marriage, only that he spoke with Claude while in Lyon that summer. The financial details of the marriage had probably been arranged before Pierre arrived in Rouen, because parents usually waited until those matters had been settled before presenting a potential groom to their daughter. Soon afterward, they all traveled to Paris to celebrate the wedding.

Following common practice, Pierre's marriage served as an opportunity for Louis to transfer most of his properties to his son. These included a building on the rue de l'Hospice in Lyon valued at 25,000 francs; the house where they lived on the rue neuve Saint Roch that was valued at 36,000 francs; and property in Longes called Lacombe valued at 6,000 francs. Amélie's dowry was roughly equivalent and included 50,000 francs in cash and a trousseau valued at 6,000 francs.[35] The contract is relatively short and straightforward, much of it filled with standard legal language. It is a bit over six pages long, with the signatures on the bottom of the seventh page. This length is consistent with the contracts of Amélie's parents and grandparents.

The witnesses who gathered in Paris at the notary's office to sign Pierre and Amélie's marriage contract included both close family members and old friends from Lyon. They were identified by name and their relationship to the couple, with the men's professions indicated as well. In addition to Amélie's parents and Pierre's father, the signers included Anne-Françoise Adelaide Vincent, wife of Pierre-Marie Arnaud-Tizon, *négociant* in Rouen, paternal aunt of the bride; Claudine Françoise Adelaide Arnaud-Tizon, first cousin of the bride; Pierre-Louis Arnaud-Tizon, brother of the bride; Françoise Montagnat, wife of Vital Roux, *négociant* in Paris, friend of the bride and groom; Anne Marie Tournachon, wife of Jean Jacques Fournel, *négociant* in Paris, friend of the bride and groom. It is interesting that the women signed the document rather than their husbands, who were no doubt there with them.[36] Regardless of who placed their names on the document, this gathering was an opportunity to build and reinforce ties between not only the two families directly implicated but also their friends and allies.

One striking absence from the list of signers is Pierre's mother, who did not travel from Lyon to attend the wedding. Marguerite probably learned about her son's plans from Louis, as Pierre does not seem to have written to her during the weeks leading up to his wedding. In fact, Pierre's correspondence journal has very few entries during this period. It included one short entry dating from early November in which he simply recorded "Voyage to Rouen." The next entry, dated from over a month later, was a summary of a letter to his mother: "19 Frimaire [December 10, 1801], wrote about my marriage which took place on the 12th of this month. Our friend Marduel has arrived. Amélie attached a letter to mine."[37] It seems astonishing that it took Pierre a week to write to his mother about his wedding, though his father had likely shared details with her earlier. Unfortunately, because we do not have Marguerite's letters from these years, we cannot know how she reacted to the news of Pierre's marriage.

In contrast to his slow pace when it came to communicating with his mother about the wedding, Pierre wasted no time in facilitating a marriage that would link his wife's family to one of his closest friends, Gabriel Suchet, younger brother of the future Napoleonic marshal. Two weeks after marrying Amélie, Pierre wrote "*au papa* Arnaud-Tizon" and "*à la cousine* Adèle."[38] Adèle was Pierre-Marie Arnaud-Tizon's only daughter, and thus his sole heir. Pierre seems to have been quickly ingratiating himself with his in-laws.

Gabriel Suchet joined the army with his brother in 1793 and left the military in 1800 after a less-than-illustrious performance. A biography of the marshal includes details on the younger brother's civilian career. "He opted for civil administration, and he must have been quite successful because he was named director of the Rouen tax office in 1808. The two brothers had earlier agreed to allow their uncle [Louis] Jacquier to oversee the family's business in Lyon."[39] In the meantime, the elder brother continued his brilliant military career, becoming a marshal of France in 1811 and receiving the honorary title of duc d'Albuféra. Although the Suchet brothers remained close to Pierre throughout their lives, status and fame created some distance between Pierre and the marshal.

Several weeks after their wedding, Pierre and Amélie traveled to Rouen, giving Pierre and his in-laws a chance to discuss this possible marriage. During his stay, Pierre communicated regularly with his father and sent two letters to Gabriel Suchet.[40] After returning to Paris in February, Pierre wrote to Catherine, who seems to have been the other matchmaker involved in arranging the Suchet marriage.[41] Shortly afterward, she traveled to Paris and then Lyon, perhaps to meet with the Suchet brothers' uncle and to learn more about the family's wealth and connections.[42] This was the first of many instances when Pierre and Catherine would collaborate on family matters.

Catherine must have been satisfied with what she discovered about the Suchets in Lyon, as the steps toward a wedding continued. Not long after that trip, Pierre asked his father-in-law to propose a convenient date for Suchet's voyage to Rouen. The visit, which took place in early April, was an opportunity for him to meet his future bride and her parents.[43] They then began planning the wedding. Weddings always required a trip to Paris to purchase the necessary items. Adèle and her mother, Anne-Françoise, went to Paris in early June and then returned to Rouen along with Pierre and Amélie about ten days before the wedding took place.[44] Adélaïde Claudine Françoise Arnaud-Tizon married Gabriel Catherine Suchet in Rouen on June 21, 1802; he was twenty-eight, and she was nineteen. Pierre and Amélie remained in Rouen for a month after the ceremony.[45] By that time, Amélie was about five months pregnant. After returning to Paris, Amélie wrote to her cousin Adèle, who suddenly became "Madame Suchet" in Pierre's journal.[46] Marriage signified a change in status and the transition to adulthood, which was made visible in part through these naming practices. Once married, women became "Madame X" even among their close friends and relatives.

While the arrangements for the wedding were being settled, the groom's brother, General Suchet, was in Paris, having been assigned the task of improving military hospitals. One of his biographers draws attention to Suchet's social skills and connections and his ties to Rouen:

> The big project Suchet was working on did not keep him from participating in Parisian high society. He regularly attended receptions at the Tuileries where the Bonapartes welcomed him warmly. He was one of the few generals who knew how to carry himself in a salon. It did not take long for Talleyrand, *très veille France*, to notice him. Suchet also spent a few days in Rouen to attend the marriage of his brother, who married a well-endowed heiress. . . .
>
> At the end of October 1802, Suchet took a few days off to visit his brother. This trip coincided with Bonaparte's voyage to Normandy. On November 1, the First Consul organized an elaborate dinner, and knowing that Suchet was in Rouen, he invited him.[47]

The general probably also visited with his brother's in-laws during that visit. The Arnaud-Tizons must have been delighted to form this alliance, which connected them to high-ranking members of Napoleonic society, while Suchet no doubt appreciated the wealth that came with marrying the only daughter of a rich man.

The marriage, which cemented long-standing ties between the Vitet and Suchet families, boded well. The couple settled in Rouen, where Gabriel worked in the local tax office. They went on to have two sons and a daughter. In 1807, Gabriel purchased the Château de Saint Just near Vernon, between Paris and Rouen.[48] A secondary residence in the country served as both a status symbol and a potential refuge from the political and social disorders that plagued cities. Unlike most of his friends, Pierre Vitet never purchased a country home, perhaps because he already owned so many properties in and around Lyon. But he and Amélie often visited their friends' homes, where they enjoyed the fresh air and relaxing atmosphere.

A Young Couple in Paris

Soon after their December 1801 wedding, Amélie and Pierre settled into life on the rue neuve Saint Roch with Louis. Amélie got pregnant almost immediately after marrying, which was exactly what young brides were supposed to do. Sex was not a subject that was broached in these families' letters, at least not directly. In mid-August, a Vitet family friend, Marduel, referred to the subject obliquely while discussing his interactions with Pierre's mother in Lyon: "I often see Madame *la chère épouse et mère*. She is greatly satisfied to learn from your letters that the dear daughter-in-law is progressing well in her pregnancy. She will have been married for nine months on September third."[49] It is interesting that people took note of the nine-month mark after a wedding, as if they even expected that a bride conceive on her wedding night.[50]

Health was a common topic of discussion, especially regarding pregnancy and childbirth. In June 1802, Pierre wrote to Louis to announce his and Amélie's arrival in Rouen, where they would be attending Suchet's wedding. In that letter, he wrote that Amélie was feeling better; she may have been experiencing morning sickness before their trip. After about six weeks in Rouen, they returned to Paris for the remainder of her pregnancy.[51] Amélie gave birth to Louis, whom they called Ludovic, on 26 Vendémiaire Year XI (October 18, 1802), ten and a half months after their wedding. Louis, now a grandfather, may have assisted at Ludovic's birth, as midwifery was among his areas of expertise. In contrast to the long delay in writing to his mother after his wedding, Pierre wrote her immediately to inform her of Ludovic's arrival. The same entry in his journal includes a list of friends and family in

Lyon to whom he wrote to share the news. These included Mr. Marduel, Amélie's brother, whom he called "Arnaudtizon *fils*"; Louis's cousin, François Vitet; and other unnamed "principal acquaintances."[52] He did not write to Claude, probably because Catherine was with them to attend the birth, as was a common practice, and no doubt wrote to her husband herself. She and Louis served as the witnesses on the official record of Ludovic's birth.[53] Catherine arrived about a month before Ludovic's birth and returned to Rouen when Ludovic was five weeks old.[54] Pierre wrote to his mother the day Catherine left, sharing that news with her and informing her that Amélie and Ludovic were doing well.

Even though maternal breastfeeding had grown more common in the eighteenth century, Pierre and Amélie chose to send Ludovic to a wet nurse. Despite arguments in its favor, most famously Jean-Jacques Rousseau's, many upper-class women chose not to breastfeed their babies, either for health reasons or because of their lifestyles. Many believed that country air was healthier for babies and that they would be better off with wet nurses in rural villages than in the city with their parents.[55] Other reasons could be categorized as more selfish. Common knowledge dictated that nursing women should abstain from sex, something that young husbands probably found hard to bear. Nursing a baby also tied women to the home and, like many women of her class, Amélie may have preferred to be free to socialize as she wished. In his study of the wet-nursing business, the historian George Sussman referred to the contemporary social commentator Louis-Sébastien Mercier, who declared in 1783 that "the fashion of maternal nursing among Parisian women had passed."[56] The desire among upper-class Parisiennes to be free of the constraints imposed by breastfeeding may explain the apparently brief period during which maternal nursing was à la mode.

Amélie and Pierre were rarely apart during the first years of their marriage, and aside from at least one monthlong trip to Rouen each year, they stayed in Paris most of the time. After returning to Paris from Rouen in early 1803, Amélie sent her parents an update on Ludovic.[57] They had probably visited him on their way back to Paris. Unlike poorer families, who sent their babies far away from the city to wet nurses who charged less, Pierre and Amélie could afford to pay the higher prices charged by wet nurses in villages nearby and could thus visit Ludovic regularly. Sussman explained: "Wealthy families in the eighteenth century found wet nurses through personal contacts—friends, relatives, rural tenants, or servants—and maintained personal contact with the nurse during the period the baby remained with her through correspondence and frequent visits."[58] With Ludovic cared for by his wet nurse, the couple was free to devote their attention to each other while no doubt strengthening their bond through their shared affection for their son.

Pierre, Amélie, and Louis also traveled together to Lyon in May 1803, while little Ludovic was still with his wet nurse. This was the first time that Pierre's mother met her daughter-in-law, though she had seen Amélie's face in a portrait Pierre sent to her not long before Ludovic's birth.[59] They were gone about six weeks, but since the trip from Paris to Lyon took a minimum of four days, they had about five weeks in Lyon.[60] This visit appears to have been Louis's only trip to Lyon since the few months he spent there in 1794 and 1795; it was probably also the first time he had seen his wife in eight years.[61] They timed their trip to be there when Amélie's father, Claude, was also in Lyon.[62] Whenever Claude was there, he would visit with Pierre's mother, who wrote about his visits in her letters to Pierre. This trip thus gave Pierre and Amélie an opportunity to bring both sides of their family together. Like their correspondence practices, such visits reinforced their bonds.

While their trips to Lyon were infrequent, Amélie and Pierre visited with Amélie's family in Rouen regularly. In 1804, they traveled there three times. During the first trip, which took place in January, they left Louis home in Paris and Ludovic, who was getting close to the age when he could be weaned, with his wet nurse.[63] In March, soon after returning, they brought Ludovic home; he was sixteen months old.[64] One study found that most parents who hired wet nurses retrieved their babies soon after their first birthday.[65] However, the statistics that produced that average included poorer families for whom the fees charged by wet nurses were a considerable burden. For wealthy families like the Vitets, it seems to have been common to leave babies with their wet nurses until fifteen or eighteen months of age.

Sending frequent updates to his mother, who stayed in Lyon during these years, was one responsibility that Pierre made sure to fulfill. In May 1805, for example, Pierre announced that Ludovic would be receiving his smallpox inoculation, another big event in a young child's life. Since the process involved introducing live cowpox virus, it carried some risk. Pierre kept the family informed about such matters and sent updates once Ludovic had fully recovered.[66] Later that year, he also sent his mother a dress, asking his father-in-law, Claude, to deliver it on one of his many trips to Lyon.[67] This work of kinship, which we often associate with women, counted among Pierre's duties.

As a good *père de famille*, Pierre devoted much time to staying in touch with family and friends through letter writing and visiting. In June 1804, Amélie and Pierre brought little Ludovic with them to Rouen for the first time.[68] Pierre's father joined them, staying for about ten days during the middle of their visit. Until Louis's arrival, Pierre wrote several letters to his parents, but during his father's stay, Pierre did not add any entries to his correspondence journal.[69] He must have been busy visiting with family and taking his father sightseeing. Their travels seem to have included a trip to the seaside, as Pierre sent a package of shells to some friends in Paris. Pierre and Amélie stayed in Rouen for two months, only to return a few months later to celebrate New Year's.[70] Despite Pierre's use of the Revolutionary calendar in his journal, marking the traditional new year remained a family tradition, as did remembering people on their saint's day. During their stay, Pierre wrote to his mother to send her their well wishes, and a few days later, he sent his father a similar note: "My wife and I write to wish him a happy new year. Ludovic scribbled a few lines."[71] Such practices and the expressions of affection they contained reinforced familial ties. Having both sides of their family together in the same space, particularly once Ludovic could join them, gave Pierre and Amélie an even more effective way to build friendly relations among the in-laws and across the generations.

A momentous event in French and world history took place just before Pierre and Amélie traveled to Rouen for Christmas and New Year's: on December 2, 1804, Napoleon Bonaparte crowned himself emperor. Pierre's journal makes no mention of the coronation. There is little doubt that he and his father were opposed to the Empire, but their purely domestic existence means they left few traces of their political views. They, like many of their compatriots, seem to have acknowledged that the Revolution's experiment in democratic, participatory politics was over. It was time to focus on family and salvaging their patrimony while doing all they could to help their allies succeed in this new world.

Chapter 3

Turning the Page

Negotiating a New World in the Nineteenth Century

The early nineteenth century brought rapid change to France with a succession of political regimes, extraordinary military successes and debacles, and occupation. After the unstable Directory regime proved itself unable to handle either the economic difficulties caused by inflation and an unreliable currency or the brigandage of the countryside, Napoleon Bonaparte's coup d'état seemed to offer a solution.[1] His military credentials promised a courageous leader who would know how to end the chaos, and many people were willing to risk losing some of their freedom in exchange for law and order. Louis Vitet, ever the man of principle, refused to lend his support to what was clearly an unconstitutional and antidemocratic power grab. Aside from Louis, whose position as a deputy made his opinion public knowledge, it is impossible to know what our "characters" thought of the 1799 coup or Napoleon's 1804 coronation as emperor. They probably felt a mixture of hope for stability and concern that all they had fought for with the Revolution could be lost. Was Napoleon saving the Revolution or killing it? In 1799, as today, that was not a simple question to answer.

With Napoleon's rise to power, the swinging pendulum that characterized nineteenth-century French politics began. The Napoleonic Era (1799–1815) brought its own challenges: nearly constant warfare and thus heavy conscription; censorship and a virtual police state to silence opposition to the regime; and grave economic difficulties as the Empire began to collapse. It also brought some significant benefits: the Napoleonic Code, a standardized civil law code that permitted families to strategize and plan for the future; opportunities for career advancement and enrichment through the Napoleonic system of rewarding merit and loyalty among soldiers and administrators; and space for industrial and technological progress in the context of the continental blockade that protected French manufacturers from British competition.[2] These legal reforms, which remain the basis of the French civil code to this day, proved long-lasting, as did the administrative system in the provinces with prefects overseeing each department and reporting back to Paris.

The Empire collapsed abruptly when Napoleon abdicated in 1814 in the wake of military defeat, and the Bourbons returned to the throne with the first Restoration. The new government lacked popular support, however, as suggested by the willingness of millions of French to rally to Napoleon when he returned from exile in March 1815 and tried once again to lead France to victory during the period known as the Hundred Days, an interlude ended by the Battle of Waterloo. The Bourbon king, Louis XVIII, then returned to Paris once again, this time accompanied by hundreds of thousands of occupying troops who remained in France until 1818.[3] Charles X inherited the throne from his brother in 1824, then lost it in July 1830 in a relatively bloodless revolution. Pierre's son, Ludovic, participated in the political movements that contributed to that revolution.

The Vitet and Arnaud-Tizon families lived through this succession of political, economic, and legal changes, doing their best to ride the waves, but they did not emerge unscathed. The Arnaud-Tizon enterprise was hit by the repeated economic crises that struck France between 1811 and 1815. Some bad investments eroded much of their capital, and at the same time, they had to find the financial resources to provide a dowry for their youngest daughter, Adèle, who married in 1816. As they faced this new world, they relied on lessons learned as Lyonnais bourgeois of the old regime: being suspicious of outsiders; trusting only family and long-standing allies; working to get allies in positions that would benefit everyone; and building and relying upon the resulting network to accomplish personal and professional goals. The rules underlying the game may have changed with the abolition of privilege and merit in theory replacing birth when it came to selecting who would rise to the top—changes that made education more important, especially for boys. However, the strategies these families employed to navigate this new world resembled those they had mastered before the Revolution, particularly networking and knowing the right people to access positions of power and prestige. Such connections proved essential for young men seeking to build careers in a world where expanded educational opportunities among wealthy families increased the competition for many high-ranking positions.

Familial Transitions: Marriage, Property, Death

With some brief exceptions, Pierre and Amélie Vitet spent the first two decades of the nineteenth century living in Paris and raising Ludovic, who remained at home rather than attending a boarding school as most boys from wealthy families did. Pierre never practiced a profession and instead divided his time between working with his father, pursuing his interest in the arts, overseeing his son's education, and gathering with friends and family. Since Pierre did not work outside the home, he and Amélie were constantly available to each other and to little Ludovic, on whom they lavished attention. They spent much of their time socializing and partaking in the capital's many attractions and cultural events. They attended the theater and musical performances on a regular basis, and as an amateur painter, Pierre looked forward to each year's artistic salon, sending the catalog with commentaries to Amélie's family in Rouen. They also typically spent two months in Rouen every year in late summer and early fall, where they socialized with that city's wealthy industrialists and administrators.

During the last few years of Louis's life, Pierre's mother, Marguerite, joined them in Paris. She had never expressed any interest in visiting the capital and had lived apart from her husband and son for many years. What exactly convinced her to move to Paris is unclear, though seeing her grandson seems to have been her primary motivation.[4] She came for a visit in July 1806 and returned to stay with them that fall. It seems likely that her affection for Ludovic and her desire to be near him as he was growing up played a role in her decision to move to Paris. We know little about her relationship with her husband, as virtually none of their correspondence has survived, though one Lyonnais historian makes a strong case that theirs was an unhappy marriage.[5] Whatever her motivation for staying in Paris, Marguerite took her second voyage at a fortuitous moment. She arrived in October 1806, during Pierre and Amélie's annual visit to Rouen.[6] Two months later, Louis was involved in an accident; he was struck by a carriage while out for a walk, and Marguerite nursed him back to health. Aside from occasional trips to Lyon, she stayed in Paris for four years and was there when her husband died unexpectedly in June 1809.[7] He had nearly finished his last book, *Le traité de la sangue*, which Pierre completed and saw through its posthumous publication. About a year later, Marguerite left Paris precipitously and returned to Lyon, where she remained for the rest of her life, living with her trusted servant Marion in a building she co-owned with her sister.

While Louis and Marguerite Vitet chose to live apart for much of their lives, there is much evidence to suggest that Pierre and Amélie's relationship was based on mutual affection and even passion. In 1809, during one of the rare moments they were apart, with Amélie in Rouen and Pierre in Paris, Amélie received a letter from Mery Fournel, the wife of the Vitet's longtime friend Jacques Fournel. Madame Fournel drew attention to Pierre's devotion to Amélie: "You may complain that we are keeping Vitet too long. I am not the only guilty one in this affair as you will understand when I say that he has not yet dined with us. He has promised to come on Wednesday. Thus, I am the cause of one day's delay. But you should not get upset. For you must know how much it pains him to be unable to speak with his Amélie. Just among us, is there a husband who is more attuned to the wishes of his wife?"[8] Along with enjoying each other's company, Pierre and Amélie also slept in the same bed, a practice that was common among poorer couples but less so among the upper classes.[9]

After his mother's death in 1820, Pierre traveled to Lyon to handle inheritance matters. The long letter he sent to Amélie upon his arrival provides a glimpse of his personality, his sense of humor, and his physicality:

> I wrote to you from Chalons, my dear Amélie, to inform you of my safe travels up to that point. Now I hasten to let you know that I am in Lyon. . . . I arrived at the rue des Bouchers at 5:30 in the morning. I felt bad about showing up so early and serving as everyone's alarm clock. But in Lyon we are more diligent than in Paris. My aunt got up immediately, even though I had begged for her not to be disturbed. She wanted to be the first to embrace me and to express our mutual affection during this difficult first conversation. . . .
>
> I then washed up and got a shave as I had had no chance to even think about that since leaving Paris. Once I was cleaned up, it began to feel like the whole voyage, including my three nights in a carriage, had been a dream. I did not feel fatigued. The stagecoaches are quite comfortable; we covered the distance in exactly sixty hours. One of the voyageurs got off at Auton, which left just me and Labarolière's son in the carriage and we were able to make ourselves more comfortable. . . . As you can imagine, I took advantage of my talent for sleeping [*faculté dormitive*] to make do without my bed. It was not sleep that I missed but rather my dear companion. I thought about you a great deal but was unable to dupe myself with these illusions. Only writing to you

and imagining that we are taking up a conversation can begin to compensate for not seeing you. To attain this compensation, don't forget to reply and send me your news.[10]

Pierre's lighthearted account of his voyage, his reflections on Lyonnais versus Parisian attitudes, and his affectionate banter reflect the closeness and intimacy that marked his everyday interactions with Amélie.

Pierre was nearly fifty at the time of this trip, and his ability to bounce back after three nights in a carriage suggests that he was in good shape for his age. He seemed proud of his stamina and his approach to maintaining his health: "First, I can tell you that I am feeling very well having taken care to control myself at the dinners that I have been attending in town and when I accept generous invitations that are difficult to refuse. This precaution has helped me avoid the dangers associated with this lifestyle. In addition, I have been returning home early every evening to have a light snack with my aunt and get to bed early. Thus, my dear Amélie, there is no need for you to worry about my health."[11] *Dinner* here refers to the main meal of the day, which people typically ate in the early afternoon. Avoiding heavy foods and late nights was the main prescription for maintaining one's health, and in mentioning those details, Pierre sought to reassure Amélie that all was well, just as he had with his father twenty years earlier.

Family Ties and Tensions

Claude and Catherine Arnaud-Tizon's marriage was a similarly successful partnership that appears to have been based on mutual affection. For the first fifteen years after moving to Rouen, they spent a great deal of their time apart, because Claude returned frequently to Lyon along with his son, Ludovic, who, once he was old enough, remained in Lyon most of the time to oversee the family business. That changed in 1811, when Claude sold his business in Lyon, allowing him, Catherine, and Ludovic to focus on the factory and their growing family in Rouen. The Arnaud-Tizons also established strong relationships among the Rouenais bourgeoisie, forging friendships and attending social events where they could mingle with the "right" people.

In 1808, Claude and Catherine's second daughter, Victoire, married Jacques Barbet, a Protestant from Rouen whose father was an extremely wealthy textile manufacturer. The marriage contract includes some revealing details. Like her older sister Amélie, Victoire received a dowry of 50,000 livres plus a trousseau. Jacques's father contributed 15,000 francs' worth of objects—10,000 in silver and 5,000 in furniture. He also promised to give them 50,000 francs four years later. Until paying that sum in full, he agreed to pay them 5 percent interest annually on the amount.[12] Finally, the contract stipulated that Victoire had agreed to convert to Protestantism.

The issue of Jacques Barbet's religion, which never seems to have been a matter of concern to his in-laws, serves as an occasion to discuss these families' attitudes toward religion. With one important exception, the men and women in these families appear to have felt little attachment to religion. Louis and Pierre Vitet and Claude and Pierre-Marie Arnaud-Tizon were all Freemasons. Lyon was known as the capital of French Freemasonry in the eighteenth century, and Pierre drew masonic symbols, such as equilateral triangles, in his journal.[13] Louis supposedly labeled Catholicism "a Cinderella doctrine suitable for wet nurses and infants on the breast."[14] The Vitet and Arnaud-Tizon men were probably deists, while the women in these families seem to have held on to key traditions, such as baptism, without much attachment to religious belief beyond those rituals. The subject almost never comes up, except occasionally in the negative. For example, Catherine complained about how some people questioned her decision to allow her daughter to marry a Protestant.[15] In another instance, she told Pierre that she was feeling too ill to withstand the cold church where a mass was being held in honor of Louis XVI.[16] Her excuse sounded very much like someone who simply did not want to participate in the commemorations for the dead king.

One person held beliefs that contradicted these generalizations: Pierre's mother, Marguerite, whose letters stand out for their frequent references to religion and the importance of living as good Christians. Her emphasis on religious matters makes their near total absence from all the other family members' letters even more striking. When writing to her daughter-in-law, Marguerite emphasized the importance of religion, as she did in one letter she sent on Amélie's saint's day, *la sainte* Marie. (Amélie's full name was Amélie Marie Josèphe.) "My dear daughter, I am writing to wish you a *bonne fête* and to repeat my compliments on the good fortune you have for being under the special protection of the mother of God, the patron of all Christians and the protector of all French since Louis XIII, the Pious, consecrated all his kingdom to this good mother. This devotion is detailed in *Les Heures* de Noailles. On August 15, I encourage you to devote yourself to her at this special time."[17] Napoleon had designated August 15 "Saint Napoleon's Day," but Marguerite wanted her daughter-in-law to remember its earlier significance with a reference to Louis XIII's pledge to dedicate his kingdom to Mary.[18]

In addition to connecting the Arnaud-Tizons to a very wealthy Protestant family, Victoire's marriage to Jacques also initiated an important business relationship. Forming a partnership with Jacques, they purchased a factory in

1808 that used the period's cutting-edge technology to produce printed cotton fabrics known as calicos or *indiennes*; they thus became *indienneurs*.[19] Victoire's brother, Ludovic, who had been living and working in Lyon, moved to Rouen to engage in this new enterprise in 1811. Victoire and Jacques went on to have three children: Juste was born in 1809, Marie in 1810, and Henry in 1812.[20] After buying the factory, which was in a Rouen suburb called Bapaume, they moved into a house on-site. Then, in 1813, after his father died, Jacques left the partnership with his in-laws to work with his brothers.[21] A few years later, he bought a chateau called Ecorchebœuf near Dieppe, thus fulfilling a key aspiration of bourgeois families: owning a secondary residence in the country where one could appreciate the clean air and vistas and, if necessary, escape urban crowds.

Jacques's later trajectory illustrates broader trends among the French bourgeoisie. In 1822, he purchased the house and factory at Jouy that had belonged to one of France's most celebrated and successful *indienneurs*, Christophe Philippe Oberkampf.[22] At that point, Jacques began using the name Barbet de Jouy, though that new appellation only became official in the 1850s. Jacques's desire to acquire an aristocratic-sounding name reflects another aspect of postrevolutionary continuity: titles still mattered. A new, more confident bourgeois political identity may have been taking shape in these years, thanks to the growing visibility of the liberal opposition to the Restoration. However, Jacques's story demonstrates that wealth and connections continued to function as stepping stones toward more aristocratic aspirations. Jacques no doubt hoped that the name Barbet de Jouy would help his sons gain access to positions and opportunities that had remained closed to him.

The two younger Arnaud-Tizon siblings, Ludovic and Adèle, married into families from the same milieu. Ludovic's wife, Marie Françoise Julie Thiébault, went by the name Amélie, yet another example of shared first names in this story with two Ludovics, two Adèles, and three Amélies. Ludovic Arnaud-Tizon's Amélie came from a family of wealthy merchants. Her father had died when she was young, and her mother had since married a *négociant* named Marc Antoine Brunet. Her mother and stepfather signed her marriage contract, which stipulated that she would receive 60,000 livres in dowry. Ludovic's parents promised the same amount, and Ludovic provided twenty-five thousand from his own savings.[23] Taking advantage of this opportunity to reinforce both families' ties to their wealthy and well-connected allies, the witnesses who gathered to sign the contract included several high-ranking members of Napoleonic society, among them the banker Jacques Récamier and Jacques-Fortunat Savoie-Rollin, the former prefect of the Seine-Inférieure. The couple settled into the house and factory at Bapaume, where Ludovic ran the family business. They had four children who survived infancy, three boys and a girl—Claudius, Marc, Marie, and Auguste, born in 1814, 1815, 1820, and 1826.[24]

Once Ludovic Arnaud-Tizon married, only one child remained in Catherine's household. Several years separated her youngest daughter from her three older children. In fact, Adèle was only four years older than her nephew Ludovic Vitet, and the two played together when they were children. Unlike the others, who had spent their early years in Lyon, Adèle grew up in Rouen. At the age of fifteen, she began attending balls there with her mother to be "seen" in society, but unlike her sister, she did not marry someone from Rouen. In 1816, at the age of eighteen, Adèle married Jean-Christophe Riocreux, whose family ran a business that made silk ribbons in Saint Etienne, a large town not far from Lyon.[25] Christophe handled his family's business dealings in Paris, and the Riocreux couple settled there, something that pleased the young bride, who had always enjoyed visiting the capital. A few years later, in 1821, Claude and Catherine moved to Paris as well. At that point, the only family members who remained in Rouen were Claude's brother, Pierre-Marie, whose wife died in 1817, and Ludovic and Amélie Arnaud-Tizon along with their children.

Despite doing everything possible to ensure their children's happiness and to provide them with the financial resources to succeed, all was not smooth sailing, and financial matters precipitated three family crises that caused tension and anxiety among the Arnaud-Tizon and Vitet families. One crisis involved Pierre-Marie's son-in-law, Gabriel Suchet. In 1817, it became clear that Suchet was facing serious financial problems. He had been unable to keep up with his obligations to his creditors and was facing bankruptcy. To save the family's honor, Suchet's brother and father-in-law came to his rescue, but he never fully recovered solvency and struggled with debts for the remainder of his life. While the families had cooperated to save Suchet from catastrophe, the stain of financial ruin continued to mark his and his children's lives.

The second crisis revolved around a dispute among the Arnaud-Tizon brothers-in-law. The economic turmoil that accompanied the last years of the Empire hit the Arnaud-Tizon business hard, and it was a struggle to make the textile factory at Bapaume profitable. Ludovic Arnaud-Tizon worked himself sick trying to turn it around, and his aging father continued to work by his side. By the early 1820s, Claude and Catherine had largely distributed their wealth to their children. To reduce their living expenses, they moved in with Victoire and Jacques, first in Rouen and later in Jouy and Paris. In 1825, tensions arose regarding the business arrangements that had been made in 1813, when Jacques had left the family partnership, as well as about Adèle's dowry, which had not been paid in full at the time of her wedding. As Claude and Catherine struggled to make the scheduled payments, the younger men disagreed about their commitments vis-à-vis those obligations. Accusations of dishonorable or untrustworthy behavior flew in every direction, particularly between Pierre and Jacques, until the family orchestrated a reconciliation.[26] With family members relying upon each other for life's most important matters, conflict and distrust could have dire consequences.

The third crisis involved a dispute between Claude and Victoire that was significant enough for Claude to announce his refusal to continue living with her and Jacques and causing him to leave precipitously for Paris in November 1831. Catherine wrote to Pierre the next day to express her sorrow about the situation and ask if they could move in with him and Amélie. He responded positively but explained that he would have to ask his tenant to leave to make space for them. Claude then traveled to Bapaume to stay with his son and daughter-in-law, while Catherine remained in Jouy.[27] She was upset but accepted the situation, which remained tense until she and Claude moved into the house on the rue neuve Saint Roch at the end of December.[28] None of the family members included details in their letters about the dispute, which they explicitly stated they would only discuss in person. Regardless of its causes, the quarrel had immediate (and eventually fateful) consequences for Catherine and Claude, who had to pack up and move abruptly to Paris.

Following the Next Generation

By the mid-1820s, the succeeding generation was coming of age just as the political situation in France was evolving. Ludovic Vitet proved to be an extraordinarily intelligent young man. After receiving various prizes during his last year in lycée, he went on to study law, though it appears he never completed his degree.[29] Instead, he devoted himself to writing, socializing, and immersing himself in liberal politics. In July 1824, Ludovic set off on a trip with a man who would remain a lifelong friend, Charles Tanneguy Duchâtel.[30] They traveled to Switzerland, retracing the footsteps taken by Pierre and Louis thirty years earlier.[31] While in Switzerland, they visited people who had befriended and assisted Ludovic's father and grandfather during their year in exile and spent a few days at Coppet, Madame de Staël's chateau. She had died in 1817, but her home remained a gathering place for leading liberals, including her son-in-law, Victor de Broglie, a prominent abolitionist. From Switzerland, Ludovic headed into northern Italy and then finally to

Lyon before returning to Paris. In addition to enabling him to fulfill a traditional rite of passage for wealthy young men, Ludovic's voyage permitted him to rekindle alliances and tap into broader familial and political networks as he entered adulthood.

Soon after that trip, Ludovic emerged as an influential figure among the growing liberal opposition, a movement that gained momentum when Charles X inherited the throne. Ludovic numbered among the founding members of François Guizot's association Aide toi, le ciel t'aidera, and pursued a career as a writer and art critic, serving as one of the editors of the *Globe*, an important liberal publication launched during the last years of the Restoration. In a study of the publication and its contributors, Jacques Goblot listed Ludovic among a group of young men whose taste and experiences shaped their approach to journalism: "These young men from good families had nonchalantly studied law, or were in the course of studying it, all the while enjoying the pleasures of socializing and throwing themselves into diverse intellectual pursuits. They traveled; they performed plays in chateaux filled with the best people and there encountered scholars, society women, and statesmen. These experiences shaped their tastes and manners."[32] Guizot, who was fifteen years his senior, took Ludovic under his wing when they met at the Ecole Normale, and the two men became lifelong friends.[33] The two shared interests that combined history and politics. After some early attempts at writing historical fiction, Ludovic went on to publish several influential historical studies, including a work on the French wars of religion and numerous books on the history of art and architecture.[34] In 1830, when the July Monarchy replaced the Bourbon Restoration, Ludovic became inspector general of historical monuments, a position created for him by Guizot. Ludovic's story illustrates the continued importance of networking and patronage in the postrevolutionary period, as it was largely his friendship with Guizot that propelled Ludovic into his political career.[35]

The early years of the July Monarchy brought many challenges to these families. The 1832 cholera epidemic struck them hard. Catherine Arnaud-Tizon died of the disease. Her daughters Amélie and Adèle caught cholera too, and Adèle died the following year, perhaps from its repercussions.[36] Ludovic Vitet nearly succumbed to the disease and spent a year recuperating, traveling to various spa towns to take the waters and rest. His illness, as well as the deaths of so many family members, forced him to delay his wedding for several months.[37] In October 1832, Ludovic married Cécile Périer, niece of Casimir Périer, a wealthy banker and the first prime minister of the July Monarchy.[38] (He also died during the epidemic, as did Cécile's mother.) Guizot lavished praise on Ludovic's wife, seeming almost jealous of their relationship: "Outwardly, she appeared to be the coldest person, beautiful, with no striking traits and no movement, without language, saying nothing and seeming unconcerned if no one said anything to her. In reality [she was] full of passion, wit, and had a strong taste for noble pleasures, while giving and showing none of that except to her husband. Never has a man possessed so exclusively a woman, and never has a woman so merited being possessed."[39] In addition to this apparent love and passion, the marriage brought a sizable dowry to Ludovic and reinforced his family's connections with the Périer family that dated back to prerevolutionary Lyon, when the Périer brothers attended the same school as Pierre. Once again, the family continued to rely on older networks. The Vitets may have settled permanently in Paris, but the foundations of their most important relationships remained grounded in long-standing Lyonnais connections.[40]

And we are not yet done with Pierre and Amélie Vitet's story. In 1822, when their son Ludovic was twenty, they had a second child, also named Amélie but whom the family called Mimi. They all went on to live long lives. Ludovic and Cécile had no children and lived with Ludovic's parents in a building the Vitets had constructed for them on a new street near the Luxembourg gardens in the late 1830s, the rue Barbet de Jouy.[41] The Barbets built a home there as well. Pierre Vitet lived to a ripe old age, passing away after a lengthy illness in 1854 at the age of eighty-two.[42] Ludovic's wife died quite young in 1858, leaving him a grieving widower living with his elderly mother, Amélie, who died two years later, at the age of seventy-five.[43] Ludovic's sister married Eugène Aubry, and the couple also took up residence on the rue Barbet de Jouy. Their two children took the name Aubry-Vitet, perhaps out of a desire to maintain the Vitet name, which otherwise would have died out for this branch of the family. Ludovic's niece and nephew became his heirs, and he later lavished attention on his nephew, much as his father had done with him. That nephew, Eugène Aubry-Vitet, carried on both the family name and his uncle's profession, as he too published works on literature, art, and history.[44]

As for Claude and Catherine's other descendants, Ludovic's sons, Claudius and Marc Arnaud-Tizon, created a partnership in 1845 called Arnaud-Tizon frères, out of which they continued to run the family business that had been launched by their grandfather, while their younger brother, Auguste, established a new branch of the business in Le Havre. Prior to that, in the late 1830s, Claudius had moved to Scotland, where he opened a textile factory and learned about new techniques that he then brought back with him to Rouen. Marc later left the partnership to travel far and wide. He made two trips to the Pacific during the 1850s, dying in the Philippines in the 1860s.[45] The Barbets' sons went on to illustrious careers, particularly Henry (1812–

1896), who became director of the Louvre during the Second Empire. In 1834, after Adèle Riocreux's death left her husband a widower, Pierre agreed to serve as guardian of their three children.[46] Thus, late in life, Pierre (who was sixty in 1832) and Amélie continued to occupy their time with children—their own daughter as well as their nieces and nephews.

Of these family members, Ludovic Vitet is the one whose life and career is most remembered today. As mentioned earlier, he held public office throughout the years of the July Monarchy. In the 1840s, he used his family connections in Rouen to gain election as a deputy to the National Assembly from the Seine-Inférieure (today the Seine-Maritime). His friendship with Guizot kept him close to circles of power throughout the July Monarchy. After the Revolution of 1848, he returned to serve as a deputy and joined the monarchist majority. His opposition to Napoleon III's acquisition of power led to his arrest and brief exile in 1851. The last years of Ludovic's life brought both loss and new opportunities. He remained in Paris through the Commune, a frightful moment for wealthy Parisians with its widespread property destruction and its empowerment of the popular classes. He then served once again as a deputy early in the Third Republic and became vice president of the Chamber of Deputies. He died in 1873, leaving behind his dear friend Guizot, who published a long and moving eulogy of Ludovic, whom he described as a "a beautiful soul."[47]

Ludovic's life choices reflect long-term continuities in bourgeois lifestyles, strategies, and practices. While holding public office and committed to political liberalism, Ludovic led a life of the mind, researching and writing about history and architecture. Like his parents, he and his wife hosted frequent gatherings in their home and shared an appreciation of the good things in life: art, intellectual pursuits, stimulating conversation. Politically, too, his views were consistent with those of his father and grandfather; he even chose exile rather than support another Napoleon. When viewed in this multigenerational context, Ludovic's life reflects the decades-long effort to put into place the ideas, values, and practices first launched in 1789 by men like his two grandfathers.[48] Liberal constitutionalism remained the guiding light of these three generations of men and women, whose words, reactions, and strategies are the focus of the chapters that follow. Beyond politics, though never separate from it, the private lives of these "bourgeois" families reflected those values as they focused on doing all they could to ensure the happiness and prosperity of succeeding generations.

Part Two

Life Goes On

Chapter 4

Marriage

The Most Important Alliance

Finding suitable spouses for their children was arguably parents' most important responsibility. The alliances forged through marriage served as both an ends and a means: They were a consequence of the nonstop network building these families engaged in as well as an opportunity to build new connections that could benefit not only the individuals directly involved but also many others in their kinship and friendship networks. Negotiating a proper marriage nearly always required the involvement of one's allies, who, recognizing the far-reaching consequences of such connections, readily assisted and often initiated the matchmaking. While a child's "happiness" mattered as parents considered potential spouses, that happiness was assumed to be based on finding a person from the "right" background and with complementary tastes and ways of life. Ideally, love and passion would develop between the two people whose lives would be forever linked, but happiness did not depend on these emotional matters. Rather, happiness meant above all economic security, with parents deemed most capable of deciding these matters.

As these families' key correspondent, the center of their overlapping networks, Pierre Vitet was at the heart of virtually all their marital negotiations. As discussed in chapter 2, soon after his own marriage, Pierre played a role in orchestrating the marriage of Amélie's cousin Adèle to the younger Suchet brother, an alliance that linked the Arnaud-Tizon family with General (later

Marshal) Suchet. That episode set the stage for Pierre to become Catherine's most trusted collaborator and confidant as she worked to arrange the marriages of her own children. This chapter examines the steps they took in each case and considers the practical and emotional concerns that drove parents and other family members as they worked to make this most important decision for their children. The letters the family members exchanged reveal the practices and strategies they employed as well as the views and attitudes they expressed regarding marriage.

Although the ideal relationship between romantic love and matrimony was evolving during these years, the consensus was that marriages of convenience—when two people of similar backgrounds united for larger familial concerns rather than flights of passion—would be built on a more solid foundation than love matches. However, marriages of convenience could result in high levels of spousal infidelity. While such behavior may have been accepted, if not expected, of the aristocracy before the Revolution, it appeared deeply threatening to a new social order based on stable, patriarchal families. And with a new inheritance system based on equal distribution among all heirs, not primogeniture, female infidelity seemed especially unacceptable.[1] One of the interesting facets of this moment of transition, from the aristocratic model of marrying for the sake of maintaining or improving a family's social and political position to the perhaps more bourgeois model of companionate marriage, is that marriage was supposed to accomplish two potentially contradictory goals at the same time. Spouses were picked by families, and marriages were arranged with larger familial, political, and economic goals in mind. At the same time, however, couples were expected to lead their lives together and thus to be compatible—and preferably even to love each other.

The transition to the companionate model of marriage in Europe has been studied by many scholars using a wide variety of approaches. Although there is disagreement over its extent, timing, and significance, most historians date this transition to the late eighteenth century, and most refer to the Enlightenment emphasis on individual autonomy as essential to understanding its origins.[2] Despite this consensus, the historian Adeline Daumard argues that bourgeois families in France continued to select spouses for their children well into the nineteenth century: "Most marriages in bourgeois and aristocratic society were marriages of convenience [that] could [also] be marriages of inclination. . . . It is nonetheless obvious that love could not develop between people who had never had the opportunity to meet [and] that depended on their parents' choices [*habitudes*]."[3] Other studies make the case that while love and happiness may have grown in importance over the course of the nineteenth century, emotions remained secondary to matters of interest.[4] Alain Corbin similarly argued that "sexuality, a central part of every modern marriage, in the nineteenth century was merely a backdrop to married life. What usually held bourgeois households together was the need to protect inherited wealth."[5] It was only at the end of the century that love and sexual passion began to be viewed as essential components of marriage.

Arranged marriages thus coexisted with the companionate model. How did these two seemingly contradictory systems overlap? How did individuals and families reconcile the need to launch marriages that would further family members' larger goals of building and strengthening their social and economic positions with the new idea of finding personal happiness and satisfaction through a marriage based on love and affection? What, then, was a "happy" marriage? It appears to have been one that made both families feel confident that the spouses would care for each other in every sense of the term: emotionally, financially, and physically. In other words, interest and "love," which signified compatibility more than romantic passion, were both essential in the minds of those who sought to construct happy marriages for their children. The companionate model did not replace the process of arranging marriages but rather became integrated into it, and the couple emerged as the essential unit defining the family, slowly replacing previous models of the family based on lineage.[6]

It is also likely that a familial conception of identity continued to dominate over a newly emerging sense of the individual. As Honoré de Balzac famously put it, "the basic unit of society is not the individual but the family."[7] A passage from an 1834 article by the conservative Catholic writer François-René de Chateaubriand suggests that he too believed that French society continued to be "organized around groups and by families" and not yet "the individual, the way it seems to be becoming, the way one can already see it in formation in the United States."[8] In her work on French suffrage legislation from 1789 to 1848, Anne Verjus has postulated a "*familialiste*" approach to voting laws, which granted suffrage not to individual men but to men designated as heads of household.[9] This *familialisme* encouraged men to play the role of good fathers who participated in raising and educating their children. Domestic bliss was a goal for men and women alike, and texts and images encouraging male involvement in the household, the space in which good citizens would be raised and trained, multiplied during the Revolutionary period.[10] Conceptions of marriage and conjugal satisfaction similarly reflect the centrality of family and domestic life to the economic and emotional stability these men and women desired.

Successfully navigating the social world in which these marital strategies operated required an all-hands-on-deck approach. Catherine Arnaud-Tizon's letters provide granular detail on how these negotiations took place as well as her sense of what the responsibilities of motherhood entailed.[11] She depicted herself as driven solely by the desire to ensure her children's "happiness" as well as eternally grateful to her "dear friend" Pierre for his unending patience and willingness to help her and the rest of the family accomplish their goals. Her long, frequent letters to Pierre at these key moments in their lives allow us to enter her world and to see how a bourgeois matron envisioned her roles and responsibilities and how she depicted her feelings while fulfilling those roles. A central part of her worldview and that of those she corresponded with is the subjugation of the individual to a greater good: the family.

Seeking a Husband for Victoire: Business and Family Interests Intersect

The first case of marital negotiations explored in this chapter, those for the second Arnaud-Tizon daughter, Victoire, highlights the material and business concerns that drove parents' efforts to find suitable spouses for their children, especially girls. The first steps took place in 1806, when Victoire turned sixteen and began to appear in society—in other words, to dance at balls where eligible bachelors and young, unmarried women could see and interact with each other. Until they married and began to exercise freedom as matrons, French girls led fairly secluded lives, but at these late-night events, Victoire could chat with other girls her age and put herself on display among the Rouennais upper crust. For her, there were never enough balls, and she enjoyed hearing about those that her sister attended in Paris as well. Catherine commented on her daughter's enthusiasm in an 1807 letter to Pierre and Amélie: "So you have inaugurated the [season of] balls. Victoire is looking forward to hearing about your activities (*plaisirs*). I think she will be disappointed this year because dancing has not taken root here. We have nonetheless subscribed to one."[12] There was a ball season—late winter and early spring—but the preparations were already in full swing in the Arnaud-Tizon household by early December. Mother and daughter alike needed suitable gowns for these events. Having relatives in Paris gave them access to the latest fashions; Pierre and Amélie contributed to their allure by sending them fabric and accessories.[13] Catherine's letters from this period cover a seemingly unending series of balls and the various preparations necessary to participate in them.

When a marriage prospect for Victoire emerged in fall 1807, Catherine discussed the man's strengths and reflected on her role as the mother of a marriageable daughter.

> I still plan to go to Paris once the person in question has arrived. . . . But for now, nothing is settled. First, the young people must see each other and agree [to the match]. I confess that the solidity of this person pleases me. Mr. Fournel spoke highly of the young man, and I have confidence in his judgment. I confess that all this has made me anxious. I feel the weight of my responsibility for the happiness of my dear Victoire. But in doing all that my affection for her inspires in me, I think that I have no reason to reproach myself. Having no hope of marrying her in Rouen, *le papa* is happier to see her go to Lyon, where she has a brother, than some other city where she would be completely isolated. Paris is no longer an option for us because finding a suitable person would be even more difficult.[14]

Catherine felt comfortable voicing her anxieties with Pierre and explaining how she felt about this important decision. Financial matters explain her view that finding a groom in Paris would be difficult. Parisian families had already constructed the building blocks for those alliances, and dowries there were higher as well.

If Victoire was to marry a man from a provincial city, Lyon seemed the best option, although she may not have agreed with this plan. Victoire visited Paris and Lyon with her mother in 1806. During their trip, Catherine wrote to Pierre and Amélie about Victoire's distaste for the city of her birth: "Victoire cannot stand Lyon and will be happy to travel back to Paris. Even the theater has left her unimpressed. They are nonetheless performing an elaborate opera with a beautiful ballet. It was difficult for her to admit that the theater [in Lyon] is prettier than the one in Rouen."[15] Despite the connections she had there and the city's vibrant cultural life, Victoire found Lyon unappealing. Her parents were nonetheless working toward a marriage that would require her to live in Lyon, suggesting that *happiness* referred to something other than a particular emotional state. Rather, the term implied stability and security, which in their minds revolved largely around financial matters.

Everything remained veiled in secrecy, with the initial discussions taking place through intermediaries starting in October 1807. Most letters never named the man in question, referring to him and his family members as "Monsieur V" or "Madame V." In this case, it was Vital Roux and his wife, Roux-Montagnat, who communicated with the mother of the potential groom. In late October, they sent one of her letters to Pierre, who forwarded it to Claude and Catherine.[16] Catherine responded immediately with questions, which Pierre then communicated to the Roux couple. A few days later, Pierre informed Catherine that Roux had sent a letter to Madame V in Lyon following Claude's instructions.[17] Secrecy and discretion were essential at this stage, when the first feelers were being sent, both to protect Victoire and because the family's reputation could be affected if the negotiations fell apart. "Please tell our friends, the Roux, that I beg them not to speak of our affaire in Lyon with Monsieur or Madame Suchet. It is essential not to divulge anything that has not been decided, and the Suchet household is not very discreet. I am looking forward to receiving news from Lyon. I fear that the first impression we gave the gentleman regarding Victoire's repugnance for Lyon could hurt our chances. This would be a shame because I think this could be a solid marriage. In the end, I just need to be patient, and everything will become clear."[18] Sounding anxious, Catherine was concerned that the potential groom would back out. When Catherine refers to a "solid marriage," she seems to be basing her assumption on the families' similar social and economic positions. The adjective *solid* was no accident; marriage needed to provide a strong foundation for this and future generations.

Though girls often did not know when a marriage was being considered, in this case, Victoire was aware of these discussions but took no part in them. In a letter written while she was waiting to hear that Mr. V had embarked for Paris, Catherine described her own and her daughter's feelings: "I await news from Lyon. The idea of being near you for a little while makes me happy, despite the inevitable anxiety due to the circumstances. Victoire is gay as usual. She is content to allow us to handle this affair and seems unworried."[19] Although Victoire may have accepted the situation, it is difficult to believe that she felt no apprehension when her future was under discussion, especially since she disliked Lyon and that was where she would be going if she married this man. Young women could theoretically reject a suitor that had been selected for them, but few had the willpower to stand up to their parents.[20]

Their interlocutor, Vital Roux, was busy with his own affairs, as he was about to be named to a prestigious post that would benefit his friends and allies.[21] Catherine responded to the news about his new position with enthusiasm and then returned to the issue of Victoire's possible marriage, expressing concern about the financial considerations.

> I am surprised that Mr. V is asking now about the dowry that we give to our children. I thought that we had discussed that matter in the first letter. It is one of the essential issues. I must admit that had I realized this I would not have spoken to Victoire [about this possible match]. They may think we are richer than we are. We will give to Victoire, like your wife, 50,000 livres plus a trousseau that we estimate at 6,000 livres, including diamonds. In addition, we give our word of honor that

> there will never be any inequality in our children's inheritance. That is what I wish you to communicate to Roux. Between us, I am starting to doubt the success of this matter. . . . The only regret I will feel is that I spoke about this with your sister. This could awaken in her the desire to marry, something which had not entered her mind. She is still very young and can wait.[22]

Victoire had just turned seventeen, and Catherine did not want her daughter worrying about marriage earlier than necessary. Financial matters needed to be handled first, prior to allowing emotions to enter the picture and to avoid one party or the other feeling rejected.

The potential groom may have had his own reservations, as he repeatedly delayed his trip to Paris. In late November, Pierre wrote to Catherine with news that Roux had received a letter from Mr. V announcing that he would come to Paris at the end of December.[23] In her response, Catherine sounded relieved that the arrangements were advancing and discussed next steps.

> Please tell me when he arrives, and I will go there. I want to see him and ensure that we agree about all matters of interest before he comes to Rouen. By "interest" I am referring to his role in his mother's business and the fortune he has currently. If we can believe what people say, he is quite wealthy. But since he has a sister, it is good to know how much he owns now. It would be good if our friend Fournel could repeat the praise he has offered of this young man. I need to hear this to lighten the weight of my responsibility. I am impatient to see all of this finalized. Victoire does not seem the least bit worried. She may think that we are no longer considering it. Still, she is very enthusiastic about reading your letters. When you discuss this matter, please write on a separate sheet so that I can remove it. I think it is futile to talk to her about this before Mr. V arrives in Paris.[24]

While Catherine feared the negotiations might fail, she also expressed concern about the potential groom and sought reassurance about his qualities. Her reminder to Pierre about writing on a separate sheet when discussing the negotiations reflects both Victoire's curiosity and Catherine's desire to avoid stirring up her daughter's feelings before things were settled. Because letters were generally shared and read aloud, inserting a loose piece of paper into the two-sided, folded sheet used for letters was a common practice when people wanted to write about private matters.

Catherine's response to Pierre also included the man's name for the first time: Vintrinier [*sic*]. The potential groom must have been Artus Vingtrinier, son of Antoine Vingtrinier, a wealthy furrier who had served on the municipal council of Lyon when Louis Vitet was mayor and had died in 1802 in Longes, suggesting another connection with the Vitets. Artus was twenty-nine in 1807, the ideal age for men to marry, and his family's wealth and political affiliations would have made him a likely candidate. The mother of the potential groom was Marie-Sophie Montagnat, a cousin of Madame Roux née Montagnat.[25] The Roux, Vitet, and Arnaud-Tizon families were already close allies. In pursuing this match, they were returning to their roots and reinforcing preexisting ties. Plus, the Vingtrinier family was very rich, although the fact that the man had a sister meant that some of the family's wealth would be going toward her dowry.[26]

When Pierre informed Catherine a few days later that Mr. V would soon arrive in Paris, she replied immediately to explain how they would handle his trip to Rouen if the initial discussions went well. "I hope that our friend Roux will accompany him, because I do not want you to do it. That would make too many tongues wag. We will soon be able to discuss everything in person. I will say that I am traveling for business, to purchase merchandise from Parisian manufacturers. I will only confide in my sister-in-law and my brother. I hope that Madame Roux will not speak to Suchet about any of this. You will tell him that this is a business trip."[27] Secrecy remained essential. She especially did not want Suchet informed, as she did not trust him to keep the news to himself. These important negotiations required her presence as well as the involvement of her most trusted confidants.

The meeting was delayed further when Mr. V announced that he would need to postpone his trip due to an accident. It finally took place in early January, forcing Catherine to travel to Paris at a less-than-ideal time of year. "Despite my desire to join you immediately, I am obliged to wait until after the new year. If I leave any sooner, it will cause too much gossip. I will reserve a seat on the stagecoach for January 2. . . . The news that you gave me that our friend Roux will not be able to accompany his relative to Rouen for even one day has upset me. . . . Oh, how I need to see you and speak with you my dear children."[28] Catherine's yearning to speak with Pierre and Amélie reflects her reliance upon them for support and advice, particularly at difficult moments. The word *poids* (weight) appears repeatedly in her letters; arranging her daughters' marriages was her weightiest responsibility.

When Catherine wrote again to confirm her travel plans, she continued to sound anxious about meeting her potential son-in-law and finalizing the arrangements. "I am still planning to leave on January 2. . . . I had anticipated that it would be difficult for Roux to accompany his cousin to Rouen. We will find a way to work this out because it is not appropriate to bring Victoire there [to meet him]."[29] Strict notions of propriety and etiquette governed these maneuvers. In this case, bringing Victoire to Paris to meet her future husband, rather than having him ask for her hand in her parents' home, seemed inappropriate.

Something must have gone wrong in the negotiations, as there was no further mention of this possible match. Catherine arrived in Paris as planned on January 2, 1808. A few days after her arrival, and presumably after she had met with the potential groom, Pierre wrote to Victoire inviting her to travel to Paris with her father. They arrived on January 9. Claude returned to Rouen two days later, but Victoire and Catherine remined in Paris until the end of the month.[30] In all likelihood, something blocked the negotiations, and Vingtrinier left Paris before Victoire arrived, because in Catherine's previous letter, she had said that if the negotiations went well, she would bring him to Rouen to meet Victoire. Instead, it was Victoire who traveled to Paris to visit with her sister and brother-in-law. She probably never met the man who had so occupied her mother's thoughts.

A few months later, another promising proposition emerged, and Catherine's tone became exuberant as she contemplated the end of her worries about seeing Victoire in a "solid" marriage.

> I had no time to write yesterday, my dear children, to announce some news that will please you as much as it does us. Our dear Victoire has been sought after by a young man of this region, the son of a rich *négociant* who is in the same industry as Madame Long, and whose factory is in Deville near this lady's. The final agreement was reached yesterday morning, and in the evening Victoire was introduced to her future husband, whose only flaw in my mind is that he is a bit young. He is only 23 years old. Victoire saw him last winter at all the balls and had no difficulty in reaching a decision. The young man seems sweet and very happy to ally himself with us. I will wait until we are together to share with you all the details on his fortune and his family because, in eight or ten days, I will be spending a few days with you to make some necessary purchases before the wedding. I beg you to speak to no one about my trip, not even Suchet. . . . I forgot to tell you the name of the gentleman. It is Monsieur Barbet. . . . Amélie may remember seeing him at the ball.[31]

Pierre responded immediately to Catherine's breathless account of this exciting news. The whole family would now be coordinating their efforts toward the next steps.

Victoire's future husband was Jacques Barbet, son of one of Rouen's most prominent textile manufacturers, Jacques-Juste-Bonaventure Barbet (1756–

1813), who ran a calico factory employing two hundred workers in Deville, near Rouen.[32] Barbet was Protestant, but the issue of religion never appeared in any of Catherine's first letters announcing the marriage. The only aspect of Barbet's identity that surprised anyone was his youth, as most men in these families married when they were closer to thirty. Pierre's first reference to Barbet in his journal, a summary of the letter he sent to Catherine when responding to the news, simply mentions the "forthcoming marriage of Victoire in Rouen with Mr. Barbet, the twenty-three-year-old son of a *négociant* from this town."[33] Jacques's wealth clearly pleased them, while his religion remained a nonissue. Choosing to marry their daughter to a man from Rouen reflected the Arnaud-Tizons' willingness to deepen their ties there. While moving to a new city entailed risks, in this case it also brought them an opportunity: marrying their daughter to the son of an extremely rich man.

After discussing her future son-in-law and her plans to travel to Paris to buy certain "necessities," Catherine laid out the details of how they would make room for everyone as she joyfully anticipated having the entire family under one roof.

> We are renovating Victoire's room because she will be staying here with us for a while [following her marriage]. We are setting up the one upstairs for Adèle and her maid, and there will be a third bed there for Marguerite [Amélie's maid]. Ludovic [Catherine's son] will sleep in Morel's room [their clerk], who will stay at your uncle's house. That way everyone will have space [*sa niche*] in our little house. I am anticipating with great pleasure this happy circumstance that will bring us all together. My little Ludovic will sleep in your room, Amélie, to keep the little office free for my dear Vitet.[34]

In addition to sharing her plans for this family gathering, Catherine sounded proud of her logistical skills. Pierre and Amélie's servant would be coming with them to look after Ludovic, who would be sleeping in Amélie's room so Pierre could have space to himself, presumably to paint, read, and write. The presence of servants was taken as a given; the people in these families did not do the manual labor of running a household and caring for children.[35] Rather, they occupied their days with the work of kinship, their business and other financial matters, and social activities, men and women alike.

Pierre and Amélie responded to Catherine the moment they received her letter; she quickly replied with more details on the groom and her plans.

> I had no doubt that the news of Victoire's establishment would bring you great pleasure. She is looking forward to seeing you; I hope you

> will be here within two weeks. I am planning to visit you at the end of next week, and we will discuss everything together. . . . Monsieur Barbet very much wants to meet you. He is a good-natured young man. [*C'est un bien bon enfant.*] He is mild and full of life [*doux et ne manque pas d'esprit*]. Everyone who knows him sings his praises. I hope that your sister will be happy, and I dare say I am almost convinced [of it]. . . . Please share the news of your sister's marriage with our friends the Roux and Fournel [families].[36]

It was time to publicize the upcoming wedding and to prepare for the ceremony. Once both families had agreed on the financial and other details, the wedding took place very quickly. In the meantime, the young man and woman grew to know each other as the families announced the good news to their friends.

One essential task involved preparing a *corbeille du mariage*, a gift basket filled with luxury items offered by the groom to the bride on the day the marriage contract was signed. The gifts were typically worth about 5 percent of the dowry. Jewelry and other more "practical" articles, such as gloves, handkerchiefs, and cashmere shawls, figured among the gifts, which were meant to prepare the girl for her future role as wife and mother and symbolized the moment of transition to female adulthood.[37] Giving such gifts served multiple functions, including building feelings of mutual support and obligation, demonstrating both families' commitment to the financial solvency of the couple, and solidifying their integration into larger kinship networks.[38]

Catherine's preparations for the wedding included a three-day shopping spree in Paris.[39] Upon her return, she wrote to Pierre and Amélie to ask them to handle several additional purchases, including some on behalf of Jacques Barbet.

> We need diamonds to make the clasp on Victoire's pearl necklace . . . and I would like to use the remaining diamonds to make earrings for me. I'll trust Amélie's good taste; she can decide on the setting. . . . We would like to receive everything as quickly as possible since the marriage is to take place on June 2. Monsieur Barbet would like to order a diamond necklace at the price of 5,000 livres . . . plus the pearl ensemble at 2,400. . . . Forgive us for all that we ask of you. We rely so much on your friendship. When Ludovic arrives [from Lyon] please tell him to send me Victoire's birth certificate right away.[40]

Pierre methodically recorded in his journal all the items he purchased and their cost, including a comb decorated with diamonds that Amélie's uncle had him order in Paris. He shipped the purchases to Rouen in boxes that were insured for their full value by the stagecoach service.[41] Included were diamonds, pearls, necklaces, and earrings—6,000 francs' worth of jewelry from Victoire's parents and more than 7,000 francs' worth from Jacques Barbet. These were no small sums of money. In fact, more was spent on one necklace than the average skilled worker earned in five years! However, these were not simply beautiful accessories. Besides serving as jewelry, gems were a "safe" investment that could be sold or repurposed. In addition to demonstrating to all who attended the wedding that the families had the resources to offer such extravagant gifts, these purchases functioned as insurance for an uncertain future. Any investment could go sour, but diamonds would always have value.

While these purchases were being shipped to Rouen, people were also on the move. Amélie's brother, Ludovic, stopped in Paris for a few days en route from Lyon; then they all left together for Rouen. Pierre continued to record entries in his journal that included some of the details on their stay and on Victoire's wedding. On Wednesday, June 8, Pierre left Rouen to spend a day at St. Just, Suchet's chateau, to "say goodbye to General Suchet, who came that day [to Rouen] to surprise the Arnaud-Tizon family and then returned [to St. Just] to dine."[42] Pierre returned to Rouen on June 9 to witness the signing of the marriage contract on Friday, June 10.

Appearing before a notary to sign the contract was a momentous event that brought together the couple's extended families and their allies. It carried more significance than the actual marriage ceremony, which was usually a simple gathering at City Hall followed by an optional church service. The contract stipulated that Victoire's family promised a dowry of 50,000 livres. They provided only a small portion right away, paying Jacques Barbet 5 percent interest on the remaining sum. Jacques's father promised the same amount under the same terms.[43] Men and women alike typically received their share of their families' wealth through the property arrangements laid out in their marriage contract, as marriage both symbolized and instituted in more concrete terms the transition to adulthood.[44] An exchange of gifts also marked that day; Jacques gave Amélie a pearl necklace and earrings, while Pierre and Amélie gave Victoire a pearl comb.[45] The marriage dinner took place on June 14. Forty people attended the meal, which was followed by a *soirée dansante*.[46] Pierre and Amélie then stayed in Rouen along with *le petit* Ludovic (who signed the contract even though he was only six!) for a few weeks after the wedding.

After a two-month hiatus in their correspondence, Catherine's first letter to Pierre and Amélie following their return to Paris discussed her sadness at their departure as well as Jacques's integration into the family. "I cannot tell you how much we are suffering from our separation from you. I hope that a similar reunion will take place every year. This is the only idea that helps me bear your absence, plus knowing that my dear Vitet will be coming to see us this winter. The newlyweds are counting on you. Barbet kissed his wife on your behalf. He asks that you do the same with Amélie and said he would have preferred to take on this task himself."[47] Even via his mother-in-law's letter, this new "brother" was flirting with his new "sister." Jacques's letters often included innuendos and even some explicit references to sexual conquests. He is the only one of these family members who made such remarks, at least in the letters that have come down to us. It is perhaps no accident that he was also the only one who would later purchase property that would allow him to take on the aristocratic-sounding name Barbet de Jouy. His words and behavior did not fit the image we have of bourgeois propriety and thrift; he frequently demonstrated more "aristocratic" pretensions and behavior.

Another wedding that took place in 1808 serves as an example of even more impressive social mobility. In a letter to his mother in Lyon, Pierre announced the "upcoming marriage of General Suchet with Mademoiselle D'Antoine, daughter of the mayor of Marseille and niece of the queen of Spain."[48] Marguerite responded immediately: "The news of the general's marriage surprised me, as well as your brother-in-law. We thought that he would only consider that once he was settled in Paris. But he is making an honorable, even brilliant alliance, which the emperor must have encouraged. It is a shame that the couple must live apart just as they are beginning to love each other. Please send my congratulations to your friend."[49] On October 31, Pierre wrote to Catherine to announce the upcoming wedding; she traveled to Paris shortly thereafter. Catherine was still in Paris when the general's wedding took place on November 16. It seems that Pierre and Amélie attended.[50] He and Suchet were longtime friends; there is every reason to assume that Pierre and Amélie would have been invited, and Catherine may have attended as well, as she left Paris three days afterward. At that event, they would have encountered the very highest ranks of Napoleonic society.

A few days after Suchet's wedding, Pierre wrote to Jacques congratulating him on Victoire's pregnancy.[51] The young couple had done what was expected of them and had conceived their first child shortly after their wedding. They went on to have three children, Juste, Marie, and Henry all born in quick succession. After that, they must have practiced some form of birth control, because the pregnancies stopped. No one in these families had more than four children; most had two or three. Family size, like just about everything else, seems to have been based on rational calculation, and there was strong motivation to avoid large families.[52]

An emphasis on quality over quantity seems to have been the norm, and not only vis-à-vis children. A small number of close, trustworthy friends made up their entourage, and they all worked together to make the best of the unpredictable world they inhabited. One response to the uncertainty of this period of rapid, unprecedented change was the desire to seek a quiet, domestic existence in which close family and friends—people one could rely upon because their destinies were so intertwined—lived, worked, and socialized together. Domestic space served as a haven in which to combine business, pleasure, and the emotional ties of family and friendship for both men and women. However, even though men and women performed the work of kinship side by side, they did not have the same roles or status in the family.

A Bride for Ludovic: Helping a Son "Obtain" His Choice

The marriage arrangements for the one Arnaud-Tizon son differed from those of his sisters, most significantly in that he played a more active role in selecting the potential bride. Ludovic was twenty-five years old when these discussions took place, and his parents disagreed about whether it was the proper time for him to consider marriage. In April 1812, Catherine wrote to Pierre to share her opinion that Ludovic ought to marry. Her accounts of Ludovic's life in Lyon, where he had been living to oversee the family's business and properties, give the impression that she thought he was overly fond of socializing and fancy balls. She hoped that if he married the right kind of woman, he might dedicate himself to more serious pursuits. "I think like you that a solid education and good character are preferable to a large fortune. I feel that it is essential for Ludovic to marry to encourage him to settle down and to acquire a taste for work. *Le papa* does not share my opinion and seems to think that it would be better for Ludovic not to rush into anything. In the end, this grown boy will do what he wishes, and he has decided to go to Paris to discuss all of this with you."[53] Here, we see how she bowed to her son's wishes in ways she never did with her daughters. Men generally wed after reaching the age of majority and thus had the right to marry on their own accord. In practice, however, most men needed their families' support to provide their financial contribution to the marriage. In every marriage contract I have examined for this book, the bride and groom received equivalent amounts of cash and property from their parents. Sons thus needed their parents' approval as much as daughters did unless they had already inherited their share of the family's wealth.

The following month, Catherine wrote to Pierre asking him to communicate their preferences regarding Ludovic's future spouse to Jacques Barbet, who was visiting Paris. In the letter, she articulated her views of what made a good wife. "I much prefer, for all of our sakes, that he choose a wife who is well brought up and from a good family, whose mildness and talents are suitable for a quiet lifestyle, rather than see him place wealth above all else. One can earn money, but one cannot give an upbringing to a woman who had not received it. That is my opinion, which Barbet knows. Show him my letter. He will be happy to learn about his brother's plans. [Ludovic] is working hard at the factory."[54] Catherine wanted a daughter-in-law who would be satisfied with living in a small village outside of Rouen and helping her husband run their household and factory, not someone who would be dreaming about Parisian entertainments and socializing. Two weeks later, she wrote to ask Pierre to begin the negotiations:

> Ludovic, still hoping to marry and wishing to obtain the one about whom we have already spoken, I am writing in his name and in the name of *le papa* to request that you negotiate this matter. *Le papa* would like to give 30,000 livres in cash. You should consult with Barbet about the best manner for making this offer. . . . Please believe me, my dear friend, when I tell you how much we appreciate the steps which you are taking on our behalf. You are contributing to the happiness of your brother, who is already deeply grateful. For me, I confess that I wish to see my son established and that the good that is said of the young lady upon whom he has laid eyes makes me desire ardently that he will be able to get her.[55]

Men hoped to "obtain" the women they sought in marriage; girls could only hope to be selected. This language, and the conception of marriage that it renders visible, reflected a legal system that defined men as autonomous subjects and women as subordinate.

Pierre responded with information about the potential bride and her family, details he had received from the friend who was serving as their intermediary: "I told Madame Audiffret about our hopes to receive 40,000 [livres] payable in two parts, plus the land. She thinks this should be possible. She spoke to us about the good will of the young lady's parents, and how she will do everything she can to help this succeed. But we must wait several days because Mr. Brunet is away."[56] Catherine's next letter was full of gratitude: "Ludovic is frustrated at the brief delay in our great affair caused by Mr. B's absence. He appreciates the zeal you have demonstrated in helping us with this important circumstance, and thanks his good brothers. As for me, my dear children, I owe you a great debt. [After this,] we will only have Adèle to take care of, and she still has plenty of time."[57] Catherine used this letter as another opportunity to express her appreciation to Pierre for all that he did to help the family navigate these essential matters. In the meantime, Ludovic was growing impatient as he waited for the two families to reach an agreement.

While Claude was in Paris negotiating on behalf of his son, Jacques visited the capital as well. After returning to Rouen, he sent a letter to Pierre that gives a glimpse into how the men of these families viewed marital negotiations and how they spoke to each other.

> To relax from the fatigue of a hot day, my dear Vitet, I am chatting with you and my good Amélie. I hope that my dear sister did not feel too tired after singing so beautifully Saturday evening and that the only mark left by that evening is the pleasant memory of her complete success. I assure you that I feel great pleasure in noting that my dear current and future sisters-in-law were the best part of the gathering and that is saying a lot. I spoke a great deal about them here where everyone is concerned about *le papa's* absence. Our dear brother speaks of nothing else and is waiting impatiently for your letter telling him to join you there. Days are weeks for him. I hope that in possessing this charming person, they will feel like minutes and that soon your negotiating talents will satisfy *le papa* Arnaud-Tizon and result in an alliance that will make all of us happy. . . .
>
> I would like to speak to you about Madame Suchet. How is this dear cousin? Her husband and children? How lucky you are to see her often, to enjoy her conversation. I attribute the strong feelings I experience in our gatherings to the pleasure I experience in speaking with her. My dear Vitet, I beg you, who has a reputation as such a good man [*honnête homme*] and who is so close to her [*si bien établi dans son esprit*] to let her know that I, that we, think of her often. Kiss her for me, for us, for you, for you all. With your reputation, you can go far, and I am persuaded that she would believe anything you say to her and would allow you to do anything you would like.[58]

This is a remarkable letter in many ways. First, we see the language of men "possessing" their wives. Second, Jacques's appreciation of his sisters-in-law is quite striking, particularly the flirtatiousness visible in his comments to

Pierre regarding Adèle Suchet. This kind of *galantrie*, as it would have been labeled at the time, does not appear in these families' letters, except for some of Jacques's. Was this just his way of joking, of entertaining his reader, or did he really feel the kind of passion and sexual attraction that his letter seems to be voicing? Although we cannot gauge his true feelings, the fact that he used this tone with Pierre, who probably shared the letter with Amélie, shows that these men and women may have been more comfortable acknowledging desire than most of the surviving correspondence suggests.

By early July, the Arnaud-Tizon and Brunet families were preparing for their first to face-to-face discussions. As usual, Catherine relied on Pierre as they moved toward this step.

> The family read over the part of your letter concerning the important matter we are handling. Our unanimous opinion is that you should not change your plans to come here on the 15th. . . . If [our propositions] are accepted, my son will leave immediately with his father, and if we need a plenipotentiary before that, we know Vitet's *complaisance* well enough to believe that he would be willing to make the trip if necessary. . . . As you have said, the wedding will have to take place in Paris, all without great ceremony. Part of the family will attend. Then we will gather in Rouen as quickly as possible to spend the rest of the summer together. Voilà, my dear friend, the decision made by the family council.[59]

Making sure they had the support they needed to successfully carry out these important discussions required organization and planning. Catherine's reference to the "family council" was no exaggeration.

Two weeks later, Pierre asked Catherine about the financial arrangements he needed to communicate to the potential bride's family, and she responded right away. "I am hurrying to respond to give you the information you requested: my son will receive a dowry of 60,000 livres; he has earned about 20,000."[60] As usual, money came first. Pierre wrote back to announce that he would be meeting soon with the girl's stepfather and to ask for more details.[61] Once again, Catherine wasted no time in sending her response:

> As we have already stated, my son has a quarter interest in our business, and in January he will have a third. We will leave it to you to discuss the other financial issues. It would be good to try for 40,000 livres and if that drops to 30, it will need to be cash. I don't think our pretentions are excessive. *Le papa* and Ludovic are ready to leave [for Paris] at the first sign, but they wish to avoid any financial discussions. . . . If

> it all works out, I want the ceremony to take place immediately, and very simply. I think that the Brunet family would prefer that too. You are once again demonstrating your affection, my dear friend, in agreeing to handle this for us. Your brother will owe his happiness to you because after all the good that we have heard about this young lady, I think it is assured.[62]

In addition to raising the amount of their son's dowry, the Arnaud-Tizons were willing to accept less from the bride's family, apparently because Ludovic had his heart set on marrying this woman. Even though they would be contributing more to the establishment of this new household than their future in-laws, Catherine seemed optimistic about the marriage. They were apparently willing to make this investment to satisfy their son.

When Pierre wrote to inform her of the results of his discussion with Mr. B, who, in defending the interests of his stepdaughter, had raised an unspecified concern about Ludovic's character, she again wasted no time in responding. "I appreciate Mr. B's frankness, and hope that once he knows my son, he will no longer think him capable of such stupidity. And as you say, such behavior does not correspond to the steps he took to obtain the hand of this young woman. To bring all of this to an end, and to demonstrate our desire to ally ourselves with this respectable family, my husband and son will leave Thursday morning for Paris. My son wanted to go immediately, but *le papa* could not leave any sooner."[63] That first meeting must have gone well, as the future spouses met soon afterward at the country home of the girl's family in Saint Brice. In a letter to Catherine dated August 10, Pierre described the young couple's first encounter and informed her that the bride's mother planned to hold the wedding at the end of August.[64] Once a decision had been reached, the wedding took place as quickly as possible.

Soon, everyone was busy organizing the wedding. On August 16, Claude responded to Pierre regarding the posting of marriage banns in the Rouen city hall and expressed his enthusiasm for the upcoming celebrations. "It appears that nothing should delay this wedding, which from my son's perspective cannot happen too soon. His impatience is understandable, and I share it because it will be an opportunity for us to all be together. In the meantime, you and your dear wife have a lot of responsibilities. You are beginning very early to fulfill paternal and maternal obligations, especially you who agreed to take my place [in the negotiations]. Although this serves as an apprenticeship for the moment when you . . . [reach this stage with] the other Ludovic, I am nonetheless deeply grateful."[65] Like Catherine, Claude appreciated Pierre's willingness to contribute to this important familial project. While Claude handled the legal requirements, Catherine went to Paris to meet the bride. Upon her return, she wrote to Pierre and Amélie about the young woman. "I was very pleased with my future daughter-in-law. I hope she will see us in the same way we see her. I think my son fortunate to have made such a good choice. He is very impatient. For my dear Ludovic, fifteen days seems very long."[66]

As the wedding approached, Catherine shared the news with Pierre's mother, whose follow-up letter to Pierre gives further indication of what a "happy" marriage signified among these families. Above all, she emphasized the "networking" potential of the new alliance.

> You sent me such wonderful news that I am impatiently awaiting the departure of the courier to send you my sincere congratulations. I am overjoyed that Mr. L. is marrying such an excellent young lady, whose talents and qualities will make him happy. I have congratulated his parents and thanked his mother for sharing the news of this marriage with me. They must be happy to be keeping their son near them, and to be able to serve as father and mother for his amiable wife. I beg you both to express to your brother all that I wish I could say to him, and to give him my sincere wishes for their prosperity and long lives. I look forward to meeting this future spouse who may visit our town where Mr. Brunet has many old friends. All of Mr. Ludovic's friends will celebrate his happy choice. Your [Amélie's] cousin, Mr. Bournichon, told me that he had met Mr. Brunet in Lyon and that he has fond memories of him. He is so enthusiastic about this alliance that he has visited me several times to discuss the wedding. He is considering visiting Paris on the day after the ceremony. . . . He is full of joy for both families and his affection for the Arnaud-Tizon son equals that of a father.[67]

A marriage in the family was an event to celebrate as a moment of joy and future possibilities and was also an opportunity to rekindle and reinforce older ties, even among people who were only distantly related to the couple.

The couple and their witnesses signed the marriage contract in Paris on August 28, 1812. The contract uses the term *dowry* (*dot*) to describe the property that the couple received from their parents. Ludovic contributed 25,000 francs in cash he had earned himself and 60,000 francs from his parents. The bride, Marie Françoise Julie Thiébault, who went by "Amélie" like her future sister-in-law, received 36,000 francs in cash, of which 6,000 would be paid up front and be used to construct her trousseau. The other payments of 10,000 francs were to be made on January 1, 1813, 1814, and 1815, with 5 percent annual interest added. Another 30,000 francs would come through property.

As a minor, Amélie needed her parents' permission to marry—in this case, her mother, Jeanne Françoise née Le Sage, widow of Etienne Thiébault, and stepfather, Marc Antoine Brunet. Ludovic's witnesses were Gabriel Suchet and his wife, Adélaïde Arnaud-Tizon, Madame Marie Louise Nezon, wife of M. Audiffret, *ami*, and M. Jean Fournel, *ami*. The bride's witness list was longer and included Pierre, Amélie, and Ludovic Vitet, Savoie-Rollin, baron de l'Empire, Madame Casimir Périer, and Jacques Récamier.[68] These were high-ranking members of Napoleonic society, another indication of how this marriage would assist the Arnaud-Tizon family in cementing ties to people whose connections could prove beneficial.

The wedding took place the next day, Saturday, August 29; the civil ceremony was held at the city hall for Paris's first arrondissement and the religious ceremony at Saint Roch Church. A few days later, the newlyweds traveled to Rouen along with the Arnaud-Tizon, Vitet, and Barbet families. Pierre and Amélie remained there through October.[69] They threw another party at their factory, where they hosted sixty guests for a meal followed by music and dancing. They even invited the *curé de* Saint Roch to attend the celebrations in Rouen. Not long afterward, the family gathered for the baptism of Victoire's son Henry, with Amélie Vitet serving as godmother.[70] The young couple then began to settle into their home in Bapaume, where Ludovic would oversee the family business along with his father and brother-in-law Jacques.

While the newlyweds were visiting Paris that winter, Victoire sent a letter to Amélie Vitet that suggests that the couple's first months together had not always been smooth sailing.

> You have no doubt seen Ludovic and his wife. One felt more enthusiasm for this trip than the other. I don't think I need to tell you that it was Amélie [Arnaud-Tizon] who was happy to see her dear friends, whom she misses, and to have dresses and other items made to suit her husband's taste. You cannot imagine how difficult Ludovic has been about his wife's clothing. A day never goes by without him complaining about her extreme slovenliness [*négligé*] which is still as visible as when you were here with us.
>
> I don't know if you have heard about the chagrin that hit this new household. Upon my return, Amélie thought she was pregnant and was enjoying the opportunity to voice her whims. She was already feeling cravings and did not hesitate to seek to satisfy them. Among other things, while out for a ride, she wanted oysters, which was accomplished. How disappointed she was when, five or six days later, all her dreams were shattered. At that point, rumors flew around the house.

> *Maman*, who always imagines the worst, was convinced she had had a miscarriage and sent someone to get Doctor Blanche who explained that he was not worried and that one cannot know one is pregnant until one has been for a few months, not a few days. Voilà, my dear, the news from our private life.[71]

The young wife no doubt wanted to live up to expectations as she entered this stage in her life. However, her ability to convince others to go along with her whims seems to have bothered her sister-in-law, who made sure to share the story with her sister in Paris.

This was not the only difficulty the young couple faced, and the years that followed their wedding were not easy ones. The catastrophic retreat from Russia after the 1812 invasion proved to be the beginning of the end of the Napoleonic Empire and worsened the series of economic crises hitting France. Producers of luxury items suffered as orders came to a halt. This was the context for the early years of Ludovic's marriage. These struggles took their toll on Ludovic's health as well as the family's financial well-being.[72]

A Spouse for Adèle: The Girl Is the Last to Know

The final example in this chapter highlights the differences between sons and daughters when it came to arranging marriages. While Ludovic asked his parents to help him "obtain" the wife of his dreams, the girls in the family were kept in the dark about their potential matches until the negotiations had been completed and all the essential decisions had been reached. The process leading to Adèle's marriage also contrasts with the example of Victoire's marriage in that Catherine was not involved. In this case, it was the men in the family who showed up at the family home with a potential groom, without telling either the girl or her mother!

The youngest of Catherine's children, Adèle was the only one who was born in Rouen, and her upbringing must have differed quite a bit from that of the others. She spent much of her childhood living like an only child, particularly once Victoire married in 1808. And while her three siblings had lived through difficult years as young children in Lyon during the Revolution, Adèle's teen years were touched by the collapse of the Napoleonic Empire and the confusion that ensued. In addition, by the time Adèle reached the age to be "seen" in society, her mother had lost her enthusiasm for balls and large gatherings. Marriageable girls needed to attend such events, however, and Catherine continued to perform her duty of accompanying her daughter, even if the late nights exhausted her.

Adèle turned sixteen in 1814, and the confusion and chaos that struck France in 1814 and 1815 as the Napoleonic Empire was crumbling made marriage negotiations difficult. When it became clear that foreign troops would be occupying Paris, Amélie, Pierre, and their son, Ludovic, left for Rouen, remaining there for several months. Soon after returning to Paris, they received a letter from Catherine expressing her sadness at their departure. "You cannot imagine, my dear children, the emptiness I have been feeling since you left. I haven't been able to force myself to enter your room. I would be so happy if someday we could live together permanently, but I know that is not your plan. . . . *Le cher papa* is doing better and no longer mentions his stomach pains."[73] Her mood reflected both the political situation in France and the stage in life that she and her husband were entering. She was in her fifties, her last child would soon be leaving the house, and she and her husband were beginning to feel the effects of age. From here on, her letters almost always included references to their health problems, mostly her own; she complained constantly of pain and fatigue.

Soon after Amélie and Pierre returned to Paris, Adèle joined them for several weeks, attending the balls held there during Carnival season. Catherine missed having her daughter near her but recognized that Adèle needed to escape the "sadness" of Rouen.

> This poor girl is very happy to be with you. She will spend the end of carnival season more gaily than she would have here. I miss her, but I can bear her absence when I think about how happy she is with you. . . . I assure you that despite all the difficulties we experienced during your stay with us, I have never been happier. . . . The fact that our family gets along so well makes us very happy. Such happiness is a shelter from all revolutions. By living this way, we can be happy regardless of what else may happen.[74]

It would be difficult to find a more explicit explanation of the bourgeois turn toward the family as a refuge from political turbulence. While Adèle was in Paris, Catherine seems to have gone through a period of depression, and she often mentioned her pain and loneliness. France's political situation and her frustration at seeing the Bourbons back on the throne no doubt contributed to her gloomy mood and perhaps her former Jacobin husband's stomach pains. However, she also saw other difficulties on the horizon, including financial problems that could make finding a suitable spouse for Adèle difficult. That concern may explain her reference to the "poor girl."

With Adèle away, Catherine sounded increasingly sad and pessimistic as she complained about her health and hinted at their financial difficulties. "I want to thank you for all that you are doing for your sister, but I would like her to come home. I have been feeling constantly out of sorts and my solitude has become unbearable. I would like to go the country, but I cannot do so if my daughter does not return because I do not want to leave my husband alone. As for the music lessons, I had agreed that she could take 15 or 20, but no more. We cannot afford them."[75] In response, Amélie wrote encouraging her mother to visit them in Paris, but to no avail.

> I appreciate your generous invitation to go pick up your sister and spend some time with you. Nothing would make me happier, and I would be on my way, except that I do not want to leave your father alone. . . . And I must admit that my health is also an obstacle because I am almost always in pain. The cold weather fatigues me. I have been spending all my time before the fire, often alone. I hope I can get used to this [lifestyle] because if I continue to be paralyzed [with pain] that will be my destiny.[76]

As she felt herself slowing down, she was probably contemplating the next phase in her life. Her youngest daughter would be marrying soon, Victoire and her children had left Rouen, Amélie was in Paris, and only Ludovic and his wife were nearby in Bapaume. She had them and their children to occupy her, as well as caring for her husband, but she felt old age approaching.

Catherine also took a much less active role in finding a spouse for Adèle than she had with her other children. The first steps took place in July 1816, by Jacques and Claude, who kept Catherine out of the loop. Soon after they announced their plan, Pierre shared his reflections on the man in question, Christophe Riocreux. He recorded a summary of the letter in his journal: "Regarding Mr. Riocreux and the real reason he traveled to Rouen: proposition of marriage for our sister Adèle. We think this gentleman is in every regard a very suitable person. His uncles Pailhon are very rich; one is single. Mr. Riocreux runs the Paris branch of their business. I propose to go to Rouen to discuss this affair in more detail."[77] Material concerns came first, as usual, but the fact that Riocreux lived in Paris was a plus as well. Catherine responded immediately, asking Pierre to travel to Rouen without delay. She and Claude wanted him there for the negotiations. He was their trusted adviser; they knew he would do everything in his power to work in the family's best interests.

> I am counting on your good will and friendship when asking you to travel here tomorrow. *Le papa* and I will be delighted to see you, and I am sure our visitors will feel the same way. They will be dining with

> us on Thursday. My husband and Mr. Barbet thought they were being smart in hiding Mr. R's intentions, but he was the one who let the cat out of the bag, not by saying anything but through his obliging manner. I do not know if Adèle has any idea what is happening. It is certain that she likes him, just as we do, and there will be no problem [convincing her to marry him]. She may be leaving us, but she will be near you, and she will be living in a place she likes. So everything is for the best.
>
> I cannot tell you how much the young man impressed us. I like his frankness. He is in perfect harmony with us on every matter. His type of business pleases us. Altogether, this alliance leaves us nothing to desire. I am sure that you will agree, as will all the family. . . . This marriage flatters me even more [knowing that] interest cannot be the motive. I understand, my dear children, that anyone who knows you wants to ally with you, and [thus] that your sister owes her happiness to you.[78]

When she wrote that "interest cannot be a motive," she may have been referring to the fact that their financial situation had weakened.[79] Regardless of Catherine's effort to minimize the role of "interest," it is clear that she and her relatives continued to conceive of marriage as an alliance of families and that families were much more than groups of people who might or might not get along with each other. Rather, everyone depended in an essential sense on the behavior and successes of the others.

Pierre left for Rouen immediately and wrote to Amélie soon after he arrived. All seemed to be going well. In his journal, Pierre wrote: "I found our family thoroughly satisfied and full of hope that our plans for Adèle's marriage will succeed in bringing happiness to this dear girl. I also saw our two travelers from Le Havre. The groom-to-be is enchanted with his future bride."[80] Pierre provided more details in a letter to Amélie: "I am writing to announce my safe arrival with your family, whom I found healthy and happy to see me. Our gentlemen had also arrived, but had not yet been to the house, which meant they were surprised to see me. We ate together this morning. I have already chatted with your *papa* and *maman* who told me they are happy with the man who is presenting himself for your sister. M. Riocreux's character is making them feel confident about her future happiness."[81] In a postscript, he added: "Adèle has been informed of our projects and seems happy." The girl was the last to know.

The next day, everything was decided: "Everything is going well. Our discussions have satisfied everyone. We dined with our uncle who very much liked our gentleman. The couple just made their declarations and embraced each other with joy and tenderness. Adèle received his kisses with good grace."[82] Two days later, Pierre sent another long letter to Amélie, this time with details on the couple's growing attachment as well as the broader family's interactions.

> Our young couple is learning to appreciate each other. [*Nos amoureux se conveinnent de plus en plus.*] I say *amoureux* because there is real feeling there, and Mr. Riocreux is enchanted with Adèle who is gracefully and happily accepting his demonstrations of love. They exchanged some gifts, and in ceding one of her rings, Adèle found it replaced by a pretty diamond one that her future husband had on his finger. . . .
>
> Mr. Riocreux has written to his family in Saint Etienne to inform them of his choice and to ask them to attend the wedding. Where will this wedding be happening? Rouen! Everyone has agreed that this is where it must take place. It looks like our vacation here will include this *fête de famille.*[83]

As with Ludovic, the groom made a "choice," while the bride-to-be accepted her destiny.

As usual, once the necessary agreements had been reached, the wedding took place almost immediately. Catherine traveled to Paris to purchase the necessary items for the wedding. Then everyone gathered in Rouen—Pierre, Amélie, and Ludovic arrived on August 1, Riocreux and his family the next day.[84] Pierre wrote to his mother about the festivities, highlighting the fact all these guests were staying with Amélie's family. It was quite a feat to have found space for everyone, and Pierre credited Catherine for this accomplishment.[85] The groom's friends and family stayed for eight days.[86]

Soon afterward, the young couple left for Paris with Catherine, who went to help Adèle get settled into her new home. In the meantime, Pierre and Amélie remained in Rouen for their annual vacation, a situation that frustrated Catherine to no end. While away, she sent regular updates to Pierre and Amélie on Adèle's transition to married life.

> I promised to write to you my dear children and I am keeping my word. I need it to help me bear the idea of leaving you in Rouen with me here in Paris. I owed it to my dear Adèle and I am happy to help her get settled. I must give credit to her husband, who is doing everything in his power to make her home pleasant and to keep her from suffering. He is afraid she will be bored, but I assure you his concerns are unwarranted. With a bit of effort, they will be nicely installed in their little house.[87]

So far Catherine was impressed with her new son-in-law, who was proving to be an attentive husband.

In her next update, Catherine sounded even more satisfied, though her upcoming departure was causing her concern.

> I am taking advantage of a moment of solitude to respond to your long letter. Our newlyweds are at the theater. They tried to convince me to go with them, but I persuaded them that I would be happier at home chatting with you. . . . The joy of seeing Adèle so well married helps me view my future solitude as a light sacrifice, but as the moment of our separation approaches, I am feeling less resolve and more chagrin, which I am trying to hide. I am nonetheless thoroughly satisfied with my new son-in-law. One cannot demonstrate more goodwill and amiability toward one's wife. He finds great pleasure in providing for her anything that will make her life more pleasant. He bought her a piano which was installed this morning.[88]

Again, Catherine seemed happy to announce that Christophe had taken his young bride to the theater and was trying to provide a home where she would be comfortable. Buying a piano served as proof of his desire to make Adèle happy, as he was allowing her to pursue her interest in music and keep herself occupied. Of course, music would provide entertainment both when she was alone and when they had guests. Catherine spent these first weeks with the newlyweds to help Adèle get settled and to be certain the couple got off on the right foot. Once she had accomplished those tasks, it was time for Catherine to return home to her husband. However, leaving her youngest child in Paris proved challenging.

As Catherine prepared for her return to Rouen, she expressed concern about the impending separation and worked through those feelings by emphasizing her sense of duty. "I told you in my last letter how well your servants have been treating me. If Riocreux and his wife had not insisted, I would have preferred to stay at your house. That way, Adèle would have only been seeing me for half the day, and my departure would have been easier and more discreet. But I could not do as I wished, and when I spoke of leaving next week, they did not want to consent. One morning I will reserve my place [on the stagecoach] and pack my bags without saying anything."[89] Mothers and daughters often felt intense emotional bonds that made this first separation after a girl's marriage difficult. Many novels from the period focused on this moment in a girl's life, which all assumed would be painful.[90] Adèle was simultaneously facing new responsibilities as a wife and the unknowns of marriage to a man she barely knew while living far away from the person who had always held the most important place in her life, her mother.

In the end, this moment of separation was delayed further, because when Catherine returned to Rouen at the end of August, the newlyweds accompanied her. They may have made this unplanned trip to help Adèle through this difficult moment of transition. By that point, Pierre and Amélie had left Rouen, though they returned for a brief stay in early October. [91] When Pierre and Amélie traveled back to Paris on October 15, Adèle and Christophe were already there and met them at the stagecoach. They spent that evening together, the first of many such gatherings.[92] Frequent visits with her sister may have helped Adèle adjust to her new circumstances. Once again, the family was there to support each other emotionally as well as in more material ways.

While Catherine was worrying about Adèle managing without her, she was suffering from loneliness herself. In her first letter after Pierre and Amélie's return to Paris, Catherine complained about how much she missed them. "I barely had three weeks with you . . . I often ask myself why fate must separate us from those with whom we are most compatible while uniting those who quarrel unceasingly."[93] She did not specify who quarreled. Soon afterward, she left to stay with Victoire at her country home to, as Pierre put it, "diminish her sense of isolation."[94] At the end of October, the family learned that Adèle was beginning to show signs of a pregnancy, as Catherine explained in a letter to Amélie. "It seems that Adèle is feeling sick; it is almost certain she is pregnant. I would have preferred that she had had more time to rest. In the end, if this makes her husband happy, all is for the best. I hope that she will follow your advice and be cautious."[95] Now Catherine had something else to worry about—Adèle's health: "It seems that she is feeling quite ill. She is a bit delicate and in following her instincts, she could end up really sick. If she is like me, she is not at the end of her suffering. She needs to be courageous and to continue exercising."[96] In addition to these health concerns, the upcoming birth required that the family orchestrate other plans. Very early in the pregnancy, they had already determined who would serve as the child's godparents: Christophe Riocreux's father and Adèle's mother.[97] These were moments that strengthened emotional connections across the generations. Such connections reinforced the sense of the family as a unified entity working in concert to build a solid future for them all.

Because of the connections between marriage and property, familial strategizing came first, but that does not mean that emotions were absent from these calculations. Catherine's comments on love and marriage while discussing a situation involving their friends, the Fournels, shed light on how these families weighed love versus interest. One Fournel daughter had apparently developed an interest in a man whose wealth did not live up to their expectations, and the family had to decide whether to permit her to follow her heart. In a letter to Pierre, Catherine wrote: "What you are telling me about the romance [*les amours*] at the Place des Victoires does not surprise me. The two are very close and, in my opinion, they will end up marrying because in the end there is only some wealth lacking and everything else is perfect. I must admit that I have a weakness for the gentleman. As Mr. Fournel knows his daughter's preferences, could he offer her another husband? I think he is too much a man of honor to do such a thing."[98] It appears that feelings could trump matters related to wealth and status, so long as the difference between the two families was not too great. Though fathers remained in control and had the final word, their children's feelings counted, too.

When she wrote a few days later, Catherine reflected on this situation and brought up another set of close friends, the Roux couple. This case also reveals the various concerns weighed and strategies employed regarding marriages. "The wedding your letter announced did not surprise me. I thought I had seen Mademoiselle M. showering attention on that gentleman who certainly deserves it. Now Madame Roux has completed her task. I hope this third marriage will prove happier than the first two. When the occasion arises, please present my best wishes for the happiness of her cherished daughter."[99] Jacques Fournel and Vital Roux were prominent bankers and business partners.[100] Clearly money mattered to them, but other considerations, including their daughters' emotional satisfaction, counted as well.

Marriage had always been—and arguably continues to be—at least partially about property and lineage. What was new in this period was the idea that marriage should *also* be about love and passion, but this was a very bourgeois kind of love based on being satisfied with what one was given. Based on these letters, it seems that few would have ever considered separating these two aspirations, which were so completely interwoven as to seem one. Happiness thus depended on learning to accept one's situation and to bend one's emotional life to reality, to find a way to blend utility with pleasure. Girls were trained from an early age to bow their will to that of others—first their parents, then their husbands. Having their daughters marry while they were young helped to ensure their flexibility, their willingness to learn to be the kind of wife their husband wanted them to become. To a lesser extent, good bourgeois sons were expected to bow to their parents' authority over them as well. However, they had the chance to become heads of household someday, which meant that they would have the responsibility of ensuring their own progeny's happiness by properly managing the family's assets to be able to pass them on to succeeding generations through dowries and inheritance. These men and women seem to have accepted the basic premise that one person's life was just a small component of a living, breathing, multigenerational entity: the family. The concept of the individual may have dominated the political and philosophical treatises of this period, but the family still trumped the individual in many of life's most important decisions. A happy marriage meant finding individual satisfaction while working toward the economic and social success of one's larger familial and kinship networks.

Chapter 5

Parents and Children

Generational Ties

Just as attitudes about marriage were in transition during the Revolutionary period, so too were ideas and practices related to child-rearing. In their educational treatises, both John Locke and Jean-Jacques Rousseau emphasized the importance of proper upbringing to shape the person the child would become—Locke's famous *tabula rasa*. These new ideas meant that children were no longer viewed as small versions of adults who were best beaten into submission and kept separate from polite company until ready to behave properly. Instead, creating a loving, supportive, and nurturing environment increasingly became the goal, with discipline coming more from love than an insistence on submission. This approach to child-rearing also created an atmosphere that encouraged family members to view children as cherished parts of family life. Parents, grandparents, aunts, and uncles regularly shared amusing anecdotes and offered advice as they worked toward the common purpose of raising happy, healthy, and hard-working children. The need to prepare boys and girls for their future roles was an essential—perhaps *the* essential—function of parents and the broader family as well.

Although this more nurturing approach applied to children of both sexes, the contents and methods of boys' and girls' education differed. While girls remained at home, where they learned to read and write, studied music and the arts, and mastered the skills needed to run a household, bourgeois families typically sent sons to boarding schools starting around age nine. In this context, mothers and daughters grew deeply attached to each other, as they lived side by side until the girl abruptly left this maternal environment upon her marriage, usually around age eighteen.[1] As the previous chapter made clear, this momentous transition in a young woman's life generally took place with little input from the woman herself, as her parents planned her life for her. Boys experienced the transition to adulthood through marriage as well, but later in life than girls, usually after they had established themselves professionally. Boys had to contribute to the family's economic stability, whether by taking up the reins in the family firm or completing a degree that would lead to a career. Law school was by far the most sought-after avenue. Medicine was an option, too, but it was less prestigious than the law, which opened doors into high-level government positions.[2]

Most guides to child-rearing published in the late eighteenth and early nineteenth centuries built upon the model established by Rousseau, and like Rousseau, their authors defined the role of boys' education as working toward the creation of independent thinkers able to exercise their autonomy, while girls were taught to serve others. Rousseau's popular educational treatise *Emile* encouraged parents to raise their children in a loving atmosphere, giving them time to experience nature and to develop their minds and bodies in an environment of relative freedom. *Emile* focuses largely on raising and educating boys, but the book devotes attention to raising Emile's ideal counterpart, Sophie, as well. She had to be raised to serve her husband in a world where gender complementarity was the ideal.[3] Both the content and methods of girls' and boys' education differed because of these assumptions about gender norms and the proper roles for the sexes. Girls' education remained limited and superficial, while boys encountered more complex subjects and studied them more deeply. One key distinction was that girls were seen as having no need to learn Greek and Latin, but for boys, these languages were viewed as essential to mastering French grammar and rhetoric.[4]

The Vitet couple's child-rearing methods followed these precepts, and the family certainly appreciated Rousseau and his ideas. In July 1811, Pierre and Amélie traveled to Montmorency with some friends to visit Rousseau's former home, an experience Pierre described in some detail: "Visited the Hermitage of Jean-Jacques. Noted the vanity of the owner of the property, Mr. Grétry, who is shocked that people visit the place not because of him, but for Rousseau. Reprehensible pride of this old man who should be giving an example of how to honor the author of *Emile*, while receiving just recognition of his own talents."[5] Pierre, like so many of the men and women of his generation, adored Rousseau and felt a deep connection to him, as expressed in the common reference to Rousseau as *"l'ami* Jean Jacques."[6] It seems that he also tried to live by the principles expressed in Rousseau's writings.

Amélie and Pierre devoted enormous time and effort to their son's education. The biggest crisis in Ludovic's childhood came when he reached the age when most boys in these families entered boarding school. It was a trying moment for his parents, who struggled over this important decision that could have lifelong consequences for their son. This chapter covers this episode, along with some of the other big questions of child-rearing, including pregnancy and childbirth, schooling and other lessons arranged for children, and an important moment in many young men's lives, the rite of passage symbolized by a voyage, a version of the Grand Tour taken by upper-class Englishmen. In each case, these moments contributed to the larger goal of raising children who would build upon the successes of previous generations while forging ahead into an increasingly unpredictable world. Then, as now, families had to make choices at every step about how to raise their children, starting with the question of maternal nursing and then moving on to properly educating their children based on their affinities and their future roles within the family and society at large. Making those decisions and implementing them to their best effect was not purely the domain of parents but also of the larger extended family, who viewed preparing the next generation for success as a shared responsibility. In addition, children reinforced the emotional connections that existed across the generations; the pleasure derived from sharing amusing anecdotes about babies and children and applauding their successes comes across clearly in the letters exchanged between family members.

One consequence of historians' attention to the rise of the domestic ideal for women is a tendency to ignore men's roles in the private sphere. While studies of motherhood in this period are quite common, we have fewer studies of fathers and fatherhood in part because of an assumption that men's energies were devoted largely to "public" matters: business, politics, and financial dealings. Studies examining the *"bon père de famille"* demonstrate that a new image of the father as a nurturing and supportive family member, rather than the fearsome patriarch, emerged in the literature and art of the period following the Terror.[7] Beyond this new image, it seems that Pierre's choice to devote so much of his time and energy to his son's education was far from an isolated case.[8]

Pierre's affectionate relationships with family members and the roles he played within his kinship network reflect this ideal of the good father and family man. He was certainly an engaged parent, and he had been a devoted son as well. And although his relationship with his mother seemed strained at times, his mother-in-law grew to count on him as a trusted confidant.

Besides the bonds of affection created through Pierre's marriage to Amélie and the birth of Catherine's first grandchild, Pierre and Catherine shared similar views on politics and enjoyed the same kinds of social activities.[9] In addition, as demonstrated by the degree to which they collaborated on all of life's most important decisions, men's and women's lives and responsibilities overlapped to a greater degree during the early nineteenth century than seems to have been the case later in the century.[10] Catherine participated in running the family business and kept track of financial matters, and Pierre's life story suggests that "domesticity" could offer an appealing option for men and not just women.

Pregnancy, Childbirth, Nursing

Before highlighting Ludovic's upbringing and his relationship with his parents, I want to examine other family members' experiences with childbirth and its aftermath to help us explore the practices and considerations that governed the early phases of a child's life as well as which topics family members felt merited discussion. Health remained a central concern, though other matters came up, too, particularly the issue of maternal breastfeeding. Unlike her sister Amélie, who sent baby Ludovic to a wet nurse, Victoire Barbet chose to breastfeed her children, perhaps because she lived in the village of Bapaume, where the air was deemed pure enough to raise an infant. In early July 1809, Pierre mentioned in a letter to a friend that Victoire had given birth to a boy who was nursing successfully.[11]

Breastfeeding did not always go smoothly, however, and Catherine's letters to Amélie and Pierre often discussed how Victoire and her baby were progressing. Victoire's son, Juste, was three months old when Catherine sent this report on her daughter's condition: "Victoire is doing well, so well that yesterday she made some visits with her husband, and they came to see me. Despite that, I am not without worry. Her breast is not painful or swollen, but it is still hard under the last *dépôt* [abscess]. . . . I confess that it is essential for your sister's happiness that she remain healthy because her husband does not like sick people and seems impatient with the nursing, even as he caresses his little boy who is doing wonderfully."[12] Besides voicing concerns about Victoire's abscesses, Catherine drew attention to Jacques's impatience, reminding us that child-rearing impacted husbands, too, particularly as contemporary wisdom advised nursing mothers to refrain from sex. As we will see in some later episodes, Jacques Barbet could be quick-tempered. Though he was no doubt happy about becoming a father, he clearly wanted his young wife to be available to him.

Catherine sent frequent updates on Victoire's struggles with nursing and shared anecdotes about her children. In 1809, still discussing Victoire's first child, Catherine wrote, "Your sister is doing very well. She has almost returned to her normal size. Her baby is still healthy. Since his mother's last *dépôt*, he has been behaving strangely. He refuses to nurse from the left breast unless he is turned as through nursing from the right one."[13] Victoire went through two more pregnancies, and in both cases, nursing became a matter of discussion. In April 1811, six months after Victoire gave birth to her second child, Catherine joyfully shared more family news with Amélie. "[Victoire's] little girl is doing very well. Victoire's abscesses, which we allowed to open naturally, have left barely any scar and will resemble a tiny pox mark. As for big Juste, he is like your brother when he was a child. He has a bad cold right now, but it never keeps him from running or eating. Adèle has gotten much taller and is filling out. Spending time at Bapaume is doing her a world of good, and she is wonderful company for your sister."[14] Now a two-year-old, Juste was big and strong, developing as one would hope for a little boy. Catherine's youngest daughter, Adèle, who was then thirteen, was also developing as desired—"filling out" into the young woman she was fated to become and learning about her future roles as she helped her sister run her household.

A few years later, when Adèle became pregnant, Catherine voiced concern over the preparations for the birth, asking Amélie to intervene as she grew increasingly annoyed at Adèle for acting as though she did not need or want her mother's help and advice.

> I would appreciate it . . . if you could tell me whether Adèle plans to keep her child with her or if she will send it out to nurse. I am preparing the layette, and the contents are different in each case. Has she decided on a doctor [*accoucheur*]? . . . I learned from your father that her husband brought her one that she did not like. It is necessary to defer to her preferences. . . . Also, let me know if she has thought about sheets for the birth. The two pairs I will be bringing with me will not be enough . . . and if she does not want to make more, I do not see how we will be able to manage for the birth. I am sorry to bother you with these details, but who else can I address? Adèle hardly ever responds to my letters. I don't want to make a big deal about it, but since she does not have much experience, she needs to listen to the advice [of others]. She probably has spoken to you about the fringes that I did want to make. I admit that I was hurt by the rude way she asked me to finish them by a date that was too soon for me to get them done. I

> wasn't feeling well, and it would have been impossible for me to make them so quickly.[15]

In addition to providing details on how bourgeois families prepared for a birth, this letter reveals a degree of generational conflict that is not often visible in their correspondence. Catherine sounds shocked that her daughter would not seek her advice. Adèle's apparent lack of concern regarding her mother's health also bothered Catherine, and she shared those feelings with her older daughter.

When she wrote to Amélie again two weeks later, Catherine expressed relief that some of the arrangements had been made and resignation to the fact that the young couple wanted to handle their own affairs. It was not easy for Catherine to let go.

> Thank you for responding to my questions. As you said, the most important thing has been accomplished: The *accoucheur* has been selected, and as I had hoped, Mr. Esparon oversaw the choice. Regarding the wet nurse, that is for them to decide. I just wanted to know whether the child will be staying in town to finalize the contents of the layette. Like you, I realize that our young household needs to take care of itself. We must allow them to figure things out on their own, and I assure you that I will no longer attempt to offer them advice. [When I get to Paris] I will stay with you and will go to the rue St. Denis only when my presence becomes necessary.[16]

Sounding angry, Catherine was giving Adèle space to make her own decisions. Her question about the layette reflected the fact that the clothing required for a baby differed depending on where the child would be living while with the wet nurse. If the baby was going to be with its parents, nicer, more presentable clothing was necessary, whereas if it was being sent to the country, simpler clothing would suffice. As she was with her other daughters, Catherine would be there to assist once Adèle went into labor, but she wanted to leave the young couple on their own while waiting for that moment to come, as she felt her presence was unwelcome. Sometimes the intergenerational cooperation that so marked these families' lives went less smoothly than they hoped.

Estimating due dates involved a variety of factors and led to family members debating how best to make such calculations. After Pierre wrote to Catherine encouraging her to move up her trip to Paris because he was convinced that Adèle would be giving birth earlier than they had presumed, his sister-in-law ("Madame Ludovic," as the family referred to her) wrote to say that they were following his advice. Her letter reveals how families discussed such matters.

> You so well pleaded your case, my good brother, that despite our own views, *maman* is heading to Paris this evening. She came to say goodbye to us yesterday and is spending today with Papa and the Barbet family. We checked the almanacs to calculate Adèle's due date and concluded, regardless of what you say, that she will not give birth before June 10. The months, the moons, everything supports the probability of our conjectures. We concluded that your concern for Adèle came from your desire to have our dear mother with you. Now that she has left, I hope that you were right, since the longer it takes our sister to give birth the longer you get to keep *maman* with you, and as you appreciate the pleasure of having her there, you can also understand how much her absence pains us.[17]

The affectionate language Amélie Arnaud-Tizon expressed regarding her mother-in-law may have reflected the norms of this kind of letter-writing, but Pierre's insistence that Catherine travel to Paris earlier than planned suggests there was some level of sincerity there. And, in fact, the rest of the family was correct: Adèle gave birth in early July, with Pierre serving as godfather to the child.[18]

Adèle sent her baby to a wet nurse, and in her case, choosing *not* to nurse proved difficult. She ended up with engorged breasts that formed *dépôts* that eventually burst, first on one breast and then the other.[19] Pierre wrote to Catherine in mid-July to share this news, which she viewed as worrying: "I just received your letter, my dear friend, that confirmed the fears I had about my dear Adèle's health when I noticed that her engorged breasts had not improved. We can only hope that the doctors are correct when they say she will not have any more *dépôts*. Please keep me posted because I can only count on you and Amélie to give me accurate information. I beg you not to hide anything from me."[20] Being away from Adèle at this time was difficult for Catherine, especially considering Adèle's unreliability as a correspondent.

Amélie Vitet went through a different set of problems when it came to bringing children into the world. Her son, Ludovic, arrived very early in her marriage, but no others followed until much later. It is possible that Amélie had difficulties during Ludovic's birth and sought to avoid further pregnancies. That would explain the long separation between the births of her two children. She may also have had some miscarriages, but since pregnancies could not be verified until some of the outward signs began to reveal themselves, confirming a miscarriage was not easy. With such high maternal and infant mortality rates, whenever a birth or miscarriage took place, families corresponded frequently to give updates on the health of mothers and their babies.

In 1812, after hearing about a possible pregnancy, Catherine assumed that Amélie was displeased. "The news you shared about your wife's health did not please me as I imagine she is unhappy about having another child. I encourage her to accept the situation as there is nothing that can be done and feeling upset about it only makes things worse."[21] In April, Pierre shared the news with his mother by referring to "his wife's health" and saying that a pregnancy was likely.[22] Two days later, he wrote to Catherine to inform her that Amélie had lost the baby: "Announcement that Amélie has been indisposed. Her apparent pregnancy is over as her *maladies* [her period] have returned after two and a half months. She slept well last night and is spending two days in bed as a precaution."[23] In her response, Catherine voiced concern for her daughter's health. "Make sure she takes care of herself and rests in bed for a few days as doctors often get these things wrong; it is possible she had a miscarriage. Send me news frequently. I am very disappointed that I cannot see for myself how things are going, but we cannot always do what we wish."[24] A few days later, Pierre informed his mother of the news: "My wife's pregnancy is no more. Difficult *maladies* have returned. She is resting and taking good care of herself."[25] Pierre's correspondence journal gives no indication of what kind of emotional response he and Amélie experienced because of this apparent miscarriage or their preferences about having more children.

Unlike Catherine, who assumed that her daughter did not want to have another child, Marguerite treated the miscarriage as a disappointment:

> I hesitate to express my regret to you, my dear children, regarding that which is affecting you. Although I was dubious about this pregnancy, I understand that you felt hopeful and that each day that passed gave you more confidence that you would experience the joy of enlarging your family. I know that my darling Ludovic was excited about having a little sister. His disappointment will bring him closer to God as he recognizes the need to obey His holy law. Give him lots of hugs from me and have him hug his little mother on my behalf. Be sure to encourage this dear wife to go out for a walk each morning while the air is cool.[26]

Marguerite used this trying moment to remind them of the importance of bowing to God's will, a notion that had probably helped her to cope with losing so many of her own children. In contrast, Catherine assumed that Amélie did not want more children, suggesting that the long interval between Ludovic's birth and his much younger sister's may have been the result of efforts to avoid pregnancy. Coitus interruptus was the primary form of birth control, and there is evidence to suggest it was quite common.[27]

In contrast to Marguerite's assumption that most couples desired more children, Catherine's discussion of Victoire's pregnancy that same year suggested otherwise.

> My dear Amélie, I received your last undated letter in which you reproached me for my silence. . . . All the misfortunes that have hit our society are the cause. I did not have the courage to pick up my pen. I was also delayed by the end of Carnival; we attended a few parties that helped to raise everyone's spirits. The Mardi Gras dance at Madame Lemarchand's was not very animated even though there were a lot of people. Victoire was obligated to leave at midnight because she was feeling tired. This pregnancy has been harder on her than the previous ones. I attribute this to her displeasure about it.[28]

The "misfortunes" to which she is referring are the deaths of several of their close acquaintances in Rouen. It is interesting to learn that Catherine believed that her daughter was unhappy about being pregnant. She does not explain the cause of Victoire's "displeasure," whether it involved the physical consequences of pregnancy, fear of childbirth, not wishing to have more children, or some combination of such feelings.[29] What is certain is that these families avoided having large numbers of children; the goal for most of them seems to have been two or three.

Though they could not know it, Victoire was carrying twins, which would explain why the pregnancy was more tiring. She gave birth to a boy and a girl in July 1812. Pierre wrote to his mother soon afterward to send his wishes for her health and happiness on her *jour de fête*, her saint's day, and used that letter to share this exciting news.[30] Unfortunately, before she received that letter, one of Victoire's babies—the girl—died.[31] Marguerite's response sheds light on how these families reacted to trying moments.

> I cannot get over the surprise about the augmentation of the family thanks to your sister Victoire. I imagine that this double birth will require you to serve as godfather, but since they have many friends in Rouen, I cannot guess who will be the godmother. I hope that Madame Barbet's convalescence goes as smoothly as last time. . . . I have heard of mothers who found it difficult to nurse two babies or, worried that

> they might love the one sent to a wet nurse less than the other, preferred to have both nursed out of the home. Having accomplished her task so well up to now, I think that Madame Barbet would find it difficult to follow that path. But she is in a good position to find a satisfactory solution, maybe by finding a wet nurse nearby. These concerns must be shared by *la maman* Arnaudtizon. I can see her now caring for the mother and her newborns. Please send them my regards and give me news of everyone . . . as soon as you can.[32]

Marguerite's letter acknowledges the multigenerational work of caring for young children as well as common practices regarding breastfeeding. What mattered most to her was who would serve as the godparents, though she also reflected on how Victoire would handle nursing twins.

In contrast to the disappointment she expressed when Amélie had a miscarriage, Marguerite exhibited no emotional reaction after learning about the death of Victoire's baby girl. Pierre wrote to his mother to inform her but provided little in the way of details, and Marguerite seems not to have responded to the news. Babies, especially twins, died frequently. Families thus anticipated this sad outcome. How Victoire and her husband responded to this loss cannot be known, but the lack of any trace of emotion in the letters makes it seem like their primary reaction was a pragmatic acceptance of fate. Life had to go on; the Barbets had two young children, Juste and Marie, to care for and the baby boy, Henry, for whom they hired a live-in wet nurse, perhaps because of Victoire's previous difficulties.[33] Catherine's silence on the death of the infant also reflects standard practices in her letter writing—sharing good news and amusing stories while keeping more upsetting details to a minimum.

Giving birth and caring for babies remained largely the concern of mothers (and wet nurses and servants), but as children grew older, fathers took more active roles in their upbringing. While visiting with his in-laws, Pierre wrote to his father about four-year-old Ludovic's reading lessons. In a letter written two days later to his mother, he provided further details: "Ludovic received a watch from his aunt Victoire. He is enchanted with it and proudly showed off how well he could read it." The following year, Pierre sent his mother a note with a page of Ludovic's attempts at writing.[34] The sharing of stories and advice about young children was a common feature of these letters. Although they had servants to do much of the labor related to childrearing, men and women alike, and family members across the generations, felt deeply engaged in children's social and educational progress.

Managing Boys' Education

Pierre's intense paternal engagement surfaced during an episode that left a mark on them all: Ludovic's enrollment in boarding school in the spring of 1811, when he was eight years old. While it seems unsurprising that boys struggled with leaving the family home and entering a colder, more impersonal environment, family members voiced more concern about Amélie's emotional state than her son's. Pierre, too, seemed troubled, as he mentioned the preparations for Ludovic's entry into boarding school repeatedly, even telling his business agent, Jean Costerisan, that he would not be able to travel to Lyon that spring because of it.[35] He felt he needed to remain in Paris to provide moral support to Ludovic during this trying time.

Both of Ludovic's grandmothers wrote frequently to offer advice and request updates on how Ludovic and his parents were coping. Marguerite reminded Pierre of his experience with boarding school. "I hope that your son will be as you were: very committed to entering school (*collège*), and always happy during the time you lived there, never complaining about either the food or the difficulty of the subjects taught. Your friend Bodard can also tell him that you were neither a tease nor a tattletale, and that everyone loved you. I am sure that my little one will work to live up to his father's model. I am holding back my quill which would like to say more."[36] As usual, Marguerite expressed reticence about voicing her feelings to her son. What else did she want to say, and why did she feel uncomfortable sharing her thoughts and feelings? Or was this manner of communicating a kind of manipulation that she exercised because of a sense of powerless toward her son, who by this point had taken on the role of "head of the family" in the aftermath of his father's death?[37]

While Marguerite acted as though she was holding something back when she communicated with her son, Catherine Arnaud-Tizon voiced her opinions and concerns forcefully. As the moment approached for Ludovic to enter boarding school, Amélie suffered emotionally and physically, and her mother worried (as usual) about her health. Catherine empathized with Amélie, who was struggling as she anticipated the upcoming separation.

> I just received your letter, my dear Amélie, which I was waiting for impatiently because I have been worried about your health. I see that I was right and that you have a bad enough cold to be running a fever. I hope that you are telling me the truth when you say that you are feeling better. I request a letter from my dear Vitet in the next two days to confirm your well-being and to calm my worries. I encourage you to be strong and not to let your son sense how much you are suffering as you prepare to separate from him. It is important that he maintain his

good disposition. I am disappointed that your father's absence makes it impossible for me to spend two weeks with you to distract you as I had hoped.[38]

To facilitate Ludovic's acceptance of his new situation, Amélie needed to find the strength to control her emotions, a concern also voiced by Pierre's mother, who wrote to him regarding "the cold that has been affecting your wife. This tender mother is suffering at having to separate from her son, and I share your pain in this regard. I am happy to hear that this dear boy is maintaining his resolution. He will soon come to appreciate the advantages which you are procuring for him."[39] Amélie's emotional suffering, which everyone presumed was the cause of her physical ailment, seemed natural and expected.

As the big day approached, Catherine wrote again to encourage her daughter to be strong in the face of an unavoidable transition.

> Ludovic's entry into school is thus fixed for Saturday. I am delighted that this little man remains determined. That will protect him from much pain. I encourage you, my dear Amélie, to hide the pain you are feeling as you separate from this dear child. You cannot keep him at home with you any longer without hurting him. It would be a shame not to encourage his talents. I think that during the first year it might be possible to extend his vacation a bit and I hope you will stick to your word and spend the entire vacation with us.[40]

Like Marguerite, Catherine assumed that Amélie was struggling to accept Ludovic's departure and that the family had no choice in the matter.

Pierre wrote to Catherine the day after installing Ludovic at school. He mentioned Ludovic's willingness to accept the situation but said nothing about Amélie's state of mind. It was probably not good. "Announced Ludovic's entry into boarding school on Saturday, April 27, his resignation and good will. My wife and I will be visiting him today. Thanks to Barbet for the good shad which we ate on Friday with our friends and Ludovic's."[41] They hosted a party at their house the evening before taking Ludovic to school and served fish that Jacques had sent from Rouen. Again, familial cooperation contributed to marking this important moment. Then, after dropping off Ludovic on Saturday, Pierre and Amélie visited him the very next day!

Ever the engaged mother and grandmother, Catherine continued to worry about Amélie and Ludovic and did what she could to improve the situation from a distance.

> I received your letter, my dear children, as well as Ludovic's, which renewed my chagrin at not being able to spend some time with my

> dear Amélie who must be feeling a great void. I am impressed at this dear boy's maturity [*raison*] and look forward to hearing about your first visit to learn whether any sadness has replaced the firm resolution he has demonstrated so far. Please tell me in which neighborhood is located the place de l'Estrapade and whether it would be permissible for me to send my dear boy some *mirlitons* [a kind of squash] that I think he might enjoy eating. Send him my love.[42]

Catherine transitioned from discussing all that Ludovic and his parents were going through to her own suffering caused by her husband and son spending several weeks in Lyon. Separation as a form of loss emerged as a common theme in her letters from this period, as in this passage from a letter she wrote a week later: "I saw in the letter you sent to Barbet that my dear Ludovic is adjusting well to life at school. I cannot wait to see him. The summer vacation seems so far away."[43] This important and difficult moment of transition intensified Catherine's desire to be near her loved ones.

Ludovic's initial experiences were quite positive, but he began to suffer as the newness wore off. Catherine blamed his parents' visits for his difficulties in adjusting and continued to worry more about Amélie than Ludovic. On May 9, she wrote:

> Your letter gave me great pleasure in assuring me that our dear boy is becoming somewhat accustomed to his new life. I had warned you that overly frequent visits would make him homesick. It is essential that his mother demonstrate courage. . . . It seems that the dear little mother's health is still not perfect and that she cannot fully shake her nasty cold. I assure you that if it was not necessary that I stay at home during *le papa*'s absence I would have gone to see how she was doing myself, even though you say there is nothing to worry about. I hope she will rest. She needs to put aside concerns about fashion and dress warmly until the summer heat takes hold. The fluctuating temperatures engender many illnesses in your city, particularly chest congestion.[44]

Voicing classic advice about staying warm to avoid illness, Catherine clearly felt that it remained her responsibility to care for her adult daughter. She used those concerns to build a case for Amélie to travel to Rouen (specifically Bapaume), where they would nurse her back to health with clean air, fresh food, and her mother's attention.

> We need to discuss Amélie's health. I think the fresh air at Bapaume and some cow or donkey milk would do her a world of good. We have a small cow that just gave birth and a female donkey. Barbet will coop-

> erate and can get us a second donkey. He, his wife, and I beg Vitet to send us his wife for 15 days. We realize we cannot have you both here because you don't want to abandon Ludovic. . . . I am convinced that my dear Amélie would benefit from the sweet air of our valley. She can stay comfortably at her sister's house which is set up nicely now.[45]

Catherine used every tool available to convince Pierre to send Amélie to her, but it did not work.

A few days later, Catherine wrote to say how happy she was to learn that Amélie's health had improved and then returned to Ludovic, who also seemed to be doing better. He was adjusting to school and working hard, thus living up to expectations. Trying to provide emotional support to her daughter, Catherine expressed optimism that all would be well. "Let's speak of our dear boy, of his maturity and his hard work [*sa raison et son application*], proven by the good scores he has already received. I am certain that he will soon become very knowledgeable and that the routine of the school, where it seems the students are well cared for, will be good for his health."[46] She shared similar sentiments in her next letter, expressing pride about Ludovic's abilities: "It seems that Ludovic is adjusting well to school and is happy there. I am not surprised that his teachers are satisfied with his work. He likes to study and wants to do well."[47] Here, Catherine is playing the role of the loving, supportive mother and grandmother by praising Ludovic, who was demonstrating traits that boded well for his future: a good work ethic and determination to succeed.

Despite Pierre's repeated insistence that Amélie's health had improved, Catherine continued to worry. When Pierre mentioned that they had opted not to attend the festivities held to celebrate the birth of Napoleon's son that June, Catherine took it as a sign that Amélie was still unwell. She also connected Amélie's situation to that of other family members. Amélie's sister Victoire had her own worries, as her second child, Marie, remained too weak to wean. "Learning that you chose not to mingle with the crowds made me very happy. Nonetheless you know my talent for worry and I am wondering if Amélie's health inspired your caution. Tell me the truth about her cold and whether donkey milk might help her. Victoire and her husband drink it. She is a bit worn out from nursing her little girl who cannot be weaned because she is delicate and hardly eats anything. If Victoire was weaker, we would need to find a wet nurse, which would be unpleasant but necessary to care for this dear little girl."[48] Offering advice and sharing news about how others in the family were managing their health served as a way for Catherine to feel like she was contributing to her family's well-being even when they were apart. Not long after Catherine sent this letter, her long-anticipated reunion with the Parisian branch of her family took place, as Pierre, Amélie, and Ludovic spent two months in Rouen. Catherine could thus observe with her own eyes her eldest daughter's health following her miscarriage and the fever caused, they assumed, by the emotional strain of sending Ludovic to boarding school.

The Vitets returned to Paris in October (the start of the new academic year), and Ludovic went back to school, provoking another series of animated discussions about Ludovic's studies and Amélie's health. Pierre's mother wrote encouraging words regarding Ludovic's abilities. "My dear Ludovic will courageously take up his studies, which he did not abandon [during summer vacation]. His father, who worked with him, will share in the glory of his success. I am sure I will soon hear about his accomplishments, and I will share in your joy, because our hearts are united by reciprocal sentiments. I hope that my dear daughter has completely recovered from her cold and that her health holds up. You say nothing of yours, which I hope is good."[49] Part of Pierre's role as a "good father" was to oversee his son's education, including by working with him during breaks. When he returned to school, Ludovic seemed ready to pick up where he left off, as suggested by Catherine's first letter to Pierre and Amélie after their return to Paris that year: "I admire Ludovic's resignation. I was afraid that he would be very sad and am happy that he has accepted the situation. When you see him, send him my love and his aunt Adèle's, who misses him a lot."[50] These last words about Adèle, Amélie's youngest sister, serve as a reminder that Ludovic's aunt was only a few years older than he was, a situation made quite likely when women married so young. Catherine gave birth to her youngest child just three years before her eldest daughter married.

A month after beginning school that autumn, Ludovic got sick, and his parents brought him home. A few days later, Pierre wrote to Catherine to inform her "of Ludovic's illness . . . and the concern it has caused us. He is at home with us. His treatment: leaches, baths, *vesicatoires* [blistering agents applied to the skin], quina [also spelled *kina*, probably quinine]."[51] The next day, he shared the same details with his mother. Both grandmothers wrote back immediately; Catherine was especially worried, as was her nature.

> I just received your letter my dear children, and you can imagine that it caused me pain to learn that my dear Ludovic is sick. I have every confidence in the treatments you are giving him and hope to learn soon of his recovery. Please allow me to suggest that you ask Dr. Esparon whether the dear boy has the strength to withstand entire days of

> work with only two hours of recreation. Would it now be good for his health to keep him home with you for one more year, and to accustom him little-by-little to work? His sickness seems like a nervous malady that could have been caused by work. My love for you inspires all that I am saying to you my dear children, and I hope you will forgive me for speaking to you this way.[52]

This was one of the rare instances in which Catherine suggested she may have been going too far in offering advice, perhaps because sending boys to boarding school seemed so essential.

Ludovic's illness led his parents to withdraw him from school temporarily. Catherine agreed with their decision and shared her views on why, in this case, it was acceptable for the boy to remain at home rather than toughing it out at boarding school. "Your letter, my dear Amélie, brought me great pleasure in reassuring me about our dear boy's health. . . . I completely agree with your plan to keep him home from school for the winter. He needs maternal care, which is irreplaceable."[53] Catherine's reference to Ludovic needing his mother's attentions may have been an effort to respond in advance to arguments about boys needing to experience the hardships and discipline of boarding school to develop into sufficiently strong and independent men. But Ludovic was still young, just nine years old, and apparently there was space to maneuver within this system for educating boys.[54]

However, rather than sending Ludovic back to boarding school once his health had improved, they chose a less common path. In late November, Pierre informed his mother of Ludovic's recovery and announced that he would nonetheless be staying home.[55] Pierre justified this decision by referring to the boy's delicate health, but the emotional stress they had all experienced when Ludovic entered boarding school the first time probably contributed to Pierre's assessment. He later sent Catherine details on the arrangements they had made to allow Ludovic to continue his studies. "Informed her that I pulled Ludovic out of school and have engaged a tutor who will come three evenings a week to give him lessons, along with André Pradher, whose father also canceled his enrollment, and who will be studying the other days of the week at the Conservatory."[56] André Pradher was the son of the well-known pianist, composer, and music teacher Louis-Barthélemy Pradher, who taught at the Paris Conservatory from 1800 to 1827.[57] Ludovic would be in good company.

Catherine reiterated her view that he would benefit from staying home. "The details you sent regarding Ludovic's health and the plans you have adopted for his education brought me great pleasure. I am persuaded that this dear child needs maternal care for a few more years. Plus, because he is growing at an extraordinary rate, the boarding school diet cannot be suitable for him. I am convinced that thanks to your attention, his studies will not suffer. He will just complete them a bit more slowly, something which is of little consequence for children who are not destined for business."[58] Catherine's reference to "maternal care," even though it was Pierre who handled Ludovic's education, reflects her blindness to the roles of fathers, a kind of refusal to acknowledge Pierre's intense engagement with his son's upbringing. The reference may also reflect her desire to underline the value of maternal care to reinforce her own sense of worth, while reiterating that it was Ludovic's health (not his parents' weakness) that justified this unusual decision. Another point she raised in support of their plan came out of her assumption that Ludovic would not be entering the world of business, so any delay in his education would have little impact. His family's background and wealth meant that he would not need to contribute to their economic well-being, and his obvious intellectual abilities already put him on a path toward a more scholarly trajectory.

Pierre's mother also voiced support, emphasizing how much pleasure Amélie must be taking at having her son at home. Marguerite then turned her attention to a subject that was very important to her: religion.

> I see that my dear Ludovic is writing as though he had never been sick. He is keeping busy and will not make you regret keeping him at home. I appreciate how happy this must make his mother and hope that she will make sure he receives his catechism training. Whenever you like I can send you the excellent catechism from Montpellier that was bought for you and is suitable for every age. We just read the first volume, or more accurately I heard it read at my sister's house, where I regain that which my weakened eyes have forced me to lose to my great chagrin.[59]

Ludovic's religious education emerged as a major preoccupation for Marguerite. In a letter to Ludovic sending birthday greetings, Marguerite expressed her desire that her grandson focus his efforts on becoming a good Christian, implying that his parents' concerns lay elsewhere.

> I want to remind you that I ardently wish that you learn as much about virtue as science, and to apply yourself in your study of religion to become a true Christian by practicing under the supervision of a good teacher. I hope that this will be Auguste Hochet's. His parents have been happy with him, especially since his First Communion. It always gives me pleasure to receive a few words from you, and I believe you

> are honest enough to tell me frankly how you are progressing. It will make me happy to think of the joy you will give your parents with your docile obedience, by telling them everything, and by showing them affection. The affection I feel for you will last as long as my life, and I hope you will not forget me. Accept this book that I told you about and model yourself on he who will pray for you if you invoke him with confidence.[60]

Although she does not specify which book she sent, presumably the model Marguerite was encouraging Ludovic follow was that of Jesus. In Marguerite's telling, obedience, virtue, and open communication with one's parents and other family members developed on a bedrock of affection and respect. It was love that made children want to be good.

In addition to religious instruction, music and exercise were important aspects of a child's upbringing. In a letter to Amélie dating from when Ludovic was nine years old, Catherine emphasized the importance of physical activity. "So my dear Ludovic is taking dance lessons. I worry about his strength because of his extraordinary height. But this exercise can only do him good, especially in this season when we cannot go for walks."[61] He also took piano lessons from Mr. Pradher, one of the most accomplished musicians of the period. After pulling their sons out of boarding school, the Pradher and Vitet families maintained the same routine, with the boys studying Latin together at the Vitet home. A letter from André's mother announcing that he would be missing those sessions for two weeks makes it clear that the families took these lessons seriously. "André will not be able to attend Latin lessons for fifteen days. He is still feeling unwell and Dr. Esparon recommends that we take him out a lot for walks, and to keep him active [*ne pas trop le laisser tranquille*]. I do not want him doing work that would be too tiring for him right now, that he is not in a state to do."[62] Finding the proper balance of physical activity and intellectual work was an important part of parents' role in ensuring their children's health while positioning them for success.

Besides demonstrating his and his wife's willingness to go against the norm, choosing to educate Ludovic at home meant that Pierre was committing himself to ensuring that his son would receive a suitable education, both by teaching him some subjects himself and by hiring tutors.[63] While Pierre's interest in being a "good father" seems to have gone further than most, his deep engagement with his son's education does not seem to have surprised anyone. He happily took on this responsibility and developed an extremely close relationship with his son. And his efforts paid off: Ludovic later entered law school, where he excelled.

A letter Catherine sent to Pierre in 1817 demonstrates the extent to which Ludovic's education was a top priority for everyone—a shared commitment:

> I am sad to learn that I will not be seeing you and Ludovic this fall. Despite the chagrin that this news causes me, I must accept your reasoning. Time is precious for his studies, and if you want him to take courses at the college, it is essential that he prepare himself to make a good impression there. It requires great effort on my part to accept the situation, but we must sacrifice our pleasure in the interest of our children. You promise to send me Amélie for two weeks. I will be very happy to see her. Her presence will partially make up for not seeing you. I will wait until she arrives to visit Ecorcheboeuf [the Barbet's chateau near Dieppe] and will join her at Bapaume. While in Rouen, she can sleep in my bed, which is very big. That way I won't miss out on any time with her.[64]

Catherine's constant desire to be with her children (even to the point of sleeping in the same bed!) was a running theme in her letters, but she understood that Ludovic's education, which Pierre was overseeing so attentively, had to take priority.

Educating Children: A Family Affair

Pierre demonstrated an interest in the education of other children as well, suggesting once again strong complicity among the members of these families. Years later, when Pierre and Ludovic visited with the family in Rouen while Amélie stayed home in Paris with their baby daughter, Pierre sent Amélie descriptions of her niece and nephews, including some comments about their behavior and education.

> We received hugs in bed this morning after our little niece Marie came with Claudius to knock at our door. The dear child's rapid growth astonished us. She is strong and chubby, with a freshness that inspires joy and envy. Like our little girl, it's constant movement and petulance with her and she never stops babbling. Her big brother has grown and seems healthy. I cannot tell you anything about Marc. After he revolted against his tutor and announced that he did not want to work during vacation, they sent him back to the boarding school for three days to make him change his mind. The treatment seems to be working already, and the penitent should be returning to the paternal abode tomorrow.[65]

While young children's "petulance" could be endearing, as boys entered school age, they had to live up to high expectations and submit to their parents' rules. The threat of being sent back to school when they could otherwise live at home served as an incentive to behave properly.

Pierre expressed his views on the proper timing and approaches to educating boys in a long letter he drafted in the blank spaces on a letter that Amélie Arnaud-Tizon sent to Amélie Vitet in 1818. The draft letter is undated; we cannot know when and to whom he wrote, though it likely was meant for Catherine, as he mentions Victoire's son, Henry, and Mr. Lemarchand, a Rouennais acquaintance of the Arnaud-Tizons'. "Regarding education, it seems that Mr. Lemarchand is upset about his son's naughty and disobedient character and wants to remove him from his boarding school to enroll him at one in Juilley . . . [where he hopes] he will bend under the more severe discipline and will apply himself to his studies. . . . [Gustav] will fall in line as he remembers the hugs and attention he received from his aunts and uncles. . . . We must encourage him to remain obedient, gay, and affectionate and to apply himself to learning to read and write."[66] Turning to the Barbet children, Pierre reflected on the ideal age to enroll boys in school. "Despite [Juste's] understandable desire to have his younger brother with him as a comrade, I do not agree with the idea of enrolling Henry. He is not yet six and he barely knows how to read. Nine years in boarding school risks turning him off studying and becoming what we call a kid [*gamin*] rather than a studious schoolboy [*écolier*]. It is common to criticize parents who delay sending their children to boarding school. They lose precious time, and it is nearly impossible to catch up. But enrolling them too early can cause just as much damage."[67] Pierre had well-developed ideas about how best to educate boys to help them acquire the character traits and skills they needed to be successful. Though he believed that the timing of enrolling boys in school was important, he also emphasized the importance of finding the right balance of discipline and positive reinforcement through familial displays of affection.

Pierre's interest in his nieces and nephews is apparent in a note dating from 1819, in which Catherine thanked Pierre for some gifts he had sent. She discussed her grandchildren's progress in learning to read, write, and, in the case of the girl, play the piano.

> I distributed the gifts to the children who were very happy with them. Juste followed your advice and took his books to his boarding school. I am pleased to see that he enjoys reading. Marie loves the fur and the dress on which it is to be attached is already at the seamstress so she can wear it on Sunday. Henry put his beautiful book in his mother's desk

> for safekeeping. The dear boy will go to boarding school after the winter. He is learning to write and knows how to read quite well. Barbet's three children are writing well. After only six weeks of lessons, Marie wrote a new year's greeting to her father that was really well done. She is also progressing with her music. She is already doing difficult exercises and enjoys putting in the effort.[68]

Catherine enjoyed voicing her pride in her grandchildren. She seemed similarly happy to announce her grandson's successes in a letter she sent to Pierre the following year:

> We were eating breakfast when Barbet received a letter from Mr. Pinel informing him that Juste was first in his class of 48 and he is the youngest. You can imagine how proud he was, and he pleaded with his *papa* and *maman* to go see him. We immediately set up the carriage, as the walk was a bit long for me, and we went to congratulate him. We found him decorated with a medal and wearing his Sunday clothes to make it more visible. He asked me to send you and his aunt his regards and to share the news with his cousin.[69]

Celebrating children's successes encouraged them to work harder while reinforcing affection and demonstrating support across the generations. Such stories brought the family together, creating a sense of closeness even when apart.

Desiring Togetherness

Another common theme in Catherine's letters was parents' desire to be near their children and grandchildren. She frequently complained about not being able to see Amélie and Pierre as often as she wished and empathized with others who felt similarly. When the Suchet couple moved to Paris in April 1812, Catherine commented on how sad her sister-in-law was at their leaving: "Everyone misses them, and we feel intensely the emptiness in the house. As for us, I admit that this is making us very sad. I feel awful for my poor sister-in-law. She cannot speak about her grandchildren without crying. If I was in Monsieur and Madame Arnaud-Tizon's place, I would soon be joining my children."[70] Catherine desired togetherness, with multiple generations in frequent contact—if not physically together, at least through their correspondence. In 1810, when her then twenty-five-year-old son, Ludovic Arnaud-Tizon, was running the family business in Lyon and had not written for a while, Catherine wrote to Amélie to complain. Catherine hoped perhaps that a letter from his sister would inspire her son to reply to her own letters. "I have had no news from Ludovic. Our business correspondence never mentions him; it is as though he doesn't exist. I admit that I am beginning to worry and cannot forgive your brother for his silence. In the end, one must be patient while summoning the carefree [*mandant les insouciants*]."[71] As she did in many other instances, Catherine was implementing a standard parenting tool: using one child to intervene with another who was not meeting her expectations, in this case by not communicating with her regularly.

In the spring of 1812, after Amélie suffered her probable miscarriage, Catherine used every possible argument to convince her to come sooner than usual for their annual visit.

> My dear friend, you ask about when your sister will be giving birth so that you can be available to serve as godmother. She thinks she will have the baby between August 15 and 20. I hope that my dear Vitet will decide to spend the month of July with us. It disappoints me that you always visit us in the fall. The long days of summer are much better for enjoying the countryside, and I must admit that I am also desperate to see you. . . . I am convinced that the change of air would do wonders for my dear Amélie. We would lead a tranquil life and would do whatever she would like.[72]

Catherine combined the pleasure of spending time together with improving her daughter's health to build her case.

Catherine's letter sending New Year wishes in January 1813 reiterated her never-ending desire to live near Pierre and Amélie, though she recognized that while she and her husband remained in Rouen, that would be impossible.

> I am hurrying to reply to your lovely epistles and to express my appreciation for your affectionate words. The assurance of your friendship is very important for me. The love I feel for my children is the source of my happiness and the only thing that one can count on with any certainty. If you speak of us often, my good friends, I can assure you that a day never goes by without us conversing about you. We regret that we do not live in the same city. We would be able to spend our time together as a family and see outsiders only occasionally to make us appreciate our family gatherings even more. But fortune has not given me this kind of complete happiness, and Rouen is too gloomy to hope that you would ever move here. Believe me when I say, my dear children, that I pin all my hopes on your annual visit. I wish you both all the happiness that you deserve.[73]

The pleasure of spending time together as a family, without "strangers" in the mix, is something that comes up repeatedly in her letters and reflects her understanding of what family members should feel for each other and the roles they play in each other's lives. As a mother, she viewed her happiness as inescapably linked to her children. She wanted to be near them, participating in their lives as much as possible. Her avoidance of "outsiders" and desire for insularity represented a form of security as well, a way to feel protected and safe.

Part of what made family life so attractive was the socializing that took place at home, and music and dancing were frequently part of those events. Boys and girls alike took piano, singing, and dancing lessons and then performed at family gatherings. Ludovic became quite passionate about the piano, as did his aunt Adèle, whose parents purchased a piano for their home in Rouen so she could pursue her studies on that instrument, which also helped with her singing lessons.[74] Pierre encouraged his sister-in-law Adèle in her studies, sending instructions on how she needed to proceed as she neared the age at which young women married. "Encouraged [Adèle] to continue her studies—of music and of writing and grammar. She needs to practice writing her own words and not just copying. One good method is to read the letters of Madame de Sevigne, then to try to write on the same topic and correct her mistakes by comparing her work to the model."[75] When some friends visited with Amélie and Pierre in Paris, they reported back to Catherine that Ludovic had become an accomplished piano player: "They told us about the delightful way you were celebrated. They said that my dear Ludovic played the piano like an angel. I look forward to judging his progress myself."[76]

Ludovic continued to live with his parents as he pursued his education, another sign of their close and amiable relationship. In April 1816, Pierre wrote to his mother with an update on their situation: "I am still in the national guard, but am serving less frequently, which permits me to spend time in the country. We are all doing well. My wife did not cough all winter. Ludovic is getting stronger and can go out now or down to our garden. . . . My son's first communion has been delayed due to Mr. Roman's absence. While we wait, we have been handling his religious instruction. . . . As for me, my health continues to be excellent except that I am starting to lose my hearing because of a gunshot in Rouen."[77] Pierre seemed most interested in assuring his mother that all was well, though he did share the bad news about his hearing.

In March 1817, Marguerite wrote to encourage Pierre to enroll Ludovic in a boarding school she had heard about. Pierre wrote back saying that he rejected her "plan to place my son with the priest Paneur who recently opened a *pension* in Paris. We will have him prepare for his first communion in a different manner." Pierre later reassured his mother that Ludovic would be studying with a priest at Saint Eustache.[78] He made his First Communion in July 1817, when he was fourteen. Pierre marked the occasion by sending a thank-you gift to the priest who prepared Ludovic for this important rite of passage: twelve bottles of Bordeaux wine and twelve jars of jam. He also made sure to send his mother the good news, which he included in his letter wishing her a happy saint's day.[79] Catherine wrote a note "congratulating [her] dear Ludovic on his first communion," adding that "his grandmother must have been happy to receive this news."[80] Drawing attention to the religious fervency that Marguerite demonstrated in contrast to most of her family, Catherine's comment about Ludovic's other grandmother underlines the ways that religion could also reinforce generational ties. Later that summer, Pierre and Ludovic traveled to Lyon, an experience that no doubt strengthened their already strong bond; it was not the only time the pair traveled together.[81]

Ludovic's education remained a topic of discussion once he began attending school again in his teens. In March 1818, Catherine applauded his early successes. "Congratulations to you and my good Ludovic for his high rank at school. This dear boy is seeing his hard work rewarded, which must make him want to work even harder. Kiss this big boy for me as heartily as I love him. I can see him now as a distinguished man of thirty and hope to live to see it."[82] While ensuring their children developed the skills to succeed in life and fostering their talents were the primary responsibilities of parents, sharing and following the details on their progress became a central theme in their correspondence, making the larger family feel implicated. Ludovic entered the Collège Bourbon in October 1818 and quickly rose to the top of his class, again offering Pierre a chance to brag about his son's accomplishments. Catherine's response gives an inkling of what he must have written to her.

> I learned with pleasure that my big Ludovic was first in his class. It's just as you say: finishing the year this way portends well for the year to come. Give the dear boy lots of kisses from me and make sure he knows how much I share his well-deserved satisfaction. Juste was overjoyed when he heard the news and immediately grabbed his quill to congratulate his cousin. Henry speaks to us often of Paris and all your kindness to him. He will be joining his brother at boarding school after New Year's Day. Marie handles her piano lessons like a girl of fifteen and has progressed measurably. I think she is well-disposed for music, which pleases her mother.[83]

All the family took pleasure in each other's successes—at least that is how Catherine portrayed everyone.

Ludovic was clearly the pride and joy of his parents and his grandparents, whose enthusiasm for his successes knew no bounds. In January 1819, Pierre wrote to his mother that Ludovic had been invited to attend the annual Saint Charlemagne dinner at his school because of his academic accomplishments; he was first in his class.[84] In August 1820 and again in 1821, Pierre shared news of Ludovic's achievements: in 1820 he received prizes in Latin and history, and in 1821, he received first place in philosophy.[85] Ludovic then began studying law, the most prestigious career for men of his class and thus an unsurprising choice for such a talented student. Although he never demonstrated great passion for the law and did not receive a degree, he became a devotee of one of his professors, Théodore Simon Jouffroy, a disciple of Victor Cousin, who taught psychology in his home after being forced out of his position at the Collège Bourbon. It was at those gatherings that Ludovic made many of the contacts that would lead him to journalism and a writing career, including Sainte-Beuve and the duc de Broglie. He also formed a close, lifelong friendship with Charles Duchâtel.[86] While building upon the connections and reputations of earlier generations, Ludovic was beginning to create his own network of friends and colleagues.

Transitions: A New Baby and New Life Stages

Around the time that Ludovic was completing his studies, in January 1822, Pierre and Amélie had another child, a girl they named Amélie, like her mother, and whose nickname became Mimi.[87] The family's correspondence from these years allows us to see how the couple handled this late-in-life enlargement of their family. They sent Mimi to a wet nurse, just as they had with Ludovic. The woman they found was the wife of a gardener who lived in Bourg-la-Reine, a town about five kilometers south of Paris.[88] They visited their daughter regularly and reported on her health to the rest of the family. When she turned one, Pierre wrote to his aunt in Lyon that the little girl had five teeth and was lively and happy.[89] In April 1823, they began making plans to bring her home. To decorate her room, they ordered fabric from Ludovic Arnaud-Tizon in Rouen. Pierre explained to his sister-in-law that his wife wanted "a piece of calico to make curtains and other things for our little girl upon her return from the wet nurse. Amélie went to see her; she has teeth and is ready to be weaned."[90] They brought her home at the end of May, when she was about eighteen months old. Pierre referred to the "difficulties of weaning" as the little girl adjusted to her new home, and they incorporated her into their lives.[91] Pierre's mother had died by this point, and Amélie's parents were dividing their time between Jouy and Paris, which means that fewer letters exist to flesh out the details.

Catherine's letters do not explain why she and Claude decided to move to Paris, but as they aged, it seems they no longer wanted to live on their own. In addition, they had always planned to leave Rouen once they retired. They first moved in with Jacques and Victoire and later with Pierre and Amélie. Catherine had already been complaining about physical ailments for years, as in the following letter from 1816. She probably wanted to avoid the stresses and costs of running her own household. "You ask about my pains. I am still suffering a lot and from time to time I have episodes where I cannot move for two or three hours. Afterward, I feel very tired. Despite all of this, I am doing well. I am eating as usual without any problems and that helps me tolerate the pain. *Le papa* is doing marvelously despite his concerns about the complete stagnation of business."[92] Catherine was fifty-two when she wrote these words; her husband was sixty-three. Age, physical disability, and financial concerns led them to the decision to move in with their children and eventually away from Rouen.

Once Catherine and Claude left Rouen, their daughter-in-law, Amélie Arnaud-Tizon, replaced her as Pierre and Amélie's main correspondent there. Her letters offer a rare opportunity to consider the experiences of a young mother working to raise four children, run a household, and support her husband in the family business. Her views reflected prevailing attitudes regarding the education of boys and girls, but her comments demonstrate that she felt confident developing her own opinions and was not afraid to share them. In one 1821 letter, Amélie began by discussing the Barbet children, starting with Marie.

> This little girl is still very sweet. She puts a lot of effort into her studies. One cannot say the same thing about Juste who has disgraced himself to the highest degree. His teachers complain not just about the quality of his work but also his character. He is defiant toward them and responds insolently. All these grievances have made Victoire anxious and sad. She does not yet know what her husband will decide to do, but she too sees the necessity of removing him from [the school run by] Mr. Pinel who has no idea how to inspire fear in his pupils.[93]

As with Ludovic's education, it was Juste's father who would decide how to handle his son's schooling, while his mother anxiously waited to see what her husband would decide.

Amélie then turned to her own children's progress. Based on her comments, it seems that she was handling her sons' education, in part because they were still young but also because her husband (unlike Pierre and Jacques) had to work full-time overseeing the family's textile factory.

> Children cause so much worry; the pleasure they engender often costs a great deal. Mine, for now, have been doing wonderfully. Claudius already needs to work several hours [a day], but he applies himself willingly. He can learn things by heart with ease and his writing is not bad for a child who is not yet seven. Marc is more distracted and less interested in learning. Seeing that I could not make him progress in reading, I decided to leave him in peace for a few months. I hope that pride will inspire him to catch up to his brother. As for your goddaughter, she is still a very good girl, very strong, very fresh; she has two teeth and seems very precocious. You can see, my dear friend, as I enter into all of these minute details, how much confidence I have in your affection for these children. I know that you love them like a mother and that you feel for them as we do for your son. . . . [Ludovic] holds the same place in my heart as my own children. I feel as proud for his success, for his good behavior, as I would for my own son, and I speak about him with as much pride as a mother.[94]

Sharing these details demonstrated her devotion as a mother, which she also assumed on the part of her sister-in-law. Amélie made frequent reference to her attachment to her nephew Ludovic, a model young man in her eyes, whose mother no doubt enjoyed hearing such praise of her son.

A few years later, when Amélie Arnaud-Tizon was nursing her fourth child, Auguste, she seemed both happy and fearful that her good fortune could end.

> I am happy to let you know that my big baby is thriving. He is truly a wonderful child. He is good-natured, never cries, and is not at all demanding. To satisfy the family, I am starting to let him eat a little, but I assure you he doesn't need it. He is rarely hungry . . . and can easily go two or three hours between feedings. At night he only nurses once and very quickly. You can see that he is not difficult. I do not feel at all tired. . . . I still have lots of milk, and my doctor insists that it will continue as long as I keep up with it. His little sister is crazy about him and not at all jealous as I had feared. His brothers also love to hug him. You cannot imagine a more beautiful scene than these four children whose happiness and good health bring me such contentment. I appreciate my maternal blessings and can only hope that through some enchantment my good fortune will continue, as I know that it is

> impossible that the future will not cause me some worries, privations, and perhaps sorrow. Whatever we say about the joy of large families, they also multiply the risks, and it is rare to have four children remain perfectly healthy. I would then say goodbye to my happiness which I am appreciating now, knowing that it is ephemeral. Though these reflections are sad, they are true.[95]

In speaking from the heart and sharing her joys and fears, Amélie Arnaud-Tizon expressed the friendship and trust she felt for her sister-in-law.

A year later, while responding to an invitation to visit with the Vitets in Paris, Amélie sounded less satisfied with her life as she complained about her many responsibilities, but such complaints were also a way to build intimacy.

> It is difficult for me to leave my house. I would be deserting four children, a big household. Supervising it along with our business requires my constant presence. This life so full of unpleasant activities is tiring. I am in constant physical and moral activity which is wearing me out. . . . Many would nonetheless envy my situation, and thus I must try to be happy. I know that children require sacrifices, and we are lucky when we can profit from them. Tell dear little Amélie that her cousin Marie has begun her education. She has six lessons per week and is willing and talented. Amélie [aka Mimi] will need to do the same thing soon, and then both of our daughters will honor and please us. Our schoolboys are not doing badly either, though we had to delay their return to school because of a bout of boils.[96]

Following the norms of the time, her sons were in boarding school while her daughter received lessons at home. Amélie does not mention the subjects covered in those lessons, but they presumably included reading and writing, some arithmetic, music, and perhaps art and needlework, all skills deemed essential for women of this milieu.

The final stage of Ludovic Vitet's education came in 1824, when he took a long trip with his best friend, Charles Duchâtel.[97] Ludovic retraced his father's and grandfather's footsteps to a degree, as he went to Switzerland, Italy, and then Lyon before returning to Paris. The voyage lasted more than three months; they left Paris on July 10 and returned on October 18.[98] On the way to Switzerland, they stopped to visit the fort where Toussaint Louverture died. Ludovic described the site in a letter addressed to his mother:

> Upon our arrival in Pontarlier, we made the heroic resolution to go on foot to Pontets. We were happy with this decision because the route was so diverse, and so rich in beautiful sights of every kind, that we

> would have certainly missed a lot in a carriage. At one league from Pontarlier, we passed below the Fort de Joux, where poor Toussaint Louverture died. The position [of the fort] could not be stranger or more savage. It is suspended like a crow's nest on a black boulder underneath which is a rapidly flowing stream and surrounded by pine trees and other huge rocks.[99]

Ludovic's prose, with its emphasis on the powerful effect that this natural terrain and its ancient fortress had upon him, is reminiscent of the romantic literature of the period. The reference to "poor Toussaint" speaks to Ludovic's immersion in liberal and abolitionist circles. His education and entourage, and his parents' inculcation of such values throughout his life, placed him firmly within those movements.[100]

The people and places Ludovic visited included both well-known sites and his family's close friends and allies. While in Switzerland, they visited Coppet, another place where Ludovic could reinforce his liberal pedigree and meet with prominent abolitionists, such as Victor de Broglie, Madame de Staël's son in-law.[101] They also stopped at the homes of people who had befriended Pierre during his time in exile.[102] After a few days in Milan, Ludovic spent several days in Lyon, demonstrating respect for his Lyonnais connections and for his parents by visiting with his relatives there. Unfortunately, his timing was not ideal; he arrived shortly after the death of Jean-François Vitet, his grandfather's first cousin. Pierre rushed off a note to announce this news to Ludovic and to remind him to wear mourning clothes while in Lyon.[103]

The letters Ludovic wrote during this trip give insight into the close and friendly relationship he had with his parents. He used the informal *tu* with them, something that Pierre did not do with his mother, though he did say *tu* to his father. In closing his letters to his father, Ludovic used affectionate phrases such as "your son and friend" or "your loving son." In contrast, Ludovic closed his letters to Amélie with the phrase "your devoted son," expressing his love and filial obligation. The fact that Ludovic and his parents lived together when they had a townhouse built for them on the rue Barbet de Jouy similarly reinforces the sense that there was little in the way of generational conflict among this family. Ludovic remained close to his parents all his life, and although he had no children of his own, he was close to his niece and nephew, who became his heirs. All three generations of Vitets (and Aubry-Vitets) lived in the same building from the 1830s through the 1850s and beyond.[104] Family was clearly the centerpiece of their lives. By this point, Ludovic Vitet held high-level public positions, but his choices about where to live and how to spend his time demonstrate that his father was not alone in appreciating the private sphere and the pleasures of socializing as a family.

Bourgeois families placed children at the center of their worlds. Children served as the glue to bind generations, as parents and grandparents shared news about their successes and struggles. It was a constant effort to do all that was necessary to ensure that they had the abilities, values, behaviors, and social skills to fit into their world. Children also added joy to family gatherings, such as by playing musical instruments to entertain and impress guests. The pleasures of family life, which often involved multigenerational gatherings featuring music and dancing, kept everyone close and ensured that the collaborative work of preparing future generations for success could take place. Writing about those gatherings and sharing news about children's health and progress also reinforced the emotional bonds of people living far from each other. All this kinship work depended on the financial foundations that wealth and bourgeois approaches to property and investments provided.

Chapter 6

Le Patrimoine

Property, Business, Wealth, and Honor

Although a good education and proper upbringing were vital to setting up children for success, providing them with a stable economic foundation was even more essential. However, the massive changes unleashed by the Revolution—new inheritance laws, new forms of property ownership, and the economic hardships caused by war—meant that families struggled to accomplish this goal. Intergenerational tensions also increased, as the new political system and its emphasis on change and experimentation seemed to favor youth over experience.[1] Regardless of these innovations, risk-averse investment strategies focused on landed wealth dominated for the most part among these families, with one prominent exception: the textile factory operated by Claude in partnership with his son and son-in-law. This business was a risky enterprise subject to larger military and economic realities over which they had no control.

In theory, the Revolution ushered in the age of the individual, a system in which rights and duties were acknowledged or assigned to people (men) as individuals and as citizens, not because of their position within a particular family or their pedigree. As this book makes clear, however, family ties and support remained vital. *Family* here refers not to the nuclear family, although those ties seem to have been growing stronger in these years, but rather the older sense of the term, meaning kin, a multigenerational unit with many branches that included cousins, aunts, uncles, and so on.[2] This multigenerational family remained fundamental to people's identities and life choices. Despite new investment opportunities and inheritance laws, early nineteenth-century practices regarding property resembled those of the old regime.[3] The French Revolution may have ushered in the age of the individual in terms of the discourse of rights, but in practice, the individual did not count for much. Anyone who privileged individual happiness and pleasure over larger familial considerations undermined the goals and strategies that lay at the heart of bourgeois existence.

This chapter traces the strategies the Vitet and Arnaud-Tizon families implemented regarding their businesses, property, and investments. Both families struggled to navigate through the turmoil of the Revolutionary decade and to some extent came out worse for wear, but they managed to hold on to their social and economic positions and sometimes even improve them. They did so by making the most of their wealth and connections to build on the successes of earlier generations. Similarly, each death in the family brought opportunities to review investments as properties were bought and sold, renovated, and repurposed. While losing a loved one caused pain and grief, death was an anticipated part of life, and families moved on quickly, focusing on making the best of the situation in economic terms. However, mismanagement of family resources could lead to a fate worse than death in their eyes: financial ruin and its resulting loss of honor (and credit).[4] The Arnaud-Tizons faced such a calamity in 1817. In response, the entire family—parents, siblings, cousins, and in-laws—came together to save the family's honor. That dramatic moment illustrates not only familial solidarity but also how an individual's standing could not be separated from that of the family. One person's successes or failures affected all.

Intergenerational Cooperation: Strategizing to Maximize Familial Success

Both the Vitet and Arnaud-Tizon families built on foundations laid by earlier generations. In addition to following in his ancestors' footsteps professionally, Louis Vitet benefitted from their wealth and connections. His father, Jean François Vitet, became wealthy enough to purchase a title of nobility.[5] Louis inherited his father's title and properties in Lyon and Longes and, when the opportunity arose, purchased *biens nationaux* in the same village.[6] An only child, Pierre acquired those properties and eventually all that his mother brought to the marriage, enough to allow him to live as a *rentier*. To manage his properties, he relied on his trusted friend and business agent in Lyon, Jean Costerisan, with whom he corresponded frequently to discuss the harvest in Longes, repairs on his houses, and dealing with tenants.

Like Pierre, the Arnaud-Tizon brothers benefited from their ancestors' successes. Their father, who ran a thriving textile business in Lyon, amassed a huge fortune. Toward the end of his life, Claude *père* composed two wills. The first, dating from July 1781, when his daughter married, indicates that his three children were to receive 110,000 livres at their marriages. The second, dated August 3, 1791, six months after Claire's death, provided additional funds to her son and designated Claude's two sons as his sole heirs.[7] The money and property Pierre-Marie and Claude *fils* inherited upon their father's death in May 1793 included nearly 400,000 livres held in the family business and two houses in Lyon valued at 100,000 livres that produced 4,800 livres in annual rent.

The chaos of the Revolutionary decade made managing those resources difficult, and the brothers' strategy appears to have been to hedge their bets. While Claude was serving as a municipal officer in the Jacobin-dominated city government, Pierre-Marie moved to Rouen with his wife and daughter to live with his in-laws, the Vincent family.[8] They left in February 1794; Catherine and her children seem to have joined them in 1796, while Claude continued to run the business in Lyon.[9] The archives tell us little about Catherine's first years in Rouen, though we know she gave birth to her fourth child, Adèle, there in September 1798, while her husband was in Lyon.[10] Claude spent more than a decade living apart from his wife and children much of the time, with his son, Ludovic, joining him in Lyon when he became old enough to work. In contrast, Pierre-Marie sold his properties in and around Lyon, while his holdings in and near Rouen expanded when his wife came into her inheritance.[11]

Matters related to property and business were family affairs, with women involved in making decisions about how to run them. Catherine's engagement comes across in a letter she sent to Amélie in 1805. "I want to tell you about some changes we are making in our house. Your father has decided to run his own business affairs. The shop we have will suffice. The only change we needed to make was the addition of a small bathroom [*cabinet de bain*] in the courtyard. We will hire a clerk who will sleep in the room near the dining room. Your son's room will serve as our office, and he will use the little room behind his aunt's."[12] As in artisanal workshops, employees became part of the household, and Catherine oversaw the necessary arrangements to house them. A few weeks later, she sent reassuring news:

> The days seem so short that we never have time for ourselves, but do not worry that we are overworking. We spend evenings at the theater or socializing as usual. It is only the day that we make our payments that your father works until eight, but it does not tire him. If I noticed that the record-keeping was too much for him, I would hire a second clerk immediately. For now, I can assure you that all is well, and he has never been happier. Morel's training is nearly complete. In another month, it will feel like we have been doing this work all our lives.[13]

Although we cannot be certain of Catherine's precise role in the business, she clearly participated in hiring decisions, and her use of *we* suggests that she was involved in other matters as well. In this and many of her letters, Catherine portrays herself as competent and confident regarding business and financial matters.

Catherine sounded even more enthusiastic when she shared details on an ambitious project they launched in 1808, when Claude and Jacques formed a partnership to run a textile factory in Bapaume, a village outside of Rouen.

> Yesterday, Barbet purchased a calico factory that is ready to put into use having been built only a few years ago. He and Victoire will be living on the premises, and we will be storing the finished goods here until they are sold. This new enterprise will be incorporated into our current one, and I am certain that it will be profitable. As for Barbet, running this factory will permit him to maintain his expertise in this area. He was raised in this business. He likes it and can only succeed. Plus, he will only be responsible for the factory itself. My husband will handle the purchasing and correspondence. Victoire is happy about living in the country. . . . They will be thrilled to welcome you to their little hermitage, and I will be overjoyed to take my little Ludovic there to breathe the healthy air. This place will serve as our country home, something I have desired for a long time. . . . The views there are beautiful. My dear Vitet will certainly find pretty sites to paint.[14]

Feeling implicated in these matters, Catherine referred to "our business" as she described their plans. And, as usual, Catherine used every opportunity to encourage Pierre and Amélie to visit.

A year into this venture, Catherine sounded optimistic. The business was going so well that they were expanding into a second factory:

> We finally completed our inventory last night. The results were better than we had hoped. All is going well, and we are confident it will con-

> tinue. We are preparing [to launch] a second factory on Girod's land . . . and are decorating two bedrooms in the house, one for ourselves and the other for you, my dear children, with a smaller room for Ludovic. This way we can gather as a family at Bapaume, and when my dear Vitet does his painting lessons with his friend Dunouy, there will be space for him to come and go as he likes.[15]

This was a family endeavor that she hoped would prove beneficial for all.

Everything changed when Barbet *père* died in 1813 and Jacques came into his inheritance.[16] A year later, Jacques purchased an estate near Dieppe. When Claude visited the property, Catherine reported on his impressions: "*Le papa* visited Ecorchebœuf with Barbet and his wife on Sunday and was very satisfied with it, both the land and farms as well as the house, which is very spacious and solid. It will be in perfect condition with very little expense."[17] This purchase would provide the entire family with a country home at which to gather.

After the house underwent more than a year of renovations, Catherine visited in April 1816. The night after she arrived, a rare spring snowstorm hit, causing excitement and worry.

> At 8 a.m., the servant entered my room to light the fire and with a sinister air announced that six inches of snow had fallen. . . . I was comfortable in the big, beautiful, well-heated house, but we were expecting *le papa et l'oncle* at 2 p.m. . . . I was concerned about the danger of driving in their carriage without marks on the road. But you know Barbet: He is fearless. He left in his carriage to find the gentlemen, and everyone arrived safely. . . . The next day they were able to visit Barbet's new property and were very impressed. . . . Barbet's house leaves nothing to be desired in terms of comfort. . . . Your room and Ludovic's are ready, as well as his study for we cannot forget that. His little wife [Victoire's daughter] loves the country air and is fat as a pig.[18]

Besides taking advantage of this opportunity to encourage Pierre and Amélie to visit, letting them know that their creature comforts would be satisfied in this new family home, Catherine highlighted her son-in-law's bravado. It is unclear how she interpreted his fearlessness—was she applauding or criticizing him? It is also interesting that she referred to the property as "Barbet's house," which it technically was, even though it was Victoire's home as well. In later letters, she refers to it as Victoire's house.

Returning for another stay two months later, Catherine reiterated how much the family appreciated having a country home. "Victoire continues to enjoy living in the country. . . . They say there are many nice places to visit in the vicinity. . . . We spent part of a day in Dieppe. I appreciated the beauty of the calm sea. Fishermen's boats were everywhere. . . . Our city [Rouen] has never been so empty. Everyone has left for their country homes after being unable to do so for the past two years."[19] After years of disruptions, wealthy families were returning to their earlier practices. For the Arnaud-Tizons, having a home where they could enjoy the fresh air and pretty views improved their quality of life. Barbet's new property served as an investment while contributing to the family's happiness and well-being.

As in the case of Jacques's father, Louis Vitet's death in May 1809 unleashed a series of changes, including new financial arrangements between Pierre and his mother. As a widow, Marguerite regained control over the property she had brought to the marriage, but a week after Louis's death, Pierre created a document that transferred his mother's wealth and property to him, except for a building she and her sister had inherited from their father. In exchange, Pierre promised to pay her an annuity of 2,000 livres.[20] Marguerite appears to have accepted this arrangement on the grounds that it made sense for her son to oversee her investments. Pierre shared this news with Costerisan: "I informed him that we will be keeping my mother with us and that I made an agreement with her that suits us both."[21] Two weeks later, they all left for Rouen.[22] While there, Pierre continued handling legal matters related to his father's death, sending Costerisan documents and calculations regarding his inheritance and mentioning that his mother was "not presenting herself as an heir and wanted nothing."[23] This was Pierre's reading of his mother's views, of course, but they are in line with other evidence.

In addition to dealing with financial matters, Pierre worked to ensure his father's intellectual legacy. Most significantly, Pierre completed Louis's book, *Traité de la sangsue médicinale* (*Treatise on the medicinal leech*), seeing it to publication just two months after Louis's death. In a prefatory note, Pierre expressed his love for his father and his zeal for doing this work: "In the depths of grief, I found some solace in the idea that I was rendering homage to the best of fathers."[24] Pierre distributed copies of the book to friends and family and followed up with contacts in Lyon, hoping to convince someone to review it.[25] Political divisions dating from the Revolution continued to shape Lyonnais reactions to Louis and his work. When Ballanche *père et fils*, printers of the *Bulletin de Lyon*, refused to publish Louis's obituary and later a book review, Pierre wrote to the son of Louis's collaborator, Petitin, asking for help finding another newspaper.[26] In the end, Pierre gave up on the Lyonnais press but succeeded in getting an article published in the *Mercure*, which he distributed to friends and family.[27]

In the months after Louis's death, Pierre and Amélie renovated their apartment. Leaving the rest of his family in Rouen, Pierre returned to Paris to supervise the work. While there, he sent updates to Amélie: "The house is horribly filthy. . . . Happily, [the masons] have finished their work in the kitchen and elsewhere. Everything looks as I hoped."[28] In his next letter, he announced that the work was nearly done: "I ordered the connecting door for your room. . . . It will be installed on Thursday. . . . I know you are impatient for me to return, but I will not be able to leave until then, because the upholsterer who was supposed to come today won't be here until tomorrow, and I want to watch him set up the bed on the ground floor. [He] . . . will move the bed we want to put in our room. I also asked him to find a good used mahogany desk for my mother."[29] In addition to highlighting his efforts to be an accommodating and attentive husband and son, Pierre's letter makes clear his and Amélie's sleeping arrangements: They had their own rooms with connecting doors and a bedroom (and bed) that they shared.

After Pierre returned to Rouen, his friend Jacques Fournel sent news on their apartment and life in the capital, including an update about the reorganization of the Paris National Guard.

> The Parisian Guard has been suspended; people are saying that it's been abolished. This circumstance has not stopped the brave *épauletiers* from running from one social engagement to another. Today they will be at a fancy dinner at the archchancellor's home. For us poor soldiers who do not dine with *les grands* [high-ranking people], we hope that this rumor of ending the guard becomes a certainty.
>
> I visited your apartment. The paint smell is still strong and unpleasant. It will take a good ten days for it to dissipate, and even then, it will be necessary to leave the windows open. Everything else is finished, except for positioning the furniture and hanging the wallpaper. I encourage you to see the apartment of Besson *fils*, who found some lovely wallpaper.[30]

Fournel's discussion of the National Guard expresses a clear sense of "us" and "them"; he labeled himself (and presumably Pierre) "poor soldiers" and drew a contrast between their lifestyle and that of high-ranking officers. He then jumped from criticizing "*les grands*" and their frivolity to making suggestions about wallpaper, including advising Pierre to visit the home of a friend to get ideas about interior design. Pierre and his male friends found such topics worth their time, just as women like Catherine could discuss politics and economic developments. The Vitets did more work on their apartment the following summer, with Marguerite staying to oversee the workers while Pierre and Amélie were in Rouen. Pierre sent his mother instructions and reminded her to keep their servant, Jaunette, busy with cleaning the house, including the recently emptied cellars, and caring for her.[31] Ever attentive to spending wisely, Pierre wanted to ensure that his servant would not be idle in his absence.

In September 1810, Pierre traveled to Lyon to inspect his properties, including those in Longes, which he visited with his father-in-law and Costerisan. He shared news with Amélie on what he found and his assessment of their value.

> We inspected both domains and drew up an inventory of the house and its contents. We received a visit from Mr. Fleurdelix of Rive de Gier, who seems interested in buying our properties. He ate with us and examined the house and its surroundings. Our former servant, the Rive de Gier innkeeper Renau, who is now living off his rents, also visited and would like to buy la Combe. The two farmers would also like to buy it and are ready to pay 20,000 livres, but I am asking 27,000. . . . I was satisfied with the condition of the house and with our farmers. Your father found it much better than he had expected. These gentlemen are convinced that I should be able to get at least 60,000 francs altogether.[32]

As distant landlords, they could not be certain of the properties' condition and the productivity of the agricultural lands until visiting them.

In a letter to his mother, Pierre described all that he and his companions did, emphasizing how well they had managed to care for themselves. Although he included details on their creature comforts, he did not discuss financial matters with her, as he had with Amélie. He may have wanted to hide the value of these properties from Marguerite.

> We traveled by carriage as far as Bellevue. There, our two farmers arrived with three good horses, and once we had eaten and rested, we slowly made our way through the mountains without suffering from the heat. . . . Not having a cook, we brought some provisions with us, and the evening we arrived, Catherine Ferrande came to serve us. . . . We did not waste any time during our stay. We inspected both domains, drew up an inventory of the house, and made and received several visits with people interested in our property. . . . We invited Mr. le Curé to

> eat with us. He asked me to send you his regards, as well as that of his mother and sister.[33]

It is interesting that Pierre described the men who picked them up as "our farmers," making him sound like a seigneur talking about "his peasants." In mentioning the "three good horses," he perhaps wanted to suggest that the farmers were prospering. Catherine Ferrande must have been a local woman who demonstrated her goodwill by helping them. Though he had not visited his ancestral home in Longes for many years, Pierre felt a strong connection to the members of this community, who seem to have welcomed him warmly. Finally, in bringing up the priest and his family, Pierre clearly hoped to please his mother.

In the remainder of the letter, Pierre reported on his trip back to Lyon and sent an update on the building Marguerite and her sister had inherited from their father.

> We stopped to visit the famous reservoir built by the Chartreux. . . . From there we headed to Rives de Gier where Renaud had invited us to spend the night with him. We had time that evening to explore some business ventures, and the next morning, we visited Mr. Fleurdelix who showed us his mines and fire pump. . . .
>
> Regarding the rue des Bouchers [apartment], all is going as you wished. Tomorrow, [your tenants] will give me their outstanding rent and the keys. . . . I purchased from them a pretty mirror that had been placed above the fireplace in the bedroom that faces the street. It would have been a shame to have it removed. . . . We haven't found new renters, but as soon as we have the keys and make a few repairs, someone acceptable will come along.[34]

Although Pierre mostly sought in this letter to reassure his mother that all was well and that he was following her instructions, he included some interesting details about his return voyage. His discussion of the "business ventures" he and Claude explored as well as the mines and fire pump they visited suggests that they took advantage of their trip to learn about the local economy and the technologies that the region's entrepreneurs were employing, perhaps with the goal of learning about investment opportunities. And he apparently thought Marguerite would find those details interesting as well.

Pierre's approach to selling his properties followed the norms of the times: owners decided on a price and then waited to find interested buyers. It took years before Pierre received an offer he was willing to consider. After selling la Jurary in 1817 for 36,000 francs, he thanked his notary for negotiating the sale and requested some items from the house. "I indicated which books I would like: the letters of Mirabeau to Sophie . . . the works of Molière, and the story of *Théodore et Tiberi* for my son's library. I invite him to choose whichever engravings will make him happy."[35] The contents of homes, even books and artwork, remained with the houses, a common feature of real estate purchases in these years.[36]

Satisfied with his work in maximizing his inheritance, Pierre sent an update to Amélie as he was preparing to leave Lyon, ending his letter on an affectionate note.

> My dear Amélie, I am behind in our correspondence, and this is unfair because you have never ceased to write regularly. But my dear, I have been very busy since our return from Longes. . . . Yesterday I received a visit from our farmers who . . . had brought the things from Longes that I had put aside, [and] I finished dealing with the heirs of my mother's tenant. . . . As I complete these tasks, it fills me with joy to think that I will soon be with you and will have the pleasure of kissing you tenderly.[37]

As usual, Pierre sounds like a loving and devoted husband. After staying in Paris for a few days, Pierre and Claude continued to Rouen, stopping in Jouy to visit the Oberkampf factory, which produced the famous toile de Jouy and which Jacques Barbet would later buy.[38] They made time during their travels to view sites of interest to an entrepreneur like Claude, who may have been searching for new ideas for his own business.

Gender and Generational Tensions

While in Rouen in fall 1810, Pierre received a letter from his mother that initiated a difficult moment in their relationship and sheds light on wealth-management practices and generational dynamics. Marguerite had mentioned a few months earlier that she might return to Lyon to live with her sister or perhaps enter a convent, a proposal Pierre labeled bizarre.[39] Now, having received an invitation to travel there with a friend, she announced that she was leaving Paris immediately.[40] In his response, Pierre expressed shock and begged her to stay long enough for him to travel there with Amélie to say goodbye. It is one of the rare instances when raw emotions, in this case anger and frustration, emerge in the letters he preserved.

> I could never have imagined that I would receive the letter you sent me on the 8th. I just received it today, the 9th, at 3 p.m. because my wife

> and I had been in Bapaume with Madame Barbet. This delay kept me from replying immediately, which added to the extreme displeasure that you are causing me. Then another contrariety added to the mix: Determined to say our good-byes to you tomorrow morning, we sent Marguerite to Rouen to reserve two places for us. But all was in vain! There were no places on any of the stagecoaches, not inside or on top! This situation left me with no choice but to send my letter with the driver . . . to inform you that we will be leaving for Paris tomorrow evening. . . .
>
> I hope, my dear mother, that our rush to see you will convince you to delay your departure. Since the man who is taking you on this voyage is so nice, he should be willing to do you this favor. Our unexpected trip to Paris should demonstrate the extent to which you have misjudged the situation. I do not know if this will lessen your suffering, but you could not behave more heartlessly toward your children.
>
> And on the eve of your departure, there are countless things we need to discuss, to prepare for your arrival in Lyon. . . . Nothing could justify such a departure. That is why I am going to such lengths to see you for at least a few minutes; my wife agreed. If you had told me earlier, if you had expressed your desire to have us return to you, do you think we would have hesitated?
>
> I have no more strength to express my chagrin. It is late and I need to bring my letter to the driver.[41]

Pierre's motivation for rushing to Paris involved more than a desire to say his adieus. After convincing his mother to postpone her trip, Pierre had her sign a document transferring her remaining property to him in exchange for an annuity.[42] She left for Lyon a week later, never to return. In a letter to Costerisan, Pierre wrote that he had "settled matters" with his mother and asked him to pay her five hundred francs in January.[43] As an adult male *rentier*, Pierre viewed it as his right to oversee his mother's property while placing her in a subservient position. He would provide for her basic needs while profiting from the properties he now managed.[44] Legally, widows regained control over property they had brought into their marriage or inherited afterward, but we see in this example how in practice, adult sons often staked claim to those properties for themselves.

Throughout her remaining years, Marguerite corresponded regularly with Pierre, often voicing her affection, especially for Ludovic.[45] A dutiful son, Pierre kept up his end of the correspondence, but his letters tended to stick to business. Five years after making these arrangements, Marguerite voiced pent-up frustrations in a letter that stands out for its emotional tone. She feared that she may have disadvantaged her sister and her sister's children, because if Pierre died without a direct heir, the property would go to Amélie's family, who could then force her sister or her heirs to sell their part.

> The document you had me sign was drawn up at a moment that was unsuitable for making such an important decision. Absorbed by the fear of hurting my children as I was leaving them, and not wanting to appear ungrateful, I was not fully myself. My lack of knowledge and experience in such matters should have made me stop to reflect on what I was signing. I was suffocating with the pain of leaving you. . . . I should have delayed my departure, but you wanted to return to Rouen. I tried to calm my worries as I persuaded myself that I would see you in Lyon. . . . I beg you now out of a sense of justice and friendship for your mother to revise this document and correct whatever might prejudice my sister.[46]

By depicting herself as inexperienced regarding financial matters, Marguerite seemed to be suggesting that Pierre had manipulated her into giving up control over her property. Pierre waited two weeks to reply and made no reference to the subject she had broached after all these years of reticence.[47] He knew that she was mistaken; his wife and her family would not inherit the house, even if Ludovic predeceased him. However, his refusal to discuss the issue may also reflect his views toward his mother and "his" property. He felt under no obligation to discuss these matters with her now that he was in control.

Rethinking the Arnaud-Tizon Business Model

While Pierre was transferring his mother's property to himself, his in-laws were laying the groundwork for a transfer of wealth to the next generation as well. They did this by providing ample dowries to their daughters and setting their son up in what they hoped would be a profitable enterprise. The economic downturn that hit France in 1811 caused Catherine to worry, particularly as they were in the process of launching major changes to their business. "Our town is still very gloomy. New bankruptcies continue to be announced, and it is impossible to guess when this horrible crisis will end."[48] In his response, Pierre referred to the "business crises [and] multiple bankruptcies [and] encouraged her not to lose herself in sad thoughts and to come visit us as promised at the end of March."[49] Catherine followed his advice, arriving in February. "*La maman* Arnaud-Tizon [spent] three days with us to inform us that their associates in Lyon were unhappy with the costs of running the Bapaume factory and wanted to dissolve the business. As a result, *le papa* intends to sell his business in Lyon."[50] This plan pleased Catherine, because it meant her husband and son would live in Rouen: "[Ludovic] seems happy to live near us and is well disposed to work alongside his brother-in-law to learn about running the factory. Furthermore, this type of occupation suits him as he prefers not to remain sedentary. He will nonetheless handle some of the correspondence to assist your father who, like me, is not getting any younger."[51]

In March 1811, Catherine confirmed these arrangements and expressed joy at seeing her family reunited.

> I just received a letter from *le papa* who is doing well and seems happy with the decision he has reached to settle in Rouen definitively. What may surprise you is that Ludovic shares this opinion and is happy to join us here. All that remains for our family reunion to be complete is you, my dear children, and that happens much less frequently than we would like. I find it sad that I only see my little Ludovic during vacations, but I understand that it is essential to take advantage of his natural talents and make sure he is receiving proper instruction.[52]

Though she wanted her family members near her, Catherine understood the benefits of living in Paris, particularly for Ludovic's education. Her letter underlines how being a good mother and grandmother required sacrificing for the next generation.

In her next letter, Catherine sounded more optimistic, both about her husband's prospects in Lyon and the general economic situation. "I am sending you good news from *le papa* who writes often. Several buyers have expressed interest in our house on the rue Sirène. He is hoping that this competition will bring a good price. I am impatient for him to complete this business. . . . Commerce seems to be picking up here; at least there is less talk of bankruptcies. The sunshine is improving people's moods. One can only hope that this terrible economic crisis has reached its end."[53] Fully engaged in her husband's efforts, Catherine spoke knowledgeably about the real estate market. "I received a letter from *le papa* who still hasn't sold his house, but who just signed a lease at a good rate of 8500F. . . . Now I think the sale will take place quickly, as buyers wanted to be sure the house had been rented."[54] She wrote again the next day, mostly to grumble and complain: "I am growing impatient, and the nice weather and longer days, which might bring pleasure to some, only make me feel worse. Business is horrible, but we are nonetheless obliged to spend the entire day at home, which is very boring when there is nothing to do. It is unfair of me to share my worries and my bad mood with you, but I am confident in your friendship and ask that you indulge my rambling."[55] Two months into her husband's stay in Lyon, Catherine shared good news: "I am happy to tell you, my dear children, that *le papa* has finally completed the negotiations for the sale of his house. He got a good price: 150,000 livres with all fees paid by the buyer except for 1,500 francs commission. It is a good price, and good agreement, with the payments due over a short period."[56] With the sale finalized, the family had cut their economic ties to their native city.

The last years of the Empire and first years of the Restoration brought new challenges. Despite Ludovic and Claude's efforts, the family's business suffered, in part because the economic climate was not propitious. With Ludovic Arnaud-Tizon and his wife running the factory, Catherine often commented on their business and the economy more generally. "For the first time this winter, we all went to dine with our Bapuamiens. . . . Ludovic is working very hard, and we cannot complain about sales at this moment, which are very active. . . . In times like ours, we must take advantage of such circumstances. The dear brother is pushing production as much as possible."[57] Ludovic struggled to make the business profitable enough to support his own growing family and fulfill his parents' commitment to pay the remainder of Adèle's dowry. Inter- and intragenerational cooperation and support lay at the heart of their efforts to keep the family business afloat while setting their children up on solid foundations.

Facing Death and the Catastrophe of Financial Ruin

In 1817, the family encountered difficulties that required intense collaboration. Catherine's niece, Adèle, had married Gabriel Suchet, brother of the future marshal, in 1802. Although this alliance boded well, it did not take long for Suchet's behavior to raise eyebrows. For example, in 1807, while describing one of his many parties, Catherine mentioned Suchet's conspicuous consumption. "We will be attending a soirée at Mr. Suchet's on Saturday. . . . His carriage is the talk of the town: it is the prettiest in the city. On New Year's Day he had it painted with his brother's colors, blue and orange. He lacks nothing, and our nephew has a grandly decorated house."[58] Catherine clearly disapproved of Suchet's spending habits.

By 1814, Suchet's financial situation was becoming untenable. When Marshal Suchet visited Normandy that year, Catherine expressed hope that he might be convinced to buy his brother's home:

> Instead of acquiring a property that he does not know, it would be good for him to look at St. Just. *L'oncle* ardently wishes him to do so, but he does not dare say that to him. . . . How can Suchet dream of keeping a property purchased entirely on credit, that produces next to nothing, that he cannot enjoy, and from all perspectives becomes more onerous to him day-by-day? I admit that I have often criticized *l'oncle* for his anger toward his children, but in this case, I cannot help but agree with him and I am sure that you feel the same way.[59]

Catherine's reference to her brother-in-law's temper hints at tensions that rarely emerge in her letters. Since he had only one daughter, when she referred to "his children," she must have meant his daughter and son-in-law. As a man who had spent his life nurturing the fortune he and his wife had inherited, he no doubt felt angry about his son-in-law's imprudent financial decisions.

In another letter, Catherine described her interactions with Marshal Suchet and reflected on Pierre-Marie's mental state:

> I am not surprised that you found your uncle looking unhealthy. . . . He is upset and worried about his son-in-law and does not have enough strength of character and frankness to insist that Suchet sell a property that is causing him to lose a lot of money. . . . When the Maréchal brought it up, I spoke frankly with him. He asked if I knew St. Just and the embellishments that have been done on it. I told him no, but that I found the location charming and the chateau, while not beautiful, convenient and spacious. He told me that it was not suitable for Gabriel. . . . I responded, "it would suit you much better Maréchal, and I am certain that the air, which is very sweet, would suit Madame la Duchesse."[60]

Catherine portrayed herself as speaking confidently with the marshal, who did, in fact, buy the property two years later, in 1816.

Although this purchase inspired hope that Suchet's situation would improve, Catherine remained pessimistic.

> The news you sent about St. Just gave me great pleasure. It had the same effect on my brother and sister who told me the Maréchal paid 372,000 francs. . . . That rids our relative of a property that was inap-

propriate for him considering his current position, and which, between us, was never appropriate. God willing, he will change his way of life, which is detrimental to his health and his wallet. I admit that having participated a bit in his marriage, I feel great chagrin about this and fear discord between the husband and wife, which would be the worst possible outcome.[61]

Catherine disapproved of Suchet's lifestyle not just because it contradicted her own aversion to risk but also because of its consequences for his family.

More bad news came in 1817, a year that brought pain and suffering in the context of an economic slowdown that compounded their private struggles. As Catherine put it that January: "Business has never been so dead."[62] Their real misery began in February, when Catherine's sister-in-law died at the age of fifty-seven. Catherine's letter announcing the news differs visibly from her other letters. Her handwriting is large and messy; she was probably crying as she struggled to hold her quill in the dim candlelight. "Our poor sister [is] no more. Take pity upon us my dear friend; take pity upon her poor husband. I do not know what I am saying. I can barely hold my quill. . . . Why must life be sown with so much sadness and why are those who do only good in this world taken from their family and friends?. . . Please go see Madame Suchet immediately and tell her to bring her children with her."[63] Catherine must have sent her letter on the morning stagecoach, which would have arrived in Paris that afternoon. Pierre carried out her request: "Response to the sad news she sent of the death of our dear aunt Arnaud-Tizon. I fulfilled the difficult task of informing Monsieur and Madame Suchet. . . . Madame Suchet has decided to travel to Rouen with Clémence and Eugène [her children]."[64] Catherine responded with details about Anne-Françoise's illness and death. Though still in the depths of mourning, she appeared more composed as she listed the treatments offered.

I am still staggering under this terrible blow. . . . I spent Thursday evening with her at Madame Vincent's house. She seemed her usual self and partook in the little snack these ladies make every evening. On Friday around 2:00, she felt unwell and went to bed . . . Monsieur Pilore applied eight leeches which stopped her spitting blood. On Sunday, she seemed no worse. They applied mustard to her feet, which she could only bear for twelve minutes. On Monday, they put *vésicatoires* on her legs. She did not feel them. . . . At this point I began to suspect the gravity of her condition. . . . I left her on Tuesday evening at 8:00; *le papa* left at 11:00. At 3:00 a.m., I heard the doorbell. I jumped out of bed and found the clerk who had been sent to get us. She was no more. She

> expired painlessly in her husband's arms. There had been no time to tire her with the apparatus of religion. She did not experience the horrors of death and said nothing to indicate that she thought she was in danger.
>
> My brother is very upset, but he is handling everything courageously. He carried out his final duties to his wife and, despite our efforts to convince him otherwise, attended the burial. He will be happy to see his daughter and grandchildren. My husband will meet her at the stagecoach with a carriage.[65]

Like other momentous events, death brought families together as they sought solace with their loved ones and handled the practical matters required at such times.

As Pierre-Marie was recovering from the shock of losing his wife, Catherine sent news about how he and his daughter were managing and voiced concern about Suchet. "My dear brother is still very sad. He has nonetheless managed to return to running his business. We hope that this will distract him. Unfortunately, business is slow, and in the end, we can only count on time. In his place I would not be able to bear the isolation in which he will find himself once his daughter leaves. . . . I think we will be seeing Monsieur Suchet. He owes this mark of deference to his father-in-law, but . . . I will count on him only when I see him."[66] Suchet's unwillingness to travel at this significant moment did not instill trust.

In his response to Pierre's letter of condolence, Pierre-Marie expressed his love for his wife of nearly thirty-eight years. "My dear nephew, I did not have the strength to respond immediately to your obliging letter inspired by the irreparable loss of my excellent friend, my dear spouse. You will forgive me easily because you are good and kind. I am weeping for her. I miss her every moment and look for her in vain in her habitual places. We do not recognize happiness until we lose it irrevocably. The days are long, and the nights longer still!"[67] While Pierre-Marie seems to have felt sincere pain at losing his wife, he was not too sorrowful to handle practical matters. The day before he responded to Pierre, he deposited a copy of his wife's will with a notary. Aside from the thousand francs she donated to a local charity and half of her movable possessions, which she wanted to go to her grandchildren, she left everything to her husband and stipulated that she wanted "to be buried simply and without ostentation."[68]

A few days later, more bad news hit the family. On March 1, Pierre sent two letters to his in-laws. The first, addressed to Catherine, shared standard information. The second, addressed to Claude, announced "Suchet's awful situation. I beg him, on behalf of Suchet, and in the interest of us all, to accept the sad task of sharing this news with our cousin and her father by giving them the enclosed papers tracing Suchet's financial affairs."[69] Pierre viewed Suchet's difficulties as a problem that the men in the family needed to face head-on; it was essential that they cooperate and mobilize their resources to find a resolution.

As the family began to appreciate the magnitude of Suchet's problems, they entered crisis mode. Catherine's response to Pierre addressed the gravity of the situation and Pierre-Marie's resistance to sacrificing his capital to rescue his son-in-law. "He is firm in his resolution to preserve his fortune for his daughter and grandchildren. He does not want to encumber his properties, and his liquid wealth is far from sufficient to cover the deficit. Plus, the balance sheet that Monsieur Suchet sent inspires no confidence. It shows more than 400,000 francs of debt and very little of anything real to cover them. How could this poor man have blinded himself to such an extent? In what grief he is throwing his family!"[70] The intense emotional tone of her letter reflects how shocking and reprehensible Suchet's behavior appeared; it placed the entire family in danger. The stain of dishonor could impact them all in both tangible and intangible ways.[71]

After changing subjects, Catherine returned to Suchet's problems: "When you look closely at his affairs, you see the enormity of his debts, and good God what debt! Notes on the order of 272,000 francs with only distant and imaginary revenue to cover them: The estimated value of his wealth is only 60,000 francs. I must stop my long jeremiads which are as unpleasant as they are useless."[72] Despite her efforts to avoid the topic, Catherine could not resist harping on Suchet's selfishness and bad judgment. "What damage vanity can do! It destroyed poor Suchet. He sacrificed everything to it."[73] Her explanation was simple: He had chosen to lead an extravagant lifestyle focused on appearances and luxury rather than living within his means. Suchet's behavior contradicted her most deeply held principles.

Catherine sent another long, emotional letter to Pierre the next day that began by expressing her gratitude for his comforting words and support:

> I received your letter of the first, my very dear friend. How good and consoling it was! In my mind, you have always been *l'homme par excellence*. I assure you that we have great need of consolation. The section of your letter that discussed Suchet distressed me. . . . We can only expect the worst from such an undisciplined man who builds everything on lies. We never predicted such a catastrophe; we are stuck in a state of immobility which we leave only to be insulted. He sent his wife a letter that was as twisted as his behavior.[74]

Catherine's praise of Pierre as the person she most trusted and relied upon contrasts sharply with her reading of Suchet's behavior. As she continued analyzing the situation, she sounded increasingly hopeless. "The Maréchal is behaving as a good brother and a man of honor. He has his sister-in-law and her children in mind. . . . Having contributed to arranging this fatal marriage, I cannot express the depths of my sorrow. Our position is unimaginable my friend. . . . This misfortune consoles me for the loss of my poor sister. I thank providence that it took her in time to save her from the most violent of chagrins. I assure you my friend that life is full of bitterness."[75] Catherine's letters rarely expressed such intense emotions. Her gratitude that her sister-in-law had died before the family learned of Suchet's situation suggests how desperate everything seemed. Suchet's behavior disturbed and shocked Catherine because, unlike illness and death, this path that brought the family face-to-face with catastrophe could have been avoided if he had made different choices.

Two days later, Catherine wrote on behalf of her husband, adding her views about how to resolve the crisis and explaining why Pierre-Marie was refusing to aid his son-in-law.

> *Le papa* . . . read your letter carefully, and after thinking it through, has decided not to show it to his brother whose decision is irrevocable. Like us, our dear brother has seen the depth of the abyss and does not want to throw himself into it. . . . Some may criticize my brother, but later they will recognize that he was right. . . . Would you like to know my opinion on all of this? Suchet should flee to America. He might be able to pull out a success from this business. For you must agree, an explosion is inevitable, and with it the loss of his position, etc.[76]

Her suggestion that Suchet should flee reflected her sense that nothing could be done to avert catastrophe.

After Pierre-Marie announced his refusal to rescue Suchet, Pierre shared his reactions with Catherine. "I saw the letter [which was] full of moderation and dignity. The son-in-law is acquiescing and will seek help from his brother and other places. . . . I understand the powerful motives that drove [my] uncle and I think I can guess why he refused to come to Paris: he does not trust his own resolution."[77] This crisis renders visible the difficulties of balancing interest and emotion and of planning for the future while focused on the here and now. As the back-and-forth continued, Catherine bemoaned their situation: "It is consoling to speak with you of our suffering. I assure you that we are very sad. . . . My heart is heavy . . . for I contributed to this alliance, even though I was not directly involved. Do not think that my chagrin has been intensified by indirect criticism. My brother has behaved in these circumstances with strength and magnanimity. . . . No one here [in Rouen] knows about this unhappy affair, though I fear that trips to Paris and Madame Suchet's sadness will betray our secret."[78] The scandal of bankruptcy and a legal separation was almost more than she could bear.

Like Catherine, Adèle Suchet felt comfortable sharing her feelings with Pierre. In one letter, she lamented her situation and laid out what she saw as her contradictory obligations.

> My beloved cousin, your old friendship requires that I explain the motives that are guiding me in this difficult moment. Divided between the interests of my children and my husband, my heart is being torn apart by a thousand agonies that my weak health is struggling to resist. An even more sacred duty . . . is to conserve the life of my father, who has been fatally shaken by these shocking developments. . . .
>
> Tell our friends to stop insisting that my father travel to Paris. He could never survive the trip, and I don't want to see him die. Think of the horror of my situation if that last great misfortune should strike. I am the most unfortunate and unhappiest of women, reduced to appreciating the fact that my mother died before receiving this terrible news. If this misfortune had preceded her death, I would have spent my life wondering if it had caused her death.[79]

Adèle's references to death reveal how catastrophic her situation appeared. The fact that she and her children were being comfortably lodged and fed in her father's home in Rouen apparently did nothing to relieve her chagrin. Of course, she had no doubt grown accustomed to the luxurious accommodations and extravagant socializing that she and her husband had enjoyed (on credit) and probably found her parents' old house and her father's frugal lifestyle less than appealing.

In another letter, Adèle returned to her "competing interests" and raised a new issue: Her husband had announced that he had not received any of her letters.

> Your last letter, my dear cousin, voiced the wisdom that has always distinguished you. . . . Think about how unhappy I am, divided between these competing interests while doubting my husband's good faith. Hearing that my husband has not received my letters surprised me. Since the news of this disaster arrived, I have written to him three times, always with a tone of moderation which others . . . might have dispensed with out of indignation for . . . I have been wronged, shame-

> fully wronged. . . . Please investigate the disappearance of my letters and confirm that it is not somehow related to efforts being made to hurt me.[80]

The news that Suchet had not received her letters intensified her suspicions that he was trying to cheat her further.

Catherine was convinced of Suchet's bad intentions, too, and thus of the necessity of protecting the family from further harm.

> I see no way to come to an arrangement and even wonder if it would be a good thing. For what can we hope from a man who, after committing so many grave errors, continues to behave arrogantly toward his friends and his brother? . . . His letters to his wife have a menacing tone. Hasn't this poor woman suffered enough in losing part of her fortune? . . . Monsieur Suchet's refusal to return his wife's belongings to her is unbelievable. As for her diamonds, I am sure that he cannot return them because he sold them long ago.[81]

In the moral universe of these families, it would be hard to imagine more egregious behavior. A man who could not safeguard the family's wealth and honor, its *patrimoine*, could not be trusted with anything.

A week later, Pierre sent a package of documents to Adèle and her father proposing a resolution. Marshal Suchet would oversee the liquidation of his brother's assets under the condition that Adèle and her father cover a mortgage payment of 26,000 francs. In exchange, they would receive Suchet's property in Corby. Pierre added that they should insist that Madame Suchet's jewelry and silverware be returned to her.[82] Pierre-Marie then traveled to Paris with Jacques to discuss the details, inspiring some optimism in Pierre: "I hope that their presence will smooth out many difficulties."[83] The day they arrived, Suchet signed a document giving his father-in-law power of attorney and allowing him (and not Marshal Suchet, as Pierre had proposed) to oversee the liquidation of his assets.[84] Though this agreement boded well, Catherine remained suspicious: "I continue to fear for the future. Will we later regret having acted this way? . . . At my age one no longer loses oneself in illusions and I find it difficult to believe in such radical change. . . . What bothers me most is seeing my poor brother so unhappy. He would gladly sacrifice money, but he is not happy about having to take on such a heavy burden of responsibilities."[85] It was difficult for them to know how best to proceed; whatever path they chose brought risks.

The roles played by the two brothers-in-law in convincing the older man to save the family's honor draws attention to the shifting balance of generations and their differing perspectives. Pierre-Marie viewed his wealth as something to preserve at all costs for his grandchildren. While he sought to conserve his real property and cash reserves, Pierre and Jacques were more concerned with the symbolic wealth associated with honor and reputation. In the end, Pierre-Marie would bow to the pressure; saving Suchet and thus the family's honor took precedence.

Another twist in the story came when Pierre announced that Suchet was suffering from stomach pains and encouraged Adèle to return to Paris: "Would it not be a good idea for his wife to travel to Paris to care for her husband and to oversee the upcoming move?"[86] Appearances mattered, and Adèle's presence in Paris might calm rumors. Catherine agreed and convinced Pierre-Marie to allow his daughter to go.

> Prolonging her stay here would have started people talking. Besides she should oversee the move. Nothing is better in these circumstances than the presence of the mistress of the house. I hope that Suchet will be able to attend the meeting with Barbet to seek a reduction in the large payment [*terrible fardeau*] my brother must pay. For any other man, this burden would be less taxing, for after working through the calculations, it is reasonable to think that he will only have to make these payments for four or five years. . . . This is a sacrifice his fortune can support, but he does not view things this way. . . . As we cannot change men, we have no choice but to watch him suffer.[87]

Familiar with the settlement details, Catherine felt comfortable criticizing her brother-in-law for his stubbornness.

Over the next few months, the family moved toward the liquidation of Suchet's assets, with Pierre and Jacques continuing to serve as intermediaries between the various parties. A repayment agreement was finally reached at the end of June, with everyone involved meeting in the presence of a notary. The document began by listing the key players: "Pierre-Marie Arnaud-Tizon, Gabriel Catherine Suchet . . . his Excellency Monsieur Louis Gabriel Suchet, Maréchal de France, and Madame Honorine Anthoine, his wife."[88] Madame la Maréchale came from a wealthy family—her father had been mayor of Marseille, and she was the niece of Joseph Bonaparte's wife. It was partly her dowry that would cover Suchet's debts. Next came the document's purpose: "Wishing to reach a definitive agreement to help Monsieur le Chevalier Suchet honor the numerous debts he contracted, [the parties] have come to the following agreements with him and in the presence of their family and friends who have signed below."[89] The first article stipulated that Suchet promised not to amass any further debt, to avoid any sort of speculation, and to focus on fulfilling his functions in the office of indirect taxation. He also agreed not to enter into any business agreements without the approval of his brother or father-in-law, "a measure which has become necessary to save his children from total ruin."[90]

Details on the debt repayment plan followed. Article Two specified that Pierre-Marie would take possession of Suchet's property in the Eure (Corby) and use the rent from that property, or the proceeds from its sale, to pay off Suchet's debts. Article Three stated that the Maréchal and his wife were giving 200,000 francs to Pierre-Marie as an advance to accelerate the liquidation. Article Four named the men who would oversee the liquidation, including the family's longtime friend and banker, Jacques Fournel. Finally, Pierre-Marie stipulated that the agreement did not relinquish his daughter's right to pursue a *séparation de biens*.[91] As his only child, Adèle, and eventually her children, would be inheriting his fortune, and without a *separation des biens*, her husband would have control over those assets. Pierre-Marie, and perhaps Adèle herself, feared the consequences of the huge power granted to husbands in French civil law. About a dozen people gathered in the notary's office to sign the document, which they hoped would protect later generations from the stain of financial ruin and block Suchet from causing further harm. In the process, the family and their allies demonstrated their commitment to ensuring the implementation of the agreements outlined in the document.

But this is not the end of the story. Adèle Suchet traveled between Rouen and Paris repeatedly over the next few years. She did not have the means to support herself in Paris but hated living with her father. Although Catherine understood her niece's feelings, she was losing patience with Adèle's inability to accept her situation: "I am happy to hear that Madame Suchet's health is improving. She needs it to bear the cruel position in which she finds herself, for the future does not offer her anything to calm her worries. With a man like that she will never be free from anxiety. It would be best for her to live with her father, but she will never take that step voluntarily."[92] Catherine believed that her niece needed to protect herself and her children by returning to Rouen. Pierre agreed: "Our cousin seems to have decided to stay in Paris even though it would be in her best interests to go to Rouen."[93]

When Pierre-Marie asked Pierre to convince Adèle to return to Rouen, Catherine took stock of the situation:

> I agree with you that *l'oncle* has put you in an uncomfortable position in asking you to speak to his daughter. . . . Everyone is surprised that she is not coming to live with her father, and some have even spread ter-

rible rumors about her. . . . He has decided to give her control over the household. In the end, the house is hers and she should take possession of it for the sake of her children. . . . Please keep all of this between us. I have already told my niece how I see things. We disagreed and I do not want to repeat that.[94]

Catherine preferred to share her feelings with Pierre, who, as usual, served as her main confidant and collaborator; one of her primary concerns was the circulation of rumors that could damage the family's reputation. Adèle grudgingly moved to Rouen, but, as Catherine explained, she did not hide her displeasure. "She and Clémence came to spend the evening with us yesterday. She . . . did not speak a word while she was here. Her father is making a mistake if he is forcing her to stay."[95] Even if Catherine believed that this move was the right decision, she empathized with Adèle, who resisted living under the watchful eye of her bad-tempered father.

A letter Pierre-Marie sent to Marshal Suchet in December 1819 indicates that even after two years, much remained unsettled. New creditors had emerged, just as the marshal announced that he would no longer help his brother. This led to another face-off. Pierre-Marie's indignation comes across despite his effort to speak politely. "I understood, and my family and friends who were present and who signed our three-way agreement understood likewise, that in guaranteeing the necessary assets you were responsible for covering his debts. . . . I would like you to send me in writing your assurance that you will pay all his debts. . . . If you do not want to do this, I will cancel my promise to come to your unfortunate brother's assistance because I refuse to destroy my fortune. . . . Doing so would hurt my daughter and her children."[96] Focused on preserving his wealth for his heirs, Pierre-Marie used every tool at his disposal to build his case. It seems that Marshal Suchet paid these creditors, straining the brothers' relationship further. The marshal remained on good terms with Pierre-Marie, however, who invited him to hunt on his properties.[97]

Like her brother-in-law, Catherine grew exasperated as the problems dragged on. Her reactions alternated between frustration and pity, with some guilt added into the mix. Catherine's analysis of the affair three years into it serves as a perfect example of bourgeois mentalities.

I gave your note to Madame Suchet, but I did not read the rest of your letter to her. . . . Had [she] heard your reflections, she would have viewed them as coming from a source of authority. . . . I feel sorry for Mr. Suchet as there is no position worse than his. I think others would

> be willing to sacrifice for him if he seemed more reliable, but between us, he is a deluded child who cannot be trusted. It is nonetheless essential that his circumstances improve. His daughter is growing up and will soon need to marry. She is developing nicely but loves pleasure too much and seems unaware of the significance of her father's situation. If she were my daughter, I would try to make her understand without hurting her feelings by helping her envision a happy future. But for the moment, I find these ladies out of place in high society. I may sound old-fashioned, but I cannot think differently.[98]

In depicting herself as "old-fashioned," Catherine was drawing a contrast between her eighteenth-century upbringing and the attitudes of younger women who had reached adulthood since the Revolution. She viewed frugal, modest lifestyles as the way to ensure the slow growth of wealth and status over generations. Adèle Suchet was acting as though her husband's loss of honor could be ignored, that life could go on as usual. Catherine disagreed.

Some good news arrived in December 1820 when Jacques returned from Paris to announce that a partial solution to Suchet's problems had emerged: the sale of Adèle's diamonds. Catherine responded with relief: "It appears that the diamonds will be sufficient to bring him his freedom. That is something. . . . Madame Suchet has probably written to thank you for working with Fournel to sell them. I hope we can bring this matter to a close. Clémence is seventeen and the time to marry her is approaching. It will not be possible to find her a suitable match in her current situation."[99] As usual, Pierre was at the center of these efforts. He informed Adèle that he had sold her diamonds for 15,225 francs and would be transferring the funds to Suchet.[100]

Another positive development took place when Suchet finally traveled to Rouen in February 1821. Catherine reported on his visit:

> He was well received by the entire family. He dined *chez la bonne maman* [Adèle's grandmother] on Sunday, and Thursday *chez* Barbet with the whole family and some friends. . . . His presence will have a good effect as the public is willing to excuse errors once the family appears to have forgotten them. It is important to remember that Clémence is seventeen and that the years leading up to the age of twenty do not seem to have twelve months. I hope this poor boy will succeed in liberating himself. This will facilitate his daughter's establishment. In short, all this must come to an end, and we must hope he will face up to reality.[101]

If a girl reached the age of twenty without marrying, people began to wonder if there was a problem. The family had to appear united if they wished to find Clémence a suitable husband.

Suchet's difficulties continued throughout the 1820s. When Marshal Suchet died in 1826, he left a lifetime annuity to his brother of 4,000 francs, but he was no longer there to provide larger cash infusions.[102] Clémence also married that year.[103] She was twenty-three, beyond the typical age for women in these families to marry. Although getting her settled must have been a relief, Suchet's problems were far from over. In April 1829, Pierre sent him "consolation for the worries and difficulties that had forced him to flee ten days earlier" and advised him to remain in hiding until the crisis passed.[104] The stain of dishonor had lasting effects for the entire family. In the end, no real resolution was reached; they simply did their best to minimize the damage. The fact that Clémence married suggests that the family had at least partially succeeded in its efforts, but Suchet's children did not climb to the heights of officialdom like their cousins, and their father's demise may be one explanation for their relatively lackluster careers.[105]

The members of these families spent their lives cementing their reputations as honorable and credit-worthy men and women while working closely with trusted allies and friends to avoid dealing with strangers. Financial ruin was catastrophic in a business and kinship model based on trust, as credit was not purely about money. One man's poor decisions and subsequent loss of honor impacted all those who had vouched for him as well as his children and potentially even later generations. Despite the language of individualism that had been introduced with the Revolution, no one existed in isolation. For bourgeois families, building a stable foundation for future generations was supposed to trump individual desires for pleasure or luxurious living. Suchet's disregard of this basic rule struck all involved as the worst possible crime.

End-of-Life Transitions

Besides death and financial ruin, 1817 brought another significant change: Catherine and Claude moved in with Victoire and Jacques. While in Paris to assist her daughter Adèle with the birth of her child, Catherine told Pierre and Amélie about their plans, causing Pierre to express reservations to Claude: "Discussion of the new arrangements which *la maman* told us about. It seems like a good plan for the business . . . but we disapprove of the interior arrangements: your status as a boarder in his home, and the improper dependence that will henceforth define your position. I trace all the objections that this unusual arrangement has inspired in us."[106] Pierre rarely voiced such strong views. Did he dislike the plan purely because of the dependent status it would impose on his in-laws, or were other motives at play?

In his response, Claude thanked Pierre and promised to consider his advice but made it clear that he would go along with whatever Catherine decided:

> I recognize your heartfelt concern in the advice and reflections you shared with me. I agree completely with your observations. I have not hidden my views from my wife, and if I wasn't certain that you had shared them with her, I would be sending her your letter which is in perfect agreement with my point of view. . . . Having made no definitive engagement . . . my wife and I can easily rectify all that you find inappropriate. For me, I stopped considering this move when my brother informed me that it could work against my children's interests. Their well-being has been and always will be the only goal of my actions. I would sacrifice everything to assure their happiness. My only regret is that Mr. Barbet, always quick to make decisions, has gone to some expense to prepare our rooms. I decided that it was useless to send your letter to him and his wife, and to wait to speak to him once you and my wife have come to a definitive decision. I hope we can find a way to satisfy everyone, though I think that will be difficult.[107]

Claude's willingness to acquiesce to his wife and son-in-law regarding such important matters is interesting here. This was no stubborn, domineering patriarch.

Even though Pierre and Claude opposed the move, Catherine refused to budge, demonstrating her ability to exercise her will, at least according to Pierre's response to his father-in-law: "A word regarding my previous letter and his response, which I communicated to *la maman*. Since she remains committed to the plan in question, I did not insist anymore and had to respect her decision [*volonté*]."[108] It was apparently Catherine who had the final say in this life-changing decision.

Catherine voiced satisfaction with their living arrangements in a letter she sent with her maid, Henriette: "I am settled in my new home where I feel much happier than in my big house. You cannot imagine how sad the house had become after we removed our business from the premises. I am nearly done setting up here; . . . I have two nicely furnished rooms."[109] Catherine then asked Pierre to help Henriette find employment, viewing that as her responsibility to her former servant. She also depicted Claude as happy with the situation: "*Le papa* . . . is doing very well and is adjusting nicely to his new domicile. In the end, it has not changed his way of life, except that he is less occupied, but busy enough to not feel bored. He still goes on his little outings to the theater, only now it is a slightly longer trip."[110] All seemed to be going well, though this was her plan, so she no doubt painted a rosy picture.

A few months later, she sent an update, saying that Claude was "in the best of health and getting accustomed to his new way of life. He works when he feels like it . . . and has not been bored at all."[111] They were transitioning to a new phase in their lives, becoming less autonomous while reducing their living expenses.

Another life-changing event occurred in April 1820, when Pierre's mother died at the age of seventy-five. Pierre traveled to Lyon soon afterward to handle her affairs; he hoped to sell one building while keeping the one that was jointly owned by his aunt. He updated Amélie frequently on his activities while there.

> Once I close my letter this morning, I am going to visit my tenant and, as my cousin Vitet advised, inform him that I intend to sell [the building] and propose that he make me an offer. . . . Tomorrow . . . I will visit my mother's apartment . . . and will reimburse the businesses where she had a running tab. It will be a relief to complete these sad tasks that remind me of the loss of our poor mother. After that I will spend two or three days with Costerisan to go through packets of papers, titles, books, and other objects that had been deposited with his uncle.[112]

In addition to completing his final tasks as a dutiful son, Pierre went through his mother's possessions: "I visited my poor mother's apartment with my aunt and found a copy of the will she had sent me. My aunt does not want to take all that my mother indicated, but I insisted. . . . My aunt would like to have my portrait, but I told her . . . that you had asked for it. . . . As for the family portrait, I am going to take it, but will remove the glass, which is useless because it is an oil painting."[113] *Le patrimoine* included buildings and land but also objects, some of which held emotional value, such as family portraits.

While Pierre was in Lyon, a conflict emerged with a neighbor in Paris who wanted to build a fireplace in a shared wall, forcing Pierre to send Amélie instructions about how to respond. "Regarding the fireplace . . . this is a usurpation which we are correct in refusing. . . . They will tell me: 'but your father accepted the first fireplace, why not agree to the second?' to which I would reply that the first one did not affect the strength of the wall."[114] He then told Amélie to go in his safe, where she would find "my property titles and some documents that might clarify the situation. (The key is in the small drawer where I put my rental receipts.)"[115] He hoped that the neighbor would be satisfied with the proposed concessions and, if not, that the project would be put off until his return. Pierre closed the letter by apologizing to Amélie that she had to deal with this matter. "I will end there, hoping that my suggestions will lead to an agreement . . . and regretting all the worry that this unpleasant situation has caused you in my absence."[116] It is hard to imagine Catherine needing her husband to tell her how to access their safe.

The two women's personalities and preferences may explain this difference, but generational distinctions and the nature of their investments seem relevant as well. As the wife of a *négociant*, Catherine participated in the family business and involved herself in financial matters. As the wife of a *rentier*, Amélie played a more subservient role. While Pierre kept Amélie apprised of his doings, there is no evidence that he ever asked for her advice, and he described the documents in question as "his," not "ours." Claude, in contrast, relied on Catherine's advice and assistance, and she always referred to their work as "our" business. Amélie replied to Pierre a week later with good news about the fireplace, sounding proud to report that she had succeeded in acting on his behalf. "I can announce to you, my good friend, that our neighbor seems to have given up on building a fireplace, realizing no doubt that he had no right to do so."[117] Amélie had managed, with coaching, to resolve the dispute.

Meanwhile, Pierre continued sending updates, including his plans for Marguerite's servant, Marion, for whom he expressed paternalistic benevolence. "I have rented my mother's apartment to her neighbor. That way he will have the whole floor, and . . . Marion [will be able] to stay in her room and finish her career there. This nice girl [*cette brave fille*] is touched by all that we are doing for her."[118] This "girl" was an older woman, probably around Marguerite's age. A few days later, Pierre sent affectionate words to Amélie: "My absence is becoming harder to bear, despite my many distractions, and I hope to return soon. But I must make sure that my affairs are heading in the right direction. . . . I hope to leave by the end of the month. The goal of kissing you and our dear boy is too pleasant for me not to try to complete my work as soon as possible."[119] While it is impossible to measure his degree of sincerity, by all appearances Pierre was a devoted and loving husband and father. And in managing his investments—building wealth for future generations—he was fulfilling his role as a good *père de famille* while acting as a dutiful son. "I sold some more of my mother's belongings. I got about 800 francs. . . . I will use 100 to follow my mother's written instructions to spend that amount on having masses said for her soul. One must respect the wishes of the dead. Otherwise, I would imagine my mother's virtuous soul dispensed without any expiatory ceremony. I think I could ensure it better than these priests who will be taking my money to pray for her."[120] Pierre clearly thought the hundred francs could have been put to better use, but he nonetheless fulfilled her request.

In early June, Pierre announced that he had sold the property at nearly his asking price while again voicing appreciation for his and Amélie's mutual understanding.

> I received your letter . . . my dear Amélie, just as I was about to write. It was perfect timing and very pleasant. It is as though we read each other's thoughts and respond appropriately. . . . Yesterday I nearly reserved a seat [on the stagecoach] . . . but I decided to give myself more time as I was supposed to speak with one more potential buyer for my house. I hoped to reach an agreement through a few mutual concessions. And I did it! I can announce with pleasure that I have sold my old, decrepit house for 37,500 francs. 17,500 will be paid when we sign the paperwork, then 10,000 next year, and the rest the following year.[121]

Catherine congratulated him on the sale, saying it was better to have fewer good investments than to hold on to a property that was in bad condition: "I did not expect that you would be able to sell your house in Lyon so quickly. Congratulations! It is never good to hold on to a bad house, and I think you got a good price. The ones you have left are solid and that is better than having another one."[122] As usual, Catherine confidently expressed her views regarding wealth management.

Once he had sold his agricultural and rental properties in and near Lyon, Pierre sought new investments. In 1825, after visiting possible sites with Ludovic, he bought wooded land in northeastern France. While visiting those lands, he shared details of his plans with Amélie, which included planting Canadian poplars with the goal of selling them for wood sixteen to eighteen years later.[123] It is difficult to imagine a more conservative investment portfolio.

Other changes came in November 1821, when Catherine and Claude accompanied the Barbet family when they moved to Paris after Jacques purchased the Oberkampf textile factory and house in Jouy, which permitted Jacques to call himself Barbet de Jouy (see fig. 10). In 1821, Claude was sixty-nine years old; Catherine was fifty-seven. Their son, Ludovic, had been running the family business for a decade. They had no reason to remain in Rouen, which Catherine always described as boring and sad. The move meant Catherine would be near most of her children, with all three of her daughters in Paris and only her son in Rouen. As they prepared to leave, Catherine expressed her feelings about this transition:

> Yesterday and today, we had the joy of holding a public sale to get rid of all we cannot carry or is not worth moving. . . . Tomorrow Madame Barbet will return to packing, which the sale had interrupted. Twenty-

FIGURE 10. Alexandre Hyacinthe Dunouy, *Vue de la manufacture de Jouy-en-Josas* (1824), Musée Lambinet, ville de Versailles. The people in the foreground of the image are likely some of the Barbet, Arnaud-Tizon, and Vitet siblings and cousins.

> nine cases and bundles are already on their way. . . . With a bit more patience, we will soon see the end of our worries. Only the joy of being close to you, my dear children . . . could make up for the regret I feel at leaving my son. It saddens me to see him isolated, and even if I did not love the place, it is difficult to leave the region [*pays*] where I have lived for twenty-five years.[124]

While keeping track of the details involved in moving an entire household, Catherine voiced bittersweet feelings as she prepared to enter this new phase in her life.

Pierre shared this and other important news with his extended family in Lyon in a letter he sent to his aunt: "I inform her of the transplantation of the Barbet and Arnaud-Tizon families to Paris, and the acquisition of Jouy. Also tell her that my wife is pregnant and ask if she would be godmother. Our sister Barbet will stand in for her. Death of the servant Marion; I am giving some furniture—a nightstand, table, and chairs—to her family to cover the costs of her care."[125] His responsibility toward his mother's servant extended to her family as well. He also sent an update to Ludovic Arnaud-Tizon:

> News of the family who have been living on rue St. Marc for a week. The workers are leaving and Victoire is calming down. Her sons are

> attending the Lycée Louis le Grand. . . . Marie will be taking [piano] lessons with Mr. Pradher as well as drawing lessons. How is Claudius? And how is Marie? My wife hopes for a daughter like her. In the meantime, she has chosen her *accoucheur* . . . and wet nurse. . . . She is waiting for the fabric for the birth and would like you to note these expenses so we can reimburse you.[126]

As usual, they exchanged news, goods, and well wishes, at least when things were going smoothly.

A Financial Disagreement: Brothers and Sisters in Conflict

This chapter closes with one more family crisis involving money. In 1825, a dispute emerged regarding financial arrangements made earlier to cover Adèle's dowry. It was common for families to stretch out dowry payments over many years while paying interest on the unpaid sum. However, in this case, a disagreement arose over who was responsible for making those payments. It seems that Jacques Barbet and Amélie Vitet told Ludovic Arnaud-Tizon that they believed he had agreed to cover Adèle's dowry using profits from the family business, but Ludovic believed that Jacques had promised to make the payments and took insult at their accusations.

The earliest reference to the crisis is an entry in Pierre's journal mentioning "intense discussions taking place with regard to Madame Riocreux's dowry."[127] In his long, emotionally charged reply, Ludovic Arnaud-Tizon opened his heart to Pierre and shared information on the family's financial situation.

> I want to . . . address the accusations against me that are much more serious than those about which you feel you have the right to complain. I admit that I left Paris feeling great chagrin. My last conversation with your wife filled me with cruel reflections. I would never have thought it possible that someone in my family could imagine that I profited from the debris of my father's fortune, I who always felt from the bottom of my heart the conviction that I had done and continue to do all that he could hope for from a good son.[128]

Ludovic's response focused on his sister's unfounded attacks on his character. He then provided details on the family's finances that had been hidden from Pierre:

> Since 1814, our business suffered due to repeated losses. . . . You should know, but please keep this among us, that at that point our business

> was running a deficit of almost 100,000 francs. This burden fell on me because between his children's dowries, household expenses, and the losses on our merchandise, my father found himself without resources. Despite that, I did not want to separate my interests from his. I continued to give half the profits to my father, placing hope in my courage and hard work. . . . The payments to Barbet, interest payments, and our household expenses left barely a few thousand francs per year to try to get ourselves out of the hole we were in. We hid our disastrous situation from you because we did not want you to suffer. We hoped it would improve, which it did, little by little. When my father left Rouen . . . I agreed to reimburse 24,000 francs to our business, which my father had used for the first payment of Adèle's dowry. . . . I did this on the condition that Barbet would pay what remained of Adèle's dowry, agreeing to cover it myself if Barbet did not fulfill his promise.[129]

This letter clarifies why the Arnaud-Tizon couple made the abrupt decision to move in with Jacques and Victoire in 1817 and then followed them to Paris in 1821. They wanted to reduce expenses while hiding the extent of their problems from Pierre.

Ludovic then acknowledged that they could not count on Jacques to cover the dowry. "As for the situation with Barbet, I had hoped to convince him to act upon a promise that he had frequently repeated. . . . Now I am giving up. At the first opportunity, we will discuss this together as friends, conclude this disagreeable altercation, and settle our parents' future situation."[130] He ended on a positive note, voicing optimism that the brothers-in-law would find an acceptable way to resolve the dispute.

While Ludovic expressed pain at the unfair attacks on his character, Jacques voiced outrage. In the first of two letters Jacques sent to Pierre regarding Adèle's dowry, he addressed Pierre as usual, using the informal *tu* form of *you* and closing the letter warmly. In the second, he switched to *vous* and announced that he and his family would no longer associate with Pierre. The contrast between the two letters could not be starker, and the emotions that inspired Jacques's change in tone reveal how serious such disagreements could become. With interest and emotion so intimately connected, the risk of such gut-wrenching disputes taking place remained ever-present.

The dispute exploded at the end of April 1825. An entry in Pierre's journal mentions "two letters to Mr. Barbet regarding the remaining sum due on Adèle's dowry."[131] Unfortunately, we have only Jacques's responses to glean what Pierre wrote. The first begins "My dear Vitet" and explains that he had never promised to pay the amount owed on Adèle's dowry. Jacques's letter is full of indignation:

> Thank God my reputation is well enough established that I need not fear that those with evil intentions could compromise it. . . . Only someone of bad faith would say that I promised to pay the 28,000 francs that remain to cover Adèle's dowry. In leaving Rouen, and when Monsieur and Madame Arnaudtizon decided to follow me, I promised them that if my enterprise did well, I would give them 5% of my profits to allow them to cover what they owed for their daughter. Why then did you not want to wait for that generous and selfless promise to take effect?[132]

Jacques proposed that they meet the following Wednesday and insisted they do so at his home. "That is to say that I will not let myself be insulted as I fear could happen at any other house based on how I saw my brother Ludovic treated."[133] Jacques's letter is dated April 22, a Friday. So, when he suggested they discuss these matters on Wednesday, he must have meant April 27. But that meeting never took place.

Jacques's second letter to Pierre, dated Monday, April 25, announced that he and his wife and children would no longer speak to him: "If there was a way to forget the outrageous letter you sent me on the 22nd, it would certainly be the one I received two days later. I must keep them both, sir. They will serve as a reminder of the facility with which you broke ties of friendship that had existed for eighteen years."[134] He then defends Ludovic Arnaud-Tizon, lauding him as an honorable man before providing details on their arrangements regarding the family business, an account that agrees with Ludovic's. Barbet also explains why Claude and Ludovic struggled to make their business successful, blaming early Restoration trade policies, which caused 300,000 francs' worth of merchandise they were storing to lose half its value. Then, during the months around the Hundred Days, their factory was shut down for nearly a year, while the annual cost of basic maintenance of the buildings and running their large household was nearly 20,000 francs. Things got so bad, he wrote, that "*la maman* was forced to sell her silver coffee pots to survive."[135] The business never recovered.

Two months after this outburst, the family orchestrated a reconciliation between the two men at the home of Adèle Suchet, causing Claude to voice his joy and relief in a letter to Pierre that he wrote while visiting with his son in Bapaume. "It was difficult to see this division emerge when I had sacrificed all to maintain good relations among my children who are all equally dear to me and for whom it would be impossible for me to express any preference. I am infinitely grateful to Madame Suchet and her husband for the zeal they put into bringing an end to this affair. I hope that the gathering at Jouy will be as pleasant as ever and am certain that my wife will write to me about it soon."[136] Good relations among the siblings and their spouses were essential for everyone's economic and emotional well-being, especially for Claude and Catherine, who had grown to rely on their sons-in-law in so many ways.

This family dispute illustrates two main points. First, after receiving an inheritance of nearly half a million francs in the 1790s, Claude and Catherine had lost or given away most of their wealth, largely through dowering their children. Their financial situation as they entered the last stage of their lives inspires a question: Should their story be interpreted as one of success or of failure? Jacques reflects on this point toward the end of his second letter, when he refers to his "respectable father-in-law," who can feel proud that he provided dowries of 60,000 francs to three of his children while "the goal of his efforts in his business was to provide the same thing to his youngest daughter."[137] Claude and Catherine may have been left with very little, but they had launched their children into solid marriages and established a business for their son, all strong measures for success.

During their final years, Catherine and Claude divided their time between Paris and Jouy, living with their children and grandchildren. They stayed mostly with the Barbets for nearly fifteen years, until a dispute between Claude and Victoire caused a major rift. Announcing that he refused to remain in the Barbet household, Claude left Jouy precipitously in early November 1831, went to Paris for a couple of days, and then settled in Bapaume with Ludovic and Amélie Arnaud-Tizon while waiting for a resolution. Catherine asked Pierre if they could live with him and Amélie in Paris, which required that Pierre ask a tenant to vacate his apartment. In the meantime, Pierre and Catherine exchanged many frantic letters, as she deplored the situation and expressed gratitude for all that Pierre was doing for them.[138] Their letters do not explain what happened to cause this dispute, though there seems to have also been disagreement over who was at fault—Victoire or Amélie Arnaud-Tizon. Catherine blamed the latter: "Madame Ludovic is responsible [*bien coupable*]. I have many things to say, but like her, I do not want to put them on paper; I will wait to discuss everything with you [in person]."[139] Claude's decision to stay in Bapaume also upset Catherine: "My husband's departure has caused me great pain. He had given me his word of honor that he would stay with you, taking a room in the hotel across from your house until the apartment became available. . . . I was tranquil knowing that *le papa* was near you. Then, without telling me, he departs in this season [and] at his age, putting his health at risk. [*Il y a de quoi le rendre malade.*] His lack of trust in me has broken my heart. I do not believe I deserve to be treated this way."[140] Her emotional reaction speaks to the depths of this crisis that hit them so late in their lives, when they had become dependent on their children.

Pierre's renter agreed to leave the apartment more quickly than anyone had hoped, and Claude and Catherine moved to the rue neuve Saint Roch in late December. In a letter she sent just before moving there, Catherine expressed enthusiasm about keeping her granddaughter Mimi company when Amélie went out in the evening.[141] Unfortunately, Catherine did not have much time to enjoy living with them. She died the following spring from cholera, after which Claude returned to Rouen, where he died two years later. Later, the various Parisian branches of the family lived on a new street carved out of some property they bought on the left bank near the rue de Varennes that they named rue Barbet de Jouy. Pierre and Amélie moved there in the late 1830s, along with Ludovic and his wife.[142] As Catherine so frequently expressed in her letters, this was a family that appreciated togetherness and cooperation.

It was this sense of trust and mutual support that Gabriel Suchet violated in allowing his selfish desires to trump his familial responsibilities. His story highlights the intimate connections between money and honor and how one person's behavior could affect the entire family. Suchet's betrayal shocked them to their core and made them fear the worst possible outcome: the destruction of the next generation's ability to continue the family's trajectory toward success. Saving his honor required the entire family and their most trusted allies to collaborate to avoid what they viewed as a catastrophe. The intense emotional reactions they voiced during that and the other crises discussed at the end of this chapter reflect how much weight these families placed on trust and shared responsibilities. They relied on each other for material and emotional support, without which no one could succeed.

CHAPTER 7

Networks

The Serious Business of Socializing

Having allies in the right places was essential for families to weather the storms of these years. Building and maintaining relationships that could help them accomplish their goals—what we would today call networking—was at the heart of nearly all they did, and social gatherings allowed that work to be accomplished. In addition to providing entertainment and relief from boredom for men and women with time and money to devote to nonproductive activities, social and cultural pursuits gave them an outlet for creating a sense of self and opportunities to strengthen bonds of affinity with others. Women's participation was essential to these activities; they often planned and ran the events and almost always numbered among the attendees. Bourgeois families depended on this "women's work" to accomplish their goals. Parties no doubt brought attendees pleasure, but the effort expended upon them also reflected their broader utility.

There was a daily and seasonal rhythm to socializing, with meals forming a centerpiece for many events and defining their everyday routines. In the early nineteenth century, bourgeois families ate their main meal of the day—what they called dinner—at around 2 p.m., with a lighter supper (*souper*) in the evening, a reference to the tradition of serving soup. Unless an invitation was extended for a meal, most visiting took place in the late afternoon. Carnival season, the period between Epiphany and Mardi Gras, featured elaborate, late-night balls, while summertime brought outings to the countryside for those fortunate enough to own a secondary residence.

News about social and cultural activities featured prominently in these families' letters. In January 1806, Pierre and Amélie traveled to Rouen with Ludovic for a long visit, but when Louis became ill, Pierre rushed back to Paris to care for him.[1] Pierre's letters to Amélie during this rare period of separation include lengthy descriptions of the mixed-sex gatherings that figured prominently in their lives, including one lively and entertaining Mardi Gras party hosted by some close friends. Pierre clearly found pleasure in the costumes and role-playing and relished sharing amusing anecdotes with Amélie.

> My dear friend, I promised to send you an account of our Mardi Gras festivities. Doing this will help make up for not being with you and your wonderful family. It was a beautiful day, and while touring around with Fournel and Madame Couchet, we observed many carriages circulating in two rows along the boulevards and the rue St. Honoré [and] a good-sized crowd on foot, but very few costumes and even fewer pretty masks.
>
> During the evening, my father and I went to the Fournels'. It was a large gathering, though comprised only of our acquaintances. . . . Most of the little girls were dressed as workers, shopkeepers, etc. Noémie looked very pretty under her big oyster-sellers' bonnet. (I am mentioning this to interest her little husband [presumably Ludovic].) But let's go on to the performance. Silence! Signor Purgantini is announced: Mr. Besson *fils*, carrying his violin and dressed as a village fiddler, Fournel as the charlatan's lackey, and two small, liveried jockeys precede the doctor. You have probably already guessed that it was Roux who played the role of the charlatan. He was dressed in highly ornamented fashion with a long, scarlet jacket and a frilled collar, and coiffed appropriately. He began with a preamble about his silence while speaking half in French half in Italian and performed the entire farce with such gravity that we all laughed. Then he offered his services to the group by providing consultations to the ladies to whom he presented a box of pills and a set of instructions which he sang while Maître Fournel accompanied him on the violin. . . . I regret that you were not there with us. You would have had your role in this gallant and entertaining farce which displayed Roux's mischievous spirit. My father also had a couplet which was very funny and flattering. . . .
>
> Once the performance was over, we ate, and thanks to everyone contributing their assigned dish, there was a very pretty buffet. . . . Two men joined us, a merchant named Le Danois and a young man who

was a very good dancer. The former, a big joker, played the role of a simpleton and juggler. After the meal, these two strangers performed a fricassee dance with great aplomb and silliness [*singeries*]. I left around 2 a.m. I doubt the rest of the group stayed much later. There, my dear friend, is the long story of our Mardi Gras. . . .

I just received your letter. I was delighted by the affectionate words from our dear little man [*mon petit tonton*]. I will share your expressions of affection with my father and will close my epistle by assuring you of my most tender sentiments. I wish I could include two kisses, but this evil distance prohibits that. I will instead ask Ludovic to give them to you on behalf of his *père-père*. Kiss this dear child for me and his grandfather and send my warm regards to *la maman* and *au papa zon* and your sisters. Your devoted husband, Vitet *fils*.[2]

In sharing these details, Pierre sought to entertain Amélie and her family, who knew everyone he mentioned and could easily imagine the scene. In normal circumstances, Amélie and Pierre attended such gatherings together, along with their son once he was old enough, and enjoyed the playacting, food, and dancing in the company of men and women like themselves, mostly old friends from Lyon.[3] The closing lines reveal affectionate intimacy across the generations, as Pierre refers to his son's name for his grandfather, with "zon" replacing "Arnaud-Tizon."[4]

Although they enjoyed such opportunities for amusement, socializing was serious business for these families. The Arnaud-Tizons were enmeshed in a social world that kept them constantly occupied. Amélie and Pierre were even busier, attending parties and cultural events regularly. How did these families entertain themselves? What did their socializing mean for their sense of identity? Finally, how did their socializing relate to the networks that they used to strengthen their positions and help others in the process? This chapter works though these questions while focusing on six forms of social and cultural activities: balls, weddings, dinner parties, theater and art exhibits, musical performances, and public festivals. Participants at these gatherings put themselves on display and hobnobbed with others, reinforcing valuable social connections while enjoying themselves. In most of these contexts, women's participation was essential to the successful hosting of an event and thus to allowing this important work to take place.

Dance Fever

Balls and other less formal gatherings featuring music and dance occupied a prominent place in these families' lives, requiring significant effort and expense. In a book first published in 1798 titled *Le nouveau Paris*, the author and social commentator Louis-Sébastien Mercier mocked Parisians' passion for dancing: "Each class has its dancing society, from the small to the great, that is to say, from rich to poor, everyone dances. It's a furor, a universal penchant. Parisians dance, or more precisely, they churn; because nothing is more difficult for them than to obey the rhythm, and nothing rarer among them than an ear for music!"[5] Besides mocking Parisians, Mercier makes clear that there were balls for every class. Wealthy families attended expensive ones, where they were surrounded by "the best" people, while poorer people attended dances held in lower-class drinking establishments. Mercier also contrasted women's and men's comportment at these balls: "There, the women are nymphs, sultans, savages. . . . The men in contrast are unkempt. . . . The women are more fully engaged in the pleasure of dancing."[6] And these spaces offered more than just dancing. "At each of these famous balls, there are game rooms, buffets and refreshments, illuminations on one side, and on the other, shadowy areas."[7] The expression "shadowy areas" hints at couples seeking privacy to do more than dance.

The Vitet couple's activities matched those described by Mercier, particularly early in their marriage. In December 1805, Catherine wrote to Amélie about a ball to which the young couple had subscribed: "I am happy to learn that you are satisfied with your ball and that you are amusing yourself. Hopefully your husband has not been too bored. He is so *complaisant* that I do not think he could feel bored when you are having fun."[8] Although Amélie may have enjoyed dancing more than her husband, Pierre recognized that she relished these outings.

Catherine often complained about the dreariness of life in Rouen. "Let's speak a bit about your follies. Far from disapproving of them, I am jealous, believe me. I nonetheless ask that you not stay up so late. I shared your stories with Mr. Suchet who responded with a sigh that it is only in Rouen where we are well-behaved by force. You really cannot imagine the sadness that reigns in this good city. For us, thanks to business, we stay busy. But *le papa* agrees with me that once we retire, we will move elsewhere."[9] She made similar comparisons while discussing Pierre and Amélie's plan to host a Mardi Gras party. "I arranged to have your truffles dropped off at the pastry shop and will send you the pâté on Sunday. I hope that it will meet your expectations. It seems that Mardi Gras will be brilliant this year. I have no doubt that your gathering will be very gay. . . . Carnival is very sad here; there are few gatherings except for some long, boring dinners."[10] Pierre requested a pâté from Rouen the following year as well.[11] This was apparently a Mardi Gras tradition at his home. Rouen, it seemed, had little to offer except food.

A handful of letters that Pierre received from his friends over the years give a sense of the man that we do not see in the familial correspondence. He seems to have been a bon vivant, a man who enjoyed good food and a variety of amusements, including playing billiards and other games. In February 1808, Jacques Fournel's wife, Mery, wrote to Pierre about how much they missed him and Amélie. "Our pleasures have been very restrained. There are no dinners, no dancing, no concerts. . . . We are anticipating Lent calmly and without dread. Our stomachs and our legs are not feeling fatigued, but the same is not true of our hearts. The absence of our good friends causes us regret that is only softened by the hope that they will return soon. There is still the question of Mardi Gras. We are counting on you, my dear Vitet. There is no good meal without your appetite, no dance without Amélie. You are indispensable, both of you."[12] While Mery's desire to flatter her friends may have inspired these words, it seems that Pierre and Amélie animated the gatherings they attended.

The 1812 season kept Pierre and Amélie so busy they neglected their correspondence. In January, Pierre recorded that he wrote only a few lines to his mother "because of Madame Roux's ball where we stayed until 2:00."[13] In February, he sent more details to Catherine, including news about their high-ranking friends and allies. "Dinner gala on Wednesday at the Roux's with the Maréchal's *aides de camp*. He is suffering from a fistula and hopes to have it operated on while in Paris. Bourguillon is marrying Mademoiselle Avrillion, *femme de chambre* of the empress Joséphine. Ploux served as matchmaker."[14] The people to whom Pierre referred by their last names tended to be his friends. He apparently knew both the man who was marrying this prominent young woman and the man who orchestrated the match. The Vitet couple's socializing brought them into contact with the highest levels of Napoleonic society.

Parisian Mardi Gras festivities included a variety of activities, as suggested by Pierre's summary of a letter he sent to Catherine in 1813: "Mardi Gras was very successful in Paris because of the beautiful weather. The boulevards were crowded. Amélie and Madame Suchet rode in a carriage with the children in disguise (Ludovic dressed as a harlequin). In the evening, Amélie went with her cousin to the court ball. The Roux, Fournel, and Michaud ladies attended a dance at Madame Bernard's where we were also invited. My wife preferred to see the ball at court, and I took my son to see a performance at Feydeau."[15] Attending an official court ball was an experience that Amélie did not want to miss.

Though less prestigious, the elaborate balls hosted by the Arnaud-Tizons' wealthy and well-connected circle included music, dancing, and food, with the parties continuing until dawn. Because balls occurred with such regularity and attracted roughly the same people doing roughly the same things, hosts in provincial cities like Rouen tried to make their events stand out through the décor and other touches or simply the size and extravagance. These gatherings required effort and expense on the part of both hosts and guests, as attendees needed to wear formal dress. Pierre and Amélie frequently helped the ladies in Rouen by getting their dresses mended and sending them the latest fabrics from Paris. In 1805, Pierre recorded a series of entries about the favors that he and Amélie were doing to help their family members have the right clothes. "Amélie had the crepe dress dyed [and] offered her services for any purchases they need for the upcoming ball." A few days later, he wrote to say they had "sent the gray crepe dress and ribbons for Mr. Suchet's ball."[16] Preparing for parties was a family affair, too.

Reaching the age when they could attend balls was an exciting moment in girls' lives. Although her official debut took place in January 1813, Adèle experienced her first ball in November 1811, when she was thirteen. Catherine described the event as "very enjoyable, especially for Adèle who expected to remain seated and was pleasantly surprised when she joined nearly all the contra dances even though there were many dancers. Madame Barbet also danced as did Ludovic. We left at 3:30 am, and I think the dance continued a long time after that."[17] While Adèle and her siblings enjoyed these late-night events, Catherine was frequently less enthusiastic. She already sounded blasé when she described one of the first balls of the 1813 season. "About fifty people attended. With thirteen dancing ladies, there was a contra dance of twelve going constantly. The supper was beautiful though a bit sad because the ladies were separated from the gentlemen. We left at only 2:30. Adèle enjoyed the evening. She danced a lot, as did all our ladies. You see that in our town we try to conjure away our chagrin, but it only works halfway and even while dancing we are not gay."[18] Catherine wrote these words in the context of a bitterly cold winter as well as the French retreat from Russia, which probably explains the sadness she observed.

As Adèle's debut season came to an end, Catherine had clearly had enough; in a letter to Amélie in April 1813, she wrote:

> We attended a beautiful ball chez Mr. Blanche. There were about 100 people. We arrived late after a very busy day. Our ladies and gentlemen left before the meal because it was served at 1:00 am, and that was too late for them. I stayed to please Adèle, who loves to dance, and we left at 4:00. . . . The party was very gay. They danced two contra dances in a very large salon; supper was served on small tables. Thank God these balls have come to an end. Adèle only danced twelve times for her debut year.[19]

Dancing until dawn may have appealed to teenagers and other attendees with few responsibilities but not as much to people whose work lives did not permit them to sleep all day. In a December 1814 letter, Catherine voiced her frustration. "There will be another ball on Tuesday at Mr. Lehardelay's. Adele is thus once again content. . . . I don't know why, but I am unable to amuse myself at these gatherings. I find them unbearable. If it wasn't for Adèle, I assure you that I would stay home, but as your father says, I must do for her what we did for you."[20] Though she often expressed her preference "to sit by [her] fire," Catherine had to accompany Adèle to these social events that allowed girls and women to display their beauty and grace.[21]

Their obligatory nature could diminish the pleasure these events were meant to provide. As Carnival season began in 1815, Catherine was already looking forward to its end. "There is no shortage of balls here. Today there is one at Madame Long's where the entire town is invited. It is to celebrate the Préfète of Calvados who is passing through our city. Then she will head to Caen whose curious inhabitants are waiting impatiently for her. I will send you details on this brilliant gathering. . . . There is also talk of a dance at the prefect's residence. For me, I am dreaming of summer and the time when you will be with us, and we will no longer need parties to find happiness."[22] While "brilliant gatherings" had their appeal, Catherine enjoyed more spontaneous events, including one large gala hosted by the prefect and his wife.

> Carnival season has been gay and dances numerous, not in our society but among . . . [others] and the nobility. Yesterday we enjoyed a charming impromptu [gathering] at the Prefecture. Madame de Girardin told the people she sees frequently that she would be inviting a violinist for the following Saturday. She had spoken about it to Amélie and visited me to encourage me to come. Our ladies feared it would be cold, but everyone was pleasantly surprised. Although there were no invitations, about 300 people attended and we danced four contra dances in the gallery. The salon and the bedroom were full of card tables. Around midnight, everyone was invited into the dining room where there was a well-stocked buffet and small tables. All evening, servers passed around excellent ice cream which the mothers enjoyed; there was also orange jelly, lemonade, and all kinds of little cakes. Everything was excellent and served perfectly. What made the young people happy was an invitation to repeat the soirée next Saturday. I doubt it will be as much fun because it will be too crowded.[23]

Catherine clearly appreciated the sight of such a large gathering and enjoyed the sweet treats in the beautiful space of Rouen's prefecture. A luxury item in a world without refrigeration, ice cream comes up quite frequently in Catherine's accounts of social events. Her discussion of different *sociétés* at the opening of her letter and her reference to the nobility as a group apart reveal how she understood such distinctions—her social imaginary.

A week later, Catherine wrote about more balls. While she was enjoying them, she nonetheless looked forward to the end of the season. She again discussed events that attracted elite attendees, responding to Pierre's reflections on such gatherings.

> Tomorrow a small number of us will be celebrating Mardi Gras at Barbet's. He plans to treat us to ice cream. It is the prelude to a bigger dance he will be hosting on the second Sunday of Lent. . . . He had to move it to Lent because there were so many parties. It seems the same is true in Paris. You were worried about feeling bored at the homes of high-ranking people where you would find no one you know. My reaction is different from yours; I find observing a large gathering entertaining. On Saturday we attended the second of this genre at the Prefecture. There were at least 500 people. The dancers were a bit less occupied than the first one, but we nonetheless amused ourselves. We ate well and everyone seemed gay and content. . . . I am hoping that after Barbet's ball I will be done with all these parties and will be able to go to the country to get some fresh air.[24]

Though the sight of five hundred elegantly dressed people circling through the Rouen prefecture impressed her, Catherine nonetheless complained about attending so many balls. "I hope that Easter will end the prolonged pleasures of carnival. . . . We have another ball this Sunday at Madame Prevel's. . . . [Adèle] never tires of dancing, but I am very tired of accompanying her. The balls this year don't end until 5 a.m., which is exhausting, but I must complete my task. In a few years, I'll be able to stay by my fireside."[25] Now well into middle age, Catherine was finding it difficult to fulfill her obligations as the mother of a marriageable daughter.

The 1815 season ended with Barbet's ball, the event of the year for this family. In a letter to Pierre, Catherine described the "wonderful" event in detail, drawing attention to the elite attendees whose presence reflected the family's status and reputation. When she wrote these words in late February, she could not know that a few weeks later, France would once again find itself in turmoil when Napoleon returned after being sent into exile the previous spring.

> [Barbet's] apartment is suitable for such ceremonies, and everything went well. There was even some gaiety, a rarity in Norman gatherings.

> The ladies were beautifully dressed. There were around 90 people, besides our usual group [*la société ordinaire*], there was a pretty, young bride, Madame Fontelignac, Mr. Manoury's granddaughter . . . Monsieur and Madame de Girardin were also there.
>
> A contra dance of sixteen took place in the salon, with card playing in Victoire's former bedroom, which had been transformed into a pretty little salon decorated in yellow. . . . Supper was served on a big table in the dining room, with smaller ones set up in the antechamber. There is no sign of the festivities ending. . . . We are hoping this year to catch up for lost time and dance for two years. Adèle is starting to feel like she's had enough.[26]

Hobnobbing with the political and social elite of their city and hosting balls and soirées in their own homes permitted these families to display their wealth and status while building connections that could prove useful; business, politics, and socializing went hand in hand. Catherine's name-dropping highlights the importance of such events, which permitted the family to develop ties with the right people while negotiating the transition to a new regime.

Socializing with local elites became even more frequent and elaborate during the Restoration. In January 1818, with Adèle married and in Paris, Catherine no longer needed to attend balls, but even the younger women in the family seemed unenthusiastic. "We think only of pleasure here. We are dancing at everyone's homes. Sunday there is a ball at Mr. Soyer's and tomorrow at Madame Duhamel's. Tuesday we will be *chez* Mr. Casimir Caumont. Victoire plans to attend that one. Amélie was invited to the other two, but she refused because she did not want to make new acquaintances."[27] The family's political views may explain her daughter-in-law's lack of enthusiasm for these elite gatherings.

With the growing intensity of political divisions during the Restoration, women could use spaces for socializing and networking to bring people together across these divides, as suggested by Catherine's reflections about an event held in December 1820. "The festivities are beginning and as always Madame Thézard is setting an example. She has invited 150 people to a ball she is throwing on Tuesday. She says she wants to make all opinions dance together. I am afraid we will not amuse ourselves as much as usual. I was thinking about going and judging for myself, but I think I will stay home unless I am feeling very well. In any case, I will send you details about this beautiful party."[28] While the goal of making "all opinions dance together" may have been laudable, Catherine voiced skepticism about the likelihood of its success.

When the nonstop Carnival festivities began again in 1819, Catherine bowed out, but Victoire and her husband, Jacques, maintained active social lives, which Catherine followed.

> I go out little, disliking crowded, noisy salons. Since, as you know, there are no intimate gatherings in Rouen, we mostly stay home. Victoire keeps me company most days, except when there is a ball. . . . My daughter-in-law is using the recent death in her family as an excuse to refuse invitations. I am happy with this decision because I will tell you in confidence that she is two or three months pregnant, and after what happened with her last pregnancy, she must be careful; dancing could be dangerous. I can tell you that those who like this exercise can find satisfaction this year as there is a ball almost every day.[29]

Though attending balls fulfilled important social functions, dancing was a strenuous activity. Catherine was happy that Amélie Arnaud-Tizon had an excuse to bow out during the early phase of her pregnancy.

Catherine went on to describe a "brilliant" ball hosted by Jacques Barbet's brother Henry as well as the meal that brought together local dignitaries before the ball. "All the high-ranking men [*tous les grands personnages*] were at the dinner: the prefect, mayor, general, etc. The only women at dinner were the three Barbet wives. Ice cream and small cakes were served throughout the evening, with supper announced at midnight. It was a buffet; the ladies ate off their laps in the salon. . . . Meanwhile, the workers are miserable. Business remains bad, and the thaw has caused great damage in the Deville and Darnetal valleys."[30] Catherine's attention to workers and their suffering is striking here. While her family and friends were participating in extravagant parties with the local elite, she was home worrying about the conditions of those who were less fortunate.

As Catherine slowed down, Amélie Arnaud-Tizon began to replace her as the family's rapporteur regarding balls and other gatherings in Rouen. Amélie provided trenchant observations that included sarcastic commentaries about the people around her.

> Madame Long hosted a beautiful ball in honor of Madame la Marquise Séguier, who is entering the Prefecture. . . . Dancing took place in two rooms and card-players occupied two others. Supper was served on small tables and was badly received by the *gourmands* and the gourmandes. Unfortunately for our sex, the ladies of Rouen like to criticize and imitate the charming behavior of our lovely youth. They behaved as though there was nothing refined or elegant [at the ball] and made these criticisms loudly enough for them to be heard by the obliging

> hostess who, as usual, was doing all she could to make sure that her guests were satisfied. The silent listeners were the only ones who felt uncomfortable.[31]

Besides defending the lady of the house, Amélie criticized what she viewed as the bad manners of the day, a reflection of broader Restoration-era images of disorderly young men.[32]

In January 1821, Catherine raved about a gathering hosted by Jacques and Victoire. Besides removing furniture, they had taken doors off their hinges to facilitate movement and create space for the three principal activities: dancing, card playing, and eating.

> Barbet's first attempt at hosting a ball was a big success. 120 people attended. . . . The party was gay and animated until it concluded at 4 a.m. . . . There was plenty of room to dance rounds of sixteen in the salon. . . . Gaming tables were set up in the small salon and the antechamber. From about 11:00 to 12:30, they passed around ice cream and cakes. Then they served a buffet of cold meats, pastries, compotes, etc. The large mahogany table in the dining room was covered with carafes and about fifteen place settings. Without interrupting either the dancing or games, they began calling fifteen to twenty people at a time into the dining room to eat, continuing this way until everyone had eaten. . . . After supper, ice cream was distributed again followed by punch. . . . I must not forget to mention the decoration on the staircase which looked wonderful. Madame Hanguet sent some pine branches that we attached to the banister all the way up to the second floor.[33]

Hosting a ball required significant effort, with friends and family contributing. In this case, Catherine seemed proud of her children's success at orchestrating such an elegant event.

Catherine continued sending updates on balls, even if she was not attending them herself. She began one such letter to share news that "Madame Ludovic" had returned from visiting her mother. "Her husband was happy to have her home. During her absence he played the bachelor and danced with enthusiasm. . . . As you know, we are dancing in Rouen more than ever. Victoire made her new year's visit at the Prefecture yesterday, and since they were hosting a dance as they do every fifteen days, she stayed for that."[34] Socializing with local authorities remained essential (and newsworthy).

In February 1821, Catherine described a different kind of gathering that she appreciated more than balls: hearing plays read aloud. Catherine's pessimism regarding the political situation of the early 1820s came across as she described their need for distraction:

> [Our neighbor] is coming today to read us two new plays that are being performed at the Gymnase. I find this a pleasant way to spend evenings. We do not invite chatterboxes or people who would find it boring to listen. We only admit real theater lovers. That way our reader is happy with his audience. We need to find distractions to avoid thinking and talking about politics, though our orators of the left are doing us honor. They were superb during the last session. It seemed to me that Mr. de Lafeyette especially demonstrated nobility and unrivaled logic. . . .
>
> There is nothing new here except the continuation of balls. Victoire has already attended thirteen or fourteen and has four more to withstand. They are starting to bore her, and likewise Barbet who accompanies her and sometimes attends the dinners.[35]

With so many people of their milieu wanting to display their wealth and taste, balls were an obligation that could not be avoided if one wanted to maintain valuable social ties.

Wedding Parties: Obligatory Celebrations

Like balls, weddings featured food, music, and dancing that went on until dawn. As usual, Catherine shared her opinions on these gatherings, though her reactions made them seem even less entertaining. In many cases, she and her family attended them purely out of a sense of obligation.

In July 1806, Catherine's friend Madame Long threw an extravagant celebration for the marriage of her only daughter, Charles-Aimée Long. Like the Arnaud-Tizons, the Long family had origins outside of Rouen. The bride's father moved there from Marseille in the 1770s and became a successful *indienneur*. A widow, Madame Long ran the textile business that her husband had founded and her daughter and son-in-law, Louis-Frédéric Fouquier, would eventually take over.[36] Catherine sent Pierre and Amélie details on the party, which seemed to impress her more than most.

> I will begin by telling you that there were at least 150 guests and the gardens you have seen were illuminated artfully. Across from the house was a portico of columns representing a temple of Hymen. . . . Underneath was transparent fabric where one could read the words "love

> brought them together." Spread around the garden were transparent sheets with pretty sayings about the guests of honor. . . .
>
> We arrived as they were serving the meal which displayed luxury in a grand manner. A 200-foot-long tent was set up in the courtyard of the factory. It was made of white cotton fabric, draped on the interior and at the entrance to look like an elegant salon. . . . A table was set with 140 places and covered with the most elegant platters set on a *lit de mousse* that covered the middle of the table. Rows of candles and chandeliers lit up the tent in the most agreeable manner. . . . We left *sagement* at 4 a.m., but the party continued until 6:00.
>
> You cannot imagine the stories that are circulating around town about all of this. One must be crazy to waste so much money. I would not want to spend 4,000 livres on a party. A word about the ladies' dresses: the bride was in a muslin gown with silver embroidery and all her diamonds; her mother's dress was embroidered with white flowers. . . . She looked as young as her daughter.[37]

Although she viewed it as a waste of resources, Catherine enjoyed the party and appreciated the décor, food, and fashionable attire. Going to such expense demonstrated a family's wealth and social connections, thus enhancing their status in this new postrevolutionary society.

Though such gatherings featured flamboyant displays of luxury and consumption, in their everyday lives, bourgeois families counted every penny. In a study based on painstaking research in notarial records and account books, Jean-Pierre Chaline emphasizes this essential quality of the bourgeoisie, which was to practice frugality in daily life while reserving extravagance for special moments. Chaline found that the average amount spent on food per family member was less than two francs per day, only twice that of workers who earned barely enough to stay alive. He contrasts this modesty with the same family's expenses for clothes and maintaining a carriage. He concludes that "the heart of the conception of the familial budget was to strike a balance between the desire to save and the demonstration of prestige which is, without doubt, one of the characteristic traits of bourgeois behavior."[38] Everyday frugality permitted these families to spend their money on exceptional displays of wealth and generosity when necessary.

In February 1812, Catherine described herself as frugal in the context of discussing another wedding and its associated celebrations. "You may think I was done with soirées, but we attended another one yesterday at Madame Bourgeois's where we were planning to dance. However, as there were too few people, we just played some games after dinner and danced a few Béarnaises. I hope that we are now finished with gatherings until the wedding. As a frugal woman, I am waiting until then to host a soirée to kill two birds with one stone."[39] Catherine sought to maintain appearances and fulfill her social obligations while limiting expenses.

A few weeks after the Long-Fouquier wedding, Catherine described another "fabulous party" held to celebrate the newlyweds by the Longs' neighbor, Mr. Desmarest.

> After Madame Long came to see me and pressed me to accept, Mr. Desmarest came himself and I had to capitulate. We had no regrets. . . . We came home in broad daylight at 5 a.m. Mr. Desmarest hosted like a very experienced woman [*une femme très entendue*]. He has a beautiful garden and we strolled in it until the dancing started at nine o'clock. It had rained heavily in the morning and to avoid ruining the dancers' white shoes, he had the garden covered with dry sand. There were around eighty people. A table was set up in a large hall that was decorated with white curtains and mirrors. Next to this hall was a tent with a second table for the young men. . . . I don't need to tell you that the pathway that led from the house to the dining area was beautifully illuminated.[40]

The effort and expense devoted to these gatherings, which were meant to entertain while displaying one's good taste and the wherewithal to throw such elaborate parties, demonstrate their importance. It is interesting that Catherine described the host, Mr. Desmarest, as receiving guests like an experienced woman, suggesting that it was typically women who orchestrated such gatherings that brought together the "right people." It is also clear from her comments that attending parties was an obligation that could not be avoided. Families like hers needed to participate in the social life of their city, to see and be seen among people with whom they shared a set of common experiences.

While describing a ball held in honor of the new prefect's wife in January 1816, Amélie Arnaud-Tizon discussed the work and social lives of the hosts, Madame Long and her daughter, Madame Fouquier, whose wedding Catherine had attended ten years earlier and who, along with her mother and husband, ran one of the most successful calico factories in the region.

> Madame Séguier was charming, dancing a lot, chatting with everyone, and practically helping Madame Fouquier do the honors. Mr. Fouquier appeared at the ball but only stayed about an hour. . . . He lost his colorist, is working hard at his factory and has experienced considerable

difficulties. . . . Madame Fouquier keeps the books and handles the correspondence and sales. She is seconding her husband at the factory and fortunately knows how to do everything. She also manages to fit in four trips per day between Rouen and Déville. You see that she can brag that she manages her schedule like a minister. To compensate for her solitude, Madame Long prioritizes socializing, making visits daily and hosting dinners. That is how we make friends in our city.[41]

Besides helping her husband run the family business, Madame Fouquier and her mother also accomplished the "work" of fulfilling the family's social obligations.

When another of the Arnaud-Tizons' close circle, the Ballicornes, announced their daughter's wedding, Catherine sent biting comments about them. The family she mentioned was likely Pierre-Marie's in-laws; Anne-Françoise's sister married into the family, and the couple lived near the Arnaud-Tizons on the rue au Ours. A few days before the wedding, Catherine wrote:

The groom does not seem enthusiastic. He is saving his energy for the big day. It is difficult to be more useless, and he is at an age when a man should be mature. Madame Ballicorne is giving up some of her diamonds for the family. This is all making me laugh as this lady had criticized my behavior in this regard. The matter of religion also amuses me as they could not understand how I could give your sister to a Protestant. I am dreading the boredom of the day as they say we will be invited to the ceremony, something I would have preferred to skip.[42]

The Ballicornes were apparently willing to marry their daughter to a Protestant despite having criticized Catherine for doing the same and the fact that the groom could not, in her eyes, have been "more useless."[43]

Catherine later shared her reactions to the event, which was worse than she had anticipated.

[The wedding] could not have been sadder. We arrived for dinner at 7 p.m. . . . [and] appreciated the view of the whole crowd as we entered. We kissed the bride who looked very pretty in her virginal costume, a lined crepe dress adorned with a garland of lilies with her hair decorated to match and her diamond comb. We sat down to eat at 7:30 and good God we only left the table at 11:00! We then returned to the salon, where, after a moment of confusion, everyone took seats and poets from Caen . . . entertained us with songs, each worse than the other. Then, worse still, came a reading of an allegory in prose that was

> as long as it was ridiculous. It was hard not to laugh. At midnight, as everyone was heading to the church, I asked if I could bow out, which I did, along with Victoire and Madame Suchet who needed to rest for the next day.[44]

In contrast to the smaller, more impromptu gatherings that Catherine praised, weddings required elaborate preparations that she found forced, even ridiculous.

When Jacques Barbet's brother August married in November 1813, Catherine sent details on the preparations and mentioned repeated delays due to illness and then waiting for important guests to arrive.[45] Soon after the wedding, Catherine sent a long account of all that took place.

> I waited to reply to your letter . . . to include details on the wedding which was held at City Hall on Monday instead of Wednesday. This last-minute change allowed us to skip the morning ceremony which pleased us. We were invited to supper on Wednesday along with about thirty people. We arrived at 9 p.m. At eleven, they served a superb meal that no one ate, which added to the gaiety of the soirée. At 1 a.m., we went to the Church of the Madeleine where the spouses received the benediction. It was very cold, but luckily there were no adverse consequences, and everyone has remained healthy. After the church service, we went home to bed. It was almost 3 a.m. The bride was very pretty and beautifully dressed in a white satin gown with overlaying lace, her diamonds in her hair, an English veil, and a crown of orange flowers. . . . I have rarely seen a gloomier wedding, even though they are not generally very gay. . . . But let's put aside the wedding and turn to more interesting topics.[46]

The wedding may not have been an "interesting topic," but she nonetheless described it in detail.

Her description of another wedding that took place about a year later is similar, though it includes more mocking comments, no doubt to amuse her readers.

> My dear friend, I owe you a response and the details I promised about the parties thrown for the Prevel wedding, which were limited to a dinner on Wednesday and a ball on Saturday. As I mentioned, *le papa*, Adèle and I were not invited to the dinner. Only Ludovic and his wife were subject to this first chore. As for the ball, as you can imagine, we did not miss it. . . .
>
> I had not yet seen the bride who came with her mother to pay me a visit on Friday while I was going to visit them. I can tell you that

> I saw her dancing because she never left the dance floor all night. I was unable to find a moment to offer my congratulations. She seemed more interested in amusing herself than her guests. She did not speak to anyone. She was dressed beautifully: a gown bordered with chenille and ribbons and a garland of tuberoses. . . . She had her diamonds; the comb is beautiful, but the earrings are unattractive and even a bit old-fashioned. The necklace is barely larger than Victoire's. . . . She was coifed with the hairband that we purchased at Nicolas's. . . . I won't say anything about the father and mother who, between us, seemed quite vulgar. . . . The gathering was very large; it was too crowded for the dancers to be able to enjoy themselves. I do not know if this ball will be followed by many others. . . . As for me, I will not be hosting a dance and will instead invite them for a boring dinner at some point, letting others who are more impatient do so first.[47]

In addition to attending weddings, guests were expected to reciprocate by hosting gatherings in honor of the newlyweds. Catherine's choice to host "a boring dinner" rather than a dance may reflect her desire to avoid unnecessary expenses. By creating real and symbolic connections between families, weddings were important events, not just for the couple involved but also for their entourage. Their broader social and economic significance was reflected in the practices associated with them, which included a whole series of balls and dinner parties hosted by the newlyweds' larger network of friends and family.

Dinner Parties and Male Socializing

While balls occupied much time and energy, dinner parties filled important functions as well. Often male-only gatherings, dinner parties and other opportunities to share food and drink took place frequently. In a letter to Pierre dating from early 1813, Jacques Barbet analyzed the attraction of these events. "I can assure you that our young ladies are satisfied. They have been dancing a lot. And their dance partners do not disappoint. They are truly indefatigable because aside from all these dances, these gentlemen gather weekly at soirées and dinners where they inebriate themselves, no doubt to drown their sorrows due to the current circumstances."[48] Here, Jacques was likely referring to the calamity of the French retreat from Russia.

Because they were less ostentatious, dinner parties satisfied people's desire to socialize at moments when balls seemed inappropriate. In late December 1816, Catherine sent a long letter to Pierre in which she reflected on the dire economic situation and its consequences for social life, drawing attention to the stark contrast between life in Paris and the provinces. The presence of impoverished people roaming the streets caused fear among Rouen's wealthy residents.

> The life you are leading in Paris differs a great deal from ours. There are no gatherings here, and the Rouennais woman who most likes to host elaborate galas told me recently that we cannot think about amusing ourselves this year while there is so much misery. You can guess, no doubt, that I am referring to Madame T. This lovely lady is hosting only small dinners for administrators who rave about the delicious dishes [*mets friands*] she serves.
>
> We are limiting ourselves to family gatherings. We dined on Tuesday at Barbet's with Madame Hanguet and some people from Dijon who had been recommended to Barbet. A few friends came for the evening, but we stayed in the small salon to avoid having bright lights on the street. . . . We regret not living in a place where we can forget all this misery and where we feel greater freedom than in the provinces. It saddens me to think that we were together at this time last year and that this year we must be content with sending new year's greetings on paper. If this were a more propitious time with a stronger economy, a short visit of fifteen days during this season would be wonderful. Let's hope such a time will come, but while hoping life passes and comes to an end.[49]

Catherine rarely expressed such sadness and despair. Concerns about disorders in the city led these wealthy families to change their standard practices. Hosting smaller dinner parties was one way to socialize without attracting attention.

In 1821, after Carnival season ended, Claude attended a gathering that included many high-ranking local officials and their wives, and Catherine made sure to share the news with Pierre. "So Lent has not brought an end to balls in Paris. We are much better behaved here. We must content ourselves with some meatless meals [*dîners maigres*]. One took place on Sunday at Mr. Lemarchand's with all the local officials: the prefect, the mayor and his wife, the first president and his wife, several judges, and some *négociants*. Barbet and his wife attended. My husband went to the soirée [after the meal]. There were a lot of people. Ice cream, cakes, and punch were served."[50] Events such as this brought together the business elite and city leaders to cement their relationships. Though some of the officials' wives attended, these dinner parties functioned primarily as spaces for male socializing and networking.

Another example of male socializing appears in traces of a regular gathering of Lyonnais in Paris. Among Pierre Vitet's papers is a short invitation, written in the hand of Marshal Suchet, inviting Pierre to join them (see fig. 11). He wrote: "The Maréchal Suchet sends his warm regards to Mr. Vitet and requests the honor of his presence at a dinner at his home next Friday, the 17th, date of the meeting of old comrades of Lyon. Paris, Saturday, April 11."[51] In addition to enabling the men to reconnect and reminisce, dining (and no doubt drinking) with old friends from Lyon must have served as an important opportunity for networking. Pierre's oldest and most trusted friends and allies were fellow Lyonnais like him, and this invitation provides evidence for the existence and strength of their network in Paris.[52]

A letter from Louis Pradher, Ludovic's piano teacher and one of Pierre's few non-Lyonnais friends, gives a sense of the male-only socializing that Pierre enjoyed. Pradher described an evening out with a mutual acquaintance. "After dinner, we played billiards at the Café des Milles Colonnes. If I had any modesty, I would not talk about my triumphs, but . . . without exaggerating, I can tell you that of thirteen games, I won ten, seven in a row. Whenever the games were going badly for him, he would say 'Ah! my friend Vitet, where are you?' He apparently counts on you to be his victor, and he would be correct . . . because I would be more caught up in the pleasure of seeing you than in the game."[53] Gambling and playing games seem to have occupied a great deal of these men's time.

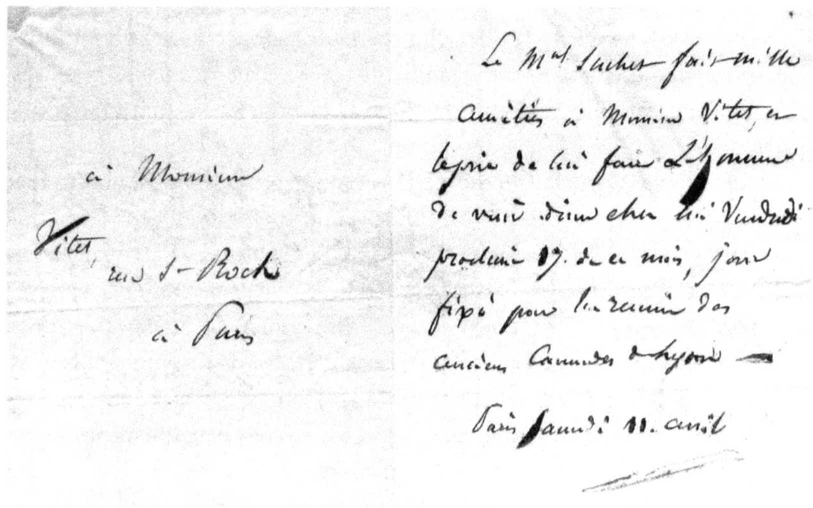

à Monsieur
Vitet, rue St-Roch
à Paris

Le Mal Suchet fait mille
amitiés à Monsieur Vitet, et
le prie de lui faire l'honneur
de venir dîner chez lui Vendredi
prochain 17. de ce mois, jour
fixé pour la réunion des
anciens Camarades de Lyon —
Paris Samedi 11. avril

FIGURE 11. Note from Marshal Suchet to PV, Ville de Lyon, Archives Municipales, 84II/11, photo by author.

Besides male-only dinners and gaming, another mostly male activity was Freemasonry. Pierre rarely discussed Freemasonry in his letters, but he drew Masonic symbols in his correspondence journal. These drawings hint at a silence, a topic of discussion and a practice of everyday life that did not appear in these letters. Aside from these and a handful of other venues and activities from which women were excluded, social life in this period among families of this class tended to bring together both sexes. And even Freemasonry was not a purely male activity; Pierre wrote to Catherine about a Freemasons ball he and Amélie attended in March 1807.[54]

Restaurants could also serve as spaces for social networking and seem to have attracted mostly male customers, although women could patronize them as well. Both of Amélie's brothers-in-law enjoyed restaurants. When Jacques visited Paris in 1812, he hosted a dinner at the restaurant Grignon for Pierre and some of his closest friends—Fournel, Roux, Michaud, and Pradher.[55] Amélie's other brother-in-law, Christophe Riocreux, was also a fan of restaurants and tried to convince his more old-fashioned mother-in-law that dining out could be a pleasant experience, something she admitted in an 1816 letter to Pierre.

> It seems you took advantage of the pleasant weather to stroll in the Tuileries as a family and while there to dine at the Frères Provençaux. Despite my distaste for restaurant dinners, I was forced to admit that we eat very well at the Frères Provençaux. The food is served in a very appetizing way, and in the room where we were seated, we felt completely at home. My dear Riocreux loves these sorts of dinners, and if the weather had been better during my time in Paris, I think he would have given me a complete course in them. It is always good to learn, and I must finish my education.[56]

Both restaurants, Grignon and Les Trois Frères Provençaux, were in Pierre and Amélie's neighborhood, near the Tuileries. The Palais Royale was just a few blocks away as well. Their home was ideally located for Catherine to "complete her education" while staying with them.

Out on the Town

In addition to attending balls, soirées, and meals in people's homes and restaurants, bourgeois men and women amused themselves in more public venues, particularly theaters and art exhibits. Provincial theaters followed a seasonal rhythm, opening for one or two seasons during the cooler months of the year and closing during the summer. Wealthy inhabitants often purchased annual subscriptions, which gave them access to regular performances. Subscriptions typically cost a hundred francs for men and fifty for women, while renting an entire box (*loge*) for a season could cost hundreds of francs, a significant expense.[57] Most subscribers attended a few times a week, with the performances taking place in the late afternoon. However, exceptional performances, such as those featuring visiting actors, required even subscribers to purchase tickets.[58]

Renting a loge, as the Arnaud-Tizon family did, could require some planning, particularly if the space was to be shared with friends and family. In April 1811, Catherine asked Pierre to see whether Suchet still wanted his spot. "Monsieur Suchet has the fourth seat in our loge this year. I would like to know if he plans to keep it next year. If not, it would be nice for us to take all four of them for our family. I would like a response as quickly as possible."[59] Her daughter Adèle had reached an age when she would appreciate the theater; Catherine may have wanted the seat for her. Sitting in a loge permitted wealthy people to watch performances from balconies overlooking the parterre, the area in front of the stage. Seats began to be installed in the parterres of Parisian theaters in the late eighteenth century, but most provincial theaters continued to have standing parterres, which were often quite rowdy spaces, well into the nineteenth century.

Although she and her family attended theatrical performances regularly, Catherine complained about their poor quality. "While you are enjoying so many wonderful new plays in Paris, our theater is getting worse and worse."[60] She nonetheless mentioned the theater frequently, suggesting it occupied a prominent place in their lives. "Our theatrical season just finished and to save us from suffering without a theater, it reopened the next day. We have kept our amiable singer Mademoiselle Lalande, but lost Mademoiselle Renaud to the Feydeau."[61] Catherine was less enthusiastic about attending these performances than the rest of her family and eventually canceled her subscription. "Our theater is reopening today. Everyone in the house has subscribed as usual, except for me. I am renouncing this pleasure for a good reason: the theater bores me when there is not a large crowd, and the heat tires me out when there is one."[62] It was the audiences that made the theater appealing to her, not what happened on stage.

While performances often disappointed, special guests inspired enthusiasm and drew larger crowds, as suggested by Catherine's 1809 account of one visiting actor's reception.

> "As you sent updates on the Parisian theaters, I will send an account of the brilliant performances taking place in Rouen. *La Vestale* is rendered beautifully. . . . Monsieur Spontini has been receiving accolades. The

audience called him back on stage at both the first and second performances. . . . I have never seen so many people at our theater. I gave the two seats in our box to Barbet and his wife, who were only able to come from Bapaume at 7:00. At 3:00 I sent Morel to reserve a place for me, and he took the last one that remained in the first balcony."[63]

If nothing else, it was entertaining to observe the crowd and their reactions, though Catherine did not always appreciate that part of attending the theater: "To attract more people to the theater, the director has brought the dancers from the Gaîeté Theater and the family of Mr. Hullui, a former dancer at the Opera. Despite the unimpressive performance, people are going in droves and yesterday, Sunday, it was so crowded that *le papa* was forced to sit in his box. As for us, I think that we will not give them our money. I prefer to stay by my fireside."[64] The reference to Claude having to sit in his box suggests that he ordinarily stood in the parterre. Perhaps he preferred the atmosphere there.

When famous actors performed in provincial cities, audiences poured into theaters. In 1817, Catherine wrote that "Mademoiselle George has been here for two weeks and is attracting large crowds to the theater. She brought a young man with her to play Talma's roles with whom people are also satisfied. There is a good opera. Fans of the theater are in heaven, including *le papa*."[65] A few years later, when France's most famous actor appeared in Rouen, his visit inspired excitement. "Talma has been here since Tuesday to great acclaim. Seats in boxes are selling out at 6 francs. . . . I was hoping they would stage *Marie Stuart*, in which case I would have tried to go, but it seems it will not be performed. Our gentlemen have been skipping dinner as they rush to take their seats."[66] The Rouennais upper crust relished the opportunity to see and be seen at these performances.

Audiences could have a powerful impact on performances and performers by voicing their satisfaction or dissatisfaction. Such reactions seemed newsworthy, as when Catherine recounted an instance when audience members forced an actor off the stage. "Madame Lemarchand must have already told you about the disruptions at the theater and the forced exit of Madame Pouchard due to whistling. The spectators were very unhappy, but the lady made peace with them and was applauded when she returned to the stage on Monday. . . . *Le papa*, still a great fan of the theater, was happy to see Madame Pouchard perform."[67] Spectators expressed their pleasure or disapproval vociferously, shaping the experience for all.

Pierre's letters included frequent references to the theater, too. He and Amélie attended both the elite Théâtre Français and more popular Salle Feydeau, named after the street on which it was located since the 1790s. In

1801, the Feydeau merged with the Opéra-Comique, which became its official name, but Pierre continued to refer to it as "Feydeau." Just a few blocks' walk from their home, the Feydeau staged comic operas, a uniquely French genre that combined drama and comedy with music and song. The theater appealed to the French and foreigners alike. John Carr, an English barrister who traveled to Paris in 1803, described the Feydeau as "very elegant" and lauded its "excellent arrangements, good performers, and exquisite machinery."[68] Although Pierre often mentioned the theater, he only gave details on special events like premieres, including one of *Koulouf*, which they saw in December 1806.[69] In one case, he discussed an accident that took place at the opera during the ballet *Ulysses*, when an actress fell off the stage.[70] He thought Catherine would be interested in anecdotes about unusual events or performances.

Going to the theater with such regularity could lead to boredom, and directors recognized the need to introduce innovations to keep spectators coming, something Catherine acknowledged in a letter dating from 1816: "So Amélie was happy with *La journée des aventures*. As you say, Feydeau needed such novelty to reanimate its performances which have grown dull. I took note of this play's success to ensure I attend when it is staged in Rouen."[71] In February 1818, Pierre described audience reactions to a play starring Mademoiselle Mars, one of France's most acclaimed actresses, referring to the boredom felt by frequent theatergoers. "Our gentlemen were bored. The public was unhappy. Whistles brought an end to the performance. Interrupted while singing a long song, Mademoiselle Mars was annoyed that she could not show off the beautiful dress that she had reserved for the final scene of *L'ami Clermont*. [Her frustration] was compensated [*dédomagée*] by 28,000 francs net in receipts."[72] Pierre's commentary on the actress's feelings and dress seems surprising. How did he know that Mars was annoyed? Did he mention her reaction because he thought it would interest Catherine? Regardless, Pierre seemed to have inside knowledge about the theatrical world, perhaps through his friend Pradher.

In November 1813, Pierre informed Catherine that they had rented a spot in a loge at the Feydeau for the year, but just for Amélie, perhaps because it was so expensive—a hundred francs.[73] Catherine's response suggests that, as in Rouen, the experience revolved as much around the spectators as the performances: "So you have rented a box at the Feydeau. That should be very pleasant. If the performance does not entertain you, you will be in too good company to get bored."[74] Though the social aspects of theater attendance clearly appealed, the cost of renting a loge did not always seem worth the expense. A month later, in a letter in which he listed a series of social events hosted in honor of a wedding, Pierre announced that they had sold their recently purchased subscription at a profit. "Pensée Roux married her cousin, [Henri] Roux. Madame Fournel hosted a gathering to celebrate the wedding last Sunday. Barbet danced with the bride before boarding the stagecoach. Madame Suchet's party was last Thursday and there is another one at the Fournel's next Monday. Our loge at the Feydeau sold immediately. We got to use it for one month for free."[75] Attending party after party, in this case to honor the newlyweds, was par for the course, as was Pierre's contentment about the good price he received for their loge. As a frugal *rentier*, he sought to make the most out of every investment.

Despite his active social life and his responsibilities overseeing Ludovic's education, Pierre had time for other pursuits, particularly his passion for art. In addition to developing his skills as a landscape painter, he assiduously attended the annual Salon de Paris. Catherine also appreciated art and timed her 1808 visit to correspond with the exhibit: "You will soon be enjoying the opening of the beautiful exposition of paintings which has been announced for the 14th. I can tell you my dear children that I do not need that event to motivate me to visit with you before winter."[76] A few days later, Pierre wrote to say that they were awaiting her arrival with impatience and sent more details about the salon.[77] Catherine replied with enthusiasm. "My dear children, I received the issue of the *Mercure* and the Salon catalog that you had the goodness to send me. I enjoyed reading over the list of masterpieces being exhibited, which inspire curiosity. I think several people from Rouen are travelling to Paris. For me, my dear children, the principal goal of my trip is to see you, and I am delighted that I will be able to spend a week with you while business is calm."[78] The 1808 Salon displayed Jaques-Louis David's painting of Napoleon's coronation for the first time, a moment depicted in a painting by Louis-Léopold Boilly (see fig. 12). It is easy to imagine the Vitets and Arnaud-Tizons among the well-dressed crowd. Like most of the social gatherings discussed in this chapter, art exhibits brought together men, women, and children whose presence contributed to the experience.

Famous works of art no doubt attracted many curious spectators, but when provincials visited Paris, they flocked above all to theaters where they could enjoy better-quality performances and see famous actors. When Jacques Barbet visited Paris in 1812, he frequented the elite Théâtre Français and, in the process, seems to have become infatuated with France's most famous actress at the time, Mademoiselle Mars. His account of how he approached this celebrity is quite astonishing, particularly when one considers the fact that his wife gave birth to twins only about a week later. It is unclear whether his story had any basis in reality or if it was a joke or an

FIGURE 12. Louis-Léopold Boilly, *The Public Viewing David's "Coronation" at the Louvre* (1810), image copyright © The Metropolitan Museum of Art. Image source: Art Resource, NY.

elaborate fantasy. At the beginning of the letter, he addresses both Pierre and Amélie using *vous* but then switches to *tu*, addressing Pierre. Would he really have shared this story with his wife's sister?

> You know, my good friends, what tribute I paid to Mademoiselle Mars during my stay in Paris, that to please her and make this charming actress notice me, I visited frequently the first, second, and third balconies of the Théâtre Français. . . . Mr. Le Brun and I made a deal with the theater's Swiss [Guard] whose job is to keep good-looking boys [away from her].
>
> Having noticed all I did to please her, and seeming very sensitive to it, she has secretly arrived in Rouen, and I will be meeting her this evening. I count on your discretion, my dear Vitet. You understand the enormity of the secret that I entrust to you. This charming compatriot (because, you know, she is from Rouen), having noticed the impression she made on me in *Le Misanthrope* and *Les fausses confidences*, will be here playing roles as a means of seduction this evening. (It is thus solely due to me that we have Mlle Mars in town, and it is well proven.)[79]

The light-hearted tone of this letter makes it difficult to interpret. Was Jacques joking about having personally convinced Mademoiselle Mars to come to Rouen? Or was he bragging about a sexual liaison with France's most famous actress while his pregnant wife sat at home? Stories abound of young, bourgeois men becoming infatuated with actresses, who seemed to be flaunting their sexual availability by appearing on stage.[80] Based on this letter, it seems that middle-class men could recount (or joke about) such adventures without causing shock. Regardless of this story's relationship to reality, Mademoiselle Mars never came up again in Jacques's letters.

It was not just good-looking actresses who appealed to spectators. While in Rouen, Pierre and Amélie received updates on Parisian cultural life from Louis Pradher. In 1812, he reflected on how to ensure a play's success: handsome actors.

> The audience listened to the work without any sign of disapproval or the constant whispering we often hear during long performances. There are six musical pieces worthy of the best composers and in the role of Pancredi, Lavigne acts and sings as we haven't seen in a long time. This young man combines a pleasant physique and height, an expressive face, and a warm, enchanting voice. I am confident that he will help the box office because he will attract the ladies. And when one cannot count on the success of a particular production, an author must be prudent enough to place a talented actor on the stage, and especially a handsome one.[81]

According to Pradher, attracting "the ladies" was the surest way to help the box office.

In another letter, Pradher shared his reactions to a performance and recounted a conversation he had with some mutual friends. Aside from the music, the opera, which was composed by Etienne-Nicholas Méhul, disappointed him. "Having just left the Feydeau, Monsieur and friend, I am fulfilling my promise to send you my thoughts on *Le prince troubadour*. Unfortunately, it was disappointing; the only good thing is the music."[82] After writing several lines about the poor writing and acting, Pradher turned to more personal stories.

> If only you were there, Monsieur and friend. I see your zeal for what is truly good, and you would have seconded my efforts to support it. I can also imagine Madame Vitet saying correctly that it is unfortunate that such good music must be paired with such awful lyrics. Then she would look to her right to comment on a lady's dress, would recognize without admitting it the people who were entering the second bal-

> conies, and would ask about who was seated above us. . . . Before we knew it, the bad performance would be forgotten. . . .
>
> Madame Suchet, Madame Fournel, Mademoiselle Félicté and Monsieur Richard were in the third balcony as well. I visited them and learned that Madame la Maréchale has given birth to a big, healthy boy and both mother and child are well. I would be happy to be the first to share this news with you that I am sure you will find agreeable. One would hope that in a sprawling four-page letter there would be one bit of news that touches you![83]

Pradher's account makes clear the social aspects of theater attendance. Was he seeking to flatter his reader? No doubt, but his description of Amélie's behavior and the interactions that took place among audience members is nonetheless instructive. Besides offering entertainment and diversion, theaters were important locations for socializing, for seeing and being seen.

In 1826, Amélie received a surprising letter from Pradher in which he announced that he planned to marry an actress. After mentioning that he was sending Amélie some sheet music she had requested, Pradher launched into a passionate account of his feelings for his future wife and lauded her virtues:

> I am getting married! To my taste, but not everyone's. The woman I am marrying is pretty and has stayed innocent in a career she has been in for twelve years, which is proof of her virtue. She resisted all the temptations she encountered and instead of having gentlemen supporters, diamonds, and cashmeres, has remained simple and humble. Some narrow-minded people will be displeased, but happily I have plenty of friends who do not think this way. . . .
>
> After all that I have told you, you must have guessed that I am marrying Mademoiselle More, member of the Feydeau Theater. Yes, my friend! I love her and she loves me! . . . As for the future, I will let destiny guide me. I will not change my lifestyle [and] will always conduct myself in a manner deserving of the respect that I enjoy. I will do my best to make her happy and thus avoid distress.[84]

He ended the letter by expressing hope that they would remain friends, which seems to have been the case, based on their continued correspondence. Félicité Pradher, formerly Mademoiselle More, became one of the July Monarchy's most successful actors, while her husband became Louis-Philippe's children's music teacher.[85] Amélie and Pierre no doubt continued to socialize with this power couple in the world of French music. This domain of the cultural elite and other high-ranking members of Restoration society was the world that Ludovic Vitet was born into and would join himself as a young man.

Musical Performances in Public and Private

In addition to the theater, which often incorporated music, dancing, and singing, various kinds of concerts figured prominently in bourgeois socializing. One space in which members of the Parisian social and cultural elite gathered was the Conservatoire de Musique, an institution founded in 1795, with a new concert hall inaugurated in 1811. Pierre and Amélie attended concerts and prize ceremonies at the Conservatoire on a regular basis and sent descriptions of them to Catherine.[86] Catherine had strong opinions about the best kinds of spaces for concerts. "I just received your lovely letter, my dear Amélie, and am happy to hear that you are all enjoying good health and are making good use of your time by going to see the latest performances and the brilliant exercises at the Conservatoire. . . . I agree that large rooms take away from musical performances. The small room felt more like a private gathering and give it its charm."[87] As at the theater, the atmosphere created by other attendees contributed to the experience of attending concerts.

Theaters and concert halls were not the only venues where musical performances could be enjoyed; they often took place at private gatherings. Music and singing served as the centerpiece of social events with friends and family across the generations. Girls and boys alike learned to play instruments, particularly the piano, and then entertained their family and friends by performing. In 1809, after responding to an account of one of Pierre and Amélie's evenings out, Catherine mentioned that some friends had organized a series of regular performances in their homes. "I am not surprised to hear of Amélie's success. The pleasant evening that you spent at Madame Hochet's made me envious. I am sure they made beautiful music. We had a good concert at Saint Ouen, as Madame Suchet must have told you, and we have one every fifteen days at Madame Goulé's which is less impressive this year. I have been taking Adèle to try to develop her taste in music, but for now she only likes her doll and is still quite the child despite being eleven and a half."[88] A large gothic church, Saint Ouen served as a suitable venue for such concerts, but smaller ones also took place in people's homes, where friends gathered to make music and provide entertainment for their social circle.

Many years later, in 1820, Catherine wrote about a series of concerts organized by a group of friends: "Victoire and her husband have signed up for the concerts being hosted by Monsieur and Madame Fouquier where there will be beautiful music. They take place every fifteen days. Madame Suchet has also subscribed."[89] At the biweekly concerts she mentioned, a group of friends shared the costs of hiring musicians and committed to attending regularly.

Catherine enjoyed such private gatherings but, even as early as 1812, tended to avoid more formal concerts: "There was a dazzling benefit concert at the Saint Ouen to support Mademoiselle Laroche, an actress of this region. *La papa* and Ludovic attended, but Victoire and I stayed at home fearing the cold and humidity of the place. There was a large, beautifully dressed crowd."[90] Less eager than usual to take advantage of this opportunity to socialize, perhaps because she was worried about Victoire, who was pregnant, Catherine nonetheless enjoyed sharing details about the event and assumed that Pierre and Amélie would appreciate reading about them.

While Catherine generally preferred informal events featuring amateur musicians, sometimes such gatherings were less successful, as revealed in an anecdote she shared with Pierre and Amélie in January 1815. "So, Madame Michaud's concert disappointed you. As you said, events that are announced so far in advance and with such fanfare rarely succeed. It lacked singing, which in my view is the heart of a concert. I attended one last week where that lack was not the problem, but rather an abundance much more annoying: novice singers who try to show off like the Vestals. Nothing is crueler than having to suffer through pieces that we have heard sung so beautifully."[91] As usual, Catherine felt comfortable sharing her views on many subjects and did not hold back on criticizing ridiculous behavior.

She and Claude continued to attend parties featuring music and dancing after their children had married, and she enjoyed sharing accounts of their socializing with Pierre.

> My dear friend, I wanted to respond yesterday to your lovely letter, but I was denied this pleasure because I woke up late, for as you know I went to Madame Thézard's party on Sunday. . . . I had decided not to go, but when I visited the lady, she made me promise to attend. I did not regret it. The party was very pretty if smaller than the preceding ones. People made music and danced for two hours. We returned home at 2:30 very happy with the evening. *Le papa* came along and enjoyed the music.[92]

Small-scale gatherings featuring music appealed to them, and now that she no longer had a marriageable daughter to chaperone, Catherine could skip the larger ones.

Men and women alike devoted significant time and energy to developing their musical talents. In a letter dating from 1818, Catherine voiced her enthusiasm for events where friends provided the music. "We have been in the tumult of planning a fancy dinner and dance hosted by Barbet. Everything went well. Everyone contributed. The Curnier ladies and Ludovic kept everyone dancing all evening by playing the piano. Everyone appreciated their skill. I don't know why, but this manner of dancing is always more fun than having a paid orchestra."[93] They preferred to socialize frequently with a small circle of close friends of their own background and social status over attending larger, more formal events.

Amélie and Pierre participated in similar concerts in their Parisian friends' homes. In February 1810, Pierre praised Amélie's performance when she sang at a concert hosted by Madame Hochet, during which people enjoyed music provided by Pradher as well as Frédéric Duvernoy, a well-known hornist.[94] Amélie sang with her brother at another gathering held in December 1812, which Pierre described as a "very pleasant *soirée de musique*" and where Pradher performed a duet with a harpist.[95] Earlier that year, Pierre mentioned that they would be attending a concert at Madame Audiffret's, where they would be seeing Mademoiselle Brunet (Ludovic Arnaud-Tizon's future wife) and Amélie would be singing.[96] When he became old enough, Ludovic Vitet demonstrated his talents as a pianist at such gatherings, including at the June 1816 celebration of Pierre's saint's day, when "Ludovic played a sonata on the piano accompanied by his friend André Pradher. The young Hersch impressed us with his precocious talent and brilliant execution. We ended the evening with refreshments and ice cream."[97] In his letter sending New Year's greetings dated December 31, 1816, Pierre also shared their full social calendar. "Story of our week: Monday, familial ball at Madame Senevas's; Thursday, Riocreux's feast day, we dined at his place; Friday, Fournel's feast day, a bit of music: Félicité accompanied Mery's air, Ludovic played a rondo, and Noémie made a portrait of her sister. We danced and then had punch and ice cream."[98] Music and dancing enlivened these gatherings of close friends and family, people who socialized regularly and supported each other through thick and thin.

At an 1813 soirée hosted by Marshal Suchet, Pradher performed again, this time accompanied by a Spanish guitarist. Pierre ended his journal entry about this event with the cryptic phrase "*observations particulières sur les invitations des grands*" (reflections on invitations from people of high rank).[99] It seems that Suchet's rank and status put strains on their relationship. Despite growing up with the Suchet brothers and despite his own wealth and prestige, Pierre did not feel part of this most elite echelon. Such comments never arose about gatherings they attended with their more intimate friends, where multigenerational and mixed-sex socializing took place in warm and convivial atmospheres.

In March 1816, Pierre recorded a more detailed summary than usual of a letter he sent to Catherine in which he complained about Marshal Suchet's rudeness while mentioning the weekly musical performances Suchet hosted with his wife.

> Account of our Carnival celebrations. Attended Jeudi Gras dinner *chez le Maréchal* who seemed impolite and almost disrespectful. He acted as though they would not be inviting us to their ball this Sunday and to their regular Sunday *soirées de musique*. Warning to readers not to be duped by these people should they pass through Normandy. The Mardi Gras party at Madame Blanc's was pleasant and well organized; the ladies danced until six in the morning. Thanks for the good *paté* sent by the *maman* which we shared with our friends Baudin and Fournel. The following Thursday, dinner chez Suchet and *soirée de musique*. The Maréchale and Amélie sang. . . . The Institute is being reformed and purged. . . . A word about politics: abolition of divorce under discussion in the Chamber.[100]

In 1816, the Restoration government renamed and combined two schools of art and music to create the Académie des Beaux-Arts. As a frequent attendee of both concerts and art exhibitions, Pierre followed these discussions closely. His use of the term *purged* suggests that he disapproved of the government's actions. And, as suggested by his closing sentence, he knew that his mother-in-law followed with interest all that happened in the legislature.

Responding to Catherine's December 1816 letter describing how her friends were avoiding extravagant socializing because of the extreme poverty in Rouen, Pierre contrasted her account with one depicting the festive atmosphere in Paris and brought up another of Suchet's snubs.

> The misery visible in Rouen is not evident in Paris. . . . The reason for this difference: the constant activity of Paris—the egotism, luxury, and spectacles of the city—distracts for better or worse. This evening, we are attending a ball at Madame Sevenas's where Ludovic hopes to dance. We are also dining at Madame Fournel's with Madame Suchet, Madame Roux, etc., a small daytime dance as usual. We received a visit from the Maréchal and Maréchale. Ludovic earned their applause by playing the piano. We visited with them Saturday evening. They talked about inviting us to St. Just, but did not mention their Sunday soirées.[101]

Although Pierre felt insulted at not receiving this invitation from Marshal Suchet, it did not seem to have lasting consequences, as Pierre and Amélie continued socializing with him.[102]

In December 1817, Pierre wrote to Jacques Barbet about the difficult political situation and then turned to the informal gatherings that he and Amélie had been attending. "Reflections on the difficult years that have been following one after the other, on the budget, liberty of the press, and the Concordat. . . . Ball at Madame Thézard's [in Rouen]. For us in Paris, we have been avoiding such brilliant gatherings. We are going on Sunday . . . to Madame Roux's because we are not required to wear formal dress. Tomorrow, we will be going to Fournel's to celebrate his saint's day. This evening, we are celebrating Riocreux's saint's day and will be dining with him. Saturday is now his day to receive friends."[103] Pierre's passing reference to Riocreux's "day to receive" refers to the common practice of people hosting weekly gatherings in their homes on the same day and time, reflecting once again how seriously they took their socializing.

Public Festivals

Music and dancing figured prominently in more public official celebrations as well. During the Empire, large annual festivals took place on August 15, Saint Napoleon Day, which corresponded to the Catholic holiday of Assumption. Catherine wrote to Pierre and Amélie with details on the August 1807 festivities in Rouen and commented on their account of what had taken place in Paris.

> Thank you for sending me the details on the beautiful festivities that you witnessed. I was even more impatient to receive your news because sometimes accidents can happen in crowds, despite taking precautions. My dear Amélie is very curious, and this time her curiosity was satisfied. The gathering in Notre Dame must have been tiring too, as I doubt you could have left earlier than 2 a.m. As for the ball, when we are dancing, we never feel tired. . . .
>
> I have not yet told you about our festivities, but they were more widespread and joyful than usual. On the fourteenth, while the theater staged a free performance, we had a beautiful concert at City Hall where the garden was nicely illuminated. Our administrators did their best to celebrate properly this double festival. Can you believe that I was at the Champ de Mars to see the dances at midnight on the fifteenth? We had gone to see the fireworks from Madame Bazile's belvedere and as we were coming home with some gentlemen, they sug-

> gested we go for a stroll, and we accepted. It was a beautiful evening; we got home after midnight.[104]

Middle-class women could enjoy these public events, roaming around the city and mingling with others in the process.

A few years later, when Amélie wrote about the festivities held in honor of Napoleon's wedding to Marie Louise, Catherine encouraged her to enjoy herself.

> I am grateful to Amélie for sending me details on all that she saw. This is nothing, so they say, compared to what will be taking place in May. The newspapers are announcing a ball at the Ecole Militaire where they expect 25,000 attendees. I imagine that these beautiful gatherings will delay your arrival with us. I find the desire to see all this completely natural, and so long as you give me my time, I will not complain, but as a businesswoman [*commerçante*] who knows how to count, I will keep track of the delay.[105]

It is interesting to hear Catherine describe herself as a businesswoman, though in this case she probably did not mean it literally. In her lighthearted tone, she made clear that while Pierre and Amélie could delay their visit, she expected them to stay for as long as usual.

In a June 1811 letter to Catherine, Pierre mentioned another festival and brought up his tenants, whose marital problems led to the wife and daughter leaving Paris. "I reassured her about our plans to stay safe among the crowds. Ludovic is home from school, and we will go see the parade on the Boulevard. Madame Mirvaux and Félicie have left for Lyon. Secret cause of their trip: outrageous jealousy of the husband, scandal in the home. He has asked to break his lease."[106] Concerns about crowds and potentially dangerous situations arose with regularity, yet they chose to partake in these moments of public jubilance—in this case, festivities organized to celebrate the birth of Napoleon's son. Pierre's reference to their tenants' problems reveals that even their renters were fellow Lyonnais, further evidence of the Lyonnais network in the capital.

Parades and other public spectacles seemed newsworthy. In October 1813, Pierre mentioned such an event in a letter sending saint's day greetings to his mother. "Amélie's mother has been in Paris. . . . We watched together the parade for the empress and the funeral procession for Grétry."[107] Pierre likewise updated Catherine on events held during the early years of the Restoration. "Account of all that we saw during the festivities held in honor of the arrival and marriage of the Duchesse de Berry. Lunch at Madame Hochet's to see the parade. The processions were like those of the past. The one at Saint Roch passed in front of my house. I hung out sheets."[108] Though he may not have been happy about the Restoration, he nonetheless performed the role of the enthusiastic citizen-subject by decorating his building for the parade.

In contrast to the large crowds that Napoleonic festivals attracted, Restoration festivals tended toward smaller events that would attract the "right" people. A letter Catherine sent to Pierre regarding a royal visit to Rouen in 1817 includes a savvy analysis of the situation. "We are expecting His Royal Majesty the duc d'Angoulême tomorrow. A ball will be held in the Salle des Conseils [at City Hall]. Tickets cost 60 francs. As you can imagine, they are hoping to attract elite attendees [*la compagnie . . . très choisie*]. I promise to send you details on His Majesty's visit and all the festivities. People are saying that the prince's mission is to bring together the different parties. One could not have chosen a more suitable emissary for this thorny mission."[109] The political divisions plaguing the country made the duke's goal of convincing all sides to rally around the throne a difficult task.

A few days later, Catherine sent details on the visit, which featured stops at factories belonging to the Arnaud-Tizons' friends and neighbors, including some run by women.

> He was very popular, traveling on horseback to be sure he would be visible to all. He visited the dye-shop of our neighbor, Mr. Demerest, and then went to see the view from Canteleu *chez* Madame Lecouteux and *chez* Madame Lefebvre. He went to see Mr. Pinel's spinning workshop and the calico factory belonging to Madame Long, who as usual organized everything superbly to keep the prince from really seeing the factory. The workshops were draped in calicos in an elegant manner, the stairs were covered in rugs, and there was no activity taking place whatsoever. People are saying that Mr. Fouquier wants to sell and is working very little. This gentleman was absent, and in his absence, Madame Fouquier explained everything to the prince. I heard from an eyewitness that it was a funny situation.
>
> The prince attended the theater where they staged *Le Nouveau Seigneur*. . . . The crowd was very large. Seats cost 6 francs. They placed chairs in the parterre, which was filled with women. A ball was held on Wednesday. The only lady in our circle to go was Madame Lemarchand. At 4 a.m., the cardinal said a mass for the prince in the chapel of the Prefecture, and most of the women who were leaving the ball went to the mass to pray for the success of His Majesty's voyage. As he was

> leaving, he expressed regret at not being able to sit down to share a meal with the manufacturers of the town due to the brevity of his visit and promised to return to see these precious establishments that are so interesting and which he would continue to support.[110]

It is impossible to know if Catherine viewed the duke as sincere, though there is no doubt that she thought it significant that he highlighted the importance of industry. Running a textile firm was an essential part of her conception of self, and hearing such a high-ranking person express an interest in manufacturing impressed her. The Restoration government's efforts at public relations seem to have had some impact on her.

Networking remained an indispensable tool for success throughout the early decades of the nineteenth century and beyond. Gatherings such as balls and soirées and other events that drew people together were the primary spaces in which such relationships took shape. And these venues nearly always included women. More than that, in many cases, women served as hosts, and they were often key participants in and contributors to the success of events like concerts and balls. Thus, the interconnected "work of patronage" and "work of sociability" were both defined as women's work, just as they had been in the eighteenth century.[111] Bourgeois men depended on the women in their lives to create and animate the spaces in which they forged and cemented relationships that could have concrete impacts on their businesses and careers. Just as marriages could lead to business partnerships, a ball or dinner party could open doors to countless opportunities. Theater performances, concerts, and art exhibits similarly appealed to and brought together both sexes and multiple generations.

Although most spaces for socializing and entertainment included men and women of all ages, some attracted more homogeneous groups. Meals were one prominent example of male-only spaces, though some meals, like the one hosted by Henry Barbet for local political elites, included a few women. Others were purely male, such as the dinners hosted by Marshal Suchet for his fellow Lyonnais comrades. Interestingly, meals served as moments for same-sex conversations even in mixed-sex gatherings, as in the case of many balls. It would not be surprising if the topics of conversation varied depending on the gender makeup of the group. However, it appears the Arnaud-Tizon and Vitet families primarily chose spaces and gatherings that permitted men and women across generations and of similar social backgrounds to mingle and observe each other and to develop and strengthen valuable relationships in the process.

Even gatherings that could be labeled as political or intellectual events appealed to women as well as men. In a June 1819 letter to Catherine, Amélie mentioned that she and Pierre would be attending a speech at "l'Institut." The speaker, Pierre-Edouard Lemontey, had served as deputy to the Estates General from the Rhône department and, like Pierre and Louis, had fled to Switzerland during the Terror. After publishing an influential study of the reign of Louis XIV, Lemontey was invited to join the Académie Française. So, "l'Institut" must mean the Académie Française. As Lemontey was a fellow Lyonnais and prominent writer, the Vitets and Arnaud-Tizons no doubt felt proud that their "compatriot," as Catherine referred to him in her response, had reached such heights.[112] Attending such events allowed men and women to exchange ideas and discuss political developments. The networking that could take place in those contexts served as a tool to help them understand and navigate France's rapidly evolving political environment.

Chapter 8

Politics

Riding Out the Storm

Until the 1820s, Pierre and his correspondents rarely discussed politics, but we can discern the perspectives of the men who held public office—Louis Vitet, Ludovic Vitet, and Claude Arnaud-Tizon—based on their actions. As explained in part 1, Louis served as mayor of Lyon early in the Revolution and then as a deputy to the Convention and later the Council of 500, only leaving public life when Bonaparte took power in 1799. His grandson Ludovic participated in the Revolution of 1830 and held official positions during the July Monarchy, the Second Republic, and the Third Republic, refusing, like his grandfather, to serve under a Bonapartist emperor, Napoleon III. Claude's public life presents a third window into the difficult choices faced by Revolutionary actors. Claude left behind few traces of his views, but his actions suggest that he supported the Revolution unwaveringly, even during its most radical phases, a path that nearly cost him his life. These men epitomize those for whom the ideals of the Revolution resonated and who worked to see these ideals enshrined in political institutions.

Although Pierre's correspondents sometimes shared their political views and analysis, it is essential to keep in mind the performative aspect of letter writing. Letters may not provide direct evidence of the writers' real feelings, but they do provide a window into how people discussed these topics among their loved ones and other trusted confidants. Catherine's letters occasionally include her reactions to political events and debates. A pragmatist and patriot, she voiced enthusiasm for France's military victories and sadness when her country faced defeat and occupation in 1815. Above all, she expressed a desire for political and economic stability—in other words, an environment where their business could thrive. Amélie Vitet seemed less interested in politics than her mother, perhaps because she had been so young in 1789, but later in life, she and her sister-in-law followed political debates closely. Under the Restoration, especially, political developments took center stage in their letters. This attention to politics emerged just as a clearly defined "liberal" opposition began to take shape. Throughout the period, conversations about politics and current affairs must have been commonplace, both in the Vitets' apartment in Paris and when they were visiting with the Arnaud-Tizons in Rouen. Domestic life may have offered a retreat from the chaos and competitiveness of the public sphere, but political discussions nonetheless frequently took place in such spaces.[1]

Political developments shaped people's lives in myriad ways, including by influencing their decisions regarding where to live, how to run their businesses, and whom they could trust to form alliances that would help them survive over the long term. This chapter focuses on the relatively rare moments when the Vitets and Arnaud-Tizons shared their reactions to high-level political developments. The chapter also draws attention to the emotions they expressed while living through moments of intense political drama and shows how their "keep calm and carry on" attitude represented a new "emotional regime" of bourgeois restraint that was emerging during this turbulent period marked by warfare, military defeat, and political change.[2]

The Depoliticization of Public Life

Both the Arnaud-Tizon and Vitet families had to rebuild their lives after the Terror. As a former "Robespierrist," Claude probably tried to lay low during these years, as did his brother, Pierre-Marie. Unlike Claude, Pierre-Marie never held political office, and that did not change once he settled in Rouen. His passion in life seems to have been money—nurturing the fortune he and his wife had inherited. We thus have more traces of his activities in notarial records regarding the sale and purchase of property than of any political or intellectual activities.[3] He and his brother must have discussed politics, but the documentary traces we have do not provide access to their views, a fact that highlights the frustrating gaps in our knowledge about these men's ideological commitments.

Louis Vitet also resettled during the Directory, moving to Paris in 1795 to serve as a deputy to the Council of 500. Louis seems to have attended legislatives debates conscientiously without participating often. When he did speak, it was at moments when subjects that were dear to his heart came up for discussion. His one major contribution came in late 1798 and early 1799, in a proposal for reorganizing the medical schools of France. He opposed the domination of the school in Paris, whose budget and salaries, as defined by a law dating from December 1794, were higher than those of provincial medical schools. His proposal argued that in the name of *égalité*, the other medical schools should receive equal support. His frustration with Parisian preeminence in education reflected his provincial identity as well as his own professional background, which included studying medicine in Montpellier and teaching in Lyon. His proposal received some support and has come up in histories of medicine and medical education in France but was never voted into law.[4] The fact that one of his rare attempts to shape policy related to countering Parisian dominance suggests that his Lyonnais identity continued to influence his perspective.

Differing views on religion may explain the strained relationship between Louis and his wife, Marguerite, who remained in Lyon when they moved to Paris. It is unclear if this decision was based on practical concerns—someone needed to stay behind to oversee their many properties there—or if she preferred to reside in her native city for other reasons, perhaps not realizing that Louis would rarely return. What is clear, however, is that Louis and Marguerite held contrasting views on religion, as Louis was probably a deist, while she remained sincerely attached to Catholicism. She spent much of her time socializing with the Marduel brothers in Lyon, one of whom was a priest, who remained on good terms with Louis, too.[5] When Marguerite visited Paris in 1806, it was Marduel who arranged her travel.[6] Though Louis may not have been as strongly anticlerical as his political foes suggested, his "scientific" perspective on the world no doubt contrasted with Marguerite's more spiritual one.

Louis's involvement in public life ended once Napoleon Bonaparte came to power in 1799. He spent the rest of his life focused on research, writing, and socializing with Lyonnais scientists and writers—men like Antoine Laurent de Jussieu and Pierre-Simon Balanche, regular attendees of Madame Récamier's famous salon in Lyon and later Paris.[7] A letter from Louis's old friend Pierre Davallon, written soon after Bonaparte's coup d'état, provides a glimpse into their shared political views. Davallon underscored the dangers of the moment by recounting a story about a man who was murdered in Lyon because of his political views. He then voiced some of his own:

> Despite the constraint and circumspection that I promise myself to maintain, I am unable to stop myself from sharing my opinions and I cannot stand men who are always ready to announce their support for the triumphant party, though sometimes it is necessary for circumstances to arrive to uncover them. . . . How events teach us about men! . . .
>
> To return to our representative system: some believe it will diminish the number of malcontents, particularly among nobles who are now represented. . . . People are saying that positions will be created with life appointments, subject to payment of a certain sum to ensure that the people are well represented. People are saying that everyone who made sacrifices for the cause of liberty will receive offices so that they can continue to make their sacrifices for the happiness of all and to provide life pensions for the representatives of our former [nobles].[8]

This close friend and ally distrusted the new regime forming around Bonaparte, and Louis and Pierre probably held similar views. They feared a return of aristocratic power and an end to all that they had tried to build with the Revolution.

Unfortunately, we have no record of how the men and women of the Arnaud-Tizon family reacted to the first steps toward creating what would become the Napoleonic Empire. We do know, however, that they did not shy away from creating alliances that connected them to Napoleonic high society. By arranging the marriage of Amélie's cousin Adèle to Gabriel Suchet, the Arnaud-Tizons cemented a link to a prominent Lyonnais family and a man whose career in the military would bring him to the very top of the Napoleonic elite. They also participated in social events that brought them into proximity to the emperor. Whether they did this for practical reasons or because they supported the regime, we cannot know. The best way to make sense of their reactions during these tumultuous years is to recognize that their desire to see their country succeed militarily and economically trumped whatever political ideologies they may have espoused.

Claude was probably a die-hard republican. Many republicans supported Napoleon as the safest assurance against a return to the monarchy. Of course, it was also necessary to survive, and survival meant demonstrating a willingness to work with those in power. It meant knowing when to lie low and when it was in one's best interest to work on building the right connections for oneself and one's children. How did Claude and Catherine view Napoleon's regime? Their letters give little indication. In fact, it is striking how little politics arose in their correspondence. While this silence may have been due to fear that their letters might be read by government censors, Claude seems to have acquiesced to the idea of the Consulate and then the Empire, as he worked with local administrators and encouraged the women in his family to attend social events where they could hobnob with the Napoleonic elite. How else could one ensure that one's family would be well positioned to succeed? Under the Bourbon Restoration, the family continued to socialize with local officials and others whose political views differed from theirs. In stark contrast to the depoliticized nature of public life under Napoleon, however, they acknowledged those differences and sometimes opted out of certain gatherings because of them.

An important book by the historian Pierre Serna sheds light on this behavior, which can appear to be driven by hypocritical self-interest and a willingness to seek individual gain. Analyzing the image of the *girouette* (weathervane), Serna argues that the ease with which French politicians and others who were less active in political life rapidly shifted their allegiances during this period was not a reflection of their hypocrisy. Rather, a deeper consistency lay beneath this back-and-forth: a desire to serve France.[9] Marshal Suchet fits Serna's portrayal of someone who sought to serve his country, regardless of the regime in control. He rose through the ranks after 1793 and throughout the Empire and then returned to public service during the First Restoration before supporting Napoleon again during the Hundred Days.

Though far from being enthusiastic supporters of Napoleon, the Arnaud-Tizons had reason to appreciate some of his regime's policies and practices.[10] The Continental Blockade sought to improve the situation for entrepreneurs like the Arnaud-Tizons by minimizing competition from England. They also saw family and friends rising through the Napoleonic system of military honors and promotion based on merit. Besides Suchet, their old friend Vital Roux was named a director of the Bank of France in 1806, while his wife, who went by the name Roux-Montagnat, became the official flower maker of the emperor.[11] Remaining in a system they had mastered and in which they had ties to people of high rank seemed preferable to the unknown future that awaited them once the regime fell apart. Despite these benefits, however, the Arnaud-Tizons probably felt growing dissatisfaction with the Empire. The economic crises and food shortages that struck France starting in 1810 hurt the Arnaud-Tizon enterprise, and military defeat took an economic toll and cost the nation nearly a million lives.[12]

And how did Pierre and Amélie view the Napoleonic regime? Again, we have no direct evidence of their opinions. Amélie's few letters from these years make no mention of politics aside from her enthusiastic accounts of participating in events featuring the political elite. All the evidence suggests that Pierre venerated his father and agreed with him on most things. So, he probably disapproved of Bonaparte's coup and disliked the authoritarianism of the Empire. Nonetheless, he did not isolate himself from Napoleonic high society. To the contrary, Pierre and Amélie's entourage included many prominent members of the Napoleonic elite. Does this mean that Pierre and Amélie liked Napoleon and the regime he created? Certainly not. But they had to go on with their lives, and nurturing these connections to high-ranking men could help them accomplish their goals.

The exhibition of David's painting of Napoleon's coronation at the Louvre in February and March 1808 inspired Pierre to voice some rare, implied criticism of the regime. While in Rouen, and before seeing it, he wrote to his father about the painting, which had been announced with great fanfare. After viewing it, he sent Catherine an engraved copy of the painting and complained to his friend and business agent, Costerisan, of its depiction of a "*nouvelle noblesse*."[13] It seems that Pierre disapproved of Napoleon's efforts to create a new class of nobles and a court-like atmosphere around him.

A good example of the families' acceptance of the Napoleonic state and its leaders came in 1810, when Napoleon married Marie-Louise. The Vitets and Suchets attended events in Paris that allowed them to see the bride, inspiring curiosity in Catherine. "Turning to all the marvelous things you have seen, I would like Amélie to send me details on her dress and her impression of our new empress's face, which we have a hard time judging based on engravings. I have seen three of them and they look nothing alike. In a letter, Mr. Suchet said that she had a nice figure. Please send details about the dress embroidered with diamonds that the newspapers mention."[14] Regardless of their views on the Napoleonic regime, the family was fascinated by the people at its top, suggesting a precursor to modern celebrity culture.[15]

Not long afterward, Napoleon traveled through Normandy with his new empress. The voyage included a stop in Rouen, where the city's elites organized elaborate festivities to honor the dignitaries. Amélie went to Rouen to partake in the events, sending Pierre, who had stayed in Paris, two letters with details on all she saw, beginning with the emperor's long-awaited arrival.

> The Rouennais finally saw the emperor arrive in their city yesterday. They received him with dignified enthusiasm. . . . As for us, we waited patiently for their entrance at Madame Long's, but we saw little and were unable to distinguish anything in the carriages. But we were amply compensated that evening when we attended the ball that the town organized for the sovereigns. Having arrived early, we were well positioned to see the smallest movements of the emperor and empress.

> I was especially lucky because I was dancing when the empress decided to take part. You can imagine how delighted your wife was to be holding hands with the empress and the King of Westphalia at the same time! . . .
>
> Since I am telling you about our pleasures, I must also share our disappointments. . . . We expected the emperor to arrive on Monday [the previous day] and prepared for the ball around this idea. . . . When we arrived at around 6 p.m., I had the impression that I was entering a tomb. The only lighting for the entire space was the ordinary chandelier. An additional six or eight chandeliers filled with candles were not to be lit until the guests of honor arrived, and we spent two or three hours waiting in this obscurity. After all this time waiting, we were told to go home. . . . Before we left, the master of ceremonies had the candles lit. . . . I assure you that it was not impressive, because despite the additional lights, we could barely see.[16]

Having grown accustomed to Parisian festivities, Amélie found the lack of flair demonstrated by the Rouennais authorities disappointing.

A few days later, she sent an account of the second day of festivities:

> It was very beautiful, even if it had a more bourgeois air than the first. There were only seven or eight hundred people, whereas people say 3,000 attended the first. . . . It was at this second *fête* that they presented the famous basket. This went very well. The demoiselles, among whom numbered Adèle, were seated by the master of ceremonies on benches located at the back of the room, across from the throne with the basket in the middle. Once their majesties had made their entrance, the little troop began to walk forward, led by two gentlemen from the Chamber of Commerce carrying the basket. . . . The thirty young ladies followed behind, walking in neat rows of five, in height order. . . . The girls made a curtsy when they left their places, another in the middle of the room, and a third at the foot of the throne. They saluted all together, which was charming. Then Mademoiselle Lebruman . . . offered a compliment to the empress. When she finished her speech, the empress placed around the neck of the little orator a necklace of pearls from which hung a small watch surrounded by diamonds. . . . I did not dance this time with her majesty for the simple reason that she did not dance. She was no doubt tired from the long exertion of the previous day when we danced *à l'anglaise* along the whole length of the theater.[17]

Amélie relished these opportunities to mingle with "royalty" and to see her younger sister Adèle chosen to play a role in the event. Of course, Napoleon was at the peak of his power and prestige. He had just married the daughter of the Austrian emperor and taken his position among the great royal families of Europe. There was no reason to doubt the longevity of his regime.

With the spring 1812 buildup to the Russian invasion, conscription became a concern, and Catherine expressed relief that her son and son-in-law would not be required to serve. "Thanks to his army replacement, [Ludovic] is only in the second lottery. Barbet is exempt because of the arm he cannot move. This is an example of bad things having good consequences since fathers make bad soldiers."[18] Families had the option of hiring replacements, and the Arnaud-Tizons took advantage of that opportunity.[19] However, Catherine worried that her son might be drafted again.

> I appreciate your concern for your brother. Like you I read the law and found it unclear. The article says "all conscripts having a man already in the army. . . ." Although his replacement is dead, I have been told that his number cannot come up having already satisfied the call. . . . My husband will introduce himself to the prefect, as will my son, since our factory often obliges us to deal with the authorities. That way, if my son is called up, we can justly claim he is needed for our factory. . . . Returning to the subject of my son's replacement, his death is a double misfortune for us because we had to pay his heirs the agreed-upon sum which we would still have if he had lived.[20]

Catherine's unfeeling reaction to the death of the man whom they had paid to replace their son in the army is revealing; what mattered was keeping their son safe. The "double misfortune" refers to the additional money they had to pay and the risk that Ludovic could be drafted again.

She also worried about food shortages and their consequences, providing frequent updates on the price of bread and the weather. "We need a good harvest to keep bread from reaching seven sous a pound, which is very expensive for workers. Fortunately, they are employed, and work in the countryside will begin soon. Many laborers are willing to work for free in exchange for food."[21] Two months later, in August 1812, she continued to express hope despite the prevailing pessimism. "There's nothing new in our city which remains very gloomy. Society has fragmented and everyone is staying home. For us, our greatest pleasure is to spend our Sundays in the country. The garden at Bapaume is delicious this year. We had beautiful weather which promises a good harvest and should calm the exaggerated concerns that some have expressed about a wheat shortage."[22] Catherine's astute analysis of the situation acknowledged the power of rumor, of people who stirred up trouble by voicing "exaggerated concerns."

Even as France's military situation worsened, Catherine struggled to maintain hope and searched for evidence to support such a perspective. In August 1813, she wrote: "The political horizon seems to be brightening. There is talk of success in Spain, and this morning I heard that letters have been arriving from Paris announcing our entry into Berlin and our advances on that front. I pray to God that this is true. Our august sovereign is expected here tomorrow. Everything has been prepared to receive him. . . . A triumphal arch has been constructed and there are plans for illuminations. It is said that from Caen to Rouen, his majesty will never travel more than two leagues without passing under a triumphal arch."[23] Even if she felt ambivalent about Napoleon, Catherine prayed for military success and seemed impressed at people's desire to display their support and patriotism.

Her tone grew more somber as the regime's collapse became evident and its economic consequences spread. "There's nothing new here. Everyone is very sad. Several factories have stopped production because there is no way to sell the spun cotton and it is difficult to procure money to pay workers This is all causing great misery, especially with winter coming and laborers unable to find work in the countryside."[24] Attuned to the suffering of others, Catherine could see that France was entering a difficult moment.

The Fall of the First Empire: Resignation in the Face of Uncertainty

Frustrations with the lack of reliable news and concerns about an uncertain future reverberated among these families as they saw the Napoleonic Empire crumbing and allied forces approaching French territory. In his journal, Pierre summarized the contents of a letter to Catherine as "disastrous political circumstances; sad and deplorable *Bulletin* dated [October] 30."[25] Although it was clear by late 1813 that the regime would be ending, it was far from certain what kind of political solution would be reached. If the Bourbon kings returned, would the changes introduced since 1789, including new inheritance laws and the sale of *biens nationaux*, remain in place?[26] In early January 1814, Catherine sounded desperate as she sought to understand what was happening. "You cannot imagine the consternation that reigns here. Everyone is dying for news, is searching for it, even making it up. The truth is that we know nothing. The newspapers tell us absolutely nothing and we are reduced to waiting and hoping for better times. . . . People are losing themselves in conjecture."[27] The frustration of not knowing what was on the horizon was unbearable for these men and women who were so accustomed to planning and strategizing their every move. Corresponding with family and friends in other cities helped. In early January, Pierre updated Jacques with "news of the day: the situation in Paris is less concerning, but people are very worried in Lyon since [the allies] took Geneva. Let's hope the government takes measures to protect Lyon."[28] Sharing news assuaged fears of the unknown while helping people prepare for whatever might be coming.

Despite this news, Catherine expressed resignation more than fear or anxiety. In one letter to Pierre, she discussed the difficulties faced by men serving in the National Guard and then turned to her own concerns:

> I hope that you will only be a soldier in the National Guard as the responsibilities of officers are very heavy. Poor Suchet will not be so lucky. Having served, he will necessarily be placed into a high rank. In the end, everyone has his own worries, and I assure you that in the world of business we are not exempt. If we manage to push back the enemies, we should be able to repair the damage, and everyone will be able to get back to work. The news from Lyon yesterday was more encouraging, but now we have heard that Dijon is at risk. We no longer know what to believe. Parties of national guardsmen have been leaving our city every day. Soldiers can hire replacements, and when one sees the crowd of men offering themselves as replacements, it is hard to believe that we have any shortage of men. In truth, with the factories closed, the workers are starving and are selling themselves.[29]

Catherine's concerns were not purely self-centered. As her hope that the French armies could prevail faded, she worried for her country and its people. The lack of certainty about the future, along with concerns about food shortages and their consequences, caused anxiety. Yet the resounding tone of her letter is one of resignation, of persevering while hoping for the best. She presented an image of herself as composed despite the difficulties and dangers of the moment.

With the allies closing in, Pierre, Amélie, and Ludovic moved to Rouen, no doubt because they deemed it safer than Paris.[30] In March 1814, Pierre described living conditions in the city to his mother. "We are experiencing here, as in Lyon, the inconveniences of war, lodging prisoners, and treating the wounded. My father-in-law furnished a bed; I contributed one as well in Paris. Public spirit is good, and people want to defend themselves against our enemies' fury."[31] Pierre sought to reassure his mother while voicing his patriotism, perhaps to comfort her with the image of her son living up to his responsibilities as a solid, bourgeois citizen, a *père de famille* and head of household. While occupied with the "inconveniences of war," they watched as the Napoleonic state crumbled. No one in these families mourned the demise of the Empire, at least not in the writings they left behind. Rather, they suffered as they saw their country facing defeat and feared the possible consequences.

Pierre found himself in the cauldron of the military and political chaos when he traveled to Paris at the end of March with Adèle Suchet, who was about to give birth. A letter he sent to Amélie the day after they arrived emphasized the reigning confusion but voiced hope that the allies might be defeated: "*Le Moniteur* [the official newspaper] is telling us nothing about the emperor's activities. It seems that he is still holding back the enemy."[32] Two days later, on March 29, Pierre informed Amélie that Adèle had given birth to a baby boy only thirty hours after their arrival in Paris. After expressing relief that she had not gone into labor en route, he mentioned that it was time to leave the city. He announced that he had reserved a place on the stagecoach for the following evening and voiced his opinion that "the political horizon [was] darkening."[33] His analysis was accurate. The entry of allied troops into Paris disrupted his travel plans, but he somehow made it out of the city. Upon his return to Rouen, he sent a letter to his mother describing "the sad situation in which [he] left Paris."[34] He feared the worst.

Révolution Royale: Pragmatic Optimism, Reasonable Anger

Pierre viewed the political transformations launched by Talleyrand and the allies as nothing short of a revolution.[35] He recorded in his journal a brief description of what he had observed in Paris and added his own political analysis, blaming the allies' successes on "our [military] disasters, general discontent, and acts of treason committed by some army officers and government officials." He then wrote in large letters: "*Révolution Royale. Retour des Bourbons en France. Abdication de Bonaparte et sa retraite à l'Ile d'Elbe.*"[36] For Pierre, the foundation of what would become the Bourbon Restoration was indeed revolutionary. He felt anger and frustration with the political and military elites whose "acts of treason" explained France's defeat in his eyes. Nonetheless, even in this entry in his private journal, his anger was reasonable and analytical; this was not an emotional outburst.

When Pierre and Amélie returned to Paris two weeks later to observe the king's arrival, Pierre shared his sense of relief with his mother while addressing the difficulties they faced. He described Rouen as "tranquil despite the horrors of war" and then mentioned that "business is dead, and the workers are miserable."[37] Pierre may have felt empathy for workers who had no resources to survive without employment, but his choice to mention their suffering could also reflect his awareness that his mother cared deeply about the downtrodden. He then shared his observations on all that had taken place in Paris, referring to the "astonishing changes that have taken place since the occupation of Paris" and emphasizing "the generosity of the victors vis-à-vis the city and its inhabitants."[38] Although fear of occupation no doubt dominated his thoughts, Pierre sought to reassure his mother, to convince her that for now, at least, she need not worry about conditions in the capital. In the process, he minimized the difficulties they faced.

Pierre used a similarly positive tone when writing to his son:

> *Mon cher petit ami,* we received from Madame Lemarchant the letter you wrote to your mother, and it gives me pleasure to respond and send you a description of all that we saw yesterday to make up for your not being here with us. Although the festival resembled most you have seen, we nonetheless regretted that you were not there to witness the king's entry into Paris. This is a unique moment in our history, after all the political revolutions we have experienced. It was difficult to take in, to believe, that such an event has taken place; seeing these things with one's own eyes impresses them in one's memory![39]

Though he may not have desired this outcome, Pierre appreciated the fact that he was witnessing a moment of great historical significance. He wanted his son to be cognizant of the enormity of the transition they were living through—another revolution, in his eyes.

Pierre emphasized the calm that reigned as the king arrived and described the event as resembling others but with a different atmosphere: "There was more zeal and more enthusiasm than on any other occasion." In the evening, "there were lamps up to the fourth floor in every window of our neighborhood."[40] What most struck him was the remarkable unanimity he observed. He then provided details on the parade of dignitaries and the responses he witnessed among the crowd.

> A large group of marshals and high-ranking officers preceded the king, along with several foreign generals and diplomats. . . . The crowd's attention . . . then turned to a group of old soldiers. . . . Cries of "Long live the guard, long live the brave" could be heard all around, to which they responded, "Long live the good French, long live the National Guard." (This latter group presented an impressive spectacle of at least

> 25,000 men carrying their weapons.) Cries of "Long live the king" began with his passage at 10:00 and continued until 4:30. There was music throughout [the day], followed by a serenade at the king's window in the evening.[41]

When writing to Ludovic, Pierre focused on the experience of watching the king's staged arrival. The crowd's enthusiasm inspired a sense of optimism for his country, that the years of turmoil and chaos might finally be ending. Of course, Pierre's reassuring assessment may reflect the fact that he was addressing his eleven-year-old son, whose hope for the future he did not want to undermine. It is nonetheless clear that Pierre was willing to give the new king a chance to prove himself capable of ruling under a constitution.[42]

Pierre voiced his frustrations more forcefully in a letter to Costerisan. "The fall of Bonaparte and the return of the Bourbons; reflections on the blindness of the former, on his refusal to recognize his repeated mistakes, on his lack of love for the French. On the other hand, hopes for a better future based on how the great powers are working together to create peace and in observing their truly generous behavior. It is important to admit this fact, regardless of whatever wounds to national pride it might cause."[43] While blaming Napoleon for his demise, Pierre placed little hope in the Bourbon kings. Instead, he expressed gratitude that the allied powers had demonstrated their desire for peace and a stable government for France, which suggested that, to the extent that he felt optimistic about the new order, it was not because of anything the king had said or done.

In a May 1814 letter to Pierre, Catherine focused on concrete economic matters and voiced hope over fear, again perhaps to cope with her anxiety amid so much confusion. "The mood here among businessmen is one of impatience mingled with fear as we wait to learn the conditions of peace. . . . It is astonishing that the newspapers have been permitted to express their opinions. In the end, we must hope that we will not remain in this period of uncertainty for very long, and that soon we will be able to work in security."[44] By work, she meant getting their factory back into production, which required that they receive and fill orders from around the country. Ending the war would help them gain access to raw materials and markets, but even more importantly, it would permit her family to achieve what they truly craved: normalcy and routine—a return to their regular lives and business activities.

In describing local political festivals, Catherine emphasized continuity despite the new circumstances. "Tomorrow we will be celebrating a memorial service for Louis XVI. The ladies of our family plan to attend, but I plan to bow out because the cold air in the church might worsen my chest congestion. I prefer to stay by my fireside. On Sunday, they will be distributing fleur-de-lis awards to the National Guard. There are plans for a banquet after that event. For in this regime, as in every other, everything must end with a meal."[45] This last line epitomizes Catherine's pragmatic and nonideological attitude toward politics: regimes would come and go, and political opinions would be voiced or silenced, but in the end, the basic practices—such as a meal being served to mark the end of the festival—would remain in place. Before expressing this cynical perspective on local and national politics, however, she voiced hope that the current troubles would soon be ending. Her desire to escape uncertainty trumped any attachment to a particular regime or ideology.

Such pragmatic cynicism no doubt dominated the thought processes of many French as they observed what was happening and attempted to keep their businesses operating and their families safe and secure.[46] Catherine may have skipped the service to avoid worsening her "chest congestion," but the other "ladies" of her family attended. Events orchestrated by the city's political and business leaders represented an opportunity to see and be seen among local elites. They could not shut down their socializing because the new regime contradicted their principles, which in the end were more pragmatic than ideological.

In June 1814, Catherine sent a long update that included her analysis of the political situation:

> The Russians were here yesterday, two or three hundred soldiers with General [Fabien Gottlieb von der Osten-]Sacken. They are going to board a ship at Le Havre. An even larger number passed through Caen en route to Cherbourg where a Russian fleet is waiting.
>
> I was happy to see the duc d'Albuféra on the list of the Chamber of Peers. I think this will bring him back to Paris where he will be able to deal with his brother's situation, because the brother of a Peer of France cannot be left without a title or at least a position of the first order.
>
> People seem satisfied with the Constitutional Charter. I found the king's speeches well done. They say he writes them himself, which is even better. It's too bad he's sixty. In the end, we must enjoy the peace and tranquility and not think too much about the future. Everyone must accept their role [*que chacun se range à son numéro*] and leave luxurious consumption to those who are obligated by their status to show off. Everyone should learn to find pleasure in their private lives and with their families. That is where we find happiness in my opinion.[47]

Catherine sounded optimistic as she observed the new constitutional monarchy taking shape and the reactions of the people around her. Her preference for a frugal, family-oriented existence reflects the political and economic uncertainties of the moment and her philosophy more generally.

The summer of 1814 brought more difficulties, as workers in and near Rouen staged walkouts. Local circumstances continued to pose challenges to the family's efforts to rebuild their business. "Our workshops remain empty. The authorities are intervening. I do not know how this will end. What is sure is that this is hurting us a lot. We have a lot of orders that we cannot fulfill and once we can, our customers may no longer need the merchandise. This new setback caps a year full of worries. There has been resistance here to paying taxes on drinks. A deputation of cabaret owners left yesterday for Paris. An invisible hand seems to be ripping away the tranquility which we so desperately need. God willing, everything will settle down soon."[48] Catherine's analysis of the situation reflected her awareness of larger economic issues that affected their ability to run their business.

As the economic outlook improved, Catherine sounded more optimistic. In late September, she mentioned that their factory was running at full capacity: "[Ludovic] is working day and night. . . . We cannot complain about how busy we are, and just hope it continues." Then she talked about how honored they had been when Marshal Suchet, duc d'Albuféra, visited their factory. "We needed to be a bit daring to invite His Greatness to pass through the little stairway at Bapaume, but he did it with a grace that equalled our eagerness [to welcome him] and our sense of friendship."[49] The family's economic and social position seemed more secure than it had for a long time, and Catherine was happy to voice hope and pride as she recounted the story of this encounter.

An Astonishing Revolution: Desiring "Happiness" and Peace

An unexpected event curtailed their efforts to find normalcy. On March 1, 1815, Napoleon Bonaparte fled Elbe, landed near Cannes, and began marching toward Paris, amassing an army of followers with every step.[50] To gain supporters, Napoleon promised a more liberal regime than his previous one. His strategy worked, as many high-ranking generals returned to his side, and even his staunch critic, the liberal political theorist Benjamin Constant, backed him.[51] Louis XVIII fled Paris on the night of March 19; Napoleon arrived in the capital the next day. People like Marshal Suchet, who had served under Napoleon and then professed loyalty to the Bourbons, faced a difficult choice. Suchet chose to fight alongside his former emperor, who sent Suchet to defend his native Lyon.[52]

Those who did not hold public office tried to maintain low profiles as they followed the unbelievable events unfolding before their eyes. For many who lived through this moment, time seemed to slow down; so much happened so quickly that each day felt like several.[53] In a letter to Catherine dated March 20, Pierre announced the king's departure the previous night. There was, he wrote, "no shock, no civil war in Paris. Bonaparte is going to return to the city this evening without striking a blow. [This has been an] astonishing revolution. Let us hope that it will not bring war with the great powers of Europe, and draw us back into the painful experiences of last year."[54] Again, he applied the word *revolution* to these rapid changes.

In her response, Catherine voiced a sense of shock mingled with resignation: "What an astonishing thing is happening. . . . It is impossible to imagine such a revolution without a single blow. How lucky it is that no blood was shed. The idea of seeing French fighting French was very cruel. I wish I could see a few months into the future. In the end, we must trust in Providence, which has protected France so many times during the past twenty-five years. Our city was, like Paris, very calm thanks to the wisdom and care of our administrators."[55] Surprise and concern for their country dominated both Pierre's and Catherine's reactions. Catherine trusted her city's leaders, whose social backgrounds resembled her own. These solid bourgeois businessmen prioritized political stability and economic prosperity over ideology.

Despite her fears, Catherine's tone remained cool, and she continued to find something positive to say about the situation: at least no blood was shed. She not only demonstrated emotional restraint herself but also described her city and its inhabitants as calm, just as Pierre had attributed calmness to the crowds gathered in Paris to observe the king's return a few months earlier. It seems that they believed—or at least hoped—that if they and others demonstrated and pursued a calm demeanor, the dangers wrought by emotional excess and the excitability that had taken over during the Revolutionary decade could be avoided.[56]

In commenting on the "astonishing events" that had taken place, Catherine voiced her desire for a particular kind of "happiness," one that depended above all on economic stability. "As for me," she wrote, "I feel like I am dreaming. . . . Business has come to a halt, but we have not suspended production at the factory as we are hoping that sales will pick up. May God bring us peace and tranquility, for without these two things there can be no happiness, especially for *négociants*."[57] Catherine's understanding of the events she was observing reflected her sense of belonging to a particular social group, the *négociants*, who depended on stability for their economic well-being. She was clearly worried, but again, her emotional tone remained subdued; they had to hold on and hope for peace, tranquility, and economic stability—in other words, "happiness," as she defined it.

Catherine sounded more optimistic when she heard that Napoleon had returned to power. In early April 1815, she wrote:

> I just received your letter, my dear friend, whose contents brought me pleasure. As you say well, we need to communicate in moments like these. . . . For me, I admit that I only fear internal dissension, and [on that point] your letter is reassuring. It was also important for us to get word from Bordeaux, as we have orders ready but fear sending anything. That city is finally obeying, and it appears that only a handful of intriguers had opposed that decision. . . . To feel more comfortable, I would need to hear that the empress and her son were in Paris. . . . We would be happiest if we could live in some secluded place where we could avoid having to listen to people crazy enough to wish to see foreign troops on our soil again. All we can do is hope that Providence, which has provided so many miracles during the past month, will see its project completed.[58]

Pierre had apparently tried to build a case that war was not inevitable, but Catherine remained unconvinced. In addition to expressing frustration that the confusion of the moment made it difficult to run the family business, she voiced her political preferences: she wished to see the empress and her son in Paris because their presence would lend the regime an air of solidity. She preferred to see Napoleon back in control than to face more bloodshed and another occupation.

Like Catherine, Pierre expressed no regret about Napoleon's return. He and Amélie remained in Paris throughout April and into May, but when it became clear that war was looming, they rushed to Rouen, seeking the relative safety of the provincial city.[59] In a letter to Jacques Fournel, Pierre described public opinion in Rouen as "mostly good," by which he meant supportive of the emperor, with only a few groups demonstrating "stains of monarchism," while the National Guard displayed "good will and patriotism."[60] When news came that the French armies had been defeated at Waterloo, he used the term "disaster."[61] In a letter to his mother, Pierre mentioned that Marchal Suchet had been removed from the list of peers and added a telling line: "*Bonheur de la médiocrité*" (the happiness of mediocrity).[62] Pierre appreciated his ability to remain out of the public eye. His choice to lead a largely private existence focused on his family and their patrimony paid off at such moments.

A Second Occupation: Muted Sadness and Anger

Expressions of mourning over France's defeat and concerns about the ensuing occupation remained prominent in letters from the summer of 1815. Pierre, Amélie, and Ludovic stayed in Rouen during the first months of the second Restoration, leaving their two servants in Paris to safeguard their property. Fournel sent updates about the second occupation in Paris and its environs, highlighting the damage done north and east of the city, including in Garges, where Vital Roux had a home.

> The allied armies have been the masters of the capital for three days and are occupying it in a less courteous manner than last year. . . . R[oux]'s house was sacked, all the mirrors, doors, windows, and woodwork smashed, and 250 horses bivouacked and continue to bivouac in the garden. His sister took refuge in the church along with a few other inhabitants of the area. Even the temple of God was not respected, and she was forced to hide for three days in the bell tower. The sacred vessels, statues of saints and the Virgin, all became victims of an enraged soldiery. This was a particularly ironic scene considering that the troops had been sent to place a very Christian king back on his throne. Peasants' houses were no more spared than bourgeois ones. . . . How can such memories ever be effaced?[63]

Fournel wanted Pierre to hear about all that their mutual friends had endured, experiences he felt would mark them forever. He also voiced his reactions to this moment of collective suffering and his sensation that they were living through events of great historical importance.[64]

A week later, and with initial fears about the occupiers' potential violence subsiding, Fournel turned to the monarchists' efforts to reconstruct the government: "For the moment, the government appears to be moving toward a liberal and constitutional system, to the great disappointment of the so-called 'pure' royalists, who are clamoring against the king in the most disrespectful manner. If the government perseveres in its efforts to create [a constitutional] system, it will do a lot of good and prevent many ills."[65] Like Catherine, Fournel hoped for the best while trying to analyze the situation and prepare for what was to come.

Fournel's optimism that political tensions would subside, or at least that a satisfactory compromise would emerge, ended quickly. When he wrote again, he included an excerpt from a letter dated August 5, 1815, that he had received from an unnamed "cold and impartial man" in Lyon. That person described the theft and destruction committed by the Austrians in Lyon as well as atrocities in the south. The letter detailed the "new horrors committed . . . by the white Jacobins" in Avignon, including the murder of Maréchal Brune, whose throat was slit on the night of July 31, and the killing of "three supposed *fédérés*" in broad daylight.[66] The inclusion of letters within letters speaks to the desire to communicate news that was hard to come by and to share in the experience of living through defeat and occupation.

Violence and fear surfaced in Paris, too, though some Parisians apparently tried to resume their ordinary lives. Fournel described eight evenings of "serious troubles at the Tuileries"—a short walk from the Vitets' home—during which several people were killed, including when two people died after the National Guard attacked a crowd that had been shouting slogans against the monarchy. Fournel concluded by criticizing Parisian frivolity, remarking that people had returned to their usual behavior of "flying from one pleasurable activity to another. This evening, Madame Catalini is performing a concert that sold out the day it was announced."[67] In offering this scathing judgment of Parisians, Fournel depicted himself as above such frivolous behavior.

Fournel was not the only friend who sent news from the capital. Amélie received a letter from a former neighbor, Madame Hochet, describing the atmosphere in Paris that summer, and she too commented on the deplorable frivolity of Parisians. "You must have seen in the newspapers that *les plaisirs* [pleasurable activities] are the order of the day for many women [here]. As for me and my family, we will feel no desire to sing and dance as long as we remain surrounded by encampments and see our poor country being destroyed by foreign troops. I am French and I cannot respond with joy when my country is invaded. Once all these gentlemen have left, and we have a solid peace and a stable government, I will celebrate."[68] Madame Hochet counterbalanced her patriotism by criticizing those who sought amusement in this context, voicing both sadness about the occupation and anger about her compatriots' willingness to ignore their national humiliation. In sharing those feelings with Amélie, she assumed her friend would deem such behavior inappropriate, too.

A Lyonnais acquaintance living in Paris, Gabriel Terrasson de Senevas, sent Pierre a long letter describing his experiences of living under occupation. Like Madame Hochet, he complained about the divisiveness of Parisian society before highlighting his good fortune regarding the foreigners lodging in his home, who were far from ordinary soldiers.

> The salons have become an arena where the most insignificant beings debate with as much vivacity as if their opinions could influence the destiny of our country. All the parties are divided, and their passions

> elevated, while the only thing that can save France is unity and resignation to withstand the injuries that we must suffer because we did not know how to prevent them. We are waiting for the peace treaty, which we have been promised in vain. In the meantime, we continue to be weighed down by the cost of housing foreign troops. In our case, we were lucky to have lodged the head of the Austrian emperor's chapel, a premier violinist and one of the most famous composers of Germany, and a young painter who is also attached to the emperor. Both are very discreet and so delightful to have around that we regretted their departure. . . .
>
> The spoiling of the museum is a great misfortune for the arts. With all the masterpieces scattered, artists will no longer be able to study them. . . . I wish the government could have received permission to allow our best artists to copy them, and to replace the statues with plaster casts. At least then these copies would have filled the void. But everything was taken from us at once. All we have left are memories and regrets.[69]

Terrasson closed his letter by mentioning that his son, Hypolite, sent his regards to Ludovic. Hypolite, who was close in age to Ludovic, became a salon artist. His father's comments on the loss of models for art students thus had direct relevance for him.[70] Otherwise, this letter gives a sense of the atmosphere in Paris during the occupation. In Terrasson's case, his fellow Parisians annoyed him more than the upper-class Austrians he was lodging.

Although most of Pierre's correspondents expressed resignation, living under occupation could cause anger and a sense of violation, particularly when people or property came under attack. One of the sharpest comments of this nature appeared in a letter Fournel sent in October 1815. He included a list of items that had been removed from the Louvre, ignoring the irony that many of these works had been taken from lands Napoleon had occupied. Fournel lamented that aside from a handful of French paintings, "everything, absolutely everything has disappeared. . . . You will find the superb galleries where our antiquities were on display emptied of their great works. As you cross the lonely vaults, your heart will be broken like mine, and you will deplore as bitterly as I the destruction of the most beautiful monument that earthly powers have ever elevated to artistic genius."[71] Fournel's emotional response to his country's violation comes across forcefully here, along with his assumption that Pierre would respond to the experience similarly.

Pierre voiced sadness and resignation when writing to his mother as well. At the end of September, he wrote: "We have prolonged our stay in Rouen in response to the circumstances. The situation in Paris and of France as a whole remains critical. Spoilation of our museum and other monuments, Corinthian horses removed by armed Austrians. Rouen has remained calm, but we still have English troops to lodge."[72] Six weeks later, they were "still in Rouen. The worrying arrival of 15,000 Prussian troops that must be lodged and fed *chez les bourgeois* led us to extend our stay with our family."[73] Those with resources had more to contribute and thus more to lose as the occupation continued.

After postponing their return several times, Pierre and Amélie finally traveled back to Paris in January 1816.[74] As they resumed their routine of socializing with their mostly Lyonnais friends in the capital, the difficulties of the period continued to weigh on everyone, as suggested by details that Amélie Arnaud-Tizon included along with her New Year's greetings in December 1816. "Maman shares your news from your letters, and I learned with pleasure that the public misery, the general calamity, and the other scourges that are making our country suffer are not keeping you from dancing and partaking in the pleasures of the capital. At the same time, we provincials are groaning and hoping for a better future. Some expect this improvement to come quickly while others see it far off, and while maintaining hope, we are experiencing a very sad winter."[75] Amélie viewed the defeat and occupation of France as a catastrophe for both personal and financial reasons and because of her sense of nationalism. In his response, Pierre "discussed the news of the day, which some view as favorable and others reject, regarding the removal of foreign troops and the methods agreed upon for paying our reparations."[76] The continued uncertainty made everyone seek news and rays of hope.

Catherine focused more on the suffering of others, perhaps because of her own life experiences. "The weather has not been good, but at least it hasn't been cold, which is one less calamity for the destitute whose numbers are growing daily due to the inactivity of the factories. . . . This is an impossible situation, and with sales so slow, we fear a complete crash, despite what they are saying in the *Gazette de France* where they are reporting that we have more orders than we can fill. It is awful to say such things in the newspapers, which are increasingly read by the multitude."[77] Catherine's observations suggest that she feared the consequences of extreme poverty and was aware that "the multitude" could be influenced by what they read in the press.

In January 1817, the Restoration government established new policies regarding taxation and food distribution, causing disturbances to break out in Rouen and elsewhere. Catherine followed the situation closely, sending frequent updates to Pierre.

> Our situation regarding food supplies is unusual. We are facing a famine while surrounded by food. . . . The city does not lack wheat, but buyers from I don't know where are purchasing the wheat sight unseen and at any price. . . . The day before yesterday, people stormed the bakers on the rue de Martainville and when they saw there was no bread, at 9 p.m., they broke all the windows up to the third floor of the bakers' houses. . . . There is nothing of this sort happening in our neighborhood. The Royal Guards are patrolling frequently, as are the mounted police. I am sharing these details to keep you from worrying if you hear about all of this. We are tranquil and have plenty of bread. . . .
>
> Saturday, there will be a benefit concert in City Hall to help the poor organized by some local gentlemen. People are rushing to sign up, but the tickets are only 3 livres, so we won't raise much. This will be a small treatment for large wounds because there is great misery.[78]

Ever attentive to the potential dangers of crowds, particularly in the context of food shortages, Catherine wished that more was being done to help the poor.

In her next letter, Catherine referred to Pierre's apparent concern about her mood, which he had shared with Victoire. "Madame Barbet told me that you found the tone of my last letter a bit dark. Our city is calmer now. There is no shortage of bread, but it costs seven sous and wheat is getting more expensive." She went on to discuss the economic situation, commenting on the plight of the poor and efforts to alleviate their suffering: "Business remains slow, but the last market was a little better. . . . One must hope that the situation will continue to improve, but when an illness is severe, the convalescence is long. One good thing: winter has not been too rigorous. . . . A concert is being organized to raise money for the indigent despite remarks in the *Gazette de France* that religion might take offense at this manner of raising money. This assistance will never suffice, and I believe a tax will be necessary."[79] Catherine's concerns about the indigent weighed heavily on her as she feared further turbulence and disorder, but in presenting her analysis of the situation to Pierre, she also found rays of hope, perhaps to lighten her "tone" in response to his comments.

She brought up the food shortages again ten days later, suggesting the importance of this issue in her mind.

> Food shortages are causing justified concern. Calm has not been reestablished at the marketplace. . . . I fear that cultivators will refuse to supply the market. [It is unclear] what is to be done. Troops are being sent. God willing, they will succeed in bringing tranquility. . . . People

> are collecting money to help the poor. The king granted 150,000 francs to the department and . . . [others] are following this example offered by the chief of state. . . . Citizens are now rushing to sign up to provide a certain sum every month for four months.[80]

Civic pride and the desire to alleviate suffering and thus minimize the possibility of outright rebellion seemed to motivate Catherine and her fellow Rouennais.

The improved business climate that they hoped peace would bring did not live up to their expectations, leading Catherine to monitor the government's responses. In February 1817, she mentioned that the economic slump was worrying them, especially her son, Ludovic, who was running the family's textile factory. "The poor boy is very concerned about the stagnation in commerce. We can only hope that the spring will change the situation. The newspapers are telling us that the king strongly desires that things get better."[81] She voiced criticism of both the government and the press: the king did nothing but express his "desire" that things improve, while the press only offered praise for the king for his good intentions.

Pierre acknowledged Catherine's interest in politics by sending her updates on Parisian happenings. Several entries in his journal mention political brochures and petitions he sent to Rouen.[82] At the end of March, he described scenes in and near Paris as the factions expressed themselves. "Description of [the] tumult that followed the performance of the play *Germanies* [and] effervescence that reigned for two days afterwards. Some whippersnappers [*freluquets*] caused disturbances by wearing white ribbons knotted on their buttonholes [*boutonnières*] as a sign of their movement and carrying large canes called 'Germanians.' Occasional trouble arose at Versailles when the king's bodyguards insulted the National Guard."[83]

Such outbursts and other disputes caused Catherine to fret about the economic consequences of the ongoing diplomatic negotiations and intensifying political divisions. In December 1817, she wrote: "We get no political news here whatsoever. The lack of public discussion has reduced our newspapers to silence. We have only heard about a slap given and received without a word, given by *un brave* and received by a noble. It is difficult not to worry about our political and financial situation. How are we to pay these foreigners and what will happen to us if we do not? People who see the world through rose-colored glasses are the fortunate ones."[84] Frustrated at the lack of trustworthy news and concerned about growing discontent, Catherine saw the government chipping away at their rights. "I have been reading the journals with interest lately. I am afraid that despite the convincing arguments offered by several members of the Chamber [of Deputies] that liberty of the press will not be accorded."[85] She avidly followed these debates and knew whose views she supported, in this case praising Jacques Lafitte, a banker and deputy whose speech appeared in a pamphlet she must have read.[86]

Political Debate during the Restoration

Catherine clearly viewed political developments as having a direct impact on her life and thus followed them closely. The 1818 elections emerged as a prominent theme in her correspondence with Pierre, who wrote at the end of October to announce that after a valiant fight, the Liberals had failed to achieve their hoped-for victories.[87] In her reply, Catherine discussed the results and offered predictions for upcoming local elections. "It seems you have been passionately engaged in the elections and that the results disappointed you. But as you say, at least your deputy, based on his platform, is committed to the good cause. . . . I was happy to hear about Mr. de Lafeyette's nomination. . . . Nominations are still a year away and there are already intense disputes at social gatherings. I am preparing myself for bad selections because the patriots are not sufficiently unified. I fear that their votes will be diluted and thus allow the [other] party to succeed."[88] Catherine's use of the term *patriots*, the label used to designate supporters of the Revolution, suggests that she understood the emerging liberal opposition as continuing in their path, as defending the accomplishments of the Revolution, and as resisting a return to the Old Regime.[89]

In spring 1819, she again shared her reactions to legislative debates. "We have been following closely the debates in the Chamber. It seems they have been very animated. We laughed, or more accurately groaned, at our poor deputy's speech. It would have been best for him not stand at the podium because it is impossible for someone to be more ridiculous."[90] That fall, Catherine reported on a local election where the Liberals performed well, naming the men who were chosen and commenting on the length of the electoral assembly. "Yesterday's assembly lasted all day. We only dined at midnight. One inexperienced secretary made everyone wait three hours for the minutes. . . . The meeting ended with cries of long live the king. The nobles are saying that the rabble [*la canaille*] has triumphed."[91] After mentioning that her husband would be returning the next day at 7 a.m. and planned to stay again until the end of the session, she turned to their midnight gathering, where "the gentlemen in our family, [who] are gaining reputations as zealots," led an animated discussion, especially her son, Ludovic.[92]

In a November 1819 letter, Catherine drew explicit connections between politics and economics: "The political situation is worsening by the day and is affecting business. Trying to hold on to their wealth, people are buying very little. For us personally, we do not have much to complain about yet, but if this period of terror continues, it is possible that within a month the workers will be without work."[93] Ten days later, things had gotten even worse: "Business has come to a halt. Our employees are only working three days a week and if the situation continues, the factory will close in fifteen days, and it will not be the first. Everyone is complaining. It's a sad symphony. . . . Those who seek to destroy the tranquility that we were enjoying are to blame. One must maintain hope. People are making speeches everywhere that leave no doubt that the French want a constitutional government."[94] Political instability had a direct impact on her family's business; these were not distant, abstract concerns.

Unfortunately, the political situation only worsened, and Catherine sounded increasingly pessimistic. The sense of *us* and *them*, of the *Liberals* and the *Ultra-royalists* (commonly referred to as the "Ultras") that began to appear in her letters is far from surprising, but it is rare to find such clear evidence of women's political engagement, as in this passage from a letter she sent to Pierre in February 1819.

> The liberal press is explaining the situation well. I don't know if the Ultras' newspapers have replied. The large group of wealthy people who have been offering their opinions must frighten them a little. . . . It is impossible to believe how crazy those people are. In the meantime, commerce is languishing, and the value of merchandise is dropping, giving way to speculation. The factories are overflowing with cotton. If they are forced to shut down, unimaginable misery will follow. And while all of this is happening, people still manage to amuse themselves. I am sure that some are attending balls every day.[95]

Although she held back no punches in criticizing the ultra-royalists who were fighting liberal reforms at the cost of France's economic growth and social peace, she was equally critical of people who were happy to bury their heads in the sand, enjoying mindless amusements while their country was heading for catastrophe.

Catherine was not the only woman in the family who shared political news and opinions during these years. In 1819, Amélie Arnaud-Tizon analyzed the local situation: "*Maman* has no doubt already spoken to you about the agitation that has taken over here regarding politics and the legislative debates. It seems that bitterness is taking hold, and that in larger gatherings people are trying to avoid mixing differing viewpoints. It's probably for the best, a way to keep people from feeling uncomfortable."[96] Politics was affecting social life as opinions hardened.

Tensions remained high in Rouen throughout the spring of 1820, inspired in part by the government's decision to remove a popular army officer. Amélie described the atmosphere in the city and her family's reactions at length.

> The political situation in Paris is neither happy nor reassuring; our town is also anxious and sad. They are taking away from us the brave General Morin whose departure is affecting us deeply. He will carry with him the regrets and respect of all decent people. He has been receiving proof of these feelings every day. Everyone has been fighting over who will host him during his last days here. Yesterday was Barbet's turn. He threw a farewell dinner that all the Liberals attended . . . but invited no [female] family members except Madame Suchet and her daughter. . . . We have a new garrison that has been causing problems for our town. . . . The general's sangfroid forced the officers to remain disciplined, but who will keep them under control once he leaves? . . . Once again, here is more bad news for business. We are resigning ourselves to a slowdown and expect to return to the complete stagnation we already lived through for four months. Madame Suchet told me yesterday that all these problems made her feel a bit better about her husband's sad situation. Happy are those who are behind the scenes. She thinks *le Maréchal* must be worried; he is not alone there.[97]

Amélie sounded frustrated that her brother-in-law invited so few women to the dinner in honor of the general. Her musings on Marshal Suchet and her statement "happy are those who are behind the scenes" recall Pierre's "happiness of mediocrity."

The February 1820 assassination of the duc de Berry elicited extensive discussion. Two days after the duke's death, Pierre shared "disturbing" (*fâcheuse*) political news: "The ministers are exploiting the duc de Berry's assassination to accomplish their goals and are demanding laws limiting freedom of the press and individual freedoms."[98] Catherine also described the assassination's effects in Rouen: "As in Paris, we are grieving [*nous déplorons*] Sunday's fatal event. It's a great misfortune for France that we feel deeply."[99] Politics dominated their correspondence in the months following the assassination, a period labeled the Royalist Reaction.[100] Catherine appreciated the Liberals' efforts to resist legislation that would enhance the political weight of the nobility. "Since I left Paris, the newspapers have become very interesting, and our orators are speaking with force and courage to speak the truth. They deserve to receive recognition. There is no better title to hand down to your children than that of having defended one's country's liberties."[101] She acknowledged the value of political patrimony.

These debates continued during Pierre's trip to Lyon following his mother's death in May 1820. The law on the double vote, which gave the richest citizens the right to vote twice, passed on June 12. Pierre stayed informed by reading newspapers in subscription libraries. The details he included in his letters, as well as Amélie's responses, reveal their shared engagement in these issues.

> I dined with our friend Costerisan at my aunt Morel's house along with Mr. and Madame Aubernon on Sunday. Old man Aubernon is still following his good principles: he confirmed the nomination of Mr. Teissiere as deputy for Grenoble, defeating his ministerial competition, as did Mr. Lameth and Mr. Ribard. . . . [Lyon] receives all the latest news and political brochures. Besides the Cercle des Négociants . . . there are lots of reading rooms [*cabinets de lectures*] just as in Paris. They are well attended, and we can find in them all the latest pamphlets, even the most liberal ones. For the moment, everyone is preoccupied by the upcoming visit of the duc d'Angoulême.[102]

In referring to politicians by name, Pierre assumed Amélie's familiarity with them. His letter gives the impression that such topics arose frequently in their conversations.

In his next letter, dated May 6, Pierre used a lighthearted tone to describe the Lyonnais political atmosphere as inhabitants awaited the arrival of the king's nephew.

> I dined Thursday at my cousin Vitet's house. Madame Cartier was there, but less for the meal than to see the duc d'Angoulême's arrival. And sure enough, while we were eating, the prince arrived at the Archbishopric where he will be lodging. The big clock at Saint Jean chimed a few times to celebrate his entry. The ladies rose quickly, but it was already too late, and they returned to console themselves with dessert while my cousin and I teased them about their disappointment.
>
> I learned the next day from poor papa Guérin, who still holds to his laughable ultra-royalism, that [the authorities] were dissatisfied with the enthusiasm with which the Lyonnais expressed their love for the Bourbons because they had the poor taste to shout only "Long Live the King" and not "Long Live Monseigneur le duc d'Angoulême." There

> was concern that the parade . . . would be unimpressive because the National Guard has practically dissolved due to the men's refusal to serve and the lack of respect held for officers who are not elected by their companies. In addition, trips to the countryside kept a lot of men from participating. As for me, I will not be among the spectators. . . . I will be spending the day at Saint Didier with Costerisan, who wanted to show me the renovations he has made to the country house he inherited from his uncle.[103]

Pierre had no qualms about skipping the events being held in honor of the duke and was happy to mock the royalists. His analysis of the problems faced by the National Guard reveals his (and others') support for democratic principles.

Pierre's love of sarcasm, particularly when discussing royalty, is evident in a letter he sent to Amélie the next day:

> The weather yesterday was splendid, perfect for curious spectators, aside from a chilly north wind. An accident that not everyone knows about nearly ruined the festivities. The duc d'Angoulême fell as he was mounting his horse in the courtyard of the Archbishopric. I don't know whether the horse fell too, or if the prince missed the stirrup. I don't dare believe that he could have been clumsy. A clumsy prince, that's impossible! One must be a great horseman as well as a great admiral of France! It is thus the horse, the paving stones, or something else that we must accuse. We must launch a full investigation; yet a new case to handle.[104]

His efforts at humor hint at the nature of his relationship with Amélie and the types of stories and jokes they enjoyed sharing.

Pierre discussed national and local debates with Amélie in nearly all his letters. In one, he voiced his frustration regarding a religious festival. "I read with pleasure yesterday . . . about the first discussions on the election laws. The speeches by General Foy and by Français de Nantes interested me a great deal. Other meetings of a different nature are attracting attention here: the Pentecost festivities. Expensive candles are being sold to wealthy families to illuminate their houses, the proceeds of which are to be used for the processions."[105] In addition to questioning the utility of such local events and their cost, Pierre assumed that Amélie was following the parliamentary debates in Paris, and he was right.

Amélie even attended a session of the Chamber of Deputies and shared her reactions, sounding knowledgeable about the debates and referring to other sessions she and Pierre had attended. She went with Pierre's cousin Morel; they took their seats at 9 a.m. "The crowds seeking to hear this interesting discussion are still very large. One must take the same measures we did to have decent places with tickets; and to sit in the public seats, it is necessary to arrive by 4 a.m. . . . You know from the newspapers that we got to hear Mr. Bignon and B[enjamin] Constant. Their speeches no doubt interested you, but it is another thing to hear them express these truths and to appreciate the impression they made on everyone in the Assembly."[106] Amélie's discussion of these orators and her anticipation of Pierre's reactions suggest that following politics was another of their shared passions.

Pierre responded with his own reflections:

> Your account of the wonderful session that you attended interested me a great deal. There is no doubt that the outcome of this discussion has been decided against all rational arguments, lessons from experience, and the advice of wise men. Yesterday evening I re-read the excellent speech by Mr. Keretry, speaking both for himself and for Camille Jordan, and I said to myself, 'the minsters are laughing at all this; they respond to reality with the absurd. . . .' In a few days we will know if we will maintain our electoral rights and the hope of being honorably represented.[107]

Pierre assumed Amélie's familiarity with the issues and the men fighting for them. He then turned without transition to a family visit, intimating that politics entered the broader family's conversations, too. "So, our brother Barbet came to witness the conclusion of this debate about which I have a bad feeling! During political crises, it is valuable to observe up close how people react. . . . Plus, politics is not the only thing that brings him, his wife, and his daughter close to you. During the debate between <u>the left</u> and <u>the right</u>, you will be able to enjoy the pleasure of being together as a family. I regret missing the chance to spend this week with such good friends."[108]

Once the law on the double vote passed, political tensions hinged on the link between religion and the Bourbon regime. Never afraid to share her views, Amélie Arnaud-Tizon expressed cynicism toward both.

> It appears that Lent has not ended your amusements, and that you are still dancing despite the penitence and <u>sermons</u>. As in Paris, Rouen has its trends, its fashionable ladies, and even its ridiculous practices. <u>*Le dernier bon genre*</u> (the latest trend) is never to miss a sermon, vespers, etc. . . . Our elegant ladies arrive [at church] an hour early affecting to

> be responsible for an enormous prayer book that they carry around in the streets to edify passersby. They speak of nothing in the salons and even at balls except the preachers and their talents and morals. I heard Madame Gouen trying to indoctrinate people at Madame Thézard's house, using vehement language exhorting them to renounce the errors of this world. She can applaud her success at proselytizing. The officers go to the sermons too. If it is thanks to her that they owe this return to piety, I am certain that their gratitude will provide her with new tools, despite all that she already possesses.[109]

Amélie's sarcasm regarding this feigned religiosity served as a commentary on the Restoration. She also had no patience with the local nobility and their hypocrisy, as suggested by some reflections she included in a letter dating from 1826: "I think I will be working in the shop tomorrow; one clerk will be absent and thus there will be additional need. . . . Carnival season was slow for business, but very full of dancing for the nobles, who seem happy to celebrate; they must have qualified for an indemnity!"[110] Amélie was referring here to a law granting nobles an indemnity to compensate them for property lost during the Revolution. While nobles danced, she was working to keep the family business afloat.

Catherine shared news on local politics, too, including election results for Rouen, demonstrating her mastery of the names and issues at play. Prior to listing the winners and losers, she commented on national news: "I neglected to communicate the outcome of our electoral college. . . . The government was predicting that the Ultras would dominate, and the results lived up to that expectation. It seems that everywhere the 'good party' has triumphed. . . . The supporters of absolute power will be able to sweep away with ease the last few traces of our liberty. All that is left for us is to accept without complaint the taxes they will impose upon us."[111] As usual, Catherine focused on the practical consequences of political decisions.

Further exhibiting her passion for current events, Catherine shared her reactions to the Queen Caroline Affair, a scandal that emerged when King George IV tried to divorce his estranged wife by having Parliament pass a bill annulling the marriage.

> Have you seen the results of the queen's trial? We first received news about this event from Mr. H . . . who arrived from London on Saturday. His account mirrored reports in today's *Constitutionnel*. Even though it was two in the morning, the crowd's enthusiasm was unimaginable, and to satisfy it, the government ordered celebrations and illumina-

> tions. The queen was in Parliament, not in the chamber, but in private apartments they had prepared for her. She responded emotionally when she learned that, after its third reading, the bill had been put off for six months. . . . She then got into her carriage and returned to her palace accompanied by a huge crowd who slowed her passage as they cried "long live the queen." When the carriage passed before the king's palace, the guards waved their hats on their canes and shouted, "long live the queen."[112]

As a symbol of monarchical abuse, Caroline elicited sympathy from Catherine and from liberals on both sides of the channel.

However, it was domestic politics that inspired Catherine's most passionate reactions. In a February 1821 letter, she voiced concerns about the direction in which the French government seemed to be heading.

> There is nothing new in our city. People are still dancing and eating and reflecting little on the political situation. Happy are those who can avoid thinking about it because it does not bode well for the future. As for me, who stays close to my hearth, undistracted by the sound of violins, I have lots of time to worry and I am struggling to understand where this system of government is taking us. I assure you my friend that despite my confidence that you are working to defend our rights, I am happy that you are not in the thick of it. I suffer when I see the impotence of the heroic actions taken by our liberal deputies. I worry that there will be a coup d'état. All we can do is exercise patience and hope that we will be pleasantly surprised.[113]

With domestic and international affairs weighing on her, Catherine fell into the nineteenth-century equivalent of doomscrolling: "We need to distract ourselves from our depressing political situation, but I must admit that I have been sulking about it as I sit by the fire. Every day I promise myself not to read the newspapers, but my curiosity takes over. . . . It seems that after indemnifying the émigrés, they also plan to indemnify those who lost holdings abroad. The *Maréchal* we know will certainly receive something. I wish they would propose to indemnify those whom the assignats ruined; then it would be difficult for me not to approve of the system of indemnities."[114] Catherine sounded frustrated about plans to compensate émigrés and those who lost property in the colonies but not families like hers. In referring to the assignats, she may have been hinting at one factor that contributed to her family's impoverishment: the collapse of the paper currency created during the Revolution.

Growing Political Dissent and Mobilization

As Sarah Maza has argued, by the mid-1820s, there was a clear sense of *us* and *them* among those labeled the bourgeoisie, who saw themselves as distinct from both the nobles above and the workers below. In 1824, Louis XVIII died, and his more conservative brother, Charles X, took the throne, another factor that contributed to the growing politicization of the bourgeoisie. It is no accident that most references to nobles in these letters date from the second half of the 1820s, when a stronger sense of bourgeois identity emerged in the context of the political conflicts that took place following the assassination of the duc de Berry.[115]

Amélie Arnaud-Tizon took advantage of a wedding announced in June 1826 to criticize royalists and the nobility.

> You must have heard that big cousin Bergasse is marrying a *demoiselle noble* who is said to be pretty [and] blond, with nice features, a sparkling complexion, tall and slender, altogether a remarkable person. . . . I learned that there were 20,000 pounds of *rentes* in the family of three children. . . . Despite his solid principles and extreme submission to "*Vive le roi quand même*" [long live the king anyway, a phrase used by ultra-royalists], our cousin took the precaution to stipulate in his marriage contract a promise that the inheritance would be divided evenly, regardless of the law that might be in effect in the future. You see that he did not lose track of his self-interest. . . . The substitute Procureur du Roi is marrying the untitled Mademoiselle Doré, daughter of a cotton merchant with a small boutique on the Grande rue, but with a dowry of 100,000 francs. . . . There are lots of other noble marriages where they are asking for more than a name.[116]

Amélie seemed to relish mocking royalists and their hypocrisy, a criticism that was frequently raised during these years by members of the liberal opposition and their student allies. Disturbances in theaters, where students and other young men shouted for Molière's *Tartuffe*, regardless of which play was scheduled to be performed, were not uncommon and conveyed a sense of frustration with royalists' hypocrisy.[117] In this case, the royalist cousin's insistence on his in-laws practicing equal inheritance (as had been established during the Revolution) "regardless of the law that might be in effect in the future" hints at one legal tactic available to create some certainty in such an unpredictable world.

After the November 1827 elections caused the Ultras to lose their legislative majority, Amélie Arnaud-Tizon sent a long, passionate letter to Ludovic Vitet. By that point, he was writing for *Le Globe* and associating with prominent opposition figures. Amélie wrote to congratulate him on his successes and express her gratitude.

> What do you think of our victory, my dear Ludovic? It was greater than we had hoped. We are overwhelmed by our triumph; we can hardly believe we were so lucky. . . . Our triumph was as great and generous as the cause. . . .
>
> I need to get to the point of my letter, my dear friend. I have been hearing for a long time about the zeal and devotion you have been demonstrating for our cause and I wanted to offer my sincere gratitude and appreciation. . . . It is wonderful, while still so young, to demonstrate such a formidable and brilliant character, to be so <u>mature</u> and so <u>profoundly enlightened</u>. Please accept, my dear friend, the prediction of an aunt whose feelings for you are almost maternal, and who expects to see you elected to a position that will place you among the ranks of our strongest defenders as well as our best writers. Your uncle feels equally proud to have a nephew who was able to place himself on track for such an illustrious career. . . . We often think about how happy your grandfather Vitet would have been to see himself reborn in you. Your mother and father must be experiencing that feeling in his place. I have often thought about how your mother's pride must be mingled with fear every time you leave the house. I trembled when I read your name in the newspaper associated with your friend who was murdered in the street. My God, my friend, please be prudent; watch for these evil doers following so closely behind.[118]

Amélie viewed herself and her family as part of a multigenerational movement that Ludovic was now bringing to fruition, causing them to feel pride and optimism.

Her letter did not end there. Two more long paragraphs followed with details about individual politicians fighting the good fight in Rouen, demonstrating her own knowledge and passion. At one point, she reflected on her situation as a woman who cared so much about politics, anticipating criticism of her enthusiasm.

> Perhaps that's enough of a woman's political commentary. . . . I must seem like a chatterbox, but I am so excited about the topic that I feel a nervous agitation that forces me to speak despite my best efforts. Even though I am only a woman, I am caught up in the overwhelming enthusiasm [*je partage vivement l'enthousiasme general*]. I feel angry about a system that tries to hold us back, forcing us to darn stockings,

> and to work with our children as though imagination was not part of our capabilities. . . . Men have advanced too far today for women to stay so far behind. For men to appreciate our company, we must reduce that distance.[119]

These are the only words in the thousands of letters examined for this book that could be labeled "feminist." No other person drew attention to the concerns of women or to the limits placed upon them. Amélie closed her letter by asking Ludovic to respond within eight or ten days; otherwise, she would feel humiliated about writing him such a long and passionate letter. While voicing criticism of men's assumptions about women's capabilities and their efforts to keep women "darning stockings," she also seems to have absorbed some of the common clichés about women, such as their "nervous" reactions and their tendency to talk too much.

These were tumultuous years in France, as the country moved from republic to empire and then back to monarchy (twice) while enduring war and occupation. It seems that Napoleon successfully depoliticized everyday life for these families. They largely avoided public matters to focus on rebuilding their businesses and positioning themselves and their children for success. The Restoration did the reverse, bringing political debate and activities to the center of family discussions. The families' reactions to the difficulties they faced, particularly during the second occupation, which caused more strife and hardship than the first, reveal their perseverance. The resounding message of the letters exchanged among the Vitet/Arnaud-Tizon circle of family and friends during that period is resilience, a keep-calm-and-carry-on approach to life. Beneath the shock and anxiety, their letters voiced the need to push on despite the uncertainty and the desire to share news and information that would help them do so while seeking emotional solace by sharing their experiences.

There is no doubt that the women in these families followed attentively all that was happening while also managing their households and businesses. Studies of early nineteenth-century liberalism tend to assume its relegation of women to the new, more distinct private sphere, to spaces where emotions were acceptable and even desirable, in contrast to the supposedly more rational and masculine public sphere.[120] Catherine's letters suggest that women's acceptance of the new emotional regime of bourgeois restraint was perhaps more central than has been previously assumed. The relatively subdued nature of her reactions to the chaos and turmoil of these years indicates that women like Catherine played a role in constructing both the bourgeois rejection of eighteenth-century sentimentalism and the liberal, oppositional political world that emerged during the Restoration and would define the bourgeoisie throughout the century.

Political revolutions, military successes and failures, economic crises: all these events impacted these families' lives in very real ways. Letters written as these events were taking place make clear how astonishing they appeared, how people struggled to believe what was happening and to work through the implications of these multiple "revolutions." Despite the high degree of uncertainty and the enormity of the changes these men and women lived through, their need to continue working toward long-term goals related to family, property, and patrimony remained the same. Emotional restraint served as a tool with which to find the strength to persevere amid the chaos. Sharing experiences and reactions in letters strengthened emotional bonds while reassuring recipients that the writer remained a reliable and ready source of support and that they were all in this together.

Conclusion
Identities, Networks, and Emotions

Although Catherine Arnaud-Tizon and her loved ones managed to persevere through the political and economic storms of the Revolutionary decade and beyond, they were less fortunate when a different kind of threat emerged—a microbial one. An early victim of the 1832 cholera epidemic, Catherine died in April 1832. Ludovic Vitet, whose wedding plans had just been announced, nearly died, too. It took months of treatments, which included him taking the waters in various spa towns, before he fully recovered. Ludovic's poor health, along with the fact that his fiancée's mother died from the disease, forced the families to delay the wedding for several months.

When the epidemic struck, all three generations of the Vitet/Arnaud-Tizon family had recently moved into a home on the rue Trudon, a few blocks from their longtime residence on the rue neuve Saint Roch. Pierre wrote to Amélie Arnaud-Tizon in late March 1832 to announce that Catherine and Claude were comfortably settled in their rooms there.[1] Catherine died less than two weeks later, after having been sick for only twenty-four hours, by which time Amélie and Ludovic Vitet were ill as well.[2] After Catherine's death, Pierre purchased a double plot at Père Lachaise cemetery, relying on a friend to select and purchase the plot. He was too busy caring for ill family members to handle these steps himself. Pierre sent details to his sister-in-law Amélie and mentioned that they were hiding the cost from Claude.[3]

Pierre continued to support his family in every way possible through these difficult times when they found themselves powerless against this invisible enemy. Soon after Catherine's death, Claude moved back to Rouen, where he probably lived with his brother. He died not long afterward, in 1834.

Pierre was one of the few members of the family who did not catch cholera; perhaps he drank wine instead of water. A few years after Ludovic's marriage, Pierre and Amélie moved with him and his wife, Cécile, to the rue Barbet de Jouy. As usual, these families chose to stay close and to support each other across the generations. Pierre lived to the ripe old age of eighty-two, though it appears he suffered from a languorous illness during the last year of his life.[4] He died in July 1854 and was buried in the Vitet family tomb at Montmartre cemetery, where his wife, son, and daughter-in-law would be buried as well. Amélie Vitet passed away in 1860, two years after Ludovic's wife.

With much of this book focused on the nitty-gritty of these families' lives, it makes sense to zoom out and consider the strategies these families employed to survive and even to thrive throughout the chaos and unpredictability of war and political upheaval. An exploration of the various strands of these families' stories reveals four main survival strategies: geographic mobility, the cultivation of relationships with trusted friends and allies, political savvy (and luck!), and a turn inward toward private, familial life. These strategies, which reflected and shaped their sense of identity both as bourgeois and as Lyonnais implants in Rouen and Paris, represent continuities with eighteenth-century practices like patronage intermingled with new approaches inspired by the postrevolutionary context.

Movement proved essential for both the Vitet and Arnaud-Tizon families. Louis and Pierre survived the year of the Terror by fleeing France and spending several months in exile. After Thermidor, they returned briefly to Lyon and then moved to Paris, leaving Marguerite behind. Like the Vitet father-and-son team, the Arnaud-Tizon brothers and their wives also left Lyon. Catherine and her children joined Pierre-Marie and his wife, daughter, and mother-in-law in Rouen around 1796, with Claude dividing his time between the two cities until 1811, when he sold his business and property in Lyon. After all that they had lived through between 1789 and 1794, it seems that both families preferred to build their lives elsewhere. They voted with their feet, as did many of their Lyonnais friends and acquaintances.

A second strategy these families deployed was what we might call networking. Here, they built on lessons learned during the eighteenth century, when patronage networks were so vital. Patronage did not stop with the Revolution; having the right people in the right places and marrying one's children into families that would reinforce and possibly expand those networks remained essential. Socializing was the primary tool for building and maintaining networks. Seeing and being seen at the right gatherings and events, making sure that marriageable daughters attended the right balls, and hosting dinners and other kinds of soirées were necessary as these families sought to solidify their positions. It is clear from the many letters they exchanged discussing such events that these families put huge effort and expense into their socializing and that these gatherings were about much more than amusing themselves.

A third strategy involved political savvy—following the evolving political situation, knowing when and how to voice their opinions and, perhaps more importantly, when *not* to voice them. Here, too, there was the possibility of voting with one's feet, as when Louis Vitet stepped away from politics following Brumaire. The depoliticization of public life visible during the Napoleonic period meant that public matters rarely came up in their letters, except for war and economic conditions, two important topics for a family trying to run a textile factory and needing to ship raw materials and finished goods. Politics became a much more prominent topic of discussion during the 1820s, when Pierre and Amélie attended debates in the legislature and their son, Ludovic, joined the liberal opposition. Some of the women in the family, particularly Amélie Arnaud-Tizon, wrote long, passionate letters about the political situation and followed legislative debates closely. In addition to voicing what can only be labeled feminist views about the unfair limitations placed upon women, she expressed gratitude that Ludovic was fighting for liberal constitutionalism, even mentioning how proud his grandfather would have been.[5]

A fourth strategy relates to the choice *not* to engage in public affairs; many family members—men and women alike—shifted their attention toward private, domestic concerns. In addition to viewing the home as a refuge, they recognized the benefits of not appearing in the limelight and appreciating, as Pierre put it, the "happiness of mediocrity."[6] Pierre spent most of his life as a *rentier* focused on managing his properties, raising and educating his son, corresponding with his extensive network of family and friends (virtually all Lyonnais), and socializing and otherwise enjoying the finer things in life, including his passion for landscape painting, something he shared with his lifelong friend, Alexandre-Hyacinthe Dunouy, a professional artist.

These survival strategies required the entire family's cooperation, across generations and genders, and their goals and implementation overlapped as well. Political discussions arose during social gatherings, and business ventures relied upon the connections developed through networking. Public and private concerns were necessarily interrelated. It was impossible to separate them, with businesses built upon marital alliances and run out of homes that also housed clerks and with the friends and family with whom they socialized also serving as their bankers and investors. Two Lyonnais bankers who ran a business together in Paris, Jacques Fournel and Vital Roux, were particularly trusted friends and allies. They and other close friends from Lyon gathered regularly in Paris, including at Marshal Suchet's home, creating a network of allies who supported each other in their public and private ventures. The people they relied upon were virtually all fellow Lyonnais whose ties went back decades, if not generations.

The overarching goals these strategies supported could also lead to tensions, as when the Arnaud-Tizon brothers-in-law had a falling out over the question of the youngest Arnaud-Tizon daughter's dowry. Financial matters and emotions often overlapped within these relations of dependence and interdependence across the generations and the different branches of the family. When relations did not go smoothly or when someone proved unreliable, as in the case of Gabriel Suchet, who had married into the Arnaud-Tizon family and faced financial ruin in 1817, the families went into crisis mode. Such breakdowns could have dire consequences, including the inability to ensure that future generations would have the financial wherewithal to marry well and continue to build the family's patrimony. That patrimony included both real wealth and more ephemeral or emotional forms of wealth and credibility, of honor and respect. No bourgeois family could hope to accomplish any of its goals if they could not maintain the foundation upon which all else depended: honor.

For the most part, these two families successfully navigated the transition to the new regime. Claude and Catherine Arnaud-Tizon could feel proud about their children's marriages and progeny, some of whom went on to illustrious careers. Pierre and Amélie's son, Ludovic, made it to the pinnacle of July Monarchy high society, marrying the niece of Casimir Périer, holding a variety of public positions, and publishing several books. Jacques Barbet's purchase of the Oberkampf factory at Jouy had both real and symbolic significance as he began calling himself Barbet de Jouy. His and Victoire's son, Henry Barbet de Jouy, became a curator of the Louvre in the mid-nineteenth-century, gaining celebrity for his successful efforts to protect the museum's collections during the Commune. Claude and Catherine's son, Ludovic Arnaud-Tizon, was less successful. Despite his best efforts, the business he inherited from his father never prospered, and his sons sought their fortunes elsewhere. One died in the Philippines in 1860. Another launched a business in the nearby port city of Le Havre, thanks to financial assistance from his mother's family.[7]

What do these families' stories tell us about the Revolution and the bourgeoisie? The Revolution did open doors for some wealthy non-nobles. Louis Vitet's properties included several *biens nationaux*, investments that provided the financial foundation that permitted his son to live as a *rentier* and his grandson to arrive at the very top of the social and political hierarchy in the 1830s. But the Revolution did not produce unmitigated paths toward success, as suggested by the extent to which Claude and Catherine had to impoverish themselves to assure their children's future "happiness." Starting in the early 1820s, as they were reaching old age, they lived with one or another of their children, in part because they had insufficient resources to support themselves. And Claude's brother, Pierre-Marie, who seems to have been the more financially successful of the two, struggled to establish his progeny because of the bad behavior of his son-in-law, Gabriel Suchet.

As a microhistory, this book invites questions regarding representativeness, and I would like to conclude by reflecting on that issue. My answer is that these families are representative of the Lyonnais bourgeoisie, whose strong sense of local identity shaped their life choices, particularly the alliances they maintained, but perhaps less so of the French bourgeoisie more generally. Maintaining alliances with a small circle of close friends, mostly people whom they had known their entire lives, seems like a particularly Lyonnais approach and reflects their distrust of outsiders.[8] If we zoom out further to consider the Vitets' and Arnaud-Tizons' cousins and allies who did not leave Lyon, we see that those who held more prominent positions during the Revolution and/or who had allied with more radical groups were more likely to move, while the more conservative ones and those who managed to stay out of politics altogether felt comfortable staying in their native city.

Finally, the turn inward toward private, domestic life seems quite generalizable, both during the First Empire, when the depoliticization of public life discouraged debate and discussion, and during the Restoration. We see similar tendencies beyond France in Biedermeier culture with its emphasis on the comfort and pleasures of the home, which was seen as a space of refuge after the Revolution and Napoleonic wars.[9] That some men, particularly those who had supported the Revolution, may have preferred to focus their lives on caring for their families, managing their properties, and generally avoiding the limelight during the Empire and Restoration is certainly not surprising.

Such life choices also highlight the porous boundaries of the public and private spheres during this period and the lack of clearly defined, specialized gender norms as well as the intersections between "rational" interest and "emotional" concerns. Many of the spaces and activities that structured these families' lives included both sexes and involved more shared responsibilities than classic studies of the bourgeoisie would suggest. This blurriness is especially visible in the life choices of the two people whose lives and words are at the center of this book: Catherine Arnaud-Tizon and Pierre Vitet. Catherine contributed to running the family business and spoke knowledgeably about financial matters, while Pierre devoted much of his time and energy to family matters. In addition, both were young adults in 1789; Pierre was born in 1772, and Catherine Arnaud-Tizon was born in 1764. Living through the entire Revolutionary era, with the sense of hope and possibility it created and the physical and human destruction it caused, must have left deep impressions. Their letters do not refer to those experiences explicitly; they never discuss the past, only the present and future. But those memories, along with their shared goals for the future, cemented the strong emotional bond that emerged between them as they corresponded about the family's struggles and triumphs and collaborated to accomplish their aims.

Notes

Introduction

1. CAT to PV and AV, October 27, 1806, AML Fonds Vitet 84II/12. Catherine Françoise Arnaud-Tizon always signed her letters "DA" for Descheaux Arnaud-Tizon. It was common practice to use maiden names; men even used their wives' maiden names to distinguish themselves from their brothers, as first names rarely appeared, except in reference to children and servants. Although I do not know which of her given names she used, I refer to her throughout this book as Catherine. To avoid confusion with so many people having the same last names, I generally refer to the members of the Arnaud-Tizon and Vitet families by their first names. Unless otherwise indicated, all translations are my own.

2. CAT to PV, November 13, 1806, AML 84II/12. Catherine uses the term *complaisance* frequently in her letters to Pierre. Depending on context, it can be translated as "indulgence" or "kindness." I explore the relationship that developed between Catherine and Pierre in Davidson, "A belle mère idéale." See also Verjus and Davidson, *Le roman conjugal*, 37.

3. Work connecting emotions to politics during the French Revolution underlines this point. See Linton, *Choosing Terror*, and Tackett, *Coming of the Terror.* On the history of emotions, see Rosenwein, "Worrying about Emotions," and Reddy, *Navigation of Feeling*.

4. On this "bewilderment," see Fritzsche, *Stranded in the Present*. Lynn Hunt concisely summed up this hugely significant consequence of the Revolution when she wrote "tradition lost its givenness." Hunt, *Politics, Culture and Class*, 12.

5. PVCJ is in AML 84II/8 and on microfilm.

6. The American ex-wife of a descendant of the Vitets contacted me when she heard about my research. She explained that the documents had been held in the family's chateau. When the collection went up for sale in 1995, the French National Archives purchased and subsequently divided it into two parts, with the older material housed at the AML and the more recent material, circa 1827 forward, housed at the AN. Acquisition details appear in the AML's inventory of the Fonds Vitet.

7. Goodman, *Becoming a Woman*. The literature on the emergence and evolution of the self in these years is huge. Studies that have influenced my understanding of this concept include Goldstein, *Post-Revolutionary Self*, and Wahrman, *Making of the Modern Self.*

8. See di Leonardo, "Female World," and Joris, "Kinship and Gender," 248–251.

9. On the utility and limitations of letters as sources, see Chartier, *La correspondance*; Grassi, *L'art de la lettre*; and Dauphin et al., *Ces bonnes lettres*. These studies demonstrate that historians should not treat letters as reflections of actual emotions

but rather as part of a set of ritualized practices people used to classify and evaluate their relations. The articles in a special issue of *FHS* entitled "Epistolary Gestures" address these methodological questions. Most relevant to this study is Rance, "Réseaux épistolaires."

10. On evolving attitudes toward sexual passion in marriage, see Corbin, *L'harmonie des plaisirs*, and Verjus and Davidson, *Le roman conjugal*.

11. PV to AV, July 25, 1810, AML 84II/9. Further reflection on this letter and Amélie's response to it, as well as the nature of Pierre and Amélie's relationship as revealed in their letters, appears in Verjus and Davidson, *Le roman conjugal*, 50–51.

12. Napoleon launched massive improvements to the postal system. See Marchand, *Le maître de poste*.

13. On the norms and practices associated with letter writing and its importance for maintaining family networks, see Lyons, *Reading Culture*, 173–177.

14. See, for example, Garrioch, *Formation of the Parisian Bourgeoisie*, 1–7. Although most historians no longer see class conflict as the primary driver of the French Revolution, that does not mean that economics have dropped out of the causal explanations they offer. In an important recent book, William H. Sewell Jr. argues that commercial capitalism and expanding notions of choice across classes, contributed to the outbreak of Revolution. Sewell, *Capitalism*, 5–7. Sewell's argument parallels those of Colin Jones in "Great Chain of Buying" and of Jones and Spang in "Sans-culottes, *sans café*."

15. Maza, *Myth of the French Bourgeoisie*.

16. Maza, "The Bourgeois Family Revisited," 41–42. See also Garrioch, *Formation of the Parisian Bourgeoisie*, 120–121, and Marraud, *De la ville à l'état*. On the cult of family happiness see Roberts, *Sentimental Savants*, and Adams, *A Taste for Comfort and Status*.

17. Maza, *Myth of the French Bourgeoise*, and Hunt, "La visibilité du monde bourgeois," in Jessenne, *Vers un ordre bourgeois*, 371–373. Many of Balzac's novels offer insights into early nineteenth-century bourgeois life and values. See Del Lungo and Glaudes, *Balzac, l'invention de la sociologie*; and Pasco, *Balzac, Literary Sociologist*. In his comparative study, *Modernity and Bourgeois Life*, Jerrold Seigel argues for the importance of networks and communication for understanding bourgeois society, a point that my book reinforces.

18. Daumard, *Les bourgeois et la bourgeoisie*, 48–49.

19. Le Wita, *French Bourgeois Culture*, 5. Two classic methodological statements about how everyday life and practices relate to identity construction include de Certeau, *Practice of Everyday Life*, and Bourdieu, *Outline of a Theory of Practice*. See also Gillis, *A World of Their Own Making*.

20. Pellissier, *Loisirs et sociabilités*, 125.

21. Quoted in Pellissier, *Loisirs et sociabilités*, 125.

22. Covering multiple generations of a family, Christopher Johnson's *Becoming Bourgeois* relies on letters to consider everyday practices, experiences, and emotions and develops an argument about bourgeois identity and strategizing that has many parallels to the findings presented here.

23. Vera Kaplan found similar continuities regarding elites' reliance on patronage networks and the emotional bonds that developed within them across another

revolutionary divide: that of the Russian Revolution. See Kaplan, "Weathering the Revolution."

24. On correspondence and networks, see Horowitz, *Friendship and Politics*, and Hennequin-Lecomte, *Le patriciat strasbourgeois*.

25. See Landes, *Women and the Public Sphere*, and Bonnie Smith, *Ladies of the Leisure Class*. In their classic study, *Family Fortunes*, Leonore Davidoff and Catherine Hall present separate spheres as a foundational ideology of middle-class identity. For critiques of separate spheres, see Steinbach, "Can We Still Use 'Separate Spheres'?," and Joris, "Kinship and Gender."

26. While later models of bourgeois masculinity required that men launch careers in the private or public sector, during the first decades of the nineteenth century, bourgeois men could choose to lead lives of leisure and focus on their families, cultural pursuits, and hobbies without raising eyebrows. See Rauch, *Crise de l'identité masculine*, chap. 3.

27. One of Pierre's closest friends, Alexandre Hyacinthe Dunouy, was a professional artist who served as the official court painter in Naples during the Napoleonic Empire. Pierre's passion for art and his intense devotion to his father and later his son are discussed in Verjus and Davidson, *Le roman conjugal*, 36.

28. Roberts, *Sentimental Savants*, and Verjus, *Le bon mari*. Studies that trace images of the *bon père* and the *bon citoyen* into the nineteenth century include Kingston, *Bureaucrats and Bourgeois Society*, and Harrison, *The Bourgeois Citizen*.

29. On sentimentalism, see Vincent-Buffault, *History of Tears*; Denby, *Sentimental Narrative*; and Cohen, *Sentimental Education*.

30. Reddy, *Invisible Code*, and Nye, *Masculinity*.

1. Eighteenth-Century Lyon

1. On Lyon's *négociants*, see Garden, *Lyon et les Lyonnais*, 364. On the Fabrique, see Edmonds, *Jacobinism and the Revolt of Lyon*, 10–15. A good overview of the economic history of Lyon within a broader French context appears in Smith, *Emergence of Modern Business*, 15–17 and 45–48.

2. Edmonds, *Jacobinism and the Revolt of Lyon*, 23–24.

3. Benoit, *L'identité politique de Lyon*.

4. Garden, *Lyon et les Lyonnais*, 39, and Edmonds, *Jacobinism and the Revolt of Lyon*, 9. That number includes the *faubourgs*, adjoining neighborhoods that were not technically part of the city. Most of these *faubourgs* were incorporated into the city in the 1850s.

5. Richard Cobb describes how Lyon's geography shaped the city's social makeup and created a strong sense of neighborhood identity. That geography also facilitated the ability of criminals to evade capture and helped make Lyon the capital of the resistance during World War Two. See Cobb, "Counter Revolution and Environment: The Example of Lyon," in Cobb, *Reactions to the Revolution*.

6. Reynard, *Ambitions Tamed*.

7. Garden, *Lyon et les Lyonnais*, 17.

8. On the medical professions, see Ramsey, *Professional and Popular Medicine*, and Brockliss and Jones, *Medical World*. On venal offices and their significance, see

Smith, *Nobility Reimagined*, 104–105. Sean Quinlan traces changing ideas about medical authority in late eighteenth and early nineteenth-century France in Quinlan, *Morbid Undercurrents*. On the changing status of surgeons, see Crosland, "*Officiers de Santé*," 230.

9. Saussac, "Louis Vitet." An essay published after the death of Louis's grandson, Ludovic, includes details on the family's origins and the elder Louis's education and career: Sauzet, "Hommage à la mémoire de Ludovic Vitet."

10. Pariset, "Notice sur Louis Vitet," an eight-page obituary filed among Pierre Vitet's papers in AML 84II/3. It dates from 1809, shortly after Louis's death. Much of it was reproduced and merged with more details on Louis's medical career and political activities in "Notice sur Louis Vitet" (1836).

11. Trénard, *Lyon de l'Encyclopédie au pré-romantisme*, 1: 122 (quoting from a 1786 pamphlet describing the program). On midwifery, see Gelbart, *The King's Midwife*.

12. Trénard, *Lyon de l'Encyclopédie au pré-romantisme*, 1: 185–195.

13. Trénard describes Lyon as the Masonic capital of France and mentions Vitet's involvement in the Académie. *Lyon de l'Encyclopédie au pré-romantisme*, 1: 79–81. Older studies highlighted Freemasonry's subversive tendencies, while more recent ones emphasize its role as a form of sociability. See Allen, "Politics of Sociability."

14. Garden, *Lyon et les Lyonnais*, 417.

15. A copy of their marriage contract is in AML 84II/3.

16. Feuga, "Les malheurs de Madame Vitet."

17. The AML makes available digitized birth, death, and marriage records for the city and its environs, including the baptismal registries of the Saint-Nizier parish. AML, Etat Civil, accessed January 21, 2025, https://recherches.archives-lyon.fr/page/etat-civil.

18. Half of babies sent to wet nurses in the countryside around Lyon died during the first two years of life. See Garden, *Lyon et les Lyonnais*, 116–140.

19. Sauzet, "Hommage," 194–195. The references are to Camille Jordan (1771–1821) and the Périer brothers, including Casimir Périer (1777–1832), a future minister who also studied at the College de l'Oratoire. Jordan opposed the Revolution and then joined the liberal opposition during the Restoration. Tulard et al., *Histoire et dictionnaire de la Révolution française*, 902, and Rémusat, *Notice historique de Casimir Périer*, 12–13.

20. On the Oratorians, see Palmer, *Improvement of Humanity*, 15–18.

21. Chassagne, "Du drap et de la toile," 75–76.

22. CM June 17, 1781, Formental *aîné*, notary, ADR 3E/5110. The groom's year of birth appears in research notes given to me by Paul Feuga and Serge Chassagne. A nineteenth-century reference work indicates that he died in Paris in March or April 1815. Bréghot du Lut and Pericaud, *Biographie lyonnaise*, 144. However, PVCJ mentions his death in March 1814.

23. Marriage registry, Paroisse St-Candé le Jeune, Rouen, Pierre-Marie Arnaud-Tizon and Anne-Françoise Vincent, June 30, 1779, ADSM, Etat Civil, 5 Mi 0473. It was later recorded by the priest of the Saint-Nizier parish in Lyon. See also Chassagne, "Du drap et de la toile," 77.

24. Leslie Walker's study of eighteenth-century French novels and their treatment of girls' strong attachment to their mothers sheds light on this preference. Walker, *A Mother's Love*, 35.

25. Baptism recorded June 29, 1783. Digitized parish records for Saint Nizier, AML 1GG130.

26. The age of majority in eighteenth-century France was generally twenty-five, though parental consent for marriage was required for men up to age thirty. Revolutionary legislation dating from 1792 reduced the age of majority to twenty-one; under the 1804 Civil Code the age to marry without parental consent remained twenty-one for women but was raised to twenty-five for men. See Traer, *Marriage and Family*, chap. 5 and 186–187, and Desan, *Family on Trial*, 60–62 and 293.

27. CM January 23, 1783, AML 84II/7, and digitized Saint Pierre-Saint Saturin parish records, AML 1GG130.

28. Garden, *Lyon et les Lyonnais*, 358. The average dowry among *négociants* was 37,300 livres. Among *hommes de loi*, such as Louis's cousin François Vitet, the average dowry was 41,700. Only noble dowries averaged over 100,000. The Arnaud-Tizon brothers and their wives were thus very rich by any standard.

29. Testament, August 3, 1791, ADR 3E/5119.

30. Baptism, April 29, 1785, digitized Saint-Nizier parish records, AML 1GG132. On the networks visible through the signatures on such documents, see Rothschild, *Infinite History*.

31. Lyonnais godparents frequently came from within family circles. Couriel, "La place de la parenté." On aunts and uncles as godparents, see Trévisi, *Au cœur de la parenté*, chap. 4. A comparative study of godparents in European history places these practices into a broader context: Fine, *Parrains, marraines*.

32. I appreciate Paul Feuga's willingness to share his research notes on the Arnaud-Tizon brothers' involvement in local institutions.

33. Garden, *Lyon et les Lyonnais*, 530.

34. Garden, *Lyon et les Lyonnais*, 530, quoting from *Agenda du Bureau de la Charité, ou principales règles . . . lit aux recteurs nouvellement nommés*.

35. Serving as a rector on a hospital board was a prerequisite for entry into other local institutions that led to ennoblement. See Edmonds, *Jacobinism and the Revolt of Lyon*, 20–21.

36. My account of the Revolution in Lyon draws on W. D. Edmonds's deeply researched and detailed *Jacobinism and the Revolt of Lyon* as well as Wahl, *Premières années de la Révolution*. A concise and lucid discussion also appears in Hanson, *Jacobin Republic*, 139–154. A dissertation on Jean-Jacques Ampère, father of the celebrated physicist and mathematician, provides an excellent overview: Johnson, "Revolutionary Justice in Lyon." See also Johnson, *The Candle and the Guillotine*.

37. Tackett, *Becoming a Revolutionary*.

38. On how the Revolution transformed participants' views and emotional states, see Burstin, *Révolutionnaires*, and Hunt, "Experience of Revolution."

39. Blanc, *Un pasteur du temps des Lumières*, 125. Blanc describes the club as having been formed through the initiative of Vitet, Frossard, and Gilibert, with inspiration from Roland. He also mentions François Vitet's membership in the Société du Concert in the context of his election to the Conseil Général of the department (135). Nathan Perl-Rosenthal analyzes correspondence practices among the "Rolandins" and their relationship to political clubs in Lyon. See Perl-Rosenthal, "Corresponding Republics," chap. 3.

40. Edmonds, *Jacobinism and the Revolt of Lyon*, 48–49 and 65. Vitet's colleague and friend Jean-Emmanuel Gilibert served as the club's president in 1791. Wahl, *Premières années de la Révolution*, 394. On Gilibert's career as a doctor and later Revolutionary politician, see Hanson, *Jacobin Republic*, 111–112. On Claude Arnaud-Tizon's commitment to the patriot cause and his political responsibilities, see Bergasse, "Un Janseniste lyonnais," 15–16.

41. See Edmonds, "Rise and Fall of Popular Democracy," and Edmonds, *Jacobinism and the Revolt of Lyon*, chap. 3 and app. III.

42. Edmonds, *Jacobinism and the Revolt of Lyon*, 52.

43. Roland was purged from the Convention in summer 1793 and fled Paris. Before that, he had served as interior minister. The literature on Roland and his famous wife, Manon Phlipon, aka Madame Roland, and the so-called Girondins is very large. It includes Oliver, *Orphans on the Earth*, and May, *Madame Roland*. In her dual biography of the couple, *Marriage and Revolution*, Siân Reynolds explores their relationship and their political views and activities. Roland's ideas about improving society through politics are explained in Walton, *Policing Public Opinion*, chap. 8.

44. Edmonds, *Jacobinism and the Revolt of Lyon*, 89–91, and Saussac, "Louis Vitet," 22.

45. Digitized Saint-Nizier parish records, AML 1GG219.

46. *Journal de M. Suleau*, no. 5 (July 16, [1791]), 27–28. A later attack on the chateau, which ended with Guillin de Montet being killed and dismembered by the crowd, took place on June 25, 1791. On the attack on the Guillin family's chateau in Polymieux, see Johnson, "Revolutionary Justice," 80–83, and Tackett, *When the King Took Flight*, 174. Côme Simien discusses this event in *Les massacres de septembre 1792*, 140–141.

47. PVCJ, entry dated March 25, 1814, but written after April heading.

48. Claude Arnaud-Tizon appears on virtually every page of the minutes of the municipal council from 1790 to 1792. *Procès-verbaux des séances des Corps Municipaux*. His role in taking down and melting the statue appears in vol. 3, 356. Claude's political activities and affiliations are discussed in Verjus and Davidson, *Le roman conjugal*, 35.

49. Johnson, "Revolutionary Justice," 129–130, and Eynard, *Joseph Chalier*, 73.

50. Wahl, *Premières années de la Révolution*, 365–366, and Trénard, *Lyon de l'Encyclopédie au pré-romantisme*, 1: 250. Julie Johnson traces Lyonnais women's involvement in politics through the story of one activist woman, Françoise Perris. See Johnson, "The 'Fury.'"

51. When he heard about women's clubs in the provinces, the Parisian journalist Louis-Marie Prudhomme told the women of Lyon to return to their homes. "Club de femmes à Lyon," *Les Révolutions de Paris* 19, no. 185 (January 19–26, 1793): 234–235, quoted in Offen, *European Feminisms*, 61–62. On these clubs, see Desan, "Constitutional Amazons."

52. Edmonds, *Jacobinism and the Revolt of Lyon*, 109. Walton discusses the play and debates about banning it in *Policing Public Opinion*, 171–172. Rosalie Jullien, the wife and mother of two prominent revolutionaries, whose letters reflect her intense political engagement, has attracted significant attention. See Parker, *Writing the Revolution*, and Duprat, *"Les affaires d'état sont mes affaires de cœur."*

53. On this event and its consequences, see Tackett, *When the King Took Flight*, and Ozouf, *Varennes*.

54. See Eynard, *Joseph Chalier*, and Hanson, "Voices from the Streets in the French Revolution," in Vincent and Klairmont-Lingo, *Human Tradition in Modern France*, 12–15.

55. Saussac, "Louis Vitet," 24.

56. Vitet to Roland, August 25, 1792, quoted in Edmonds, *Jacobinism and the Revolt of Lyon*, 123.

57. For a full account of this event and analysis of Vitet's involvement, see Simien, *Les massacres de septembre 1792*.

58. Vitet to Roland, November 1792, quoted in Trénard, *Lyon de l'Encyclopédie au pré-romantisme*, 1: 243.

59. Pariset, "Notice sur Louis Vitet," 461.

60. Edmonds, *Jacobinism and the Revolt of Lyon*, 275.

61. See Gelbart, "Death in the Bathtub," in Vincent and Klairmont-Lingo, *Human Tradition in Modern France*, and Mazeau, *Le bain de l'histoire*.

62. Edmonds, *Jacobinism and the Revolt of Lyon*, 137.

63. Johnson, "Revolutionary Justice," 180.

64. Hanson, *Jacobin Republic*, 193.

65. Hanson, *Jacobin Republic*, 221.

66. *Procès-verbaux des séances des Corps Municipaux*, vol. 5, Year II [1793–1794].

67. Edmonds, *Jacobinism and the Revolt of Lyon*, 220.

68. Passport for Pierre-Marie Arnaud-Tizon, place St. Nizier 42, to travel to Rouen with his wife, Anne-Françoise Adélaïde, and their servant Claudine Valencot, 3 Pluviôse Year II (January 22, 1794), AML 2I/70, no. 1806. The Revolutionary calendar, which defined Year I as beginning in September 1792 with the creation of the First Republic, remained in effect through 1805. When citing documents from those years, I provide both the original date and a conversion to the Gregorian calendar.

69. ADR, 1Q 339, no. 140.

70. Vitet, *Notes et souvenirs*, 10. The manuscript is held in AML 84II/7. Hulot, *Le Maréchal Suchet*, 18, and Bergerot, *Le Maréchal Suchet*, 17.

71. Vitet, *Notes et souvenirs*, 14. Louis's arrest was announced on July 11, 1793. Wahl, *Premières années de la Révolution*, 288.

72. Vitet, *Notes et souvenirs*, 14.

73. Vitet, *Notes et souvenirs*, 17.

74. Vitet, *Notes et souvenirs*, 31.

75. Vitet, *Notes et souvenirs*, 42–43.

76. Vitet, *Notes et souvenirs*, 56. The two compatriots were Théodore Vernier and Pierre-Athanase-Marie Babey; both were lawyers and deputies from the Jura who had been purged from the Convention. For more on Louis and Pierre's time in exile, see Davidson, "*Notes et souvenirs*," 219–221.

77. See Baczko, *Ending the Terror*, and Steinberg, *Afterlives of the Terror*. Michel Biard and Marisa Linton argue that using "the Terror" to label this phase of the Revolution is misleading. See Biard and Linton, *Terror*.

78. Hanson, *Jacobin Republic*, 221.

79. "Arrêté des représentants du peuple Charlier et Pocholle, qui désigne 21 citoyens pour être saisis, conduits à la maison d'arrêt des Recluses, et de là être transférés

dans une maison d'arrêt à Paris. Commune Affranchie, 18 Vendémiaire Year III (9 October 1794)," *Catalogue de la bibliothèque lyonnaise de M. Coste*, 227, ref. 5203.

80. The list of those arrested indicates that "Arnaud-Tison, ex-officier municipale," was "arrested, taken to Paris, and released by the Comité de Sureté Générale." The arrest order, dated 13 Vendémiare Year III (October 4, 1794), came from the Comité de Sureté Générale. The documents related to these arrests are held in AML 12II/11. Another man listed among those who were arrested, but who was released immediately, was Fournel *cadet*, someone who would remain a close friend and ally of the Vitet and Arnaud-Tizon families for decades.

81. A letter dated 29 Vendémiare Year III (October 20, 1794) ordered the search and sealing of Claude Arnaud-Tizon's home following his arrest. The search took place three days later. The four-page document includes a long list of all the furniture and household items they found in each room. It was signed by Bournichon, the same man who signed the death registry for Claude *père* in 1793. ADR 1Q 678.

82. See Brown, *Ending the French Revolution*, and Sutherland, *Murder in Aubagne*.

2. Recovery

1. Two of the most valuable and relevant studies of Rouen and its inhabitants are Chaline, *Les bourgeois de Rouen*, and Daly, *Inside Napoleonic France*.

2. Chassagne, "Du drap et de la toile," 77.

3. Coincidently, when Jean-Marie Roland lived in the city as a young man, he socialized with a prominent family who lived on the same "ancient, winding, Rouen street." May, *Madame Roland*, 75.

4. On typical housing layouts and uses of space, see Chaline, *Les bourgeois de Rouen*, 170–190.

5. Acte de naissance, Adelle Arnaudtizon, 29 Fructidor Year VI (September 15, 1798), ADSM Etat Civil, 5 Mi 0566. In this document, her name is spelled "Adelle," but in the family's letters, it is spelled "Adèle."

6. On this point, see Davidson, "Local Identities."

7. "Levée de séquestre pour la maison dite de la Jurary," 28 Fructidor Year II (September 14, 1794), AML 84II/3. Although this document was signed six weeks after Robespierre's execution, the authorities continued to refer to themselves as "*sans-culottes administrateurs provisoires de la campagne de commune affranchie.*" Pierre signed the document that lifted the seals on his father's house on the rue Port Chalet. Mainlevée de sequestre, 17 Nivôse Year III (January 6, 1795), ADR 1Q/827. Louis was probably already in Paris.

8. Laissez-passer, 19 Pluviôse Year III (February 7, 1795), AML 84II/7. PVCJ includes several references to paintings Pierre sent to friends and family members during these years.

9. Mainlevée de séquestre, 22 Ventôse Year III (March 12, 1795), ADR 1Q/827.

10. See Spang, *Stuff and Money*.

11. PVCJ, draft of letter to Birbel *fils, chargé du soin de notre campagne*, Pluviôse Year IV (January/February 1796).

12. The first of these surgeries took place on 5 Brumaire Year VI (October 26, 1797) and the next one a month later. PVCJ, entry dated 5 Brumaire Year VI. He wrote in the same entry that he only began to feel better in late January (*fin* Nivôse).

13. Bill of sale dated 6 Pluviôse Year VI (January 25, 1798), AN Minutier Central, étude V, 962. The document indicates that Blondel had purchased the building that had housed the congregation of the sisters of Saint Anne on 27 Prairial Year IV (June 15, 1796) for 27,000 francs. Reflecting the confusion associated with this period, the document alternates between two terms for the French currency, *livres* (the older term) and *francs* (the newer one).

14. PV to Louis Vitet, 27 Floréal Year VI (May 16, 1798), AML 84II/9. The name *Audiffret* appears in many of Pierre's letters. One branch of an old noble family from Dauphiné, they were close family friends.

15. Brown, *Ending the French Revolution.*

16. PV to Louis Vitet, 27 Floréal Year VI (May 16, 1798), AML 84II/9.

17. PV to Louis Vitet, 27 Floréal Year VI (May 16, 1798), AML 84II/9.

18. PV to Louis Vitet, 27 Floréal Year VI (May 16, 1798), AML 84II/9.

19. PV to Louis Vitet, 27 Floréal Year VI (May 16, 1798), AML 84II/9.

20. PV to Louis Vitet, 27 Floréal Year VI (May 16, 1798), AML 84II/9. Pierre used the familiar *tu* with his father but used *vous*, the formal version of *you*, with his mother.

21. Louis Vitet to PV, 13 Fructidor Year VI (August 30, 1798), AML 84II/11.

22. Undated request by PV, *officier de santé*, to remain in Paris, AN F7 10821 B 2. In his request, Pierre explained that on 27 Frimaire Year IV (December 18, 1795), the minister of war had granted him permission to pursue his studies in Paris until his services were needed in military hospitals. He had recently returned to Lyon, where "family affairs had kept him for five months," and was now requesting permission once again to remain in Paris. A letter in the file addressed to Citoyen Vitet, *Représentant du people au Conseil des 500*, and dated 16 Brumaire Year VII (November 6,1798) requested more information. The permission was granted on 18 Brumaire Year VII (November 8).

23. See Komlos, "An Antropometric History." John Komlos based his calculations on the measurement of one "*pouce*," or what he calls a "French inch," 2.706667 centimeters. Today's "inch" is 2.54 centimeters.

24. Military orders from Joubert, Year VII, AML 84II/7. The "Army of Italy" refers to the French forces that invaded and occupied much of the Italian peninsula in the late 1790s.

25. Quinlan, *Morbid Undercurrents*, 15. See also Crosland, "*Officiers de Santé.*"

26. Bergerot, *Le Maréchal Suchet*, 54–55. Joubert died in August of that year.

27. PVCJ, entry for letter to MV, 30 Germinal Year VIII (April 20, 1800). On these practices, see Woloch, *New Regime*, 397–404, and Heuer, "Neither Cowardly nor Greedy?"

28. On the appeal of living as a *rentier*, see Alain Plessis, "Une France bourgeoise," in Burguière and Revel, *Histoire de la France*, 4: 248–250.

29. One account that cannot be verified indicates that Louis "numbered among those who resisted to the very end the invasion of the legislature at [the Palace of] Saint Cloud and presented his bare chest to the weapons of the invaders." Sauzet, "Hommage à la mémoire de Ludovic Vitet," 193.

30. David G. Troyanksy examines the practices and ideas associated with retirement and old age in France during these years, emphasizing, as I do in this book, the blending of private and public concerns, of family and careers. See Troyansky, *Entitlement and Complaint*, chap. 2, esp. 120,

31. PVCJ includes entries about his trip to Lyon in Messidor Year IX (June 1801), including the line "wrote to my father via [*par la voix de*] Arnaud-Tizon."

32. A biography of Vital Roux appears in Szramkiewicz, *Les régents et censeurs de la Banque de France*, 358–365. Roux sided with the Jacobins following the siege of Lyon and had to take refuge in Paris afterward. He probably worked alongside Claude when he was serving as a municipal officer while the city was under Jacobin control.

33. PVCJ, entry for letter to Jauntet, 7 Ventôse Year VII (February 25, 1799), "Roux & Fournel are establishing a business [*vont établir une maison de commerce*] and will be moving." Like his business partner, Jean Jacques Fournel served as a municipal officer in Lyon in 1794, and like Claude, he was briefly arrested and had his home sealed and searched. AML 12II/11 and ADR 1Q/678.

34. [Salm], "Rapport sur les fleurs artificielles de la citoyenne Roux-Montagnat par Constance de Th. Pipelet de la Société du Lycée des Arts lu par l'auteur à la 59e séance publique du 30 Vendémiaire an 7." The date of the report corresponds to October 21, 1798.

35. CM, 11 Frimaire Year X (December 2, 1801), AN Minutier Central, étude IX, 866. On marriage contracts as mechanisms for transferring property from one generation to the next, see Lanza, *From Wives to Widows*, 39–50.

36. The prevalence of female witnesses on this contract contrasts with the findings of Marion Trévisi, whose quantitative research revealed that uncles appeared in this role more often than aunts. "Even though aunts were permitted to serve as witnesses for their nephews' and nieces' marriages, they did not do so frequently, except among the most advantaged social milieu." Trévisi, *Au cœur de la parenté*, 200. The Vitet and Arnaud-Tizon families numbered among "the most advantaged."

37. PVCJ, entries dated 12 Brumaire Year IX (November 4, 1801) and 19 Frimaire Year X (December 10, 1801).

38. PVCJ, entry for letter to CLAT, 27 Frimaire Year X (December 18, 1801).

39. Hulot, *Le Maréchal Suchet*, 21. For more details on the Suchet brothers during the Directory and early Consulate, see *Mémoires de Madame la duchesse d'Abrantès*, 1: 176–178. According to d'Abrantès, Gabriel ran his brother's household near Toulon like a wife.

40. PVCJ, entries for letters to Louis Vitet, Nivôse and Pluviose Year X (January 1802). PVCJ entries for letters to Suchet, 27 Nivôse and 3 Pluviôse Year X (January 17 and 23, 1802).

41. PVCJ, entries for letter to CAT, 26 Pluviôse and 14 Ventôse Year X (February 15 and March 5, 1802).

42. PVCJ, entry for letter to MV to be delivered by CAT, who left for Lyon on 8 Ventôse Year X (February 27, 1802).

43. PVCJ, entry for letter to CLAT, 30 Ventôse Year X (March 21, 1802). Suchet left for Rouen on 13 Germinal Year X (April 3, 1802).

44. According to PVCJ, they traveled together to Rouen on 21 Priarial Year X (June 10, 1802).

45. PVCJ, "arrivée à Paris avec Mr. Arnaud-Tizon et Ludovic qui vont à Lyon," 2 Thermidor Year X (July 21, 1802).

46. "Amélie écrit à sa cousine Madame Suchet," PVCJ, 9 Fructidor Year X (August 27, 1802).

47. Hulot, *Le Maréchal Suchet*, 87–88, and Bergerot, *Le Maréchal Suchet*, 84.

48. Bergerot, *Le Maréchal Suchet*, 97. Bergerot says the Suchet brothers bought Saint Just together in 1807, but later correspondence (discussed in chap. 6) suggests that Gabriel bought it on his own.

49. Marduel to Pierre and Louis Vitet, 1 Fructidor [Year X] (August 19, 1802), AML 84II/3.

50. Corbin discusses attitudes toward sex during this period and the definition of "good sex" in *L'harmonie des plaisirs*, chap. 2. He examines the proscriptions and prescriptions regarding married couples' sexual behavior in chap. 8, "Le lit conjugal: ses interdits et ses plaisirs." The assumption that women needed to experience pleasure to conceive remained in place. See Laqueur, *Making Sex*.

51. PVCJ, entry for letter to Louis Vitet, 22 Priarial Year X (June 11, 1802), and "arrivés à Paris," 2 Thermidor Year X (July 21, 1802).

52. PVCJ, entry dated 26 Vendémiaire Year XI (October 18, 1802).

53. *Extrait de l'acte de naissance*, AML 84II/15.

54. PVCJ, entry for letter to MV, 4 Frimaire Year XI (November 25, 1802). His last letter to Catherine was dated 2 *jours complémentaires* Year X (September 19, 1802). She must have traveled to Paris right after that.

55. References to the unhealthy, polluted air of Paris abound in memoirs from the period. See Fierro, *La vie des Parisiens*, 13. Many wealthy families viewed it as unthinkable to raise an infant in that environment. On arguments for maternal nursing in the late eighteenth century, see Schiebinger, *Nature's Body*, 65–74. On wet nursing, see Sussman, *Selling Mothers' Milk*.

56. Sussman, *Selling Mothers' Milk*, 27.

57. PVCJ, entry for letter to CAT, 28 Ventôse XI (March 19, 1802).

58. Sussman, *Selling Mothers' Milk*, 36.

59. PVCJ, "to my mother: sending her a portrait that I made of Amélie with Catherine [who was traveling to Lyon]," 29 Thermidor Year X (August 17, 1802). The Catherine to whom Pierre was referring here was Amélie's childhood maid, thus his use of her first name. Also from Lyon, Catherine worked for the Arnaud-Tizons for many years before quitting to marry a man name Brun later in life. A long letter Catherine Brun sent to AV in November 1813 is quoted at length in Verjus and Davidson, *Le roman conjugal*, 119–120.

60. According to PVCJ, they left Paris on 7 Prairial Year XI (May 27, 1803) and returned to the capital on 25 Thermidor (August 13).

61. Feuga, "Les malheurs de Madame Vitet," focuses on these years of separation.

62. PVCJ, 5 Thermidor XI (August 13, 1803). "Wrote to *la maman* Arnaudtison to announce our arrival. Wrote to *le papa* Arnaudtison à Lyon."

63. According to PVCJ, they left for Rouen on 28 Nivôse XII (January 19, 1804) and returned to Paris on 7 Ventôse XII (February 27, 1804).

64. PVCJ, 17 Ventôse Year XII (March 8, 1804).

65. Sussman, "Parisian Infants," 650.

66. PVCJ, entries for letters to MV, 12 Floréal Year 13 (May 2, 1805), "upcoming inoculation of Ludovic," and to CAT 20 Floréal Year 13 (May 10, 1805); entry for letters to CAT and MV, 28 Floréal Year 13 (May 18, 1805). On inoculation and fathers' roles in the process, see Roberts, *Sentimental Savants*, chap. 3. Smallpox "inoculation," a pro-

cess that involved introducing smallpox germs under the skin, began to be replaced by "vaccination," which infected the person with cowpox (a much milder version of the illness) around 1798 (Roberts, *Sentimental Savants*, 73). Though Pierre uses the term "inoculation," Ludovic probably received the less risky cowpox vaccination.

67. PVCJ, entry for letter to MV, 13 Thermidor Year 13 (August 1, 1805), "I am sending her a dress of colored percale with Mr. Arnaud-Tizon."

68. They left for Rouen on 1 Messidor Year XII (June 20, 1804).

69. PVCJ, letters to his mother, 3 Messidor and 19 Messidor Year XII (June 22 and July 8, 1804). Louis arrived on 20 Messidor Year XII (July 9, 1804) and returned to Paris on 1 Thermidor (July 20).

70. PVCJ, "to *messieurs* Roux et Fournel, sending shells for their ladies [*à leurs dames*]," 8 Thermidor Year XII (July 27); "return to Paris," 4 Fructidor Year XII (August 22, 1804); and entries dated 19 Frimaire Year XIII (December 10, 1804) and 17 Nivôse Year XIII (January 7, 1805).

71. PVCJ, entry for letter to his father, 11 Nivôse Year XIII (January 1, 1805).

3. Turning the Page

1. Brown, *Ending the French Revolution*, and Woloch, *Napoleon and His Collaborators.*

2. Woloch, *New Regime*, and Doyle, *Napoleon at Peace.*

3. See Haynes, *Our Friends the Enemies.*

4. In an 1805 letter, Marguerite Vitet complained about not yet laying eyes on her grandson: "You are pushing my patience to its limits in making me wait until then to meet my grandson [*mon bon petit fils*]." MV to PV, July 22, 1805, AML 84II/11. Pierre was in Rouen at that point visiting with his in-laws, having postponed a trip to Lyon.

5. Feuga, "Les malheurs de Madame Vitet." For further discussion of the nature of their relationship, see Verjus and Davidson, *Le roman conjugal*, 32–33.

6. PVCJ, entry for letter to Louis Vitet, October 13, 1806: "Replied to my father who wrote to announce that my mother will be staying in Paris this winter."

7. PVCJ, entry dated December 19, 1808. "Arrival of my mother in Paris, Monday December 19, at 5 a.m. on the Burgundy stagecoach. Snowy weather, bad road conditions, Saône overflowing its banks."

8. Mery Fournel to AV, July 25, 1809, AML 84II/10.

9. On conjugal life during this period, including a discussion of this couple's relationship, see Verjus and Davidson, *Le roman conjugal.*

10. PV to AV, April 29, 1820, AML 84II/9.

11. PV to AV, May 15, 1820, AML 84II/9.

12. CM, June 10, 1808, ADSM 2E3/127, *étude* Boutrolle. Serge Chassagne discusses the Barbet/Arnaud-Tizon mariage contract in *Le coton et ses patrons*, 553. Such financial arrangements were typical among wealthy families. Susan K. Foley explores two cases in which dowries were paid over ten years with interest in *Republican Passions*, 199–200.

13. One such drawing appears above the entry for Vendémiaire Year XII (the first month of the year in the Revolutionary calendar). On Freemasonry in prerevolutionary Lyon, see Trénard, *Lyon de l'Encyclopédie au pré-romantisme,* 1: 76–79.

14. Vitet quoted in Eynard, *Joseph Chalier*, 40.

15. CAT to PV, March 28, 1812, AML 84II/12.

16. CAT to PV, May 26, 1821, AML 84II/13.

17. MV to AV, August 10, 1811, AM 84II/11.

18. Davidson, "Women at Napoleonic Festivals."

19. On the eighteenth-century "calico craze," see Rosenfeld, "Of Revolutions and the Problem of Choice." On the global context and significance of the cotton trade, see Beckert, *Empire of Cotton*.

20. Few bourgeois families had more than three children, even though women typically married very young, suggesting that they relied on some form of contraception, most likely coitus interruptus.

21. Chassagne, *Oberkampf*, 331n39.

22. For more on the Barbet and Oberkampf families, see Chassange, *Le coton et ses patrons*, 553–556. See also Chassagne, *Oberkampf*, for a history of that business from its origins in the 1760s to its liquidation in the 1840s.

23. CM, August 28, 1812, private collection. I am grateful to Monique Augustin-Normand for granting me permission to photograph this and other documents in her possession in 2007.

24. Serge Chassagne discusses the couple's progeny in "Du drap et de la toile," 78–79.

25. The business went by the name Paillot frères et Riocreux; the men involved were probably brothers-in-law. *Almanach du commerce de Paris*, 464 and 810.

26. Jacques Barbet to PV, April 25, 1825, AML 84II/9; and PVCJ, April 22 and 24, 1825.

27. PVCJ, entries dated November 11 and 13, 1831; entry for letter to CLAT, November 17, 1831, and entry for letter to AAT, November 21, 1831; and CAT to PV, November 12 and 14, 1831, AN 572AP/4.

28. CLAT to PV, November 14 and 16, 1831; and CAT to PV, November 14, 1831, AN 572AP/4. PVCJ, entries for letter to CAT, December 8 and 14, and to AAT, December 24, 1831.

29. Greene, "Romanticism, Cultural Nationalism," 488. Pierre wrote that Ludovic intended to complete his degree: "Ludovic will be returning for his last year of law school and will be working for a lawyer" (PVCJ, entry for letter to Tante Morel, October 19, 1822). However, he never practiced law.

30. Charles Tanneguay Duchâtel (1802–1867) followed an educational and career trajectory that paralleled Ludovic's: he studied law, numbered among the founders of the liberal publication, *Le Globe*, and served in various positions during the July Monarchy. Unlike Ludovic, he came from a noble family; he was a count. Picot, *Le Comte Duchâtel*.

31. Ludovic wrote frequently to his parents during this trip. The letters are in AML 84II/15.

32. Goblot, *La jeune France libérale*, 53. For an analysis of similar friendship and familial networks among men one generation younger than Ludovic Vitet, see Foley, *Republican Passions*.

33. Theis, *François Guizot*, 129. In a letter Guizot sent to his daughter shortly after Ludovic's death in 1873, he praised the man who had been such a loyal and steadfast friend. According to that letter, Guizot met Ludovic when he entered the Ecole Normale at the age of seventeen, and they remained lifelong friends from that moment on. Witt, *Monsieur Guizot in Private Life*, 349. See also Guizot's introduc-

tion to Ludovic Vitet, *Études philosophiques*. Guizot gives an overview of Ludovic's life and career, including the fact that he chose to stop studying law and focus on research and writing, first history and then art criticism. Two good online sources on Ludovic's life can be found at "François Guizot: Une vie dans le siècle (1787–1874)," accessed January 21, 2025, https://www.guizot.com/fr/amities/louis-vitet/; and Alain Bonnet's entry on Vitet on the website of the Institut National d'Histoire de l'Art, accessed January 21, 2025, https://www.inha.fr/fr/ressources/publications/publications-numeriques/dictionnaire-critique-des-historiens-de-l-art/vitet-ludovic.html.

34. Among his many publications are *La mort de Henri III* and *Études sur les beaux-arts*.

35. On this point, see Horowitz, *Friendship and Politics*.

36. Letters of condolence referring to Catherine's sudden passing appear in AN Fonds Vitet, 572AP/5.

37. PMAT refers to this delay and mentions others who contracted cholera, including Adèle Riocreux and Cécile Périer's mother, in a letter to PV, April 12, 1832, AN 572AP/5.

38. CM, October 19, 1832, AML 84II/15. One mysterious detail appears on Ludovic's marriage contract: It refers to his *soeur germaine* (sister by the same parents) as Julie Clémentine Vitet. That name appears nowhere else in the family's papers or in official documents. The only logical explanation is that the notary made a mistake when recording Ludovic's sister's name.

39. Guizot, quoted in Theis, *François Guizot*, 130.

40. On the pull of local identities and memory, see Saunier, *L'esprit Lyonnais*; Gerson, *Pride of Place*; and Davidson, "Local Identities."

41. Jacques Barbet bought this land near the rue de Varenne in 1836 and divided it into lots, which he then resold. Chassagne, *Oberkampf*, 325. A later (1929) architectural drawing of the residences along the street is in AML 84II/21. By that point, the Vitets' building had passed to the Costa de Beauregard family.

42. PV's death registry appears to have been lost, but letters held among Ludovic's papers indicate that Pierre died in late July 1854 after a year-long period when he required extensive care. He may have had a stroke. See François Guizot to LV, August 1, 1854, AN 572AP/10. According to digitized Parisian cemetery records available on the website of the Archives of Paris, Pierre was buried in Montmartre cemetery on July 28. Accessed January 21, 2025, https://archives.paris.fr/r/216/cimetieres/.

43. Amélie's death registry, dated May 21, 1860, is in the digitized *état civil* records of the Archives de Paris.

44. Serbat, "Eugène Aubry-Vitet (1845–1930)."

45. When he returned from the first trip, Marc published a report he prepared for the Rouen Chamber of Commerce: Arnaudtizon, *Exploration commerciale*. See also Cottez, "Notes sur un voyage commercial," and "Essai sur Marc Arnaudtizon." I am grateful to Madame Augustin-Normand, a descendant of Claudius Arnaud-Tizon, for sharing these articles with me. An entry devoted to one of Claudius's sons indicates that Claudius was a militant republican. Like Ludovic Vitet, Claudius seems to have followed in his ancestor's footsteps, including by passing on Freemasonry as a family tradition. "Arnaud-Tizon, Ludovic Auguste," in Van Hille, *Dictionnaire des*

marins francs-maçons, 28–29. More details on the careers and travels of this next generation of Arnaud-Tizon men appear in Chassagne, "Du drap et de la toile," 79–80.

46. The documents creating this legal guardianship over the Riocreux children, which are dated May 14, 1834, are in AML 84II/7.

47. Guizot, "M. Vitet: Sa vie et ses œuvres," 65.

48. I explore intergenerational memory among the three generations of Vitet men (Louis, Pierre, and Ludovic) in Davidson, "*Notes et souvenirs*." On memory and the significance of being the son (or grandson) of a *Conventionnel* (a deputy to the National Convention, the majority of whom, unlike Louis Vitet, voted for Louis XVI's execution), see Luzzatto, *Mémoire de la Terreur*, chap. 6.

4. Marriage

1. Mainardi, *Husbands, Wives, and Lovers*, 5–6 and 218–219. On the consequences of Revolutionary legislation on the family, see Desan, *Family on Trial*; Heuer, *Family and the Nation*; and Trouille, *Wife Abuse*.

2. The classic study on this topic is Stone, *Family, Sex, and Marriage*. Other scholars have added nuance to Stone's arguments, including Ingrid H. Tague, who argues that "love . . . was recognizable not so much as an internal, emotional state but through the conditions of marriage it created: conditions in which both partners understood and accepted their complementary roles." Tague, "Love, Honor, and Obedience," 85.

3. Daumard, "Affaire, amour, affection," 45.

4. Perrot and Anne Martin-Fugier, "The Actors," in Perrot, *History of Private Life*, vol. 4, 185–186. See also the classic article by Bourdieu, "Les stratégies matrimoniales." Bourdieu reminds us that even if marital strategies prioritized matters of interest, there was always room for the assertion of individuality. Perrot and Fugier's essay also contains details on engagements, marriage contracts, wedding gifts, and other practices associated with bourgeois weddings (309–310).

5. Corbin, "Intimate Relations," in Perrot, *History of Private Life*, 4: 593. Prevailing views regarding procreation and the necessity of female orgasm meant that female sexual satisfaction nonetheless comprised part of "successful" marriages. In *L'Harmonie des plaisirs*, Corbin argues that the goal of encouraging conjugal love became more prominent in the 1820s and was intertwined with parental and filial love (265–266). On literary representations of love, sex, and marriage, see Counter, *Amorous Restoration*.

6. See Verjus and Davidson, *Le roman conjugal*, and Johnson, *Becoming Bourgeois*. On the couple as the centerpiece of bourgeois families, see Anne Verjus, "'Révolution et conception bourgeoise de la famille': Paternalisme et légitimation de l'autorité dans les débats du Code civil," in Jessenne, *Vers un ordre bourgeois*, 366–367.

7. Honoré de Balzac, *Catéchisme social*, quoted in Jean-Yves Pranchère, "Une extension inattendue de la sociologie Bonaldienne: La guerre de sexes dans la relation conjugale selon Balzac," in Del Lungo and Glaudes, *Balzac, l'invention de la sociologie*, 70.

8. François-René, vicomte de Chateaubriand, "L'avenir du monde," *Revue des Deux Mondes*, April 15, 1824, 236–237, quoted in Offen, *European Feminisms*, 88–89.

9. Verjus, *Le cens de la famille*, and *Le bon mari*. Verjus argues that it was not the abstract male individual who was enfranchised during the Revolutionary period but rather an idealized *père de famille*.

10. See Jourdan, *La Révolution batave*, chap. 5. In *Sentimental Savants*, Meghan Roberts demonstrates that the "good father" trope predated the Revolution, emerging as a prominent theme in the self-presentation of many Enlightenment thinkers who rejected earlier models suggesting that serious philosophers should choose not to marry.

11. The three Arnaud-Tizon marriages discussed in this chapter, including the parents' roles in marital negotiations and helping their children set up their new households, are explored in Verjus and Davidson, *Le roman conjugal*, 195–207.

12. CAT to PV and AV, January 7, 1807, AML 84II/12.

13. For example, Catherine thanked Pierre and Amélie for sending fabric in a letter dated December 3, 1806, AML 84II/12.

14. CAT to PV and AV, October 31, 1807, AML 84II/12.

15. CAT to PV and AV, May 18, 1806, AML 84II/12.

16. PVCJ, October 17, 1807, entry for letter to "*le papa* Arnaud-Tizon regarding Madame Roux's activities related to Victoire's possible marriage [*l'établissement de V*]. [Sent him a] copy of a letter from Madame V. [and a] letter from Roux regarding this same matter [*sur le même objet*]." After writing "Victoire" in his journal, Pierre crossed out everything but the *V*.

17. PVCJ, entry for letter to CAT, October 29, 1807.

18. CAT to PV and AV, November 12, 1807, AML 84II/12.

19. CAT to PV and AV, November 9, 1807, AML 84II/12.

20. Dena Goodman discusses cases of daughters rejecting suitors and even resisting marriage altogether in "Letter Writing."

21. PVCJ, entry for letter to CAT, November 16, 1807. Already a regent of the Bank of France, Vital Roux was in the process of becoming "chef de division à la distribution des subsistences militaires" (head of distribution for military provisions) while these negotiations were taking place.

22. CAT to PV and AV, November 14, 1807, AML 84II/12.

23. PVCJ, entries for letters to CAT, November 8 and November 25, 1807.

24. CAT to PV, November 29, 1807, AML 84II/12.

25. A genealogy website, Geneanet, provided these details, accessed January 21, 2025, https://gw.geneanet.org/pitoire?lang=fr&n=vingtrinier&oc=0&p=antoine.

26. An indication of Vingtrinier's wealth is the fact that his father's 1791 rent assessment was 1,000 pounds while both Claude Arnaud-Tizon's and Louis Vitet's was 900. Edmonds, *Jacobinism and the Revolt of Lyon*, 313. Edmonds labels Antoine Vingtrinier a Rolandin, like Louis, and indicates that he was a furrier.

27. CAT to PV, December 18, 1807, AML 84II/12.

28. CAT to PV and AV, December 29, 1807, AML 84II/12.

29. CAT to PV and AV, December 30, 1807, AML 84II/12.

30. PVCJ, entries dated January 2, 6, 9, 17, and 28, 1808.

31. CAT to PV and AV, May 4, 1808, AML 84II/12.

32. Chaline, *Les bourgeois de Rouen*, 106–108; Chassagne, *Le coton et ses patrons*, 552–553.

33. PVCJ, entry for letter to CAT, May 5, 1808.

34. CAT to PV and AV, May 4, 1808, AML 84II/12.

35. Takats, *Expert Cook*; Fairchilds, *Domestic Enemies*; and Maza, *Servants and Masters*.

36. CAT to PV and AV, May 7, 1808, AML 84II/12.

37. Hiner, *Accessories to Modernity*, 50–54. On the trousseau, *corbeille*, and other practices related to courtship and weddings, see Bricard, *Saintes ou pouliches*, 275–319; and Perrot and Fugier, "The Actors," in Perrot, *History of Private Life*, 4: 314–316.

38. Walton, "Capitalism's Alter Ego." In his classic study, *The Gift*, first published in 1925, Marcel Mauss analyzes the ways gifts promote systems of reciprocity and mutual obligation.

39. PVCJ, entry dated May 12, 1808.

40. CAT to PV and AV, May 16, 1808, AML 84II/12.

41. PVCJ, entry for letter to CAT, May 21, 1808.

42. PVCJ, entries dated May 25, June 9, and June 10, 1808.

43. CM, June 10, 1808, ADSM 2E3 127. Over twenty-five signatures appear on the contract, including those of the parents, siblings, grandparents, and many friends of both families. Serge Chassagne discusses the contract in *Le coton et ses patrons*, 553. For an analysis of marriage contracts and their signers through the lens of network theory, see Rothschild, *An Infinite History*, chap. 2.

44. On property arrangements and marriage, see Lanza, *From Wives to Widows*, 166–169.

45. PVCJ, entry dated June 10, 1808.

46. PVCJ, entry for letter to MV, June 15, 1808.

47. CAT to PV and AV, July 14, 1808, AML 84II/12.

48. PVCJ, entry for letter to MV, October 30, 1808.

49. MV to PV, November 5, 1808, AML 84II/11.

50. PVCJ, entry for letter to CAT, October 31, 1808, and to MV, November 19, 1808.

51. PVCJ, entry for letter to JJB, November 21, 1808.

52. On the "precocious" use of contraception in France and its relationship to new ideas about marital life, see Burguière, "Les fondements d'une culture familial," in Burguière and Revel, *Histoire de la France*, 4: 101–108. Burguière argues that the transition to smaller family size was part of a "new conjugal morality founded upon self-control and respect for the partner, inciting the couple to use birth control to make life less unpredictable" (107). The Revolution seems to have hastened the transition toward smaller families. See Bardet, "Political Revolution and Contraceptive Revolution," 175–187.

53. CAT to PV, April 7, 1812, AML 84II/12.

54. CAT to PV, May 15, 1812, AML 84II/12.

55. CAT to PV and AV, May 31, 1812, AML 84II/12.

56. PVCJ, entry for letter to CAT, June 4, 1812.

57. CAT to PV and AV, June 5, 1812, AML 84II/12.

58. JJB to PV, June 12, 1812, AML 84II/9.

59. CAT to PV and AV, July 6, 1812, AML 84II/12.

60. PVCJ, entry for letter to CAT, July 11, 1812, and CAT to PV and AV, July 12, 1812, AML 84II/12.

61. PVCJ, entry for letter to CAT, July 23, 1812.
62. CAT to PV, July 24, 1812, AML 84II/12.
63. CAT to PV and AV, [July 28, 1812].
64. PVCJ, entry for letter to CAT, August 10, 1812.
65. CLAT to PV, August 16, 1812, AML 84II/13.
66. CAT to PV and AV, August 17, 1812, AML 84II/12.
67. MV to PV, August 22, 1812, AML 84II/11.
68. CM, Thiebault/Arnaud-Tizon, August 28, 1812. Private Collection of Monique Augustin-Normand. One of the signers, Madame Casimir Périer, was the mother of the woman Ludovic Vitet would marry twenty years later.
69. PVCJ, entries dated August 29 and September 3, 1812.
70. PVCJ, entry for letter to MV, September 8, 1812.
71. Victoire Barbet to AV, December 7, 1812, AML 84II/11.
72. Details on these economic difficulties appear in chap. 6.
73. CAT to PV, January 27, 1816, AML 84II/13.
74. CAT to PV, February 9, 1816, AML 84II/13.
75. CAT to PV, March 16, 1816, AML 84II/13.
76. CAT to PV, March 20, 1816, AML 84II/13.
77. PVCJ, entry for letter to CAT, July 1, 1816.
78. CAT to PV, July 2, 1816, AML 84II/13.
79. Having lost money during the economic crises and wartime dislocations that took place during the final years of the Empire, they had to borrow from Jacques Barbet to come up with Adèle's dowry. JJB to PV, April 25, 1825, AML 84II/9. Tensions caused by these financial arrangements are explored in chapter 6.
80. PVCJ, entry dated July 4, 1816.
81. PV to AV, July 4, 1816, AML 84II/9.
82. PVCJ, entry for letter to AV, July 5, 1816.
83. PV to AV, July 7, 1816, AML 84II/9.
84. PVCJ, entries dated July 13 and August 1, 1816.
85. PVCJ, entry for letter to his mother, August 4, 1816.
86. PVCJ, August 10, 1816, "Departure of the Paillon, Guérin & Riocreux families."
87. CAT to PV, August 18, 1816, AML 84II/13.
88. CAT to PV, August 22, 1816, AML 84II/13.
89. CAT to PV, August 22, 1816, AML 84II/13.
90. Walker, *A Mother's Love*, 34–36.
91. PVCJ, entry for letter to MV, October 4, 1816.
92. PVCJ, letter to CAT, October 15, 1816.
93. AT to PV, October 18, [1816], AML 84II/13.
94. PVCJ, entry for letter to MV, October 25, 1816.
95. CAT to AV, October 27, 1816, AML 84II/12.
96. CAT to PV, November 9, 1816, AML 84II/13.
97. PVCJ, entry for letter to MV, November 14, 1816.
98. CAT to PV, April 8, 1818, AML 84II/13.
99. CAT to PV, April 23, [1818], AML 84II/13.
100. Roux cofounded France's first business school with Jean-Baptiste Say in 1819. See Touzet and Corbeil, "Vital Roux."

5. Parents and Children

1. Walker, *A Mother's Love*; Rogers, *From the Salon to the Schoolroom*, chap. 1; and Reynolds, "Revolutionary Parents and Children."

2. On bourgeois attitudes toward the prestige associated with different professions and the assumption that boys needed to prepare for a career to assume masculine adulthood and its requisite level of independence, see Gutermann-Jacquet, *Les équivoques du genre*, 218–232.

3. On Rousseau's educational theories and their connections to the rise of the domestic ideal for women and the ways that women could exercise agency within the context of domesticity, see Popiel, *Rousseau's Daughters*.

4. On the contrasting content and goals of education for boys and girls, see Gutermann-Jacquet, *Les équivoques du genre*, chap. 1; and Houbre, *La discipline de l'amour*. On educational methods, particularly the emphasis on mastering Latin and Greek and pedagogical practices relying on repetition and memorization, see Chervel, *La culture scolaire*. Women's writing reflected their weaker education. Written phonetically, Catherine's letters included many spelling and grammar mistakes.

5. PVCJ, entry for letter to CAT, July 17, 1811. A composer and author, André Ernest Modeste Grétry (1741–1813) purchased the Hermitage in 1798. See Arnold, *Grétry's Operas and the French Public*, 173–175; and Brix and Lenoir, Introduction, Grétry, *Douze chapitres inédits*, 7–9.

6. Darnton, "Readers Respond to Rousseau," in *The Great Cat Massacre*.

7. Roberts, *Sentimental Savants*; Verjus, *Le bon mari*; and Hunt, *Family Romance*. On the Revolution's long-term impact on ideas about masculinity, including men's roles in the private sphere, see Rauch, *Crise de l'identité masculine*, chap. 3. In his study of early nineteenth-century eulogies, James Arnold argues that notions of domestic bliss were essential to bourgeois notions of a good life. Arnold, "'Il fut bon père."

8. Sergio Luzzatto found similar trends among the former revolutionaries whose memoirs he explores in *Mémoire de la Terreur*, 142–143.

9. They were also both part of what Nathan Perl-Rosenthal labels the "second revolutionary generation . . . [that] came to maturity around 1800" and who "took for granted that social status was changeable and not fixed." Perl-Rosenthal, *Age of Revolutions*, 7.

10. In *Ladies of the Leisure Class*, Bonnie Smith demonstrates that the model of bourgeois wives focusing on their homes while their husbands focused on their businesses was a later nineteenth-century development. Until then, most middle-class women played active roles in family businesses.

11. PVCJ, entry for letter to Baudard, July 2, 1809.

12. CAT to PV and AV, October 12, 1809, AML 84II/12. An explanation of contemporary understandings of *dépôts laiteux* (literally: milky deposits) appears in *Dictionnaire des sciences*, 8: 452–467. Common wisdom held that *dépôts*, which could appear anywhere on the body, were caused by an excess of milk circulating in the blood. The treatment was therefore bleeding.

13. CAT to PV and AV, October 21, 1809, AML 84II/12.

14. CAT to AV, April 5, 1811, AML 84II/12.

15. CAT to AV, January 10, 1817, AML 84II/13.

16. CAT to AV, January 24, 1817, AML 84II/13. When Pierre wrote to his mother to announce Catherine's arrival in Paris to assist with the birth, he wrote that she would be staying with Adèle, not him and Amélie, as she said she planned to do. (PVCJ, entry for letter to MV, May 20, 1817.)

17. AAT to PV, n.d., probably May 17, 1817, AML 84II/13. PVCJ, entry for letter to CAT, May 13, 1817. Catherine arrived on May 17 (PVCJ, entry for letter to MV, May 20, 1817).

18. PVCJ, entry for letter to Mr. Riocreux *père*, May 30, 1817, and entry for letter to MV, July 6, 1817.

19. PVCJ, entry for letter to CAT, July 17, 1817.

20. CAT to PV, July 18, 1817, AML 84II/13.

21. CAT to PV, April 7, 1812, AML 84II/12.

22. PVCJ, entry for letter to MV, April 19, 1812.

23. PVCJ, entry for letter to CAT, April 21, 1812.

24. CAT to PV and AV, April 23, 1812, AML 84II/12.

25. PVCJ, entry for letter to MV, April 25, 1812.

26. MV to PV, May 3, 1812, AML 84II/11. This example is analyzed from a different angle, that of Marguerite's seeming surprise that Amélie could have been pregnant at all, in Verjus and Davidson, *Le roman conjugal*, 71.

27. Corbin, *L'harmonie des plaisirs*, 270–271. See also Flandrin, *Families in Former Times*; McLaren, *History of Contraception*; and Tuttle, *Conceiving the Old Regime*.

28. CAT to PV and AV, February 15, 1812, AML 84II/12. She listed the names of several acquaintances who had died in a letter to PV and AV, February 9, 1812.

29. Feelings of dread regarding a pregnancy come up in a letter written by the female founder of a religious order to her sister in 1813: "I realize that this condition is a new cross for you. For no matter how much one loves the children God sends, there is still fear at their coming, a certain right and natural dread of suffering and of the burden which a large family entails." Quoted in Popiel, *Heroic Hearts*, 160.

30. PVCJ, entry for letter to MV, July 18, 1812. Sainte Marguerite day was July 20.

31. According to the official birth and death registries, Louise Adelle Barbet was born on July 16, 1812, and died three days later. ADSM, état civil, régistre Canteleu, 1812, 5 MI 2463.

32. MV to PV, July 25, 1812, AML 84II/11.

33. In a letter to her sister, Victoire shared concerns about Henry's wet nurse, who was sick with a cold and a fever. Victoire Barbet to AV, December 7, 1812, AML 84II/11.

34. PVCJ, entries for letters to Louis Vitet, May 26, 1807, and to MV, May 28, 1807, and February 16, 1808.

35. PVCJ, entry for letter to Costerisan, March 31, 1811. A legal document created in 1817 spelled his name as "Costerizan," though in his signature on the document, it looks more like an "s." *Procuration* (power of attorney document) between PV and Costerizan, recorded in Paris, January 24, 1817, AN, Minutier central, étude IX 1016. PV consistently spells it with an "s" so I do the same in this book.

36. MV to PV, March 23, 1811, AML 84II/11.

37. Davidson and Verjus, "Generational Conflict."

38. CAT to AV, April 5, 1811, AML 84II/12.

39. MV to PV, April 4, 1811, AML 84II/11.

40. CAT to PV and AV, April 1811 (postmarked April 26, 1811), AML 84II/12.

41. PVCJ, entry for letter to CAT, April 28, 1811.

42. CAT to PV and AV, April 30, 1811, AML 84II/12.

43. CAT to PV and AV, May 8, 1811, AML 84II/12.

44. CAT to PV and AV, May 9, 1811, AML 84II/12.

45. CAT to PV and AV, May 13, 1811, AML 84II/12. On bourgeois mothers' roles in treating family members' illnesses, including offering opportunities for fresh air, good food, and exercise at their country estates, see Verjus and Davidson, *Le roman conjugal*, 131.

46. CAT to PV and AV, May 17, 1811, AML 84II/12.

47. CAT to PV and AV, May 28, 1811, AML 84II/12.

48. CAT to PV and AV, June 12, 1811, AML 84II/12.

49. MV to PV, October 6, 1811, AML 84II/11.

50. CAT to PV and AV, October 12, 1811, AML 84II/12.

51. PVCJ, entry for letter to CAT, November 9, 1811.

52. CAT to PV and AV, November 10, 1811, AML 84II/12.

53. CAT to AV, November 19, 1811, AML 84II/12. This moment of transition and the decision to withdraw Ludovic from school and educate him at home are discussed in Verjus and Davidson, *Le roman conjugal*, 101–102.

54. Houbre, *La discipline de l'amour*, 51.

55. PVCJ, entries for letters to MV, November 24 and December 8, 1811.

56. PVCJ, entry for letter to CAT, December 1, 1811

57. A biography of Prader appears in *Encyclopédie de la musique*, pt. 1, 3: 1657.

58. CAT to PV and AV, December 6, 1811, AML 84II/12.

59. MV to PV, December 11, 1811, AML 84II/11.

60. MV to LV, October 16, 1810, AML 84II/15. Marguerite's attention to religious matters in connection to her grandson's education is discussed in Verjus and Davidson, *Le roman conjugal*, 83–84.

61. CAT to AV, January 25, [1812], AML 84II/12.

62. Elise Pradher to PV, May 12, 1812, AML 84II/10. Both families sought advice from this doctor.

63. Parturier, Introduction, *Lettres de Mérimée à Ludovic Vitet*. In recounting Ludovic's life story, Parturier refers to the fact that "Vitet was raised by his father and lived with him until he was sixteen" (vii).

64. CAT to PV, August 7, 1817, 84II/13.

65. PV to AV, September 13, [1823], AML 84II/9.

66. Draft letter written in the margins and on the back of letter from AAT to AV, November 13, 1818, AML 84II/13.

67. Draft letter written in the margins and on the back of letter from AAT to AV, November 13, 1818, AML 84II/13.

68. CAT to PV, January 5, 1819, 84II/13.

69. CAT to PV, March 14, 1820, 84II/13.

70. CAT to PV and AV, April 10, 1812, 84II/12.

71. CAT to AV, April 18, 1810, AML 84II/12.

72. CAT to AV, May 21, 1812, 84II/12.

73. CAT to PV and AV, January 2, 1813, 84II/12.

74. CAT to PV and AV, May 4, 1816, and May 18, 1816, AML 84II/13.

75. PVCJ, entry for letter to Adèle Arnaud-Tizon, April 22, 1816.

76. CAT to PV, July 1, 1816, AML 84II/13.

77. PVCJ, entry for letter to MV, April 13, 1816.

78. PVCJ, entries for letters to MV, March 23 and April 29, 1817.

79. PVCJ, entry dated July 12, and entry for letter to MV, July 19, 1817.

80. CAT to PV, July 18, [1817], AML 84II/13.

81. PVCJ, entries dated August 17 and 20, 1817. Adèle and Christophe Riocreux accompanied them in the stagecoach to Lyon.

82. CAT to PV, March 14, [1818], AML 84II/13.

83. CAT to PV, December 21, 1818, AML 84II/13.

84. PVCJ, entry for letter to MV, January 28, 1819.

85. PVCJ, entries for letters to CAT, August 18, 1820, and August 19, 1821.

86. Parturier, *Lettres de Mérimée à Ludovic Vitet*, vii–ix. Jan Goldstein discusses Jouffroy's theories of education in *Post-Revolutionary Self*, 161.

87. PVCJ, January 20, 1822, "Sunday . . . at 7 p.m., birth of Amélie Jeanne Claudine Vitet." He wrote the next day to his family in Lyon to share the news. There was no need to write to Amélie's family, as her mother was with them for the birth. Jacques and Victoire Barbet had moved into an apartment in Paris that fall and enrolled their sons at the Collège Louis le Grand. (PVCJ, entry for letter to LAT, December 3, 1821.) Victoire probably assisted her sister with the birth, along with their mother.

88. PVCJ, January 1822 letters announcing birth of daughter.

89. PVCJ, entry for letter to *tante* Morel, January 8, 1823.

90. PVCJ, entry for letter to "Madame Ludovic" (AAT), April 23, 1823.

91. PVCJ, entries for letters to *tante* Morel, May 16, 1823, and to Costerisan, May 31, 1823.

92. CAT to AV, December 8, 1816, AML 84 II/13.

93. AAT to AV, March 28, 1821, AML 84II/13.

94. AAT to AV, March 28, 1821, AML 84II/13.

95. AAT to AV, September 9, 1826, AML 84II/13.

96. AAT to AV, October 9, 1827, AML 84II/13, emphasis in original.

97. This kind of trip was viewed as the ideal way for a young man to complete his intellectual preparation. Gutermann-Jacquet, *Les équivoques du genre*, 66. On travel literature and national consciousness, see Gerson, "Parisian Litterateurs, Provincial Journeys."

98. PVCJ, entry dated July 10, and entry for letter to LAT, October 18, 1824.

99. LV to AV, July 19, 1824, AML 84II/15.

100. On those circles, see Jennings, *French Anti-Slavery*, 10–22. The year that Ludovic took this trip, 1824, was a high point of the French abolitionist movement and the year that Clair de Duras's nouvella *Ourika* became a huge bestseller. See Kadish, Introduction, *Translating Slavery*, vol. 2; and Mitchell, *Vénus Noire.*

101. See Miller, *French Atlantic Triangle*, chap. 9; and Isbell, "Voices Lost," 48–49.

102. LV to AV, July 28, 1824, AML 84II/15.

103. PVCJ, entry for letter to LV, September 26/27, 1824.

104. Ludovic Vitet's address, rue Barbet de Jouy, no. 5, appeared in *Almanach royal et national pour l'an MDCCCXLI*, 106. Ludovic, his wife, and his parents lived in a townhouse built in the late 1830s. Detailed drawings of the entire block of buildings dating from 1929 are in AML 84II/21.

6. *Le Patrimoine*

1. On Revolutionary changes to property and inheritance laws as well as the economic disruptions caused by Revolutionary innovations like the assignats, see Desan, *Family on Trial*; Spang, *Stuff and Money*; and Blaufarb, *Great Demarcation*.

2. See Medick and Sabean, *Interest and Emotion*, and Sabean et al., *Kinship in Europe*. On the overlapping sense of family as both *la petite famille* and larger kinship networks, see Guterman-Jacquet, *Les équivoques du genre*, 19–23. Studies that underline the weight of the lineage model of the family among the urban middle classes include Ruggiu, *L'individu et la famille*, and Johnson, *Becoming Bourgeois*.

3. On these continuities and the French preference for seeking stability in landed wealth, see Seigel, *Modernity and Bourgeois Life*, 196–197.

4. Claire Crowston explores the relationship between credit in both its material and immaterial sense and honor in *Credit, Fashion, Sex*.

5. Sauzet, "Hommage à la mémoire de Ludovic Vitet," 188.

6. AML 84II / 2 holds documents related to Louis's ancestors. Details on Louis's purchases of *biens nationaux* in Longes are in ADR 1Q / 339, no. 140.

7. ADR 3E / 5110 and 3E / 5119, minutes of Jean Guillaume Berthon du Formental. The notary was executed by firing squad in December 1793. Cuer et al., *Minutes et repétoires des notaires*, 99. See also, Chassagne, "Du drap et de la toile," 76–77.

8. Passeport for Pierre-Marie Arnaudtizon to travel to Rouen with his wife Anne-Françoise Adélaïde and their servant, Claudine Valencot, 3 Pluviôse Year II (January 22, 1794), AML 2I / 70, no. 1806.

9. Documents are sparse for these years, but in 1821, Catherine referred to having lived in Rouen for twenty-five years, which would date her arrival to 1796. CAT to PV, November 13, 1821, AML 84II / 13.

10. Acte de naissance, Adelle Arnaudtizon, 29 Fructidor Year VI (September 15, 1798), ADSM, Etat Civil, 5 Mi 0566. Claude deposited notarial documents, including a power of attorney for his brother, in Lyon around the time of Adèle's birth. ADR 3E / 8271 (Verset, notary), 24 and 27 Fructidor Year VI (September 10 and 13, 1798).

11. In 1799, PMAT and his wife sold a country estate outside of Lyon at a substantial loss. They purchased it in November 1792 for 140,000 francs and sold it for 90,000. ADR 2E / 8271 (Verset notary), 26 Ventôse Year VII (March 16, 1799). When Anne-Françoise's father, Pierre Nicholas Vincent, died in September 1800, she inherited real estate and furniture worth nearly 92,000 francs. Property transfer [*mutation*], 9 Ventôse Year IX (February 28, 1801), ADSM 3Q 38 / 84. I am grateful to Serge Chassagne for sharing his research notes with me.

12. CAT to AV, 3 Brumaire Year XIV (October 25, 1805), AML 84II / 12.

13. CAT to AV, 22 Frimaire Year XIV (December 13, 1805), AML 84II / 12.

14. CAT to PV and AV, October 20, 1808, AML 84II / 12.

15. CAT to PV, Dimanche soir [February 1810], AML 84II / 12. Dated from context: Henry Barbet's wedding, a topic mentioned in the letter.

16. The funeral was a major event: "Death of Mr. Barbet *père* in Deville Monday. I attended the funeral. A large procession of workers and orphans. Curious onlookers lined the boulevards all the way to the Protestant cemetery." PVCJ, entry for letter to Costerisan, July 3, 1813.

17. CAT to PV, December 6, 1814, 84II / 12.

18. CAT to PV and AV, April 25, 1816, AML 84II/12.

19. CAT to PV, June 22, 1816, AML 84II/12.

20. Document composed in PV's handwriting dated June 3, 1809, AML 84II/7.

21. PVCJ, entry for letter to Costerisan, June 11, 1809.

22. PVCJ, June 27, 1809: "Left for Rouen with my mother, Amélie & Ludovic."

23. PVCJ, "long epistle to Costerisan," July 8, 1809.

24. Pierre Jean Vitet, "Avertissement de l'éditeur," in Louis Vitet, *Traité de la sangsue*, ii.

25. PVCJ, July 2, 1809, list of people to whom he sent the book and in some cases an engraving.

26. PVCJ, September 22, 1809, entry for letter to Petitin. Jacques-Henry-Désiré Petitin died in 1808. See the website of the École Nationale de Chartes's Comité des Travaux Historiques et Scientifiques, accessed January 21, 2025, http://cths.fr/an/savant.php?id=955; and PVCJ, entry for letter to Louis Vitet, March 5, 1808. Pierre-Simon Ballanche and his father were prominent counterrevolutionaries. See McCalla, *Romantic Historiosophy*.

27. PVCJ, entry for letter to Martin, *médecin*, January 6, 1810.

28. PV to AV, [July 21, 1809], AML 84II/9. (The letter is dated "Friday"; context and PVCJ provided date.)

29. PV to AV, July 25, 1809, AML 84II/9.

30. Fournel to PV, September 30, 1809, AML 84II/10. *Epauletiers* was a derogatory term for high-ranking officers. Thiers, *Histoire de la Révolution française*, 5: 318.

31. PV to MV, June 9, 1810, AML 84II/9.

32. PV to AV, September 2, 1810, AML 84II/9.

33. PV to MV, September 3, 1810, AML 84II/9.

34. PV to MV, September 3, 1810, AML 84II/9.

35. PVCJ, entry for letter to Molière, February 28, 1817. A record of the sale dated May 4, 1817, which shows its price as 30,000 francs (after being purchased for 18,200 francs in 1791), is in ADR 285/Q7, Table de vendeurs, 191, no. 71. It was common to record a price lower than the actual sale price, presumably to save on fees.

36. When Pierre-Marie Arnaud-Tizon sold his estate outside of Lyon, it included the furniture, paintings, and even liqueur and wine in the cellar. ADR 2E/8271 (Verset notary), 26 Ventôse Year VII (March 16, 1799).

37. PV to AV, September 6, 1810, AML 84II/9.

38. PVCJ, entries dated September 18 to 22, 1810. See Chassagne, *Oberkampf*.

39. PVCJ, entry for letter to Costerisan, May 27, 1810; and PV to MV, June 17, 1810, AML 84II/9.

40. MV to PV, October 8, 1810, AML 84II/11.

41. PV to MV, [October 9, 1810], AML 84II/9; and PVCJ entry for letter to MV, October 9, 1810. Pierre's entire letter is reproduced and analyzed in Verjus and Davidson, *Le roman conjugal*, 232.

42. PVCJ, entry dated October 10, 1810. Bill of sale dated October 16, 1810, AML 84II/7.

43. PVCJ, entry for letter to Costerisan, October 17, 1810.

44. On these generational dynamics, see Davidson and Verjus, "Generational Conflict."

45. In a letter thanking Pierre for sending a portrait of Ludovic, Marguerite voiced her affection for the boy, mentioning that she invited his maternal grandfather to come to see it, and discussing the image as it if was Ludovic himself, before offering some "light criticism" of the image. MV to PV, June 8, 1811, AML 84II/11, quoted in Verjus and Davidson, *Le roman conjugal*, 235.

46. MV to PV, February 19, 1816, AML 84II/11. Marguerite's entire letter is reproduced and analyzed in Verjus and Davidson, *Le roman conjugal*, 233–234.

47. PVCJ, entry for letter to MV, March 5, 1816.

48. CAT to PV, January 26, 1811, AML 84II/11.

49. PVCJ, entry for letter to CAT, February 4, 1811.

50. PVCJ, entry for letter to CAT, February 17, 1811.

51. CAT to AV, March 11, 1811, AML 84II/12.

52. CAT to PV, March 14, 1811, AML 84II/12.

53. CAT to PV and AV, March 22, 1811, AML 84II/12.

54. CAT to PV, April 2, 1811, AML 84II/12.

55. CAT to PV and AV, April 12, 1811, AML 84II/12.

56. CAT to PV and AV, May 13, 1811, AML 84II/12. A summary of the sale, dated June 18, 1811, is in the repertoire of the notary, Gandilhon, ADR 3E 43627*. The price shown is 120,000 francs, lower than the price Pierre included in his letter.

57. CAT to PV, April 4, 1820, AML 84II/13.

58. CAT to PV and AV, January 7, 1807, AML 84II/12.

59. CAT to PV, August 22, 1814, AML 84II/12.

60. CAT to PV, September 17, 1814, AML 84II/12.

61. CAT to PV, March 16, 1816, AML 84II/13. Pierre made similar comments in a letter to his mother: "St. Just is inhabited by the Maréchal who now owns it. This property is more appropriate for him than for his brother." PVCJ, entry for letter to MV, October 4, 1816.

62. CAT to PV, January 15, 1817, AML 84II/13.

63. CAT to PV, February 12, [1817], AML 84II/13.

64. PVCJ, entry for letter to CAT, February 13, 1817.

65. CAT to PV, February 14, 1817, AML 84II/13.

66. CAT to PV, February 21, 1817, AML 84II/13.

67. PMAT to PV, February 26, 1817, AML 84II/13 (misfiled with letters from CAT).

68. Document dated March 21, 1814, and deposited February 25, 1817, ADSM 2E2/171.

69. PVCJ, entry for letter to CLAT, March 1, 1817.

70. CAT to PV, March 2, 1817, AML 84II/13. Longer excerpts of this and several other letters written during this moment of crisis, along with analysis of the family's response to this situation, appear in Verjus and Davidson, *Le roman conjugal*, 241–251.

71. On French bankruptcy law and the practices and significance attached to it, see Vause, *In the Red and in the Black*. On honor and masculinity, see Nye, *Masculinity*, and Reddy, *Invisible Code*.

72. CAT to PV, March 2, 1817, AML 84II/13.

73. CAT to PV, March 2, 1817, AML 84II/13.

74. CAT to PV, March 3, 1817, AML 84II/13.

75. CAT to PV, March 3, 1817, AML 84II/13.

76. CAT to PV, March 5, 1817, AML 84II/13.

77. PVCJ, entry for letter to CAT, March 7, 1817.

78. CAT to PV, March 9, 1817, AML 84II/13. Divorce, which had been legal since 1792, was abolished again in 1816. A *séparation de biens* permitted a wife to regain control over the wealth she brought into the marriage.

79. Adèle Suchet to PV, March 7, 1817, AML 84II/13 (filed with letters from CAT).

80. Adèle Suchet to PV, March 10, 1817, AML 84II/13.

81. CAT to PV, March 15, 1817, AML 84II/13.

82. PVCJ, entry dated March 20, 1817.

83. PVCJ, entry for letter to CAT, March 25, 1817.

84. Procuration, March 24, 1817, ADSM 2E2/171.

85. CAT to PV, March 29, 1817, AML 84II/13.

86. PVCJ, entries for letters to JJB, April 7, 1817, and CAT, April 10, 1817 (quotation in the latter).

87. CAT to PV, April 13, 1817, AML 84II/13.

88. ADSM, 2E2/171, *dépôt de document*, June 28, 1817. The document was produced by a notary in Paris and signed there. Pierre-Marie then deposited a copy with his notary in Rouen.

89. ADSM, 2E2/171, *dépôt de document*, June 28, 1817.

90. ADSM, 2E2/171, *dépôt de document*, June 28, 1817.

91. ADSM, 2E2/171, *dépôt de document*, June 28, 1817.

92. CAT to PV, March 14, 1818, AML 84II/13.

93. PVCJ, entry for letter to JJB, April 25, 1818.

94. CAT to PV, June 9, [1818], AML 84II/13.

95. CAT to PV, December 2, 1818, AML 84II/13.

96. PMAT to Marshal Suchet, December 12, 1819, AN 384AP/187.

97. PMAT to Marshal Suchet, letters dated October 6, 1822, and September 6, 1823, AN 384AP/187.

98. CAT to PV, December 18, 1820, AML 84II/13.

99. CAT to PV, December 20, 1820, AML 84II/13.

100. PVCJ, entry for letter dated December 29, 1820.

101. CAT to PV, February 20, [1821], AML 84II/13.

102. PVCJ, entry for letter to LAT, January 22, 1826.

103. PVCJ, October 19, 1826. Clémence married Guillaume Charles Desplanque on November 18, 1826. Archives de Paris, digitized birth, death, and marriage records, V3E/M 945 (*fichier*) and 5mil 2048 (*acte*), accessed January 21, 2025, https://archives.paris.fr/r/124/etat-civil-de-paris/.

104. PVCJ, entry for letter to Suchet, April 2, 1829.

105. The three Suchet children appear among Ludovic Vitet's survivors in an 1873 death announcement. Only Edouard Suchet's profession is listed. He was Trésorier-Payeur d'Eure et Loire. Lavigne, *État civil d'artistes*, 115. A Madame veuve Deplanques is listed between Edouard and Eugène Suchet. That must be Clémence.

106. PVCJ, entry for letter to CLAT, May 22, 1817.

107. CLAT to PV, May 24, 1817, AML 84II/13.

108. PVCJ, entry for letter to CLAT, May 31, 1817.

109. CAT to PV, July 18, 1817, AML 84II/13.

110. CAT to PV, July 27, 1817, AML 84II/13.

111. CAT to PV, October 19, 1817, AML 84II/13.

112. PV to AV, May 1, 1820, AML 84II/9.

113. PV to AV, May 4, 1820, AML 84II/9. Pierre recorded a list of furniture and other objects that MV wanted given to her sister and her servant, Marion, in PVCJ, 1820.

114. PV to AV, May 10, 1820, AML 84II/9.

115. PV to AV, May 10, 1820, AML 84II/9.

116. PV to AV, May 10, 1820, AML 84II/9.

117. AV to PV, May 18, 1820, AML 84II/11.

118. PV to AV, May 15, 1820, AML 84II/9. On the treatment and place of domestic servants within these families' lives, including their presence during many of life's most intimate moments, see Verjus and Davidson, *Le roman conjugal*, 116–122. Regarding Marion, we wrote that she was "une femme clé dans la vie de Marguerite" (an essential person in Marguerite's life) (121). She handled all the daily tasks of caring for Marguerite and her household in Lyon and took part in overseeing the family's properties in Longes.

119. PV to AV, May 18, 1820, AML 84II/9.

120. PV to AV, May 20, 1820, AML 84II/9.

121. PV to AV, June 2, 1820, AML 84II/9.

122. CAT to PV, June 16, 1820, AML 84II/13.

123. PVCJ, August 10, 1825, purchase of land near La Capelle in the Aisne department; and PV to AV, October 7, 1825, AML 84II/9.

124. CAT to PV, November 13, 1821, 84II/13.

125. PVCJ, entry for letter to *tante* Morel, November 7, 1821.

126. PVCJ, entry for letter to LAT, December 3, 1821.

127. PVCJ, entry for letter to LAT, January 31, 1825. The nature of the three Arnaud-Tizon brothers-in-law's relationship is discussed in Verjus and Davidson, *Le roman conjugal*, 236–241. A longer excerpt from this letter appears on 238–239.

128. LAT to PV, February 3, 1825, AML 84II/13.

129. LAT to PV, February 3, 1825, AML 84II/13.

130. LAT to PV, February 3, 1825, AML 84II/13.

131. PVCJ, entry for two letters to JJB dated April 22 and 24, 1825.

132. JJB to PV, April 22, 1825, AML 84II/9.

133. JJB to PV, April 22, 1825, AML 84II/9.

134. JJB to PV, April 25, 1825, AML 84II/9. A longer excerpt of this letter appears in Verjus and Davidson, *Le roman conjugal*, 239–240.

135. JJB to PV, April 25, 1825, AML 84II/9.

136. CLAT to PV, July 5, 1825, AML 84II/13. Pierre recorded in his journal that the "reconciliation [was] executed [*opérée*] since Madame Suchet's arrival and through her intervention, June 24 and 29 [1825]." PVCJ, undated entry.

137. JJB to PV, April 25, 1825, AML 84II/9.

138. CAT to PV, November 14 and 18, 1831, AN 572AP/4; and PVCJ, entries for letters to CAT and CLAT, November 11, 13, 16, and 17, 1831.

139. CAT to PV, November 14, 1831, AN 572AP/4.

140. CAT to PV, November 14, 1831, AN 572AP/4.

141. PVCJ, entry for letter to CAT, December 16, 1831; and CAT to PV and AV, December 18, 1831, AN 572AP/4.

142. They made an intermediary move to the rue Trudon in March 1832. That street, which no longer exists, was located a few blocks north of their longtime home on the rue neuve Saint Roch.

7. Networks

1. PVCJ, entry dated February 18, 1806.
2. PV to AV, February 19, 1806, AML 84II/9.
3. A classic analysis of the functions of sociability and the importance of play within such contexts is Simmel, "Sociability," 127–140.
4. In one of her letters, CAT refers to Ludovic as "Tonton" and mentions his affection for *"le papa zon."* CAT to AV, 12 Frimaire Year XIV (December 2, 1805).
5. Mercier, *Le nouveau Paris*, 3: 121.
6. Mercier, *Le nouveau Paris*, 3: 127–128.
7. Mercier, *Le nouveau Paris*, 3: 125.
8. CAT to AV, 12 Frimaire Year XIV (December 3, 1805), AML 84II/12.
9. CAT to PV and AV, January 6, 1809, AML 84II/12.
10. CAT to PV and AV, February 10, 1809, AML 84II/12.
11. PVCJ, entry for letter to CAT, February 26, 1810.
12. Mery Fournel to PV, February 14, 1808, AML 84II/10.
13. PVCJ, entry for letter to MV, January 19, 1812.
14. Entry for letter to CAT, February 7, 1812.
15. PVCJ, entry for letter to CAT, March 5, 1813. "Feydeau" referred to a popular theater near the Vitet's home.
16. PVCJ, entries dated 26 and 30 Ventôse Year XIII (March 17 and 21, 1805).
17. CAT to PV and AV, November 25, 1811, AML 84II/12.
18. CAT to PV and AV, January 28, 1813, AML 84II/12.
19. CAT to AV, April 1, 1813, AML 84II/12.
20. CAT to AV, December 8, 1814, AML 84II/12.
21. CAT to PV and AV, January 25, 1813, AML 84II/12.
22. CAT to PV, January 18, 1815, AML 84II/12. Named in Paris, prefects headed France's administrative units, the departments. *Préfètes* were their wives.
23. CAT to PV and AV, January 30, 1815, AML 84II/12. Prefect of the Seine-Inférieure from 1812 to 1815, Louis Stanislas de Girardin later represented the Seine Inférieure in the Chamber of Deputies, becoming a prominent member of the liberal opposition.
24. CAT to PV, February 6, 1815, AML 84II/12.
25. CAT to PV and AV, February 16, 1815, AML 84II/12.
26. CAT to PV, February 22, 1815, AML 84II/12. Jacques Manoury was one of Rouen's most successful businessmen and a founder of the Banque de Rouen. Chaline, "La banque à Rouen," 387.
27. CAT to PV, January 9, 1818, AML 84II/13.
28. CAT to PV, December 20, 1820, AML 84II/13. Thézard numbered among the top ten taxpayers in Rouen. Saunier, *Révolution et sociabilité*, 239–241. He and his family lived on the rue aux Ours and thus were neighbors of the Arnaud-Tizons. See Chassagne, *Le coton et ses patrons*, 307.
29. CAT to AV, February 1, 1819, AML 84II/13. This example, as well as a discussion of prevailing attitudes toward miscarriages and the precautions pregnant women needed to take, appears in Verjus and Davidson, *Le roman conjugal*, 70–71.

30. CAT to AV, February 1, 1819, AML 84II/13.

31. AAT to PV, January 27, 1816, AML 84II/13. Emphasis in original.

32. See Kroen, *Politics and Theater*, and Davidson, *France after Revolution*, chap. 4.

33. CAT to PV, January 11, 1821, AML 84II/13.

34. CAT to PV, January 30, 1821, AML 84II/13. Darnetal is a small town two miles east of Rouen.

35. CAT to PV, February 14, [1821], AML 84II/13.

36. Serge Chassagne discusses the Long family in *Le coton et ses patrons*, 557–558. The groom, who took the name Fouquier-Long, served as mayor of Déville, a suburb of Rouen, and later held a seat in the Chamber of Deputies during the Restoration, allied with the monarchists. Website of the French National Assembly, list of deputies, accessed January 21, 2025, https://www2.assemblee-nationale.fr/sycomore/fiche/(num_dept)/12065.

37. CAT to PV and AV, July 9, 1806, AML 84II/12. The "lit de mousse" was probably made with sheer fabric produced in the Long factory. Today, *mousse* means foam, among other things. *Sage* in this case means to be well-behaved.

38. Chaline, *Les bourgeois de Rouen*, 196.

39. CAT to PV, February 27, 1812, AML 84II/12.

40. CAT to PV and AV, August 5, 1806, AML 84II/12.

41. AAT to PV, January 27, 1816, AML 84II/13.

42. CAT to AV, March 28, 1812, AML 84II/12. Chassagne mentions this connection to the Ballicornes in "Du drap et de la toile," 77.

43. CAT to AV, March 28, 1812, AML 84II/12.

44. CAT to PV and AV, April 10, 1812, AML 84II/12.

45. CAT to PV and AV, November 9, 1813, AML 84II/12.

46. CAT to PV and AV, November 20, [1813], AML 84II/12.

47. CAT to PV, December 6, 1814, AML 84II/12.

48. JJB to PV, February 7, 1813, AML 84II/9.

49. CAT to PV, December 27, 1816, AML 84II/12. "Madame T" was probably Madame Thézard.

50. CAT to PV, March 20, 1821, AML 84II/13.

51. Louis-Gabriel Suchet to PV, April 11, [1818] AML 84II/11.

52. On Lyonnais identity and networks, see Saunier, *L'esprit Lyonnais*; Davidson, "Local Identities"; and Verjus and Davidson, *Le roman conjugal*, 36.

53. Pradher to PV, September 9, 1812, AML 84II/10.

54. PVCJ entries for letters to CAT, 21, March 21 and 26, 1807. Women could attend meetings and events hosted by Freemasons and even become Freemasons themselves. See Allen, *Civil Society*.

55. PVCJ, entry dated April 5, 1812. According to an 1860 magazine article, "Grignon's, in the Rue Neuve des Petits Champs, was forty years ago probably the most crowded restaurant in Paris." See "France and Paris Forty, Thirty, and Twenty Years Ago by a Man on the Shady Side of Fifty," *Fraser's Magazine* 62 (September 1860): 389–408 (quot. 398).

56. CAT to PV, December 5, 1816, AML 84II/12. Les Trois Frères Provençaux opened in the 1780s. It became a favorite restaurant of Napoleon and army officers during the Napoleonic Wars and remained a popular landmark throughout the early nineteenth century. Zeldin, *History of French Passions*, 2: 740. On restaurants as public spaces that felt private, see Spang, *Invention of the Restaurant*, 79–83.

57. Hemmings, *Theatre Industry*, chap. 3; and Clay, *Stagestruck*, 169.

58. Jourda, *Le théâtre à Montpellier*, 63–64.

59. CAT to PV, April 5, 1811, AML 84II/12.

60. CAT to PV, December 30, 1807, AML 84II/12.

61. CAT to PV and AV, April 25, 1809, AML 84II/12.

62. CAT to PV and AV, April 1811, postmarked April 26, AML 84II/12.

63. CAT to PV and AV, March 11, 1809, AML 84II/12. Pergolesi Spontini was a conductor and composer and was a favorite of Napoleon. See George Loomis, "Two Centuries Later, a Composer Gets a Second Look," *New York Times*, November 27, 2019, accessed January 21, 2025, https://www.nytimes.com/2019/11/27/arts/music/spontini.html.

64. CAT to PV, November 28, 1814, AML 84II/12. It is unclear who Catherine meant by "us"; she may have been referring to herself and her daughter Adèle and/or her daughter-in-law.

65. CAT to PV, October 19, 1817, AML 84II/13.

66. CAT to PV, April 5, 1821, AML 84II/13.

67. CAT to PV, November 26, 1819, AML 84II/13. Both Monsieur and Madame Pouchard were regular performers in Rouen. See Bouteiller, *Théâtres de Rouen*, 427 and 445–446. On audiences' power over performances and the appeal of visiting actors, see Jourda, *Le théâtre à Montpellier*, 154–157.

68. Carr quoted in Hemmings, *Theatre and State*, 71. See Letellier, *Opéra-comique.*

69. PVCJ, entry for letter to CAT, December 23, 1806. *Koulouf, ou le Chinois* was an opéra-comique written by Pixérécourt and staged for the first time at the Opéra Comique on December 18, 1806. Garreau, "Pixérécourt," 125.

70. PVCJ, entry for letter to CAT, March 1, 1807.

71. CAT to PV, November 20, 1816, AML 84II/12.

72. PVCJ, entry for letter to CAT, February 28, 1818.

73. PVCJ entry for letter to CAT, November 13, 1813.

74. CAT to PV and AV, November 20, [1813], AML 84II/12.

75. PVCJ, entry for letter to CAT, December 23, 1813. According to the Geneanet website, Louise Pensée Roux (b. Lyon, 1796) married Henri Roux. Based on the family tree available there, it appears members of the Roux and Montagnat families frequently married their cousins. "Louise Pensée Roux," Geneanet, accessed January 21, 2025, https://gw.geneanet.org/jesuisgrolee?lang=en&iz=0&p=louise+pensee&n=roux.

76. CAT to PV and AV, October 14, 1808, AML 84II/12.

77. PVCJ entry for letter to CAT, October 17, 1808.

78. CAT to PV and AV, October 20, 1808, AML 84II/12. For details on the salon and its reception, see "Journaux du 15 octobre 1808," in Aulard, *Paris sous l'Empire*, 753–754.

79. JJB to PV (and AV?), July 8, 1812, AML 84II/9. A longer excerpt from this letter appears in Verjus and Davidson, *Le roman conjugal*, 237. It is possible there was a grain of truth in Jacques's letter. Mademoiselle Mars did travel to Rouen during the summer of 1812, returning to the Parisian stage in September of that year. *Mercure de France*, no. 582 (September 12, 1812): 517. (Accessed March 3, 2025, via the BNF's Gallica collection, https://gallica.bnf.fr/accueil/fr/html/accueil-fr.)

80. Berlanstein, *Daughters of Eve.*

81. L. Pradher to PV, September 16, 1812, AML 84II/10. The play may have been *La jeune femme colère*, an opera staged at the Feydeau on September 12, 1812. Elart, *Catalogue des fonds musicaux*, tome 1, 1: 174.

82. L. Pradher to PV, May 24, [1813], 11 *heures du soir*, AML 84II/10.

83. L. Pradher to PV, May 24, [1813], 11 *heures du soir*, AML 84II/10.

84. L. Pradher to AV, October 7, 1826, AML 84II/11. Pradher's first wife died in 1825. Entry on Pradher in *Encyclopédie de la musique*, 1657.

85. Barra, "Operatic Institution," 15.

86. PVCJ, July 30, 1811: "Amélie wrote to her mother . . . Session of the Conservatory very interesting for the distribution of prizes; concert, singing, speeches [*déclamation*]."

87. CAT to PV and AV, March 7, 1812, AML 84II/12.

88. CAT to PV and AV, February 8, 1809, AML 84II/12.

89. CAT to PV, December 20, 1820, AML 84II/13.

90. CAT to PV and AV, January 16, 1812, AML 84II/12.

91. CAT to PV and AV, January 30, 1815, AML 84II/12.

92. CAT to PV, March 3, 1818, AML 84II/13.

93. CAT to PV, December 30, 1818, AML 84II/13.

94. PVCJ, entry for letter to CAT, February 7, 1810. Jennifer Ronyak explores the dynamics between interiority and performance visible in private gatherings featuring music, and especially singing, in the early nineteenth-century German-speaking world. Similar processes were no doubt at play when Amélie and other women in these families sang at such events. See Ronyak, *Intimacy, Performance, and the Lied*, 6–9.

95. PVCJ, entry for letter to CAT, December 28, 1812.

96. PVCJ, entry for letter to CAT, May 28, 1812.

97. PVCJ, entry for letter to CAT, July 1, 1816.

98. PVCJ, entry for letter to CAT, December 31, 1816.

99. PVCJ, entry for letter to CAT, October 26, 1813.

100. PVCJ, entry for letter to CAT, March 4, 1816.

101. PVCJ, entry for letter to CAT, December 23, 1816.

102. PVCJ, entry for letter to Adèle Suchet, February 17, 1819, "Bal dimanche chez le Maréchal."

103. PVCJ, entry for letter to JJB, December 17, 1817.

104. CAT to PV and AV, August 19, 1807, AML 84II/12. On women's involvement in Napoleonic festivals, see Davidson, *France after Revolution*, chap. 1; and "Women at Napoleonic Festivals."

105. CAT to AV, April 18, 1810, AML 84II/12.

106. PVCJ, entry for letter to CAT, June 9, 1811.

107. PVCJ entry for letter to MV, October 9, 1813. Grétry was the composer Pierre mentioned when describing his visit to Rousseau's former home. (See chap. 5.)

108. PVCJ entry for letter to CAT, June 25, 1816.

109. CAT to PV, October 19, 1817, AML 84II/13. The Duc d'Anoulême was the son of Louis XVIII's brother.

110. CAT to PV, October 24, 1817, AML 84II/13.

111. On eighteenth-century *salonnières*, see Goodman, *Republic of Letters*, and Lilti, *World of the Salons*. On the nineteenth century, see Kale, *French Salons*. Elisabeth Joris explores "the femininization of private sociability" and its broader consequences in "Kinship and Gender," 242–246.

112. PVCJ, entry for letter to CAT, June 16, 1819; and CAT to AV, June 19, 1819, AML 84II/13. On Pierre-Edouard Lemontey (1762–1826), see Le site d'histoire de la Fondation Napoléon, accessed January 21, 2025, https://www.napoleon.org/histoire-des-2-empires/biographies/lemontey-pierre-edouard-1762-1826-ecrivain/.

8. Politics

1. Susan K. Foley makes this point regarding politically engaged men and their families during the Second Empire. See Foley, *Republican Passions*.

2. The concept of an "emotional regime" comes from Reddy, *Navigation of Feeling*.

3. See Chassagne, "Du drap et de la toile."

4. Vitet, *Rapport sur les écoles spéciales*. Michel Foucault discusses Vitet's proposal and reactions to it in *Birth of the Clinic*, 77–78. See also Ramsey, *Professional and Popular Medicine*, 77; and Crosland, "*Officiers de Santé*."

5. Two Marduel brothers lived in Lyon during these years—Antoine and Jean-Baptiste. The latter was a vicar of the Saint-Nizier church, where Marguerite was a parishioner. A passionate bibliophile, he also founded an influential pious association, le Rosaire Vivant (the Living Rosary). Poidevard et al., *Armorial des bibliophiles*, 372–373. The Marduels' letters to Louis and Pierre dating from 1795 to 1808 include frequent references to "the dear wife and mother" with whom they visited regularly. AML 84II/3. Another Marduel, Claude, a cousin of Jean-Baptise and refractory priest, returned to his post as *curé* of Saint Roch in 1801 after the Concordat. In 1807, Jean-Baptiste joined him as *vicaire*.

6. Marduel to Vitet *père et fils*, July 4, 1806, AML 84II/3.

7. Robert and Cougny, *Dictionnaire des parlementaires*, 541–542; and Sauzet, "Hommage à la mémoire de Ludovic Vitet," 193–194. On Récamier's salon, see Kale, *French Salons*, 90–91. Récamier's circle included others who opposed the emperor, such as Gemaine de Staël and Benjamin Constant.

8. Davallon to Louis Vitet and PV, 10 Nivôse Year VIII (December 31, 1799), AML 84II/11.

9. Serna, *République des girouettes*. PV discussed the phenomenon of *girouettes* in a letter to JJB. PVCJ, entry dated February 3, 1817.

10. Both families often read and commented upon newspapers known for their anti-Napoleon stance, such as *Le Mercure*. On the press of this period, see Cabanis, *La presse sous le Consulat*, and McMahon, *Enemies of the Enlightenment*, chap. 4.

11. See Szramkiewicz, *Les régents et censeurs de la Banque de France*, 358–365. Vital Roux's economic theories and influence are discussed in Rosanvallon, *Demands of Liberty*, 124–126.

12. On the consequences of Napoleon's blockade and other economic policies, see Horn, *Path Not Taken*, chap 7. Horn argues that these policies hurt more than helped French industry. On the economic situation in Rouen, see Daly, *Inside Napoleonic France*, chaps. 8 and 9. Alan Forrest provides causality statistics in *Napoleon's Men*,

19. The broader context and significance of these military conflicts and diplomatic maneuvers are explored in Mikaberidze, *The Napoleonic Wars*.

13. PVCJ, entries dated March 5, 1808 (to Louis Vitet); March 14, 1808 (to CAT); and March 19, 1808 (to Costerisan).

14. CAT to PV and AV, April 6, 1810, AML 84II/12.

15. Lilti, *Invention of Celebrity*.

16. AV to PV, May 31, 1810, AML 84II/11.

17. AV to PV, June 3, [1810], AML 84II/11. I discuss this example in "Women at Napoleonic Festivals," 312–314.

18. CAT to PV and AV, March 23, 1812, AML 84II/12. Jennifer Ngaire Heuer treats the issue of military service and its impact on families in her recent book, *The Soldier's Reward*.

19. See Heuer, "Neither Cowardly nor Greedy?"; Woloch, *New Regime*, 397–404; and Crépin, *Histoire de la conscription*. A decade later, PV hired a replacement for his son, making use of one of the insurance companies that had emerged to handle such arrangements. Contract dated February 17, 1823, AML 8411/15.

20. CAT to PV, March 24, 1812, AML 84II/12.

21. CAT to PV and AV, April 5, 1812, AML 84 II/12.

22. CAT to PV and AV, June 13, 1812, AML 84 II/12.

23. CAT to PV and AV, August 30, 1813, AML 84II/12.

24. CAT to PV and AV, November 9, 1813, AML 84II/12.

25. PVCJ, entry for letter to CAT, November 3, 1813.

26. Waresquiel, *La Restauration*, 30–38. On rumors circulating about the confiscation of properties purchased as *biens nationaux* and other economic and political matters, see Ploux, *De bouche* à oreille, chap. 6.

27. CAT to PV, January 3, 1814, AML 84II/12.

28. PVCJ, entry for letter to JJB, January 7, 1814.

29. CAT to PV, January 16, 1814, AML 84II/12.

30. They traveled separately, with Pierre leaving Paris first and Amélie and Ludovic following a few days later along with other family members and their servants. PVCJ, entries dated January 19 and 23, 1814. As it became clear that foreign troops would be occupying the city, thousands fled Paris. Lentz, *Nouvelle histoire du Premier Empire*, 2: 553–554.

31. PVCJ, entry for letter to MV, March 9, 1814.

32. PVCJ, entry for letter to AV, March 27, 1814.

33. PVCJ, entries for letters to AV, March 28 and 29, 1814; and PV to AV March 29, 1814, AML 84II/9.

34. PVCJ, entry for letter to MV, April 3, 1814.

35. Historians view it similarly. See Lentz, *Nouvelle histoire du Premier Empire*, 2: 564; and Waresquiel, *Talleyrand*, 442–444.

36. PVCJ, entry dated March 30, 1814.

37. PVCJ, entry for letter to MV, April 19, 1814.

38. PVCJ, entry for letter to MV, April 19, 1814.

39. PV to LV, May 4, 1814, AML 84II/9.

40. PV to LV, May 4, 1814, AML 84II/9.

41. PV to LV, May 4, 1814, AML 84II/9.

42. On liberal optimism that the Constitutional Charter could establish a parliamentary monarchy on the model of England, see Rosanvallon, *La monarchie impossible*, 57–64; and Vincent, *Benjamin Constant*.

43. PVCJ, entry for letter to Costerisan, April 24, 1814.

44. CAT to PV, May 26, 1814, AML 84II/12.

45. CAT to PV, May 26, 1814, AML 84II/12.

46. Catherine's reactions mirror Serna's argument that most people's primary loyalty was to France, not to a particular regime or ideology—a sentiment he labels the "extreme center." Serna, *République des girouettes*.

47. CAT to PV and AV, June 11, 1814, AML 84II/12.

48. CAT to AV, August 6, 1814, AML 84II/12.

49. CAT to PV, September 27, 1814, AML 84II/12.

50. Sudhir Hazareesingh recounts this story and connects the Hundred Days to the image of Napoleon that would be handed down to posterity in *Legend of Napoleon*.

51. Constant initially supported Napoleon until the emperor became too much of a dictator in his eyes; he then began criticizing Napoleon at great personal risk. He supported the Restoration when it appeared that it would be constitutional monarchy. Then, Constant shocked many when, during the Hundred Days, he agreed to write a constitution for Napoleon. Vincent, *Benjamin Constant*, 166–167.

52. Hulot, *Le Maréchal Suchet*, 242.

53. Waresquiel, *Cent-Jours*, 11–21.

54. PVCJ, entry for letter to CAT, March 20, 1815.

55. CAT to PV, March 21, 1815, AML 84II/12.

56. Davidson, "New (Emotional) Regime," and Heuer, "'No More Fears.'"

57. CAT to PV, March 23, 1815, AML 84II/12.

58. CAT to PV, April 6, 1815, AML 84II/13.

59. Amélie left Paris with Ludovic on Friday, May 12; Pierre left the following Sunday. PVCJ, undated entry between May 10 and 17, 1815.

60. PVCJ, entry for letter to Fournel, May 25, 1815.

61. Entries dated June 17 and 23, 1815. Pierre recorded a long account of the return of the Bourbons in his journal, PVCJ, entry dated July 8, 1815.

62. PVCJ, entry for letter to MV, July 29, 1815.

63. Fournel to PV, July 9, 1815, AML 84II/10.

64. On the European-wide drive to share such experiences, see Fritzsche, *Stranded in the Present*; and Petiteau, *Écrire la mémoire*.

65. Fournel to PV, July 16, 1815, AML 84II/10.

66. Fournel to PV, August 9, 1815, AML 84II/10. On such violence, see Triomphe, *1815: La Terreur blanche*.

67. Fournel to PV, August 9, 1815.

68. Madame Hochet to AV, July 27, 1815, AML 84II/11.

69. Terrasson de Senevas to PV, October 13, 1815, AML 84II/10.

70. Details on the Terrasson de Senevas family are available in Révérend, *Titres, anoblissements et pairies*, 6: 331–332. Terrasson was born in Lyon and moved to Paris after the Revolution. Passionate about art and literature, he (along with his wife) translated several English novels into French. His son, Hypolite, went on to marry the daughter of a wealthy Rouennais textile manufacturer. See Niderst, "La vie de château."

71. Fournel to PV, October 17, 1815, AML 84II/10. Fournel's feelings of victimization and humiliation mingled with patriotism mirror those of Parisians more generally as they saw their city sacked and occupied. In his account of this period, Emmanuel Waresquiel argues that "all of this will be experienced with pain and humiliation, inspiring among Parisians outbursts of patriotism that will in part turn against the Restoration." ["*Tout cela sera vécu avec douleur et humiliation, tout en attisant chez les Parisiens des relents de patriotisme frustré qui se retourneront en partie contre le régime restauré.*"] Waresquiel, *Cent-Jours*, 500. On "the rape of the Louvre," see Haynes, *Our Friends the Enemies*, 93–101.

72. PVCJ, entry for letter to MV, September 30, 1815.

73. PVCJ, entry for letter to MV, November 4, 1815.

74. PVCJ, entry dated January 25, 1816.

75. AAT to PV, December 31, [1816], AML 84II/13.

76. PVCJ, entry for letter to AAT, January 5, 1817.

77. CAT to PV, November 20, 1816, AML 84II/12.

78. CAT to PV, January 15, 1817, AML 84II/13. On efforts to alleviate poverty and the problems caused by unemployment during this period, see Marec, "Pauvres et miséraux."

79. CAT to PV, January 20, 1817, AML 84II/13.

80. CAT to PV, January 30, 1817, AML 84II/13.

81. CAT to PV, February 6, 1817, AML 84II/13.

82. PVCJ, entries dated February 9 and 24, 1817.

83. PVCJ, entry for letter to CAT, March 30, 1817.

84. CAT to PV, December 10, 1817, AML 84II/13. In her letter, CAT used the word *soufflet*, which means a flat-handed slap on the face. Unfortunately, I have been unable to track down the incident to which she was referring.

85. CAT to PV, December 20, 1817, AML 84II/13.

86. *Opinion de M. Lafitte.*

87. PVCJ, entry for letter to CAT, October 30, 1818.

88. CAT to PV, November 8, [1818], AML 84II/13.

89. On the rise of the liberal opposition and their evolving tactics, see Alexander, *Re-Writing the French Revolutionary Tradition.*

90. CAT to PV, April 22, 1819, AML 84II/13.

91. CAT to PV, September 13, 1819, AML 84II/13.

92. CAT to PV, September 13, 1819, AML 84II/13.

93. CAT to PV, November 26, [1819], AML 84II/13.

94. CAT to AV, December 8, [1819], AML 84II/13, misfiled in 1820 folder.

95. CAT to PV, February 19, 1819, AML 84II/13.

96. AAT to AV, December 29, 1819, AML 84II/13.

97. AAT to AV, April 6, 1820, AML 84II/13. AAT's handwriting is not easy to decipher. I have found no General Morin who could have been in Rouen in 1820. She may have been referring to General Mortier, duc de Trévise (1768–1835), who was stationed there during the Restoration. Courcelles, *Dictionnaire historique,* 8: 97–108.

98. PVCJ, entry for letter to CAT, February 16, 1820.

99. CAT to PV, February 17, 1820, AML 84II/13.

100. See Skuy, *Assassination, Politics, and Miracles*, 16–19.

101. CAT to AV, May 20, 1820, AML 84II/13.

102. PV to AV, May 1, 1820, AML 84II/9, ellipses in original. One of the pamphlets Pierre read may have been *Opinion de M. Camille Teisseire* (1820). A brief biography of Teisseire appears on the list of deputies on the website of the French National Assembly, accessed January 21, 2025, https://www2.assemblee-nationale.fr/sycomore/fiche/(num_dept)/11505/(legislature)/. He was Casmir Périer's brother-in-law.

103. PV to AV, May 6, 1820, AML 84II/9.

104. PV to AV, May 7, 1820, AML 84II/9.

105. PV to AV, May 20, 1820, AML 84II/9. Both men whose speeches he appreciated were liberal deputies.

106. AV to PV, May 25, [1820], AML 84II/11.

107. PV to AV, May 30, 1820, AML 84II/9.

108. PV to AV, May 30, 1820, AML 84II/9. Emphases in original.

109. AAT to AV, March 28, 1821, AML 84II/13. Emphases in original.

110. AAT to PV, February [3], 1826, AML 84II/13.

111. CAT to PV, November 16, 1820, AML 84II/13.

112. CAT to PV, November 16, 1820, AML 84II/13. On the scandal, see Clark, "Queen Caroline"; and Laqueur, "Queen Caroline Affair."

113. CAT to PV, February 28, [1821], AML 84II/13.

114. CAT to PV, March 20, 1821, AML 84II/13.

115. Maza, *Myth of the French Bourgeoisie*, chap. 5. See also Alexander, *Re-Writing the French Revolutionary Tradition*.

116. AAT to PV, June 20, 1826, AML 84II/13. Emphasis in original. The cousin must be Nicholas Bergasse. See Bergasse and Lamy, *Un défenseur des principes traditionnels*, 436.

117. Kroen, *Politics and Theater*, chap. 6; and Alexander, *Re-Writing the French Revolutionary Tradition*, 226–227.

118. AAT to LV, November 26, 1827, AML 84II/13. Emphases in original.

119. AAT to LV, November 26, 1827, AML 84II/13. Further evidence of AAT's desire to do more than darn stockings is the fact that she served as president of the Rouen chapter of the Société de la Charité Maternelle. Chassagne, "Du drap et de la toile," 78.

120. See Reddy, *Navigation of Feeling*; Horowitz, *Friendship and Politics*; and Goldstein, *Post-Revolutionary Self*. The classic study of how Revolutionary discourse constructed an exclusively male public sphere is Landes, *Women and the Public Sphere*.

Conclusion

1. PVCJ, entry for letter to AAT, March 24, 1832. Pierre sent news about the family's new lodgings: "The newlyweds on the first floor; [Pierre, Amélie], and Mimi, *le papa* and *la maman* on the second . . . nicely independent rooms . . . well-lit with pretty views of the gardens."

2. PVCJ, entry for letter to Delaunay, April 8, 1832.

3. "These four square meters cost 1600 francs. . . . We plan to cover it ourselves and to hide it from *le papa* who is not up-to-date on these matters." PV to AAT, April 17, 1832, AN 572AP/5. CAT was buried on April 9, 1832. The Paris cemetery registry for Père Lachaise lists her as Tison, Arnaud née Descheaux, Catherine Françoise. During the Restoration, Pére Lachaise emerged as a site for the liberal opposition to

gather during funerals. See Perl-Rosenthal, *Age of Revolutions*, 330–333; and Fureix, *La France des larmes*.

4. Letter of condolence from François Guizot to LV, August 1, 1854, AN 572AP/10.

5. AAT to LV, November 26, 1827, AML 84II/13.

6. PVCJ, entry for letter to MV, July 29, 1815.

7. Cottez, "Essai sur Marc Arnaudtizon"; and Chassagne, "Du drap et de la toile," 79.

8. See Pellissier, *Loisirs et sociabilités*, vol. 1. Living and running businesses in port cities such as Marseilles, Bordeaux, and Nantes no doubt encouraged more outward-facing perspectives, though even in Western France, with its many connections to the Atlantic world, endogamous marriages remained common. See Johnson, *Becoming Bourgeois*, and Rothschild, *An Infinite History*.

9. See, for example, Ronyak, *Intimacy, Performance, and the Lied*, chap. 3.

Bibliography

Primary Sources

Archival Materials

Archives Départementales du Rhône (Lyon)

Series AP, Cadastres
Series 1Q, Bien nationaux and séquestres
Series 2E and 3E, Notarial records

Archives Départementales de la Seine-Maritime (Rouen)

Etat civil records (microfilmed/digitized)
Series 3Q, Property records
Series 2E, Notarial records

Archives Municipales de Lyon

Etat civil records (digitized)
Fonds Coste, 12II
Fonds Vitet, 84II
Series 2I, Police Générale

Archives Nationales (Paris/Saint Denis)

Fonds Ludovic Vitet, 572AP
Fonds Suchet, 384AP
Minutier Central, notarial records
Revolutionary Tribunal records, BB18
Series F7, police records

Archives de Paris

Etat civil records (digitized)
Registres d'inhumations des cimetières de Paris (digitized)

Newspapers/Periodicals

Frazer's Magazine
Mercure de France
The New York Times

Published Primary Sources

Almanach du commerce de Paris et des départements de France et des principales villes du monde. Paris: Bureau de l'Almanach, 1820

Almanach royal et national pour l'an MDCCCXLI présenté à leurs majestés. Paris: Guyot et Scribe, 1841.

Arnaudtizon, Marc. *Exploration commerciale dans les mers du sud et de la Chine*. Rouen: Péron, 1854.

Bréghot du Lut, Claude, and Pericaud, aîné, eds. *Biographie Lyonnaise: Catalogue des Lyonnais dignes de mémoire*. Paris: Techener; and Lyon: Giberton et Brun, 1839.

Bouteiller, Jules-Edouard. *Histoire complète et méthodique des théâtres de Rouen*. Rouen: Giroux et Renaux, 1867.

Bulletin de la Société de l'histoire de Paris et de l'Ile de France. Paris: Champion, 1904.

Catalogue de la bibliothèque lyonnaise de M. Coste. Lyon: Perrin, 1853.

Courcelles, Jean Baptiste Pierre Jullien de. *Dictionnaire historique et biographique des généraux français depuis le onzième siècle jusqu'en 1820*. 9 vols. Paris: Chez l'Auteur, 1820–1823.

Dictionnaire des sciences médicales par une société de médecins et de chirurgiens. 60 vols. Paris: Panckoucke, 1812–1814.

Guizot, François. "M. Vitet: Sa vie et ses œuvres." *Revue des deux mondes* 2, no. 1 (March 1, 1874): 33–65. https://www.jstor.org/stable/44744641.

Journal de M. Suleau, no. 5 (July 16, 1791).

Mémoires de Madame la duchesse d'Abrantès. 4th ed. 3 vols. Brussels: Société Belge de Librairie, 1837.

Mercier, Louis Sébastien. *Le nouveau Paris*. 6 vols. Brunswick: Chez les principaux libraires, 1800.

Opinion de M. Camille Teisseire sur le projet de loi rélatif aux éléctions. Paris: Hacquart, 1820.

Opinion de M. Lafitte, député de la Seine, sur le projet de loi relatif aux finances pour 1817, prononcé à la Séance du 10 février 1817. Paris: Bossange, 1817.

Pariset, Étienne. "Notice sur Louis Vitet." *Revue du Lyonnais* 3 (1836): 451–463.

Procès-verbaux des séances des Corps Municipaux de la ville de Lyon. 6 vols. Lyon: Imprimerie Nouvelle Lyonnaise, 1899–1905.

Rémusat, Charles de. *Notice historique de Casimir Périer*. Paris: Michel Lévy Frères, 1874.

[Salm, Constance de.] "Rapport sur les fleurs artificielles de la citoyenne Roux-Montagnat par Constance de Th[éis] Pipelet de la Société du Lycée des Arts lu par l'auteur à la 59e séance publique du 30 Vendémiaire an 7." Bibliothèque Nationale de France, Gallica, accessed January 21, 2025. https://gallica.bnf.fr/ark:/12148/bpt6k426676?rk=21459.

Sauzet, Paul. "Hommage à la mémoire de Ludovic Vitet." *Mémoires de l'Académie des sciences, belles-lettres et arts de Lyon* 15 (1874): 185–221.

Serbat, Louis. "Eugène Aubry-Vitet (1845–1930)." *Bibliothèque de l'école des chartes*. Vol. 91 (1930): 233–234.

Thiers, Adolphe. *Histoire de la Révolution française*. 10 vols. Paris: Furne, 1836.

Vitet, Louis. *Médecine vétérinaire*. 3 vols. Lyon: Frères Perisse, 1771.

Vitet, Louis. *Pharmacopée de Lyon, ou exposition méthodique des médicaments simples et composés: De leurs caractères, de leurs vertus, de leur préparation et administration, et des espèces de maladies où ils sont indiqués*. Lyon: Frères Perisse, 1778.

Vitet, Louis. *Rapport sur les écoles spéciales de médecine, séance du 17 ventôse an 6*. Paris: Imprimerie Nationale, 1798.

Vitet, Louis. *Traité de la sangsue médicinale*. Paris: Nicolle, 1809.

Vitet, Ludovic. *Études philosophiques et littéraires*. Edited by François Guizot. Paris: Michel Levy, 1875.

Vitet, Ludovic. *Études sur les beaux-arts. Essais d'archéologie et fragments littéraires*. 2 vols. Paris: Charpentier, 1847.

Vitet, Ludovic. *La mort de Henri III, août 1589, scènes historiques, faisant suite aux Barricades et aux États de Blois*. Paris: H. Fournier Jeune, 1829.

Vitet, Pierre. *Notes et souvenirs sur quelques-uns des principaux événements de la Révolution, sur la vie politique de mon père, ses malheurs et son exil en Suisse, après le siège de Lyon, 1792–1793 et 1794*. Paris: Renouard, 1932.

Witt, Henriette de (née Guizot). *Monsieur Guizot in Private Life, 1787–1874*. Translated by M. C. M. Simpson. Boston: Estes and Lauriat, 1882.

Secondary Sources

Adams, Christine. *A Taste for Comfort and Status: A Bourgeois Family in Eighteenth-Century France*. University Park: Pennsylvania State University Press, 2000.

Alexander, Robert. *Re-Writing the French Revolutionary Tradition: Liberal Opposition and the Fall of the Bourbon Monarchy*. Cambridge, UK: Cambridge University Press, 2003

Allen, James Smith. *A Civil Society: The Public Space of Freemason Women in France, 1744–1944*. Lincoln: University of Nebraska Press, 2021.

Allen, James Smith. "The Politics of Sociability? French Masonic Culture Before the Revolution." In *Gender and Fraternal Orders in Europe, 1300–2000*, edited by Máire Fedelma Cross. Basingstoke, UK: Palgrave Macmillan, 2010.

Arnold, James. "'Il fut bon père': The Institut de France, Funeral Eulogies and the Formation of Bourgeois Identity in Early Nineteenth-Century France." *French History* 29, no. 2 (2015): 204–224. https://doi.org/10.1093/fh/cru079.

Arnold, R. J. *Grétry's Operas and the French Public: From the Old Regime to the Restoration*. Farnham, UK: Ashgate, 2016.

Aulard, Alphonse, ed. *Paris sous l'Empire: Recueil de documents pour l'histoire de l'esprit public à Paris*. 3 vols. Paris: Cerf, 1912–1923.

Baczko, Bronislaw. *Ending the Terror: The French Revolution After Robespierre*. Translated by Michael Petheram. Cambridge, UK: Cambridge University Press, 1994.

Bardet, Jean-Pierre. "Political Revolution and Contraceptive Revolution." In *The French Revolution in Culture and Society*, edited by David G. Troyansky, Alfred Cismaru, and Norwood Andrews Jr. New York: Greenwood, 1991.

Barra, Olivier. "The Company at the Heart of the Operatic Institution: Chollet and the Changing Nature of Comic-Opera Role Types during the July Monarchy." In *Music, Theater, and Cultural Transfer: Paris 1830–1940*, edited by Annegret Fauser and Marc Everest. Chicago: University of Chicago Press, 2009.

Beckert, Sven. *Empire of Cotton: A Global History*. New York: Vintage, 2014.

Benoit, Bruno. *L'identité politique de Lyon: Entre violences collectives et mémoires des élites (1786–1905)*. Paris: L'Harmattan, 1999.

Bergasse, Louis. "Un Janseniste lyonnais: Alexandre Bergasse (1754–1820)." *Revue d'histoire de l'église de France* 38, no. 131 (1952): 5–51. https://doi.org/10.3406/rhef.1952.3123.

Bergasse, Louis, and Étienne Lamy. *Un défenseur des principes traditionnels sous la Révolution: Nicolas Bergasse, avocat au parlement de Paris, député du tiers état de la sénéchaussée de Lyon aux États*-Généraux *(1750–1832)*. Paris: Perrin, 1910.

Bergerot, Bernard. *Le Maréchal Suchet, duc d'Albuféra*. Paris: Tallandier, 1986.

Berlanstein, Lenard R. *Daughters of Eve: A Cultural History of French Theater Women from the Old Regime to the Fin-de-siècle.* Cambridge, MA: Harvard University Press, 2001.

Biard, Michel, and Marisa Linton. *Terror: The French Revolution and Its Demons*. New York: Polity, 2022.

Blanc, Robert. *Un pasteur du temps des Lumières: Benjamin-Sigismond Frossard (1754–1830)*. Paris: Champion, 2000.

Blaufarb, Rafe. *The Great Demarcation: The French Revolution and the Invention of Modern Property*. Oxford: Oxford University Press, 2016.

Bonnet, Alain. "Ludovic Vitet." In *Dictionnaire critique des historiens de l'art actifs en France de la Révolution à la Première Guerre mondiale*, edited by Philippe Sénéchal and Claire Barbillon. Accessed January 21, 2025. https://www.inha.fr/dictionnaire-critique-des-historiens-de-lart-actifs-en-france-de-la-revolution-a-la-premiere-guerre-mondiale/vitet-ludovic-inha/.

Bourdieu, Pierre. *Outline of a Theory of Practice*. Translated by Richard Nice. Cambridge, UK: Cambridge University Press, 1977.

Bourdieu, Pierre. "Les stratégies matrimoniales dans le système de reproduction." *Annales ESC* 27, nos. 4–5 (1972): 1105–1125. https://doi.org/10.3406/ahess.1972.422586.

Bricard, Isabelle. *Saintes ou pouliches: L'éducation des jeunes filles au XIXe siècle*. Paris: Albin Michel, 1985.

Brix, Michel, and Yves Lenoir, eds. Introduction to *Douze chapitres inédits des "Réflexions d'un solitaire,"* by André Ernest Modeste Grétry. Namur, BE: Presses Universitaires de Namur, 1993.

Brockliss, Laurence, and Colin Jones. *The Medical World of Early Modern France*. Oxford: Clarendon, 1997.

Brown, Howard G. *Ending the French Revolution: Violence, Justice, and Repression from the Terror to Napoleon*. Charlottesville: University of Virginia Press, 2006.

Burguière, André, and Jacques Revel, eds. *Histoire de la France*. Vol.4. *Les formes de la culture*. Paris: Seuil, 1993.

Burstin, Haïm. *Révolutionnaires: Pour une anthropologie politique de la Révolution française*. 2nd ed. Paris: Vendémiare, 2022.

Cabanis, Andre. *La presse sous le Consulat et L'Empire*. Paris: Société des études robespierristes, 1975.

Certeau, Michel de. *The Practice of Everyday Life*. Translated by Steven Rendall. Berkeley: University of California Press, 1984.

Chaline, Jean-Pierre. "La banque à Rouen au XIXe siècle," *Revue d'histoire économique et sociale* 52, no. 3 (1974): 384–420. https://www.jstor.org/stable/24084161.

Chaline, Jean-Pierre. *Les bourgeois de Rouen: Une élite urbaine au XIXe siècle*. Paris: Presses de la Fondation Nationale des Sciences Politiques, 1982.

Chartier, Roger. *La correspondance: Les usages de la lettre au XIXe siècle*. Paris: Fayard, 1991.

Chassagne, Serge. "Du drap et de la toile en Lyonnais à l'indienne à Rouen: Itinéraire d'une famille, les Arnaud-Tison." In *Les trames de l'histoire: Entreprises, territoires, consommations, institutions: Mélanges en l'honneur de Jean-Claude Daumas*, edited by Jean-Paul Barrière, Régis Boulat, Alain Chatriot, Pierre Lamard, and Jean-Michel Minovez. Besançon, France: Presses universitaires de Franche-Comté, 2017.

Chassagne, Serge. *Le coton et ses patrons: France, 1760–1840*. Paris: Éditions de l'École des Hautes Études en Sciences Sociales, 1991.

Chassagne, Serge. *Oberkampf: Un entrepreneur capitaliste au siècle des lumières*. Paris: Aubier, 1980.

Chervel, André. *La culture scolaire: Une approche historique*. Paris: Belin, 1998.

Clark, Anna. "Queen Caroline and the Sexual Politics of Popular Culture in London, 1820." *Representations* 31 (1990): 47–68. https://doi.org/10.2307/2928399.

Clay, Lauren R. *Stagestruck: The Business of Theater in Eighteenth-Century France and Its Colonies*. Ithaca, NY: Cornell University Press, 2013.

Cobb, Richard. *Reactions to the French Revolution*. Oxford: Oxford University Press, 1972.

Cohen, Margaret. *The Sentimental Education of the Novel*. Princeton, NJ: Princeton University Press, 1999.

Corbin, Alain. *L'harmonie des plaisirs: Les manières de jouir du siècle des Lumières à l'avènement de la sexologie*. Paris: Perrin, 2008.

Cottez, Jean. "Essai sur Marc Arnaudtizon." *Bulletin de la Société d'études océaniennes*, no. 121 (December 1957): 723–739.

Cottez, Jean. "Notes sur un voyage commercial de Marc Arnaudtizon aux mers du Sud et de Chine (1850–1854)." *Bulletin de la Société d'études océaniennes*, no. 117 (December 1956): 610–629.

Counter, Andrew. *The Amorous Restoration: Love, Sex, and Politics in Early Nineteenth-Century France*. Oxford: Oxford University Press, 2016.

Couriel, Étienne. "La place de la parenté dans les baptêmes d'une paroisse lyonnaise d'Ancien Régime." *Le parrainage en Europe et en Amérique: Pratiques de longue durée*, edited by Guido Alfani, Vincent Gourdon, and Isabelle Robin. Bruxelles: Peter Lang, 2015.

Crépin, Annie. *Histoire de la conscription*. Paris: Gallimard, 2009.

Crosland, Maurice. "The *Officiers de Santé* of the French Revolution: A Case Study in the Changing Language of Medicine." *Medical History* 48 (2004): 229–244. https://doi.org/10.1017/S0025727300007407.

Crowston, Claire Haru. *Credit, Fashion, Sex: Economies of Regard in Old Regime France*. Durham, NC: Duke University Press, 2013.

Cuer, Georges, ed. *Minutes et repétoires des notaires de la ville de Lyon*. Lyon: Archives départementales et métropolitaines du Rhône, 2023.

Daly, Gavin. *Inside Napoleonic France: State and Society in Rouen, 1800–1815*. Aldershot, UK: Ashgate, 2001.

Darnton, Robert. *The Great Cat Massacre and Other Episodes in French Cultural History*. New York: Basic, 1984.

Daumard, Adeline. "Affaire, amour, affection: Le mariage dans la société bourgeoise au XIXe siècle." *Romantisme* 68 (1990): 33–47. https://doi.org/10.3406/roman.1990.6124.

Daumard, Adeline. *Les bourgeois et la bourgeoisie en France depuis 1815*. Paris: Aubier, 1987.

Daumas, Philippe. *Famille en revolution: Vie et relations familiales en Ile-de-France, changements et continuités, 1775–1825*. Rennes: Presses universitaires de Rennes, 2003.

Dauphin, Cécile, Pierrette Lebrun-Pézerat, and Danièle Poublan. *Ces bonnes lettres: Une correspondance familiale au XIXe siècle*. Paris: Albin Michel, 1995.

Davidoff, Leonore, and Catherine Hall. *Family Fortunes: Men and Women of the English Middle Class, 1780–1850*. Chicago: University of Chicago Press, 1987.

Davidson, Denise Z. "'A belle-mère idéale, gendre ideal. . . .'" In *L'Histoire des belles-mères*, edited by Yannick Ripa. Paris: Belin, 2015.

Davidson, Denise Z. *France after Revolution: Urban Life, Gender, and the New Social Order*. Cambridge, MA: Harvard University Press, 2007.

Davidson, Denise Z. "'Happy' Marriages in Early Nineteenth-Century France." *Journal of Family History* 37, no. 1 (2012): 23–35. https://doi.org/10.1177/0363199011428123.

Davidson, Denise Z. "Local Identities and Internal Migration: Networking as a Survival Strategy in Revolutionary and Postrevolutionary France." In *Place and Locality in Modern France*, edited by Philip Whalen and Patrick Young. London: Bloomsbury, 2014.

Davidson, Denise Z. "The New (Emotional) Regime: Bourgeois Reactions to the Turmoil of 1814–1815." *FHS* 42, no. 4 (2019): 595–621. https://doi.org/10.1215/00161071-7689184.

Davidson, Denise Z. "*Notes et souvenirs . . . sur la vie politique de mon père*: Memory, Mourning, and Politics in the Revolutionary Era." In *Everyday Politics and Culture in Revolutionary France*, edited by Victoria Thompson, Bryant T. Ragan, and Suzanne Desan. Oxford University Studies in the Enlightenment. Liverpool: Liverpool University Press, 2024.

Davidson, Denise Z. "Women at Napoleonic Festivals: Gender and the Public Sphere during the First Empire." *French History* 16, no. 3 (2002): 299–322. https://doi.org/10.1093/fh/16.3.299.

Davidson, Denise Z., and Anne Verjus. "Generational Conflict in Revolutionary France: Widows, Inheritance Practices, and the 'Victory' of Sons." *William and Mary Quarterly* 70, no. 2 (2013): 399–424. https://doi.org/10.5309/willmaryquar.70.2.0399.

Del Lungo, Andrea, and Pierre Glaudes, eds. *Balzac, l'invention de la sociologie*. Paris: Classiques Garnier, 2019.

Denby, David J. *Sentimental Narrative and the Social Order in France, 1760–1820*. Cambridge, UK: Cambridge University Press, 1994.

Desan, Suzanne. "'Constitutional Amazons': Jacobin Women's Clubs in the French Revolution." In *Recreating Authority in Revolutionary France*, edited by Bryant T. Ragan and Elizabeth A. Williams. New Brunswick, NJ: Rutgers University Press, 1992.

Desan, Suzanne. *The Family on Trial in Revolutionary France*. Berkeley: University of California Press, 2004.

di Leonardo, Micaela. "The Female World of Cards and Holidays: Women, Families, and the Work of Kinship." *Signs* 12, no. 3 (1987): 440–453. http://www.jstor.org/stable/3174331.

Doyle, William. *Napoleon at Peace: How to End a Revolution*. London: Reaktion Books, 2022.

Duprat, Annie, ed. *"Les affaires d'état sont mes affaires de cœur": Lettres de Rosalie Jullien, une femme dans la Révolution, 1775–1810*. Paris: Belin, 2016.

Edmonds, Bill. "The Rise and Fall of Popular Democracy in Lyon, 1789–1795." *Bulletin of the John Rylands University Library of Manchester* 67 (1984): 408–449. https://doi.org/10.7227/BJRL.67.1.5.

Edmonds, W. D. *Jacobinism and the Revolt of Lyon, 1789–1793*. Oxford: Clarendon/Oxford University Press, 1990.

Elart, Joann, ed. *Catalogue des fonds musicaux conservés en Haute-Normandie*: t. 1, Bibliothèque municipale de Rouen. Vol. 1, Fonds du Théâtre des arts (XVIIIe et XIXe siècles). Rouen: Publications de l'Université de Rouen, 2004.

Encyclopédie de la musique et dictionnaire du Conservatoire. 11 vols. Paris: Delagrave, 1913–1931.

Eynard, Georges. *Joseph Chalier: Bourreau ou martyr 1747–1793*. Lyon: Éditions Lyonnaises d'Art et d'Histoire, 1987.

Fairchilds, Cissie. *Domestic Enemies: Servants and Their Masters in Old Regime France*. Baltimore, MD: Johns Hopkins University Press, 1984.

Feuga, Paul. "Les malheurs de Madame Vitet, femme du maire de Lyon." *Bulletin de la Société historique, archéologique, et littéraire de Lyon* 26 (1996): 103–121.

Fierro, Alfred. *La vie des Parisiens sous Napoléon*. Saint-Cloud, France: Napoléon 1er éditions, 2003.

Fine, Agnès. *Parrains, marraines: La parenté spirituelle en Europe*. Paris: Fayard, 1994.

Flandrin, Jean-Louis. *Families in Former Times: Kinship, Household, and Sexuality*. Translated by Richard Southern. Cambridge, UK: Cambridge University Press, 1979.

Foley, Susan K. *Republican Passions: Family, Friendship, and Politics in Nineteenth-Century France*. Manchester, UK: Manchester University Press, 2023.

Forrest, Alan. *Napoleon's Men: The Soldiers of the Revolution and Empire*. London: Hambleden Continuum, 2002.

Foucault, Michel. *The Birth of the Clinic: An Archeology of Medical Perception*. Translated by A. M. Sheridan Smith. New York: Vintage, 1975.

Fritzsche, Peter. *Stranded in the Present: Modern Time and the Melancholy of History*. Cambridge, MA: Harvard University Press, 2004.

Fureix, Emmanuel. *La France des larmes: Deuils politiques à l'âge romantique (1814–1840)*. Seyssel, France: Champ Vallon, 2009.

Garden, Maurice. *Lyon et les Lyonnais au XVIIIe siècle*. Paris: Flammarion, 1975.

Garreau, Joseph E. "Pixérécourt, René-Charles Gilbert de (1773–1844)." In *McGraw-Hill Encyclopedia of World Drama*, edited by Stanley Hochman. Vol. 4. Boston: McGraw Hill, 1984.

Garrioch, David. *The Formation of the Parisian Bourgeoisie, 1690–1830*. Cambridge, MA: Harvard University Press, 1996.

Gay, Peter. *The Bourgeois Experience: Victoria to Freud*. New York: Oxford University Press, 1984.

Gelbart, Nina Rattner. *The King's Midwife: A History and Mystery of Madame du Coudray*. Berkeley: University of California Press, 1998.

Gerson, Stéphane. "Parisian Litterateurs, Provincial Journeys and the Construction of National Unity in Post-Revolutionary France." *Past and Present* 151, no. 1 (1996): 141–173. https://doi.org/10.1093/past/151.1.141.

Gerson, Stéphane. *The Pride of Place: Local Memories and Political Culture in Nineteenth-Century France*. Ithaca, NY: Cornell University Press, 2003.

Gillis, John R. *A World of Their Own Making: Myth, Ritual, and the Quest for Family Values*. New York: Basic Books, 1996.

Goblot, Jacques. *La jeune France libérale:* Le Globe *et son group littéraire 1824–1830*. Paris: Plon, 1995.

Goldstein, Jan. *The Post-Revolutionary Self: Politics and the Psyche in France, 1750–1850*. Cambridge, MA: Harvard University Press, 2005.

Goodman, Dena. *Becoming a Woman in the Age of Letters*. Ithaca, NY: Cornell University Press, 2009.

Goodman, Dena. "Letter Writing and the Emergence of Gendered Subjectivity in Eighteenth-Century France." *Journal of Women's History* 17, no. 2 (2005): 9–37. https://doi.org/10.1353/jowh.2005.0020.

Goodman, Dena. "Marital Choice and Marital Success: Reasoning about Marriage, Love, and Happiness." In *Family, Gender, and Law in Early Modern France*, edited by Suzanne Desan and Jeffrey Merrick. University Park: Pennsylvania State University Press, 2009.

Goodman, Dena. "Marriage Calculations in the Eighteenth Century: Deconstructing the Love vs. Duty Binary." *Proceedings of the Western Society for French History* 33 (2005): 146–162. http://hdl.handle.net/2027/spo.0642292.0033.009.

Goodman, Dena. *The Republic of Letters: A Cultural History of the French Enlightenment*. Ithaca, NY: Cornell University Press, 1994.

Grassi, Marie-Claire. *L'Art de la lettre au temps de la Nouvelle Héloïse et du romantisme*. Geneva: Slatkine, 1994.

Greene, Christopher M. "Romanticism, Cultural Nationalism and Politics in the July Monarchy: The Contribution of Ludovic Vitet." *French History* 4, no. 4 (1990): 487–509. https://doi.org/10.1093/fh/4.4.487.

Gutermann-Jacquet, Deborah. *Les équivoques du genre: Devenir homme et femme à l'âge romantique*. Rennes, France: Presses Universitaires de Rennes, 2012.

Hanson, Paul R. *The Jacobin Republic Under Fire: The Federalist Revolt in the French Revolution*. University Park: Pennsylvania State University Press, 2003.

Harrison, Carol E. *The Bourgeois Citizen in Nineteenth-Century France: Gender, Sociability, and the Uses of Emulation*. Oxford: Oxford University Press, 1999.

Haynes, Christine. *Our Friends the Enemies: The Occupation of France After Napoleon*. Cambridge, MA: Harvard University Press, 2018.

Hazareesingh, Sudhir. *The Legend of Napoleon*. London: Granta, 2014.

Hemmings, F. W. J. *Theatre and State in France, 1760–1905*. Cambridge, UK: Cambridge University Press, 1994.

Hemmings, F. W. J. *The Theatre Industry in Nineteenth-Century France*. Cambridge, UK: Cambridge University Press, 1993.

Hennequin-Lecomte, Laure. *Le patriciat strasbourgeois (1789–1830): Destins croisés et voix intimes*. Strasbourg, France: Presses Universitaires de Strasbourg, 2011.

Heuer, Jennifer Ngaire. *The Family and the Nation: Gender and Citizenship in Revolutionary France, 1789–1830*. Ithaca, NY: Cornell University Press, 2005.

Heuer, Jennifer Ngaire. "Neither Cowardly nor Greedy? Buying and Selling Escape from Conscription in Revolutionary and Post-Revolutionary France." *French History* 36, no. 2 (2022): 208–226. https://doi.org/10.1093/fh/crab031.

Heuer, Jennifer Ngaire. "'No More Fears, No More Tears'?: Gender, Emotion, and the Aftermath of the Napoleonic Wars in France." *Gender and History* 28, no. 2 (2016): 438–460. https://doi.org/10.1111/1468-0424.12217.

Heuer, Jennifer Ngaire. *The Soldier's Reward: Love and War in the Age of the French Revolution and Napoleon*. Princeton, NJ: Princeton University Press, 2024.

Hiner, Susan. *Accessories to Modernity: Fashion and the Feminine in Nineteenth-Century France*. Philadelphia: University of Pennsylvania Press, 2013.

Horn, Jeff. *The Path Not Taken: French Industrialization in the Age of Revolution, 1750–1830*. Cambridge, MA: MIT Press, 2006.

Horowitz, Sarah. *Friendship and Politics in Post-Revolutionary France*. University Park: Pennsylvania State University Press, 2013.

Houbre, Gabrielle. *La discipline de l'amour: L'éducation sentimentale des filles et des garçons à l'âge du romantisme*. Paris: Plon, 1997.

Hulot, Frédéric. *Le Maréchal Suchet*. Paris: Pygmalion, 2009.

Hunt, Lynn. "The Experience of Revolution." *FHS* 32, no. 4 (2009): 671–678. http://dx.doi.org/10.1215/00161071-2009-015.

Hunt, Lynn. *The Family Romance of the French Revolution*. Berkeley: University of California Press, 1992.

Hunt, Lynn. *Politics, Culture, and Class in the French Revolution*. Berkeley: University of California Press, 1984.

Isbell, John Claiborne. "Voices Lost? Staël and Slavery, 1786–1830." In *Slavery in the Caribbean Francophone World: Distant Voices, Forgotten Acts, Forged Identities*, edited by Doris Y. Kadish. Athens: University of Georgia Press, 2016.

Jennings, Lawrence C. *French Anti-Slavery: The Movement for the Abolition of Slavery in France, 1802–1848*. Cambridge, UK: Cambridge University Press, 2000.

Jessenne, Jean-Pierre, ed. *Vers un ordre bourgeois? Révolution française et changement social*. Rennes, France: Presses Universitaires de Rennes, 2007.

Johnson, Christopher H. *Becoming Bourgeois: Love, Kinship, and Power in Provincial France, 1670–1880*. Ithaca, NY: Cornell University Press, 2015.

Johnson, Julie Patricia. *The Candle and the Guillotine: Revolutionary Justice in Lyon*. New York: Berghahn, 2020.

Johnson, Julie. "The 'Fury': The Case of an Activist Woman in Lyon, 1792–1793." *Lilith: A Feminist History Journal* 25 (2019): 63–75. https://search.informit.org/doi/pdf/10.3316/ielapa.591285781753047.

Johnson, Julie Patricia. "Revolutionary Justice in Lyon: The Case of Jean-Jacques Ampère, 1789–1793." PhD diss., University of Melbourne, 2017.

Jones, Colin. "The Great Chain of Buying: Medical Advertisement, the Bourgeois Public Sphere, and the Origins of the French Revolution." *AHR* 101, no. 1 (1996): 13–40. https://doi.org/10.2307/2169222.

Jones, Colin, and Rebecca Spang. "Sans-culottes, *sans café, sans tabac*: Shifting Realms of Luxury and Necessity in Eighteenth-Century France." In *Consumers and Luxury: Consumer Culture in Europe, 1650–1850*, edited by Maxine Berg and Helen Clifford. Manchester, UK: Manchester University Press, 1999.

Joris, Elisabeth. "Kinship and Gender: Property, Enterprise, and Politics." In *Kinship in Europe: Approaches to Long-Term Development (1300–1900)*, edited by David Warren Sabean, Simon Teuscher, and Jon Mathieu. New York: Berghahn, 2007.

Jourda, Pierre. *Le Théâtre à Montpellier, 1755–1851*. Oxford: Voltaire Foundation, 2001.

Jourdan, Annie. *La Révolution batave entre la France et l'Amérique (1795–1806)*. Rennes, France: Presses Universitaires de Rennes, 2008.

Kadish, Doris Y., and Françoise Massardier-Kenney, eds. *Translating Slavery*. Vol. 2. *Ourika and Its Progeny*. 2nd ed. Kent, OH: Kent State University Press, 2009.

Kale, Steven. *French Salons: High Society and Political Sociability from the Old Regime to 1848*. Baltimore, MD: Johns Hopkins University Press, 2006.

Kaplan, Vera. "Weathering the Revolution: Patronage as a Strategy of Survival." *Revolutionary Russia* 26, no. 2 (2013): 97–127. http://dx.doi.org/10.1080/09546545.2013.855061.

Kingston, Ralph. *Bureaucrats and Bourgeois Society: Office Politics and Individual Credit in France 1789–1848*. Basingstoke, UK: Palgrave Macmillan, 2012.

Komlos, John. "An Anthropometric History of Early Modern France." *European Review of Economic History* 7, no. 2 (2003): 159–189. https://doi.org/10.1017/S1361491603000066.

Kroen, Sheryl. *Politics and Theater: The Crisis of Legitimacy in Restoration France, 1815–1830*. Berkeley: University of California Press, 2000.

Landes, Joan B. *Women and the Public Sphere in the Age of the French Revolution*. Ithaca, NY: Cornell University Press, 1988.

Lanza, Janine M. *From Wives to Widows in Early Modern Paris: Gender, Economy, and the Law*. Burlington, VT: Ashgate, 2007.

Laqueur, Thomas. *Making Sex: Body and Gender from the Ancient Greeks to Freud*. Cambridge, MA: Harvard University Press, 1992.

Laqueur, Thomas. "The Queen Caroline Affair: Politics as Art in the Reign of George IV." *Journal of Modern History* 54, no. 3 (1982): 417–466. https://doi.org/10.1086/244178.

Lavigne, Hubert, ed. *État civil d'artistes: Billets d'enterrement ou de décès depuis 1823 jusqu'à nos jours*. Paris: J. Baur, 1881.

Lentz, Thierry. *Nouvelle histoire du Premier Empire*. 4 vols. Paris: Fayard, 2002–2010.

Letellier, Robert Ignatius. *Opéra-comique: A Sourcebook*. Newcastle-upon-Tyne, UK: Cambridge Scholars, 2010.

Le Wita, Béatrix. *French Bourgeois Culture*. Translated by J. A. Underwood. Cambridge, UK: Cambridge University Press, 1994.

Lilti, Antoine. *The Invention of Celebrity, 1750–1850*. Translated by Lynn Jeffress. Cambridge, UK: Polity, 2017.

Lilti, Antoine. *The World of the Salons: Sociability and Worldliness in Eighteenth-Century Paris*. Translated by Lydia Colchrane. Oxford: Oxford University Press, 2015.

Linton, Marisa. *Choosing Terror: Virtue, Friendship, and Authenticity in the French Revolution*. Oxford: Oxford University Press, 2013.

Luzzatto, Sergio. *Mémoire de la Terreur: Vieux Montagnards et jeunes républicains au XIXe siècle*. Translated by Simone Carpentari-Messina. Lyon: Presses Universitaires de Lyon, 1991.

Lyons, Martyn. *Reading Culture and Writing Practices in Nineteenth-Century France*. Toronto: University of Toronto Press, 2008.

Mainardi, Patricia. *Husbands, Wives, and Lovers: Marriage and Its Discontents in Nineteenth-Century France*. New Haven, CT: Yale University Press, 2003.

Marchand, Patrick. *Le maître de poste et le messager: Une histoire du transport public en France au temps du cheval, 1700–1850*. Paris: Belin, 2006.

Marec, Yannick. "Pauvres et miséraux à Rouen dans la première moitié du XIXe siècle." *Cahiers des Annales de Normandie*, no. 13 (1981): 143–170. https://doi.org/10.3406/annor.1981.3864.

Marraud, Matthieu. *De la ville à l'etat: La bourgeoisie parisienne, XVIIe-XVIIIe siècle*. Paris: Albin Michel, 2009.

Mauss, Marcel. *The Gift: Form and Reason for Exchange in Archaic Society*. Translated by W. D. Halls. New York: Norton, 1990.

May, Gita. *Madame Roland and the Age of Revolution*. New York: Columbia University Press, 1970.

Maza, Sarah. "The Bourgeois Family Revisited: Sentimentalism and Social Class in Prerevolutionary French Culture." In *Intimate Encounters: Love and Domesticity in Eighteenth-Century France*, edited by Richard Rand. Princeton, NJ: Princeton University Press, 1997.

Maza, Sarah. *The Myth of the French Bourgeoisie: An Essay on the Social Imaginary, 1750–1850*. Cambridge, MA: Harvard University Press, 2003.

Maza, Sarah. *Servants and Masters in Eighteenth-Century France: The Uses of Loyalty*. Princeton, NJ: Princeton University Press, 1983.

Mazeau, Gillaume. *Le bain de l'histoire*. Seyssel: Champ Vallon, 2009.

McCalla, Arthur. *A Romantic Historiosophy: The Philosophy of History of Pierre-Simon Ballanche*. Leiden: Brill, 1998.

McLaren, Angus. *A History of Contraception from Antiquity to the Present Day*. Oxford: Blackwell, 1990.

McMahon, Darrin M. *Enemies of the Enlightenment: The French Counter-Enlightenment and the Making of Modernity*. Oxford: Oxford University Press, 2001.

Medick, Hans, and David Warren Sabean, eds. *Interest and Emotion: Essays on the Study of Family and Kinship*. Cambridge, UK: Cambridge University Press, 1984.

Mikaberidze, Alexander. *The Napoleonic Wars: A Global History*. Oxford: Oxford University Press, 2020.

Miller, Christopher L. *The French Atlantic Triangle: Literature and Culture of the Slave Trade*. Durham, NC: Duke University Press, 2008.

Mitchell, Robin. *Vénus Noire: Black Women and Colonial Fantasies in Nineteenth-Century France*. Athens: University of Georgia Press, 2020.

Niderst, Alain. "La vie de château au XIXe siècle en Forez de Lyons: Les Senevas à Croix-Mesnil (1827–1854)." *Études Normandes* 31, no. 2 (1982): 74–81. https://doi.org/10.3406/etnor.1982.2540.

Nye, Robert A. *Masculinity and Male Codes of Honor in Modern France*. Oxford: Oxford University Press, 1993.

Offen, Karen. *European Feminisms, 1750–1950: A Political History*. Stanford, CA: Stanford University Press, 2000.

Oliver, Bette W. *Orphans on the Earth: Girondin Fugitives from the Terror, 1793–1794*. Lanham, MD: Lexington, 2009.

Ozouf, Mona. *Varennes: La mort de la royauté, 21 juin 1791*. Paris: Gallimard, 2005.

Palmer, R. R. *The Improvement of Humanity: Education and the French Revolution*. Princeton, NJ: Princeton University Press, 1985.

Parker, Lindsay A. H. *Writing the Revolution: A French Woman's History in Letters*. Oxford: Oxford University Press, 2013.

Parturier, Maurice, ed. *Lettres de Mérimée à Ludovic Vitet*. Paris: CTHS, 1998

Pasco, Allan H. *Balzac, Literary Sociologist*. Cham, Switzerland: Palgrave Macmillan, 2016.

Pasco, Allan H. *Revolutionary Love in Eighteenth- and Early Nineteenth-Century France*. Burlington, VT: Ashgate, 2009.

Pellissier, Catherine. *Loisirs et sociabilités des notables Lyonnais au XIXe siècle*. 2 vols. Lyon: Éditions lyonnaises d'art et d'histoire and Presses universitaires de Lyon, 1996.

Perl-Rosenthal, Nathan. "Corresponding Republics: Letter Writing and Patriot Organizing in the Atlantic Revolutions, circa 1760–1792." PhD diss., Columbia University, 2011. https://academiccommons.columbia.edu/doi/10.7916/D8GQ74X1.

Perl-Rosenthal, Nathan. *The Age of Revolutions and the Generations Who Made It*. New York: Basic, 2024.

Perrot, Michelle, ed. *The History of Private Life*. Vol. 4. *From the Fires of Revolution to the Great War*. Translated by Arthur Goldhammer. Cambridge, MA: Harvard University Press, 1990.

Petiteau, Natalie. *Écrire la mémoire: Les mémorialistes de la Révolution et l'Empire*. Paris: Les Indes savantes, 2012.

Picot, Georges. *Le Comte Duchâtel: Notice historique*. Paris: Plon, 1908.

Ploux, François. *De bouche à oreille: Naissance et propagation des rumeurs dans la France du XIXe siècle*. Paris: Aubier/Flammarion, 2003.

Poidevard, William, Julien Baudrier, and Léon Galle. *Armorial des bibliophiles de Lyonnais, Forez, Beaujolais et Dombes*. Lyon: Société des Bibliophiles Lyonnais, 1907.

Popiel, Jennifer J. *Heroic Hearts: Sentiment, Saints, and Authority in Modern France*. Lincoln: University of Nebraska Press, 2021.

Popiel, Jennifer J. *Rousseau's Daughters: Domesticity, Education, and Autonomy in Modern France*. Lebanon, NH: University Press of New England, 2008.

Quinlan, Sean M. *Morbid Undercurrents: Medical Subcultures in Postrevolutionary France*. Ithaca, NY: Cornell University Press, 2021.

Ramsey, Matthew. *Professional and Popular Medicine in France, 1770–1830: The Social World of Medical Practice*. Cambridge, UK: Cambridge University Press, 1988.

Rance, Karine. "Réseaux épistolaires et amitiés infra-politiques entre Révolution et Restauration: Une correspondance du comte de Montlosier avec Claude-Ignace et Prosper de Barante." *FHS* 44 (April 2021): 247–277. https://doi.org/10.1215/00161071-8810364.

Rauch, André. *Crise de l'identité masculine, 1789–1914*. Paris: Hachette, 2000.

Reddy, William M. *The Invisible Code: Honor and Sentiment in Postrevolutionary France, 1814–1848*. Berkeley: University of California Press, 1997.

Reddy, William M. *The Navigation of Feeling: A Framework for the History of Emotions*. Cambridge, UK: Cambridge University Press, 2001.

Révérend, Albert. *Titres, anoblissements et pairies de la Restauration, 1814–1830*. 6 vols. Paris: Champion, 1901–1906.

Reynard, Pierre Claude. *Ambitions Tamed: Urban Expansion in Pre-Revolutionary Lyon*. Montreal: McGill-Queen's University Press, 2009.

Reynolds, Siân. *Marriage and Revolution: Monsieur et Madame Roland*. Oxford: Oxford University Press, 2012.

Reynolds, Siân. "Revolutionary Parents and Children: Everyday Lives in Times of Stress." In *Life in Revolutionary France*, edited by Jennifer Ngaire Heuer and Mette Harder. New York: Bloomsbury, 2020.

Robert, Adolphe, and Gaston Cougny. *Dictionnaire des parlementaires français de 1789 à 1889*. Paris: Bourloton, 1889–1891.

Roberts, Meghan K. *Sentimental Savants: Philosophical Families in Enlightenment France*. Chicago: University of Chicago Press, 2016.

Rogers, Rebecca. *From the Salon to the Schoolroom: Educating Bourgeois Girls in Nineteenth-Century France*. University Park: Pennsylvania State University Press, 2005.

Rosanvallon, Pierre. *The Demands of Liberty: Civil Society in France Since the Revolution*. Translated by Arthur Goldhammer. Cambridge, MA: Harvard University Press, 2007.

Rosanvallon, Pierre. *La Monarchie impossible: Les chartes de 1814 et de 1830*. Paris: Fayard, 1994.

Rosenfeld, Sophia. "Of Revolutions and the Problem of Choice." In *Rethinking the Age of Revolutions: France and the Birth of the Modern World*, edited by David A. Bell and Yair Mintzer. Oxford: Oxford University Press, 2018.

Rosenwein, Barbara H. "Worrying about Emotions in History." *AHR* 107, no. 3 (2002): 821–845. https://doi.org/10.1086/ahr/107.3.821.

Rothschild, Emma. *An Infinite History: The Story of a Family in France over Three Centuries*. Princeton, NJ: Princeton University Press, 2021.

Ruggiu, François-Joseph. *L'individu et la famille dans les sociétés urbaines anglaise et française au XVIIIe siècle*. Paris: Presses de l'Université Paris-Sorbonne, 2007.

Ronyak, Jennifer. *Intimacy, Performance, and the Lied in the Early Nineteenth Century*. Bloomington: Indiana University Press, 2018.

Sabean, David Warren, Simon Teuscher, and Jon Mathieu, eds. *Kinship in Europe: Approaches to Long-Term Development* (1300–1900). New York: Berghahn Books, 2010.

Saunier, Eric. *Révolution et sociabilité en Normandie au tournant des XVIIIe et XIXe siècles: 6000 francs-maçons de 1740 à 1830*. Rouen: Publications des universités de Rouen et du Havre, 1998.

Saunier, Pierre-Yves. *L'esprit Lyonnais, XIXe–XXe siècle*. Paris: CNRS Éditions, 1995.

Saussac, Roland. "Louis Vitet, l'homme de compromis." In *24 Maires de Lyon pour deux siècles d'histoire*. Lyon: Éditions LUGD, 1994.

Schiebinger, Londa. *Nature's Body: Gender in the Making of Modern Science*. Boston: Beacon, 1993.

Seigel, Jerrold. *Modernity and Bourgeois Life: Society, Politics, and Culture in England, France, and Germany since 1750*. Cambridge, UK: Cambridge University Press, 2012.

Serna, Pierre. *La République des girouettes (1789–1815 . . . et au-delà) Une anomalie politique: La France de l'extrême centre*. Seysssel, France: Champ Vallon, 2005.

Sewell, William H., Jr. *Capitalism and the Emergence of Civic Equality in Eighteenth-Century France*. Chicago: University of Chicago Press, 2021.

Simien, Côme. *Les massacres de septembre 1792 à Lyon*. Lyon: Aléas, 2011.

Simmel, Georg. "Sociability." In *Georg Simmel on Individuality and Social Forms: Selected Writings*, edited by Donald Levine. Chicago: University of Chicago Press, 1971.

Skuy, David. *Assassination, Politics, and Miracles: France and the Royalist Reaction of 1820*. Montreal: McGill University Press, 2003.

Smith, Bonnie. *Ladies of the Leisure Class: The Bourgeoises of Northern France in the Nineteenth Century*. Princeton, NJ: Princeton University Press, 1981.

Smith, Jay M. *Nobility Reimagined: The Patriotic Nation in Eighteenth-Century France*. Ithaca, NY: Cornell University Press, 2005.

Smith, Michael Steven. *The Emergence of Modern Business Enterprise in France, 1800–1930*. Cambridge, MA: Harvard University Press, 2006.

Spang, Rebecca L. *The Invention of the Restaurant: Paris and Modern Gastronomic Culture*. 2nd ed. Cambridge, MA: Harvard University Press, 2020.

Spang, Rebecca L. *Stuff and Money in the Time of the French Revolution*. Cambridge, MA: Harvard University Press, 2015.

Steinbach, Susie. "Can We Still Use 'Separate Spheres'? British History 25 Years After *Family Fortunes*." *History Compass* 10, no. 11 (2012): 826–837. https://doi.org/10.1111/hic3.12010.

Steinberg, Ronen. *The Afterlives of the Terror: Facing the Legacies of Mass Violence in Postrevolutionary France*. Ithaca, NY: Cornell University Press, 2019.

Stone, Lawrence. *The Family, Sex, and Marriage in England, 1500–1800*. New York: Harper and Row, 1977.

Sussman, George D. "Parisian Infants and Norman Wet Nurses in the Early Nineteenth Century: A Statistical Study." *Journal of Interdisciplinary History* 7, no. 4 (1977): 637–653. https://doi.org/10.2307/202885.

Sussman, George D. *Selling Mothers' Milk: The Wet-Nursing Business in France 1715–1914*. Urbana: University of Illinois Press, 1982.

Sutherland, D. M. G. *Murder in Aubagne: Lynching, Law, and Justice During the French Revolution*. Cambridge, UK: Cambridge University Press, 2009.

Szramkiewicz, Romuald. *Les régents et censeurs de la Banque de France nommés sous le Consulat et l'Empire*. Geneva: Librairie Droz, 1974.

Tackett, Timothy. *Becoming a Revolutionary: The Deputies of the French National Assembly and the Emergence of a Revolutionary Culture, 1789–1790*. 1996. Reprint. University Park: Pennsylvania State University Press, 2005.

Tackett, Timothy. *The Coming of the Terror in the French Revolution*. Cambridge, MA: University Press, 2015.

Tackett, Timothy. *When the King Took Flight*. Cambridge, MA: Harvard University Press, 2003.

Tague, Ingrid H. "Love, Honor, and Obedience: Fashionable Women and the Discourse of Marriage in the Early Eighteenth Century." *Journal of British Studies* 40, no. 1 (2001): 76–106. https://doi.org/10.1086/386235.

Takats, Sean. *The Expert Cook in Eighteenth-Century France*. Baltimore, MD: Johns Hopkins University Press, 2011.

Theis, Laurent. *François Guizot*. Paris: Fayard, 2008.

Touzet, Léo, and Pierre Corbeil. "Vital Roux, Forgotten Forerunner of Modern Business Games." *Simulation and Gaming* 46, no. 1 (2015): 1–21. https://doi.org/10.1177/1046878115594321.

Traer, James F. *Marriage and the Family in Eighteenth-Century France*. Ithaca, NY: Cornell University Press, 1980.

Trénard, Louis. *Lyon de l'Encyclopédie au pré-romantisme*. Paris: Presses Universitaires de France, 1958.

Trévisi, Marion. *Au cœur de la parenté: Oncles et tantes dans la France des Lumières*. Paris: Presses de l'Université Paris-Sorbonne, 2008.

Triomphe, Pierre. *1815: La Terreur blanche*. Toulouse: Privat, 2017.

Trouille, Mary. *Wife Abuse in Eighteenth-Century France*. Oxford: SVEC, 2009.

Troyansky, David G. *Entitlement and Complaint: Ending Careers and Reviewing Lives in Post-Revolutionary France*. Oxford: Oxford University Press, 2023.

Tulard, Jean, Jean-François Fayard, and Alfred Fierro. *Histoire et dictionnaire de la Révolution française 1789–1799*. Paris: Robert Laffont, 1987.

Tuttle, Leslie. *Conceiving the Old Regime. Pronatalism and the Politics of Reproduction in Early Modern France*. Oxford: Oxford University Press, 2010.

Van Hille, Jean-Marc, ed. *Dictionnaire des marins francs-maçons: Gens de mers et professions connexes aux XVIIIe, XIXe, et XXe siècles*. Paris: SPM-Lettrage/L'Harmattan, 2011.

Vause, Erika. *In the Red and in the Black: Debt, Dishonor, and the Law in France between Revolutions*. Charlottesville: University of Virginia Press, 2018.

Verjus, Anne. *Le bon mari: Une histoire politique des hommes et des femmes à l'époque révolutionnaire*. Paris: Fayard, 2010.

Verjus, Anne. *Le cens de la famille: Les femmes et le vote, 1789–1848*. Paris: Belin, 2002.

Verjus, Anne, and Denise Davidson. *Le roman conjugal: Chroniques de la vie familiale à l'époque de la Révolution et de l'Empire*. Seyssel, France: Champ Vallon, 2011.

Vincent, K. Steven. *Benjamin Constant and the Birth of French Liberalism*. New York: Palgrave Macmillan, 2011.

Vincent, K. Steven, and Alison Klairmont-Lingo, eds. *The Human Tradition in Modern France*. Wilmington, DE: Scholarly Resources, 2000.

Vincent-Buffault, Anne. *The History of Tears: Sensibility and Sentimentality in France*. Translated by Teresa Bridgeman. New York: St. Martin's, 1991.

Wahl, Maurice. *Les premières années de la Révolution à Lyon, 1788–1792*. Paris: Colin, 1894.

Wahrman, Dror. *The Making of the Modern Self: Identity and Culture in Eighteenth-Century England*. New Haven, CT: Yale University Press, 2004.

Walker, Lesley H. *A Mother's Love: Crafting Feminine Virtue in Enlightenment France*. Lewisburg, PA: Bucknell University Press, 2008.

Walton, Charles. "Capitalism's Alter Ego: The Birth of Reciprocity in Eighteenth-Century France." *Critical Historical Studies* 5 (2018): 1–43. https://doi.org/10.1086/697032.

Walton, Charles. *Policing Public Opinion in the French Revolution: The Culture of Calumny and the Problem of Free Speech*. Oxford: Oxford University Press, 2009.

Waresquiel, Emmanuel de. *Cent-Jours: La tentation de l'impossible mars-juillet 1815*. Paris: Fayard, 2008.

Waresquiel, Emmanuel de. *C'est la Révolution qui continue! La Restauration 1814–1830*. Paris: Tallandier, 2015.

Waresquiel, Emmanuel de. *Talleyrand: Le prince immobile*. Paris: Fayard, 2003.

Woloch, Isser. *Napoleon and his Collaborators: The Making of a Dictatorship*. New York: W. W. Norton, 2001.

Woloch, Isser. *The New Regime: Transformations of the French Civil Order, 1789 to the 1820s*. New York: W. W. Norton, 1995.

Zeldin, Theodore. *A History of French Passions, 1848–1945*. 2 vols. Oxford: Oxford University Press, 1973–1977.

Index

Page numbers followed by the letter f refer to figures.

www.ingramcontent.com/pod-product-compliance
Lightning Source LLC
Chambersburg PA
CBHW020825270326
41928CB00006B/441

* 9 7 8 1 5 0 1 7 8 4 8 8 0 *